The Politics of Corporations in 'New' India

This volume examines how the rise of Hindutva to power is linked to the interests of large corporations in neoliberal India. It interprets Hindutva as a fascist force and as a capitalist counter-revolution wearing a popular mask that demands a repressive imposition of order to facilitate accumulation. The book delves into different aspects of the relationship between Hindutva and large corporations. Various chapters cast in high relief how the fascist shields of religion and nationalism are deployed to further corporate profiteering. This book is also a reminder that fascism has inherent limitations and is incapable of resolving crises that give rise to it. However, its ascendance, albeit temporary, is causing widespread destruction. The volume argues that fascist destruction in contemporary India can only be effectively restricted by containing the ravages of neoliberalism and corporate loot.

Rohit Varman is a Professor at Birmingham Business School, University of Birmingham, UK. His research interests are broadly in the field of critical management studies. He has published with the Press on alternative organizations and organizing resistance in India.

The Politics of Corporations in 'New' India

Edited by

Rohit Varman

CAMBRIDGE
UNIVERSITY PRESS

CAMBRIDGE
UNIVERSITY PRESS

Shaftesbury Road, Cambridge CB2 8EA, United Kingdom

One Liberty Plaza, 20th Floor, New York, NY 10006, USA

477 Williamstown Road, Port Melbourne, VIC 3207, Australia

314–321, 3rd Floor, Plot 3, Splendor Forum, Jasola District Centre, New Delhi – 110025, India

103 Penang Road, #05–06/07, Visioncrest Commercial, Singapore 238467

Cambridge University Press is part of Cambridge University Press & Assessment, a department of the University of Cambridge.

We share the University's mission to contribute to society through the pursuit of education, learning and research at the highest international levels of excellence.

www.cambridge.org
Information on this title: www.cambridge.org/9781009605557

First published 2025

Cover Image courtesy: Getty Images/Soltan Frédéric.

A catalogue record for this publication is available from the British Library

ISBN 978-1-009-60555-7 Hardback
ISBN 978-1-009-60550-2 Paperback

When I refused to die
my chains were loosened
I came out
Into the vast meadows
Smiling at the leaves of grass
My smile caused intolerance in them
I was shackled again

I still stubbornly refuse to die
The sad thing is that
They don't know how to make me die
Because I love so much
The sounds of growing grass

—G. N. Saibaba, 'I Refused to Die'

Contents

Figures

Acknowledgements

This collection took three years to complete. The triggers for the volume were, on the one hand, the reluctance of mainstream scholars to use the label 'fascism' to describe the rise of Hindutva and, on the other, the silence about the role of big capital in the fascification of Indian society. Identifying scholars who shared concerns about the nexus between corporations and fascism was the first real challenge to take this collection off the ground.

I must begin by acknowledging the work done on this volume by a friend and colleague, who can only appear on this page with a pseudonym—Keli Vaidyar. Their real name cannot even be mentioned. Keli, who co-edited this volume, had to withdraw their name because of the ongoing atmosphere of academic repression and harassment by Hindutva forces. Thank you, Keli, for your work and support; this volume would not have been possible without your efforts. This erasure is a stark reminder of the risks faced by scholars in India.

Over the three years that I worked on this book, I got to know very inspiring people. My foremost gratitude to the authors who inspired me and enthusiastically responded to my invitation to contribute to this collection. Despite their status as leading scholars in their fields, they responded with patience, kindness, and understanding to my requests for revisions and alignment with the goal of this collection. It was a privilege to collaborate with these scholars, and I am grateful for their decision to engage with a subject that many have chosen to overlook or avoid.

I am deeply indebted to the University of Birmingham for providing a space that nurtures academic dialogue, critical inquiry, and imaginative thought. By upholding academic freedom and fostering a liberal intellectual environment, the university has supported this work in numerous meaningful ways. The final stages of this project were completed during my study leave in India, a period that offered both reflection and renewed urgency. As I travelled across the country, the stark realities of widespread immiseration, deepening inequality, corporate plunder, and the systematic dismantling of democratic institutions became increasingly evident. Equally visible were corporate capture and the pervasive infiltration of Hindutva forces into various arms of the state. Of particular concern is the growing repression within academic institutions, where voices of reason are being silenced. Scholars are being penalized and subjected to coordinated online harassment for challenging the actions of the Sangh Parivar and governments. In this fraught context, I wish to acknowledge and commend the courageous and inspiring efforts of academics who continue to speak truth to power.

I am thankful to Cambridge University Press for agreeing to publish this volume. In particular, I am truly grateful to our commissioning editor, Anwesha Rana, for her unflinching support. I also wish to acknowledge the assistance provided by Priyanka Das and Aniruddha De of the Press and thank them for carefully copyediting the volume. Two anonymous reviewers provided timely and constructive feedback that helped us refine our arguments. I thank them for their reviews.

So many other people, including my friends, colleagues, and students, who may not appear in the pages of this book have nonetheless inspired me with their passion and commitment that reinforced, time and again, my conviction to write about fascism and corporations in 'new' India.

And, finally, where would any writing on fascism be without drawing inspiration from various activists, movements, and organizations that have continued to resist fascists and corporate pillage across India? These activists, movements, and organizations have symbolized hope and have kept me charged while working for long hours on the book. They continuously remind me that fascism will be defeated.

Rohit Varman

1

Corporations and Fascism in 'New' India

Rohit Varman

You who live secure
in your comfortable houses,
who return each evening to find
warm food,
welcoming faces …

Consider whether this is a man:
who toils in the mud,
who knows no peace,
who fights for crusts of bread,
who dies at another man's whim,
at his "yes" or his "no".

Consider whether this is a woman:
bereft of hair,
of a recognizable name
because she lacks the strength to remember,
her eyes as void
and her womb as frigid
as a frog's in winter.

Consider that such horrors have been:
I commend these words to you.

—'Shema' by Primo Levi

In his powerful poem titled ‘Shema’, Primo Levi, an Auschwitz survivor, urges the world to pay attention to the victims of the Holocaust and to never lose sight of the human monstrosity that unfolded under fascism. Despite Levi’s warning, there is a global resurgence of fascism (Mason 2021; Patnaik 2024; Stanley 2020). India seems to be in a similar situation with its embrace of fascism in the form of Hindutva. Fascism is a state of capitalism that arises because of a crisis or its possibility in which the traditional elite cannot dominate the political sphere and serve the interests of large corporations through liberal institutions (Poulantzas 2018). It is an authoritarian reaction (Desai 2016; Patnaik 2024) and a capitalist counter-revolution wearing a popular mask (Parenti 1997; Rosenberg 2016). We borrow from Gramsci (1971) to understand political crisis as the detachment of the masses from their traditional ideologies as they no longer believe in them. Such a detachment (or its threat) can create the problem of order. As a reaction, and when the working class mobilizations and left forces are weak (Poulantzas 2018), fascism comes to the fore and imposes a repressive order to facilitate capitalist accumulation. The current phase of neoliberalism that particularly favours monopoly capital increases the demand for fascist exceptionalism to maintain order in the face of increasing inequality, exploitation, expropriation, unemployment, and threats of mass unrest (Desai 2016; Patnaik 2023c, 2024).

This collection of chapters examines the phenomenon of how the rise of the Bharatiya Janata Party (BJP) as a force of Hindutva to power since 2014 is linked to the interests of large corporations. The BJP is an arm of the Rashtriya Swayamsevak Sangh (RSS). The RSS and its affiliate organizations and institutions constitute the Sangh Parivar (Sangh Family). We borrow from a rich body of work on the Sangh Parivar that interprets it as fascist (Ahmad 1993; Balagopal 2023; J. Banaji 2016; Desai 2014, 2016; A. Roy 2020; S. Sarkar 2016). In fact, Zachariah (2020) suggests, in the RSS, India has the longest-running fascist movement in the world. The contributors to this volume delve into different aspects of the relationship between the Sangh Parivar and corporations. Various chapters cast in high relief how the fascist shields of religion and nationalism are deployed to further corporate profiteering. In compiling this volume, we echo Pauwels’ (2017) assessment that Hitler was not an anomaly and fascism was not a freak accident of history. Fascism is a manifestation of capitalism (Polanyi 2018), and the ascendance of Hindutva as a fascist force requires a clear understanding of the political economy that gives rise to it (Balagopal 2023).

This volume, therefore, has two urgent imperatives: First, to train our attention on Hindutva and large corporations to understand how the two are intertwined. It seeks to expose, to borrow from Cooper (2021), the kleptocratic nature of capitalism that requires the protection of an anti-democratic state to further profiteering. Second, to use this understanding to resist the dominance of fascists. In other words, this collection is written with grave concerns and a spirit of resistance. There are grave concerns about the injuries to the health of the republic caused by the Sangh Parivar. There are fears of greater destruction that will unfold in the near future if fascists are not restricted. As Arundhati Roy (2020) warns, the infrastructure of fascism is staring us in the face, and the blaze is at our door. We are specifically conscious of the great harm fascism can cause to the working class and echo Zetkin's (2017, p. 7) sharp reminder that 'fascism confronts the proletariat as an exceptionally dangerous and frightful enemy.... It is urgently necessary that it be brought down.... It is also a question of survival for every ordinary worker, a question of bread, working conditions, and quality of life for millions and millions of the exploited.' The volume is written to document and interrogate these dangers. In doing so, the volume seeks to interrupt fascism. The contributors do it in the face of repression and fear that has silenced the voices of dissent. The volume defies what Narrain (2021) labels as 'the state of undeclared emergency in India'.

This chapter is organized into three sections. Each section answers a critical question about fascism. We first delineate the key features of fascism and explain its relationship with capitalism. We follow this with a discussion of Hindutva and fascism's specific imprints in India. We also think through various aspects of fascism and large corporations in India. In the final section, we introduce the chapters in the volume to outline how our contributors interrogate the relationship between corporations and Hindutva.

* * *

Fascism can have multiple meanings with several socio-historical variations and differences from one national setting to another (J. Banaji 2016; Mason 2021). It does not have an ideological coherence (Traverso 2019) or an ideational essence (Saull 2024). It is also marked by several contradictions (Stanley 2020) and, as Zetkin (2017) warns, fascism should not be viewed as a homogenous phenomenon. The diverse origins of those who become fascists underscore the contradictory nature of fascism (Passmore 2014). Despite these challenges, Paxton (2005, p. 218) develops a useful description of fascism as

> [a] form of political behaviour marked by obsessive preoccupation with community decline, humiliation, or victimhood and by compensatory cults of unity, energy, and purity, in which a mass-based party of committed nationalist militants, working in uneasy but effective collaboration with traditional elites, abandons democratic liberties and pursues with redemptive violence and without ethical or legal restraints goals of internal cleansing and external expansion.

While underplaying the role of capitalism, Paxton uncovers the common features of fascist politics. Fascist politics includes emphases on othering, mythic past and decline, violence to overcome humiliation, propaganda, hierarchy, victimhood, nationalism, and a dismantling of working-class movements (see also Stanley 2020). These features help understand what Arundhati Roy (2020) implies when she writes that fascism is by no means the same everywhere, but it is so recognizable across nations and histories.

In spite of its distinct features, fascism is sometimes confused with totalitarianism or authoritarianism. Although fascism shares with totalitarianism autocratic leadership, a militarist attitude towards perceived enemies, and railroading democratic opposition, it is an error to conflate the two. The reduction of fascism to totalitarianism focuses on techniques of rule and personality cults without paying adequate attention to their construction and the role of socio-economic interests they serve (Kershaw 1989). Paxton (2005, p. 217) partly amends the problem by differentiating fascism from other forms of political control when he posits,

> Although authoritarian regimes often trample civil liberties and are capable of murderous brutality, they do not share fascism's urge to reduce the private sphere to nothing…. Authoritarians would rather leave the population demobilized and passive, while fascists want to engage and excite the public.

Thus, three key features that differentiate fascism from authoritarianism are chauvinistic nationalism, inciting masses to deploy them as instruments of violence, and restricting the autonomy of the personal sphere.

A key feature of fascism is chauvinistic nationalism, which is deployed to mobilize people and to get popular support. It is used by fascists to demonstrate their superiority and 'onto which it can release the delirium of its racial frenzy' (Rosenberg 2016, p. 32). Passmore (2014) particularly highlights this feature and notes that all aspects of fascist policy are suffused with ultra-nationalism. Here, it is necessary to differentiate between nation-building and fascist nationalism. The strategic deployment of nationalism is not the same as nation-building because fascists are not interested in the socio-economic upliftment of the majority, and they seek to only use the spectacles of chauvinistic nationalism to gain political dominance (Benjamin 2008). Fascists deploy nationalism to manufacture the rage of the masses and to make it into a mass movement (Zetkin 2017) that is used to further elite interests.

Such nationalist mobilizations of the masses as instruments of violence were central to fascist Italy and Nazi Germany in their early stages of development (Desai 2016; Rosenberg 2016). It took the forms of Blackshirts as the paramilitary wing of Mussolini's Italian National Fascist Party and of Brownshirts, or *Sturmabteilung* (SA), for the Nazi Party in Germany. Both parties deployed these mobilized populations (henceforth, stormtroopers) as a key feature of fascism: to violently suppress opposition and maintain political dominance (Parenti 1997). Emphasizing their role, as Arthur Rosenberg (2016, p. 35), one of the sharpest readers of fascism from the Third International, opined,

> The government and the ruling groups do not deploy the standard or regular state-authorities against the opposition, but volunteer-corps are recruited from the mass of population to handle this job. They attack, ill treat or murder … and unleash a wave of persecution and terror calculated to drown all opposition.

Such terror by masses mobilized as stormtroopers is necessary because capitalists rule indirectly and require the support of lower classes to further their political control and destroy the opposition (Zetkin 2017).

A restriction of the private sphere is the third key feature of a fascist rule. While a liberal regime is characterized by a relative autonomy of the ideological apparatus and private sphere of citizens, fascism restricts their independence and imposes repressive measures to control people (Poulantzas 2018). It helps to achieve a transformation of society (for example, Hindu

Rashtra) that is at the heart of fascist counter-revolution. Extra-legal violence through mobs from below helps to achieve such transformations (Hobsbawm 1994). A mobilized mass ensures that any deviation from the norms in the personal sphere framed by fascists is reported and punished. These restrictions can take violent forms and invite vigilantes to punish those who do not adhere to fascist codes. For example, mobs supported Hitler's regime of public humiliation and violence against the Jews and their establishments, led the burning of books deemed non-compliant with the Nazi ideology, and provided surveillance for the police state to identify individuals who violated the miscegenation laws (Wiesen 2018).

While for brevity, we confine our reading to the historical sites of Italy and Germany, and contemporary India, it does not mean that fascism is limited to these sites. Several recent writings note the rise of fascism across the globe, including in Brazil, France, Germany, Greece, Hungary, the United States, and the United Kingdom (Mason 2021; Stanley 2020). Each of these sites of fascism has its uniqueness and shared tendencies outlined in this volume.

Our attention to inter-war Germany, Italy, and contemporary India should not mask the fact that fascism lurks permanently within liberal capitalism, though it flourishes during crises. Drawing on Black radical thinkers, Toscano (2023) argues that contemporary fascism can be better understood if we acknowledge the frequent use of fascist tools of violence by liberal capitalist states on colonized populations and ethnic/racial minorities. Put differently, fascism is not merely a reaction to revolutionary threat to capitalism, but a long-drawn process of *preventive or anticipatory violence* enacted to pre-empt threats and to *restore* exploitative and oppressive forms of capitalism (ibid.).

Despite its permanent presence in capitalism, some of the newer sites and situations are also labelled as neo-fascist because of their continuation and departure from the European fascism of the early twentieth century (Patnaik 2024). For instance, while the militia party with uniforms, symbols, and parades under the leadership of a charismatic leader may still exist, these are less important in the newer avatars of fascism (Mason 2021). Neo-fascism can also actively make use of digital technologies to seamlessly propagate their beliefs, mythmaking, and violent acts that are prefigurative and showcase the promise of another world-making. Moreover, in a departure from the past, neo-fascists may not seek expansionist wars and can be temporarily defeated through elections (Patnaik 2024). Despite these modulations, we believe that it is more appropriate to use the label of fascism to uncover the historical continuities that constitute it.

* * *

A central piece in fascism's fractured intellectual history is its relationship with capitalism. Liberal (and some critical) scholars find it misleading to treat fascism as a capitalist outcome (for example, Paxton 2005 and Mann 2004). Accordingly, capitalists are against democracy but prefer authoritarians to fascists. However, when fascists acquire power, capitalists mostly collaborate with them in order to crush any possibility of socialism. In such a reading, 'Capitalism and fascism made practicable bedfellows (though not inevitable ones, nor always comfortable ones)' (Paxton 2005, p. 208). In a somewhat similar vein, 'Fascism is neither the direct "agent of the bourgeoisie" nor even its autonomous proxy' (Mason 2021, p. 191). As another example of this reading, Passmore (2014) focuses on ultra-nationalism as a key facet of fascism but fails to analyse who bankrolls it and why. Although such writings acknowledge the relationship between corporations and fascism, there is a tendency to see it as irrationality and anti-modernism.

These explanations of fascism have serious limitations because they tend to under-theorise the relationship between the state and big capital (that is, political economy) and erroneously ascribe autonomy to the political executive with an assumption that the political sphere enjoys a primacy over the economy. As a result, the role of leading actors, such as Hitler, Mussolini, Trump, or Modi, on the political stage, develops an extreme significance, and the explanations of the character of fascism revolve around their particular intentions, ideology, and authority (Desai 2016). The aforementioned liberal reading does not explicitly engage with political crises, class relations, corporate benefits derived from fascists, and the inherent contradictions of liberalism. For instance, Paxton (2005, p. 81) writes,

> Fascism, too, has historically been a phenomenon of weak or failed liberal states and belated or damaged capitalist systems rather than of triumphant ones. The frequent assertion that fascism stems from a crisis of liberalism might well be amended to specify crises in weak or failed liberalisms.

He asserts that there is no inevitability about the rise of fascism.

Although we agree with Paxton that we should not be over-deterministic in our reading of the rise of fascism, we do believe that fascism is a natural ally of corporations in their pursuit of accumulation and arises at a specific moment when large corporations are threatened by a crisis. We find Paxton's (2005, p. 102) reading limiting when he asserts,

> [C]onservative leaders rejected other possibilities—governing in coalition with the moderate Left, for instance, or governing under royal or presidential emergency authority (or, in the German case, continuing to do so). They chose the fascist option. The fascist leaders, for their part, accomplished the 'normalization' necessary for sharing power. It did not have to turn out that way.

A question to be asked is why conservatives could not ally with the moderate left or why they did not govern through a presidential emergency to overcome crisis. We do not see these as historical accidents. When the mandate is to crush workers' unions, conservatives could not have turned to the moderate left. Moreover, as Rosenberg (2016) correctly identifies, capitalists require the support of the masses to pursue their goals, and royal or presidential authority may not serve that purpose. Hence, there is a specificity of material conditions and available political alternatives that must be understood to explain the rise of fascism.

Contemporary scholarship has revealed strong linkages between liberalism and fascism (Giroux 2017, 2021; Maher 2023; Mattei 2022). It is clear that fascism is not an outcome of *weak* liberalism (cf. Paxton 2005). Fascism is an organic product of developments largely from within liberalism. As Landa (2009, p. 13) sharply adds, 'Fascism, in spite of words and gestures, came not really to do battle with liberalism, but primarily as an ally, albeit a bullying, patronizing one, offering much-needed succor.' Liberalism, which began as a socio-economic doctrine of the ascending European bourgeoisie of the late eighteenth century to challenge the privileges enjoyed by the nobility, was a movement that demanded political rights such as constitutional and representative government. These rights were demanded because they facilitated the freedom the bourgeoisie needed to shake the burden of feudal dominance. As these freedoms were realized and helped the bourgeoisie wrest control from the nobility, it became clear that liberalism was a double-edged sword that also allowed the masses to demand their rights and freedom from bourgeois dominance. Hence, there was a sharpening of contradiction between political and economic liberalism. As much as the latter helped further the economic interests of the bourgeoisie, the political avatar became a source of crisis in the pursuit of economic goals. Here, Landa (2009, p. 13) insightfully observes,

> In order to salvage the vessel of capitalism, economic liberals were quite often ready and willing to throw overboard the excess baggage of liberal political institutions and ideals. This is what I refer to as the momentous "liberal split," whereby economic liberalism and political liberalism began drifting apart to the point of finding themselves on opposite sides of the socioeconomic divide.

Indeed, Mattei (2022) sharply documents how the liberal Anglo-American establishment worked closely with fascist Italy in the 1920s and profitted from it.

Historically, capitalism's tenuous commitment to democracy explains why liberals were not originally keen on universal franchise and restricted that right to the propertied classes. Apart from a lengthy history of colonial and neo-colonial violence in the Global South, liberal European regimes have bailed out of constitutionalism and reverted to repression when the economic interests of the bourgeoisie are imperilled (Landa 2009). Thus, the divide between liberalism and fascism is artificial, and depending on the capitalist requirements and the perceived threat of proletariat movements, big capital can switch support to fascist formations to advance accumulation (Mattei 2022). As Rockhill (2023) notes, capitalists deploy liberalism and fascism as good cop/bad cop to further their interests.

We broadly agree with the scholars who explicitly read fascism as central to furthering the interests of corporations, and fascism as a specific response to political or economic crises within capitalism (for example, Guerin 1973; Parenti 1997; Patnaik 2024; Pauwels 2017; Poulantzas 2018). Such a crisis can arise because of a loss of legitimacy of the traditional political elite, threats of mass unrest, or a falling rate of profits that hampers capitalist accumulation. Guerin (1973, pp. 27–28) interprets fascism as a capitalist requirement in such moments of crisis because of its repressive and anti-democratic propensities:

> It empties the pockets of the people down to the last centime. It resorts to what M. Caillaux, once finance minister of France, expressively calls 'the great penance': brutal slashing of wages and social expenditures,

> raising of tariff duties at the expense of the consumer, etc. The state, furthermore, rescues business enterprises on the brink of bankruptcy, forcing the masses to foot the bill. Such enterprises are kept alive with subsidies, tax exemptions, orders for public works and armaments. In short, the state thrusts itself into the breach left by the vanishing private customers. But such manoeuvres are difficult under a democratic regime. As long as democracy survives, the masses, though thoroughly deceived and plundered, have some means of defence against the 'great penance': freedom of the press, universal suffrage, the right to organize into unions and to strike, etc. Feeble defences, it is true, but still capable of setting some limit to the insatiable demands of the money power. In particular, the resistance of the organized working class makes it rather difficult to simply lower wages. Under such conditions of accumulation, a strong anti-democratic state is necessary to strip the masses of all means of defence and … [tie] their hands behind their backs to empty their pockets.

In crises, fascism offers the advantage to big capital by eliminating labour unions, destroying socialist movements, and restricting democratic rights (Hobsbawm 1996; Pauwels 2017). In response to the Great Depression, the Nazis, for instance, froze workers' wages to support big businesses (Tooze 2006). Even scholars like Paxton (2005, p. 10), who are reluctant to locate the role of big business in fascism, are forced to acknowledge that 'once in power, fascist regimes banned strikes, dissolved independent labour unions, lowered wage earners' purchasing power, and showered money on armaments industries, to the immense satisfaction of employers'.

In addition to using repression to control workers and populations, fascists also introduce pro-business policies that aid capitalist accumulation. For example, Hitler reversed the nationalization of firms, enacted laws to restrict competition to support monopoly capital, and introduced a slew of tax cuts for businesses after coming to power in 1933 (Poulantzas 2018). Fascists also use public spending to contribute to corporate profiteering (Guerin 1973). Moreover, as Tooze (2006, p. 134) adds, big banks were saved from nationalism and Hitler famously remarked that 'there was no need to nationalize German businesses, if the population itself could be nationalized'. It has to be understood that the support for Nazis was not confined to German big capital and that numerous American and British corporations, labelled as 'philofascists' by Pauwels (2017, p. 173), actively supported and profiteered from the regime. Therefore, fascism is not an accidental outcome but central to capitalism (Polanyi 2018). Moreover, fascism remains marginal with an ascendant revolutionary force and waits for the tide to subside (Poulantzas 2018). It seizes power when the left is weak or defeated (Jackson 1975). Fascism is a preventative measure to ensure future possibilities of unhindered capitalist accumulation (Marcuse 2005). Hence, the timeline of fascism requires an important clarification, and there is a need to differentiate between the rise of fascists and their ability to capture the state. While fascist forces start surfacing as a reaction to the threats of working-class resistance, they do not prevail and capture the state when left forces are strong in a society.

To come to power, fascists position themselves as anti-elite to appeal to the masses disenchanted with the traditional elite. There are, however, two important points to be understood about fascist anti-elitism. First, while it may frame itself as a rule by the petty bourgeoisie, fascist disavowal of the elite is always more of rhetoric than reality. Even when it allows the petty bourgeoisie to control the political sphere, as documented in the German context (Poulantzas 2018) or as various commentators have written about the nature of the BJP as a *baniya*/trader party in India (see Laliwala 2020), there is always a close alliance with big businesses and desire to advance their interests. As Landa (2009, p. 18) notes, 'Hitler is radically contemptuous of the masses in his written texts and in his private conversations, not so in his public speeches, where he effuses love of the *Volk* and of ordinary Germans.' Second, fascists do not attain power without the acquiescence or even active assent of the traditional elites (Paxton 2005). The excesses of fascism require active complicity among the traditional elite, including magistrates, police officials, army officers, and corporate leaders.

Fascism also helps large corporations to expand by undertaking imperialist wars. As Lenin (2020) noted, imperialism is the monopoly stage of capitalism.[1] Fascism helps monopoly capital to achieve the internal goal of a docile workforce and to meet the external objective of imperialist control of markets and resources (Patnaik 2023a). Thus, capitalism is antithetical to both democracy and pacifism (Landa 2009). Pauwels (2017, pp. 93–94) gives the example of how Deutsche Bank made money from Nazi wars:

> By trading the gold of the Nazis, or rather, stolen by the Nazis from their victims, Deutsche Bank made a lot of money. This business involved large quantities of gold of different types: gold looted from the national banks of Czechoslovakia, Belgium and the Netherlands

> (Beutegold), gold stolen from rich German Jews during in the context of Aryanization (Raubgold), and gold taken from the victims of the Holocaust in the ghettos and camps and therefore symbolically—and sometimes literally—stained with blood (Opfergold or Blutgold).

The relentless pursuit of profits causes corporations to support and manipulate fascists into unleashing imperialist conflicts and wars. We should recall that at the Nuremberg trials, an American prosecutor, Telford Taylor, declared that 'those enterprises, and not the crazy and fanatical Nazis, were the real war criminals' (ibid., p. 96). In the violence that unfolds with the rise of fascists to power, it is the lower classes who pay the price. It is significant to remember that nearly 13.5 million Germans were killed, wounded, or taken prisoner between 1939 and 1945, of which the great majority undoubtedly was of lower classes (ibid.).

Fascist rule has a specific class-based character. The upper classes rarely join fascist governments and allow the petty bourgeoisie to run them. It helps big capital to maintain distance and, when the time is ripe, to abandon fascists. As Pauwels (2017, p. 49) notes in the German context, 'they would thus be able to dissociate themselves from Nazism, blame all the crimes and the misery on Hitler and the other Nazis, and piously plead not guilty'.

As a result, the middle classes form the backbone of fascist rule (Guerin 1973; Poulantzas 2018). Middle classes have a vested interest in maintaining the status quo and in supporting big businesses to safeguard their positions of relative privilege. Furthermore, nationalism has a far greater appeal for the middle class as opposed to any other class in society (Guerin 1973).

The key positions and class interests of the upper and middle classes do not mean that fascists do not require lower classes (working classes, peasants, and lower middle classes). The consent of lower classes is required to create order through their participation as foot soldiers and stormtroopers in the political sphere. Because fascism is fundamentally against the material interests of the lower classes, they are primarily won through propaganda, which is a key fascist weapon.

Rather than change property relations, fascists misdirect lower classes with propaganda and spectacle (Benjamin 2008). The goal of fascist propaganda is not to convince the intellect, but to sway the will (Stanley 2020). As Guerin (1973, p. 96) suggests, based on his reading of the writing of Hitler and his propaganda minister Paul Joseph Goebbels,

> In Mein Kampf, that amazing handbook of a political agitator, which might have the subtitle 'Or the Art of Taming the Masses', Hitler explains: 'I was always extraordinarily interested in propaganda, an art that remained almost unknown to the bourgeois parties. Propaganda should considerably precede organization, and first win the human material to be kneaded by the latter.'

Goebbels stated later that 'propaganda is an essential function of the modern state. No one else has brought to such a degree of virtuosity the art of dominating the masses. The feeble attempts of other countries to imitate us are those of mere amateurs' (ibid.). Fascist propaganda rests on the scorn of the masses. 'Propaganda must be kept on the level of the masses, and its value should be measured only by the results obtained,' Hitler advises. And his pupil Goebbels cynically repeats: 'Propaganda has only one aim, to win the masses. And any means that serve this end are good' (ibid.).

The purpose of propaganda is to make the masses believe that their own interests demand the preservation of the capitalist economic order (Rosenberg 2016). To achieve this objective, the rage of the masses has to be manufactured and directed against the other. Such propaganda is particularly effective when there is a crisis and material structures further divisiveness and hatred. As Reich (1970) and Fromm (1994) make us understand, the effectiveness of ideologies of obedience and manufactured hatred should also be located in the repressive structures of the family and sexuality. Even prior to capturing power, Nazis recognized the power of propaganda for shaping the new citizen and infiltrated bureaucracies with its members (Rentschler 1996; Welch 2001). Once in power, a department for 'Popular Enlightenment and Propaganda' took control of all means of mass communication such as literature, theatre, music, fine arts, press, and radio to 'all tasks of spiritual direction of the nation' (Welch 2001, p. 18). Propaganda becomes potent when it accompanies a strongly organized movement, as in the case of Hindutva, which we further unpack in the subsequent sections.

* * *

The ideology of Hindutva coincides with the RSS and its affiliates (the Sangh Parivar). The RSS was founded in 1925 to advance the idea of the pure nation, and its founder, Keshav Baliram Hedgewar, created an organization for achieving Hindu mass mobilization against the ideals of a secular socialist state imagined by other nationalists (Basu et al. 1993; Mukhopadhyay 2019; Patel 2020; T. Sarkar 2022). The history of the RSS and its activities have been extensively documented (for example, Basu et al. 1993; Vanaik 2017). A founding feature of the ideology of Hindutva was the propagation of a communal division between Hindus and Muslims and chauvinistic nationalism (T. Sarkar 2022). This communalism was primarily a mid-nineteenth-century creation as part of the British strategy to divide and rule (Mukherjee 2022). It has its roots in both the objective economic relations between the two communities and the British design to deepen the divide and restrict the growing anti-colonial movement (see Casolari's chapter in this volume). The RSS has its headquarters in Nagpur and Maharashtra was a key centre in its original development. Anti-caste movements and Dalit assertions in the early 1920s in Maharashtra made the region a fertile ground for a reactionary Hindutva ideology (Basu et al. 1993). One of the founders of the RSS, B. S. Moonje, went to Italy to learn about fascism in 1931 and played a key role in the initial moulding of the organization along fascist lines (Casolari 2000). It is notable that Golwalkar (1966), the second head of the RSS, identified Muslims, communists, and Christians as threats to the ideal of the Hindu nation. Golwalkar (2020 [1939]) praised the methods deployed by Hitler in purging Jews to create a pure nation. Another important figure in the pantheon of the Sangh Parivar is Vinayak Savarkar, who invented Hindutva, romanticized the idea of being a Hindu, and instilled a sense of victimhood among them (Mukhopadhyay 2019). The Sangh Parivar specializes in using the 'hurt sentiment' (Simeon 2016, p. 161) to mobilize Hindus against its manufactured 'enemies' to further its brand of chauvinist nationalism (T. Sarkar 2022).

There has been an extensive debate among those who are critical of the activities of the RSS on whether it can be labelled as fascist (Desai 2016; Jaffrelot 1993; Vanaik 1994). On the one hand, several scholars have pointed to how the Sangh Parivar drew inspiration from European fascists (Ahmad 1993; S. Banaji 2018; Basu et al., 1993; Casolari 2000). On the other hand, scholars like Jaffrelot (1993, 2021) and Vanaik (1994), who otherwise note that the Sangh Parivar works at the grassroots to propagate and impose its views through both persuasion and coercion, do not see Hindutva as fascism. Rejecting such an interpretation, Desai (2016) urges her readers to see inescapable parallels between Hindutva and European fascism. She provides an extensive and sound critique of Vanaik's (1994) and Jaffrelot's

(1993) refusal to interpret Hindutva as fascism. We concur with Desai's (2016) reading that Vanaik (1994) exaggerates the strength of the liberal democratic model of capitalism because of the historical juncture of the fall of the Soviet Union and that Jaffrelot (1993) misreads othering, the RSS as a putschist organization, and the absence of personality cult in the Sangh Parivar. Without repeating her arguments, it suffices to say that we clearly see the current regime as a fascist one. As Arundhati Roy (2020) notes, we cannot wait for millions to be gassed to death before using the label of fascism. Moreover, the Modi regime after 2014 has shown various fascist tendencies—chauvinistic nationalism, dictatorial control to further corporate interests, the othering of Muslims as the internal enemy and making them the target of mass hatred, encouraging death-worshipping cults of unreason in the form of stormtroopers, using democratic institutions to seize power and destroying democracy, legitimizing and institutionalizing violence, and attempting to control the private sphere. A chilling instance where these tendencies manifested is the mob lynching of Mohammad Akhlaq on 28 September 2015 in Bisada village of western Uttar Pradesh. Akhlaq was killed by a mob following the propaganda by Hindutva outfits that his family was storing and consuming beef in their house. This was on the basis of propaganda that included the public announcement system at a local temple (Ramakrishnan 2015). The recent laws enacted in several BJP-ruled states to restrict inter-religious marriages in the name of love jihad[2] and using stormtroopers with a compliant bureaucracy to enforce its writ are instances of the attempt by the Sangh Parivar to control the private sphere (Strohl 2019). We concur with J. Banaji (2016, p. 225) that

> the Sangh Parivar is in some ways a purer version of the political culture of a more traditional fascism. The pogroms in India have far exceeded in scale anything that Germany saw in Weimar or the Nazi period (short of the mass extermination of the Jews when the Nazis finally turned to the 'final solution').

The Sangh Parivar has, over the last hundred years, created organizational structures to help Hindutva gradually penetrate the imagination of the masses and institutions of governance (Jha 2017). The political rise of the Sangh Parivar began in the 1980s with the introduction of neoliberalism in India, when the BJP polarized polity and created its presence as a right-wing force (Desai 2016). Despite several warnings by Jawaharlal Nehru, various Congress regimes after India's independence in 1947 allowed the RSS to spread its tentacles (Mukherjee 2022). As Simeon (2016, p. 203) insightfully notes,

> South Asian fascism is more complex than the situation in pre-war Europe. This obliges us to think and rethink its elemental aspects. Here it is not a matter of a singular event such as a seizure of power by a fascist dictator, but a slow bleeding process that builds its strength incrementally ... the continued activity of militias and vigilante groups manifests a systematic attempt to militarise public space. War has now vacated the border ... it has spread inwards, into the entrails of polity.

It has truly been what Gramsci (1971) terms as a 'war of position' or a process of gradual cultural shift in creating hegemony. We have witnessed a fascification of society over time without fascists actually in power (Patnaik 2019). A prime site of this 'war of position' is education. The decline of the public education system after the neoliberal turn has been used by the RSS to indoctrinate young minds (Bhatty and Sundar 2020). Apart from using its *shakhas*, it has set up formal schools through the Akhil Bhartiya Vidya Bharti Shiksha Sansthan and informal schools (*sanskar kendras*, or cultural centres) across the country, in addition to special schools called Ekal Vidyalayas as part of their 'tribal uplift' programme (ibid.). Today they run 12,065 formal schools catering to 3.16 million children, 7,797 informal schools,[3] and 92,066 Ekal Vidyalayas catering to 2.64 million students.[4]

The conjuncture that has helped the BJP to attain power is the crisis triggered by the collapse of the post-independence political consensus in which violent capitalist accumulation coexisted with state welfarism guided by liberal regimes. The neoliberal turn of the Indian economy in the 1980s under the Congress hastened the demise of the consensus that formerly helped the party to dominate the political sphere. Neoliberalism has resulted in high levels of inequality and the transfer of wealth to the upper classes (Chandrasekhar 2019; Das 2020; Oxfam 2023; Patel 2022; Patnaik 2021b). Neoliberalism has also contributed to the weakening of working-class initiatives and left forces. The increasing appropriation of surplus because of neoliberalism is illustrated in Figure 1.1.

The figure shows that in organized manufacturing, the ratio of profits to net value added has been rising since the 1990s. Despite an increase in

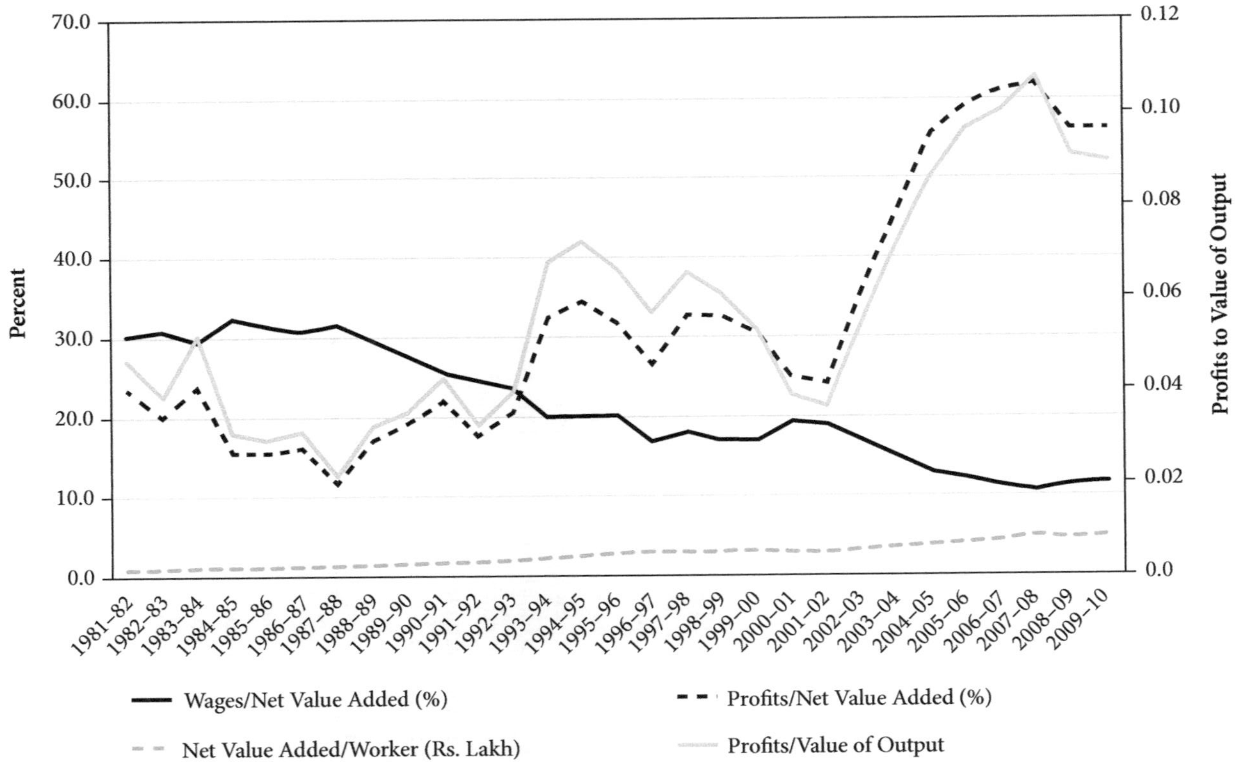

Figure 1.1 Profits, wages, and productivity in organized manufacturing

Source: Adapted from Chandrasekhar and Ghosh (2012).

productivity per worker, the wage as a percentage of value added has been falling. The surplus is being appropriated by the rich at a higher rate. This has caused an increase in inequality and abject poverty. As a result, the proportion of the population with access to less than 2,200 calories per person per day in rural India increased from 58 per cent in 1993–1994 to 68 per cent in 2011–2012 and in urban India from 57 per cent to 65 per cent (Patnaik 2021a). The Gini coefficient, a measure of inequality, shows a sharp increase after 1991 (see Figure 1.2). It has made India into one of the most unequal countries in the world (Kar 2024).

A particularly sharp manifestation of the ongoing political crisis, which coincides with the aforementioned drastic increase in inequality, was the anti-corruption movement before the 2014 elections that brought the BJP to power. The liberal political establishment's response was constrained by its own hypocrisy towards the widespread resentment against the corruption and increasing inequalities stemming from the neoliberal policies that were its brainchild. The purportedly pro-poor Congress regime set up sophisticated and oppressive security apparatuses that systematized the forced displacement of populations in favour of extractive industries while criminalizing dissent (Sundar 2016). The business elite that was immensely benefitting from the neoliberal policies, meanwhile, was alarmed by the attempts (however meagre and poorly implemented) to compensate for rising inequality through rights-based approaches to food and education and policies that protected the rights of populations threatened with displacement and irreversible damage. Neoliberalism creates an aversion among the ruling and middle classes to any state or social support for the weak (Balagopal 2023). As in the inter-war years in Germany, corporations were insatiable despite what the Congress had been offering them for decades and were surveying the political landscape to remove the meagre restrictions that remained on capitalist accumulation. As a result, the Congress regime failed at both instilling hopes for social mobility in immiserating lower classes and alleviating the economic anxieties of the middle and upper classes, thereby making the masses amenable to fascist persuasion (Varman and Vijay 2022). As Dimitrov (1938, p. 9) noted, 'fascism delivers up the people to be devoured by the most corrupt and venal elements.... Speculating on the profound disillusionment of the masses in bourgeois-democratic governments, fascism hypocritically denounces corruption.' The anti-corruption movement (that many argued was supported by the Sangh Parivar) eroded the legitimacy of the Congress to rule the country. The middle and upper classes, as defenders

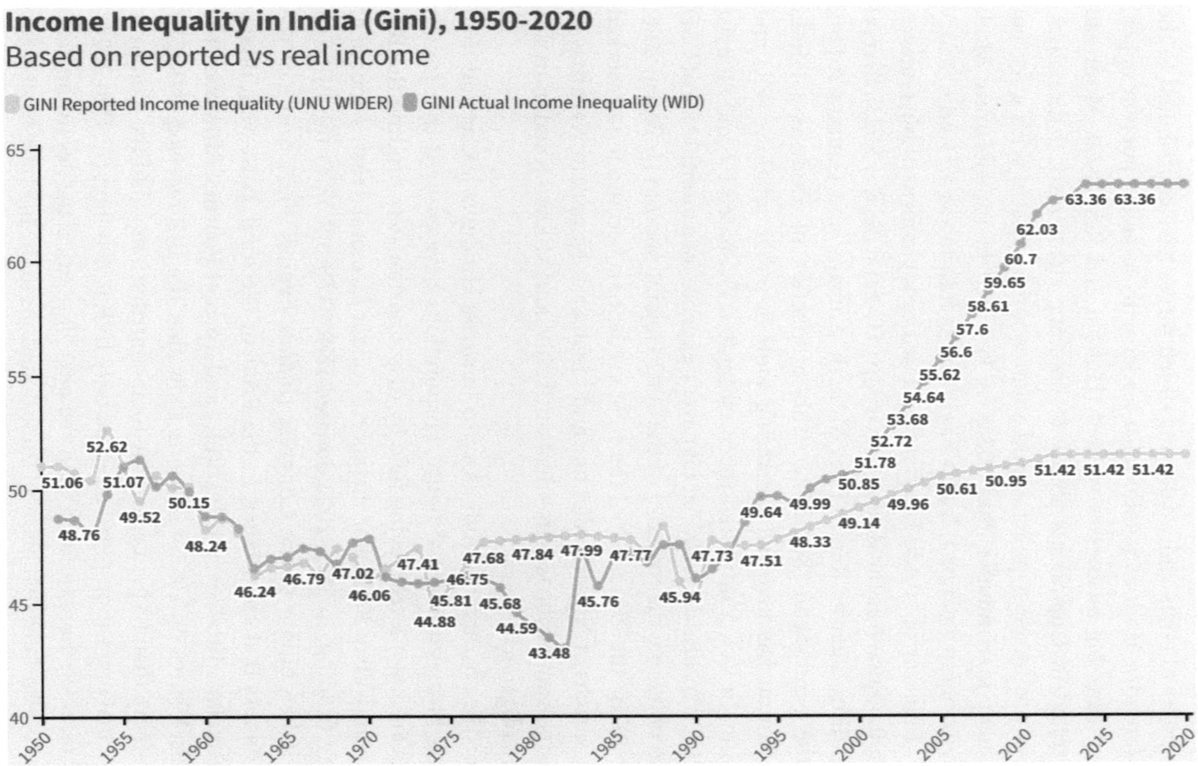

Figure 1.2 Rising income inequality in India

Source: Kar (2024).

of petty and big privileges, found expression of their grievances in a patriotic critique of the state for wasting away the nation's greatness by supporting the weak (Balagopal 2023).

The political crisis and weakening of left forces have contributed to the rise of Narendra Modi as a nationalist leader with sufficient popular appeal to deliver what big businesses wanted (Hansen and Roy 2022). Modi had demonstrated in Gujarat his ability to combine chauvinistic nationalism, aggressive pro-business policies, and suppression of dissent with a fervent commitment to Hindutva (Sud 2022). A key step in transforming Modi from a regional to a national leader has been his framing as a 'Hindu Hriday Samrat' (Emperor of Hindu Hearts) facilitated by a platform of big Gujarat-based capital known as the Resurgent Group of Gujarat (A. Roy 2023). Several big capitalists, such as Ratan Tata, Mukesh Ambani, and Gautam Adani, joined the bandwagon (Sud 2022). This production of Modi as a Hindu Hriday Samrat has involved marketing tools of public relations (PR) and advertising. In fact, Modi hired the Washington, DC-based PR and lobbyist firm APCO Worldwide in 2007 at taxpayers' expense for a monthly fee of USD 25,000 to obliterate the memory of the 2002 Gujarat pogrom (J. Banaji 2016; Jaffrelot 2021). The PR firm had the right credentials because it had worked for Sani Abacha, a Nigerian dictator and kleptocrat; Nursultan Nazarbayev, Kazakhstan's authoritarian president until 2019; and Mikhail Khodorkovsky, a Russian oligarch.

After the creation of Modi as a pro-business Hindutva leader and then launching him as a national figure, corporations have ensured that Indian elections are not a level playing field by disproportionately funding the BJP (Varman and Vijay 2022). For instance, Prudent Electoral Trust, a source of corporate funding, in 2021–2022 donated INR 33.65 billion to the BJP and only INR 1.66 billion to the Congress (*Indian Express* 2022). Some of the biggest donors that contributed to the Prudent Electoral Trust were Bharti Airtel, Arcelor Mittal, Serum Institute, and Torrent Pharma. Moreover, the recent disclosures on electoral bonds show that the BJP received INR 52.7 billion—more than 53 per cent of the total contributions—and the Congress as a principal opposition party received only INR 0.95 billion (A. Deb 2024). The BJP received more funding than the next 30 political parties in the field. The reports also show that many of these donations to the BJP have been made by corporations in return for government contracts, policy changes, and favourable tax deals (Karthikeyan et al. 2024; Tiwari and Project Electoral Bond 2024).

Big businesses require extra-legal and non-state instruments of coercion to further profiteering and do not just rely on the state's regular methods of force to secure control. Such support is offered by fascist mobs in tandem with state terror (Zetkin 2017). It is for this reason that big business in India nourishes, maintains, and promotes the BJP with all the means at its disposal in terms of political power and money. The corporate funding to the BJP helps oil its electoral machinery and produce the larger-than-life image of Modi. As we know, fascist politics destroys the relations of mutual respect between citizens that are the foundation of a healthy liberal democracy, replacing them with trust in one figure alone, the leader (Stanley 2020). The BJP both reconfigures as much as it innovates upon constitutional democracy from within (Hansen and Roy 2022). Once in power, the Sangh Parivar has used the various tools of political control already in place. The authoritarian apparatuses designed by the purportedly liberal democratic system were repurposed by the BJP with more skill and viciousness, devoid of the (liberal) hypocrisy that constrained the preceding regimes. It has used constitutional means to capture the state. 'Governmental Hindutva' makes full use of 'its discretionary authority to transform and dismantle democratic institutions, acting "as per rule" all the while' (Hansen and Roy 2022, p. 9).

The Sangh Parivar has garnered mass support by posing as anti-elite in its rhetoric. It is similar to the popular appeal of the Nazi Party that was based on their calls to overthrow the traditional German elite. As in other contexts, particularly the United States, the far-right movements funded by billionaires use the term 'elite' detached from economic status to label those fractions of the elite who oppose fascist imaginations. Hindutva's popularity, similarly, hinges on its disavowal of a section of the elite constituted by liberal intellectual classes, including international non-governmental organizations and progressive media (derisively referred to as 'Lutyens' Delhi'), while maintaining cosy relationships with indigenous plutocrats and corporations. Thus, the rise of Hindutva is situated in its appeal to both the elite and lower classes. While the current Hindutva regime furthers the class interests of the more organized elite, it garners lower-class support through propaganda and doles such as free ration.

Arendt (1966) has argued that popular support for a fascist regime shows that people overlook their rights and material interests. We offer a more careful reading of such a formulation. In our interpretation of the dominance of Hindutva, we do not see lower classes overlooking their material conditions. Instead, abject poverty, caste inequities, patriarchy, and the absence of grassroots democracy limit the lower classes' expectations of material gains to the minimal benefits doled out by the state (for example, the current offering of five kilograms of free food grain). The masses are, as J. Banaji (2016, p. 222) describes, in a state of 'manipulated seriality'. Seriality is passive, inert, and dispersed people, not the behaviour of a cohesive group. Fascists work on serialities to produce desired outcomes. Thus, dispersed masses of people are susceptible to manipulations by organized groups. The control over the state apparatus furthers the dominance of the Sangh Parivar over disorganized masses reduced to individuals.

The politics of the RSS is fundamentally casteist, patriarchal, and anti-democratic (Kasbe 2019). The control over state apparatuses helps Hindutva reinforce the stranglehold of the highly organized big capital whose interests coincide with those of the upper classes and upper castes in society (Poruthiyil 2021). Modi's record both as a chief minister of Gujarat and as the country's prime minister suggests his governments have enabled the upper castes and classes to control Indian politics and have widened inequality (Jaffrelot 2021). The current regime has strengthened the stranglehold of the elite, and the new rulers are part of the Hindutva establishment elite that is structured and sustained by the cruel inequalities of power that Sangh's anti-elite rhetoric rails against (S. Roy 2022). The ongoing control of the old elite reminds us that while fascist politics is monstrous and violent in newer ways, there is much that is unexceptional and routinized as well (Patnaik 2023b).

In sustaining the Hindutva propaganda, corporate media houses have played a crucial role (Naqvi 2019). The current Hindutva propaganda makes use of modern tools and deploys the tactics and vocabularies of anti-terrorism, anti-imperialism, digitization, and development, along with the older tropes of Hinduism present in paintings, calendar art, folk theatre, and cinema (S. Banaji 2018). Through a series of policies, this government has systematically constructed digital surveillance mechanisms by bringing streaming services into the ambit of censorship (Chisti 2023). These policies were supplemented by the vigilante mechanism of cyber and street activists and indiscriminate uses of penal provisions to criminalise content creators in the digital sphere (S. Banaji 2018). Control over these techniques of communication has turned Hindu rituals into muscular public–political spectacles that are used to threaten the other in the name of religion and nationalism. For instance, Hindutva forces make strategic use of popular music to spread their message (Purohit 2023).

Hindutva also uses monuments to further its messaging by repurposing the existing sites of cultural imagery and constructing new ones. The construction of the Ram Temple in Ayodhya on a site where a mosque existed for centuries is a prime example of such messaging. Another example is the Central Vista project that houses the Rashtrapati Bhawan, the parliament building, and other historically significant monuments. Activists and writers have noted that the execution of the Central Vista project is an attempt to re-sculpt Delhi along the contours of majoritarian Hindutva historiography (Appadurai 2021; A. Roy 2021). Such symbolism also includes the sphere of popular culture, and a cricket stadium in Ahmedabad has been renamed as Narendra Modi Stadium. A similar trend is visible in the renaming of cities and railway stations (for example, Allahabad to Prayagraj, Gurgaon to Gurugram, Mughalsarai Junction to Pandit Deen Dayal Upadhyaya Junction) as attempts to erase India's Muslim heritage.

'[F]ascists need a demonized enemy against which to mobilize followers' (Paxton 2005, p. 17). In this, Hindutva's othering of Muslims resembles the anti-Semitism of the Nazi Party. Hindutva is particularly insidious because it has been effective in deploying violent othering under the facade of nationalism, modernization, and democracy (J. Banaji 2016), and it does so by appropriating past prejudices and combining them with new ones 'skilfully dressed up as old verities, and broadcasting the resultant compound through the most up-to-date media techniques' (S. Sarkar 2016, p. 143). These conditions and strategies have helped the Sangh Parivar to recruit an army of stormtroopers, with Muslims being their prime targets (Jha 2017). The recent enactment of the Citizenship Amendment Act (CAA) is a prime example of a framing of Muslims that reduces them to second-class citizens. The act identifies Hindu, Buddhist, Jain, Christian, Sikh, and Zoroastrian as 'persecuted minorities', who arrived by 2014 from its Muslim-majority neighbours Afghanistan, Pakistan, and Bangladesh and are entitled to apply for citizenship. It omits Muslims, Jews, Bahais, and atheists from its purview, introducing a religious filter that violates the secular principles enshrined in the Indian Constitution (I. Roy 2022).

Hindutva tries to occlude the transfer of wealth to the elite and rising inequality by manufacturing a phantasmagoria of right-wing nationalism in which Muslims are framed as enemies from the past—a parade of ghosts that distracts from the real monstrosity of neoliberalism (see Varman and Vijay 2022). While the masses are kept busy with such symbolic contests and spectacles, the governmental Hindutva has ensured that its corporate sponsors are duly rewarded. After 2004, the Congress regime operated as a regulator state to support big business, the BJP government has made the state into a broker-state cutting deals and furthering the interests of corporations (Azad et al. 2019). After 2014, several labour laws have been changed to help businesses (Subramanian 2022). For instance, in July 2017, an amendment to the Child Labour (Prohibition and Regulation) Act, 1986, reduced the number of companies identified as hazardous from eighty-three to only those listed in the Factories Act that pertain to mining and explosives. In September 2020, the Lok Sabha passed three labour bills—the Industrial Relations Code, the Code on Social Security, and the Occupational Safety, Health, and Working Conditions Code Bills. The bills increase the vulnerability of the informal labour force by granting extended discretion to employers to provide social security and to terminate workers' employment. This change in Indian labour laws has certain historical parallels with Nazi Germany:

> Most remarkable is the fact that wages declined while profits were rising sharply, as we have already seen. Those two phenomena were related; they had a common origin. The Nazis deliberately chose to maintain wages at low levels in order to make it easier for the profits of their friends in big business, the corporations and banks, to skyrocket. Thanks to the services of the Nazis, German capital was able to grab a bigger share of the "pie" of the social product at the expense of labour. (Pauwels 2017, p. 77)

In addition, several other laws have been altered by the BJP government to support corporations in the mining sector. In March 2015, the Coal Mines (Special Provisions) Act was introduced, which opened India's nationalized coal mining sector to private players and set terms for the auction and sale of coal mines/blocks. Similarly, in May 2016, the Mines and Minerals (Development and Regulation) Amendment Bill was passed in Parliament, allowing the transfer of mining leases granted in auction to private individuals, pending approval by state governments.

> Within the first three months of assuming office in 2014, the Modi government issued environmental clearance to 33 out of 41 proposals, diverting more than 7,000 hectares of forestland for the purpose of mining, construction, and special economic zones. A major share of the diverted land was allocated to private corporations. (Dutta and Nielsen 2021, pp. 72–73)

A slew of other bills advanced the interests of corporations (Subramanian 2022). For instance, in July 2016, the Compensatory Afforestation Funds Act, 2016, was passed by Parliament. The act bypasses consent from village councils and other forest dwellers and allows plantation activities on protected forest lands. The Draft National Policy was released in March 2018 by the Ministry of Environment proposing the use of 'degraded forest areas' (less than 40 per cent tree canopy density) for private plantations and projects under public–private partnerships to cover over 34 million hectares of forest land. In a similar vein, the finance minister, Nirmala Seetharaman, announced the privatization or disinvestment target of INR 105 billion in July 2019, with the government seeking to reduce its stake in public enterprises to below 51 per cent. These include undertakings such as Air India, Oil and Natural Gas Corporation (ONGC), Bharat Petroleum Corporation Limited (BPCL), Bharat Sanchar Nigam Limited (BSNL), and Life Insurance Corporation (LIC), among others. The government passed the Coastal Regulation Zone Notification 2019 in December 2019 to open up India's coastline for enhanced commercial activities. It allows for construction on the previously protected 200-metre no-development zone in rural coastal areas. In 2019, the BJP government lowered the base corporate tax rate from 30 per cent to 22 per cent, which significantly lowered the corporate tax to GDP ratio in India (Chowdhury 2023, p. 155). Furthermore, the government identified in December 2019 a hundred railway routes for private carriers to operate 150 passenger trains every year. In January 2020, the Indian Railways announced that its production units will be privatized and private companies will be allowed to manage 750 railway stations across the country. Another form of benefit doled out to the big business was in the form of the three infamous farm bills in 2020: the Farmers' Produce Trade and Commerce (Promotion and Facilitation) Act, the Farmers' (Empowerment and Protection) Agreement of Price Assurance Act, and the Farm Services and Essential Commodities (Amendment). The bills were eventually withdrawn before the crucial Uttar Pradesh assembly elections because of farmers' protests.

On 12 December 2023, the union government introduced in Parliament three bills that have replaced the existing codes: the Indian Penal Code, 1860, with the Bharatiya Nyaya Sanhita (BNS-II); the Criminal Procedure Code, 1973, with the Bharatiya Nagarik Suraksha Sanhita (BNSS-II); and the Indian Evidence Act, 1872, with the Bharatiya Sakshya Bill (BSB-II). These bills equip the government with adequate power to hollow out democracy. The new laws enable the government to dramatically scale up the arrest, detention, prosecution, and imprisonment of democratic opponents, dissidents, and activists (Gopal 2023). India is on a fast track to expand state control, both by over-criminalizing and by awarding more police powers; these bills, instead of decolonizing the legal system, actually codify it by giving the state heightened control over its citizens (Surendranath and Sikora 2023).

While the BJP has enacted new laws to support corporations, in a very specific way, it has advanced the interests of the new monopoly houses of Adani and Ambanis, who have also been very proactive in their support of the Modi regime (Patnaik 2023c). For example, the adjudicating authority of the Directorate of Revenue Intelligence (DRI), K. V. S. Singh, passed an order striking down all proceedings launched by the DRI against the Adani Group firms. The firms were accused of allegedly inflating the total declared value of goods imported under power and infrastructure heads, which attracts 0 or less than 5 per cent duty to the extent of INR 39.74 billion (Narayan 2017). In October 2018, out of the 126 contracts made available to private firms to set up piped natural gas networks and fuel stations across the country, the Adani Group secured 25—the largest number awarded to a single player through the bidding process (Subramanian 2022). The Adani Group was granted (in March 2019) all six contracts for the modernizing of airports in Ahmedabad, Guwahati, Jaipur, Lucknow, Mangaluru, and Thiruvananthapuram (ibid.).

These favours should not be, however, read as crony capitalism. It misses the specificity of the connection between monopoly capital and fascism. All capitalism is crony capitalism because discretion is always exercised in how contracts are awarded to corporations and in the framing of laws to support them (Patnaik 2023c). The term 'crony capitalism' assumes that there can be a version of capitalism that does not favour specific businesses. Moreover, crony capitalism becomes a trajectory of capitalism that is a deviation from its otherwise benign path. This ignores the monopoly tendency that is central to capitalism (Baran and Sweezy 1966) and which plays a key role in supporting and benefitting from fascism. Under monopoly capitalism, the relationship between monopoly capitalists and the state becomes far closer, as is evident in the corporate–Hindutva nexus.

As a result of the corporate–Hindutva nexus, lower classes have suffered greater losses, and their lives are marked by increasing poverty and hunger (Chowdhury and Keane 2021; Varman and Vijay 2022). Data show that between 2011–2012 and 2017–2018, per capita consumption expenditure on all items in real terms has fallen by 9 per cent in rural India. Nothing of this sort had ever happened in normal times in independent India (Chowdhury 2023; Patnaik 2021a). While the poor have either stagnated or become poorer, the rich are making bigger gains than ever before. According to a recent Oxfam (2023, p. 7) report,

> The wealthiest 10 percent own more than 72 percent of the total wealth; the top 5 percent own nearly 62 percent of the total wealth, and the top 1 percent own nearly 40.6 percent of the total wealth. The country still has the world's highest number of poor at 228.9 million. On the other hand, the total number of billionaires in India increased from 102 in 2020 to 166 billionaires in 2022.

Fascism thrives when high inequality coincides with deep and easily evocable social divisions (Hacker and Pierson 2020) as in the case of India. The contributors to this volume particularly highlight this connection in their chapters.

* * *

Various authors in this volume reflect on the relationship between corporations and fascism and deepen our understanding of Hindutva. The contributors expose the forces that seek to sponsor and gain from fascism. The collection begins with Marzia Casolari's chapter, which uncovers the historical roots of the economy of hatred in India. Accordingly, the economic basis of Indian communal hatred is not a sporadic factor but a historical trend that was inaugurated by Britishers to advance colonial rule. She explains how racial or religious explanations of political hatred often conceal economic factors. She further argues that the defence of caste privileges and the related economic status was the real, underlying, initial objective of the violent resurgence of the Ayodhya issue. Casolari also points to the 2002 Gujarat pogrom to foreground the economic causes of the communal strife. The violence in such circumstances is framed as a naturalization of anger (Hansen and Roy 2022) for which no Hindutva organization can be held responsible and is allowed within the paradigm of 'permissive atmosphere' (Ghassem-Fachandi 2022, p. 289).

In her chapter, Radhika Desai casts in high relief the India Inc.–Modi bond. She questions the utility of the 'crony capitalist' frame in analyses of big capital as it reinforces a mistaken view that the business–state corruptions are aberrations. She outlines different phases of the rise of Hindutva fascism that have led to corporate support for the BJP. Her chapter foregrounds the incorporation of new 'provincial propertied classes' into the Hindutva fold aided by the dilution of Brahminism as a key point of inflection in the rise of the BJP. Drawing uncanny parallels to fascist regimes of the early twentieth century, Desai illustrates the usefulness of fascist prism to explain the links between the Modi regime and big business. She also outlines how the 'policy paralysis' of the Congress-led 2009 regime was a key turning point in the relationship between big business and Narendra Modi. Desai closes by pointing to the limits of fascism in resolving capitalist crises.

Given this background of fascism, Prabhat Patnaik's chapter implicates international finance capital in the rise of neo-fascism in India. The logic of neoliberalism breaks down the solidarity between classes, with the upper and middle classes, beneficiaries of big capital, pitted against the working classes whose lives are incrementally worsened. A neoliberal system is unable to address the crises that it spawns, and big businesses fund a neo-fascist alternative. Patnaik further points to the limits of the neo-fascist state that is trapped in the imperatives of international finance and is unable to solve the crisis that justified its existence.

In his chapter, Anand Teltumbde elaborates on the caste dimensions of neoliberalism that are driving the fascification of India. Both neoliberalism and Hindutva reject equality or fraternity. While the former considers inequality as a virtue, Hindutva is built on a caste-based and Brahmanical view of social hierarchy. They share the idea of graded freedoms depending on socio-economic privileges. Teltumbde, like Casolari, traces the conditions of fascification to the colonial regime's creation of Hindus and Muslims into distinct communities resentful of each other. However, the exploitation of these sectarian fissures for fascification required the active connivance of big capital that reaped benefits in return. Teltumbde places Modi at the centre of this mutually reinforcing project by illustrating how he consolidated a Hindu majoritarian constituency on the one hand while, on the other, initiating a wide-ranging neoliberal transformation that accelerated wealth concentration among his corporate backers. This chapter is one of the first academic works after Teltumbde's 30-month incarceration by the current regime on what legal experts have called frivolous charges; he was released in November 2022 and submitted this chapter to the collection in January 2023.

Ajay Gudavarthy and Vijay Gudavarthy identify in their chapter how the Hindutva state has benefitted from the popular consent built through a series of reconciliations of what were hitherto considered opposites. They argue that liberal institutions failed to protect or realize the aspirations of the vulnerable because of the exclusions inflicted by financial capital that cut across class, caste, and regional differences. These exclusions provided the material basis to stitch together a majority consisting of formerly antagonistic groups on the one hand and mass political participation with extra-institutional violence on the other. This manufactured but resilient block, the authors argue, provides the regime with the legitimacy it needs for authoritarian interventions that scuttle democratic institutions and facilitate further wealth accumulation for the elite.

In his chapter, Arvind Narrain demonstrates the mutually reinforcing nature of the rhetoric of ethnic superiority, mass mobilization or mob rule, and support for private capital that prop up Hindutva fascism. Individuals immiserated by unfettered capitalism compensate for their emasculation by binding themselves into supremacist mobs that engage in public assaults and humiliations of dissenters and minorities. Narrain reveals the simultaneity of vociferous support for such displays of ethnic supremacy with a silent but foundational commitment to big capital displayed by the Hindutva regime. Distractions by regularly manufactured cultural flashpoints and the tragedy of the pandemic are used to hustle through regressive labour laws and environmental clearances that further lubricate capitalist accumulation.

Ashok Kumbamu in his chapter explores the sociopolitical and economic dynamics surrounding fascist tendencies and their implications for India. He uncovers the symbiotic alliance that has emerged between Brahmanical Hindutva forces, corporate entities, and the state apparatus, analysing their collaborative strategies and modus operandi. He builds on Sartre's and Banaji's writings and deploys the concept of manipulated seriality to explain Hindutva's mass mobilization. This mobilization is not grounded in genuine inclusivity, as Hindus are divided based on castes and sociocultural practices. Instead, it relies on the calculated manipulation of collective sentiments. Kumbamu closes the chapter by examining various policies that underscore how the Modi government employs constitutional mechanisms to promote and legitimize neoliberal Hindutva politics of dispossession and violence.

Amit Shrivastava in his chapter examines the nexus between Hindutva and a handful of large corporations. This nexus has stabilized under Modi through a centralized decision-making structure that is in turn nourished and bolstered by corporate funds and pliant media to deliver a series of corporate-friendly policies. The outcome of such deepening linkages between the centralized decision-making structure and big corporations is the breakdown of democratic feedback mechanisms resulting in a callous perpetuation of precarity of the informal sector, which employs most Indians. The centralization and digitization of welfare delivery have further led to the bypassing of regional systems of accountability, with constricted possibilities for grassroot mobilization and democracy. In these undemocratic structures, Shrivastava identifies the contradictions that offer possibilities of resistance.

Rohit Chopra in his chapter charts the extension of the fascist hegemony over sociopolitical realms to popular culture, in particular films. The spike in films that propagate and reaffirm Hindutva ideology and the silencing of content that threatens the ideological tenets of Hindutva resemble those in popular culture under the fascist regimes of Europe. Chopra shows that even films that purportedly represent resistance to Hindu nationalism are forced to adhere to the dictates of Hindutva.

In his chapter, Rohit Varman builds on Casolari's emphasis on the economy of hate to examine the testimonies of the Muslim victims of the 2020 pogrom in north-east Delhi that was allegedly incited and organized by the Sangh Parivar. This chapter explains how the lower classes act as instruments of fascist violence to further political mobilization from below and to create the degraded other. Fascist violence obfuscates the role of big businesses in the immiseration of lower classes as they seek material and symbolic compensation from the other. It furthers a delusion of exalted status through the guise of distributed sovereignty. The resulting religious hierarchy and divisions become tools to establish political hegemony that advances the interests of big capital. Thus, as instruments of fascist violence, lower-class Hindus intensify structural violence of which they are, as a majority, the prime victims. As Das (2020) reminds us, Hindutva is a class war cloaked under the guise of nationalism and religion. Fascist violence is an expression of the destructive tendencies that are inherent to a capitalist class society.

Daniel Kinderman in his chapter explores the reasons for the Indian business responses to Hindutva which have ranged from silence to open support. He considers fear of reprisal to greed and the identity of corporate owners, professionals, and customers that lock the interests of businesses to the regime. Reasons such as the threat of 'stick' in the form of vindictive state agencies and the benefits that accrue from aligning with the Hindu-nationalist agendas are often tough to disentangle. Kinderman supports his argument using primary evidence from businesses that supported the Bharat Jodo Yatra, organized by opposing political formations in 2023. The chapter also traces differences in the stances of Indian corporations with that of American corporations during Trump presidency to the contrasting political economies and stages of institutional development.

The book closes with Anand Patwardhan's reflections on the making of his widely acclaimed documentary film, *Ram Ke Naam* (In the Name of God), which examines the events leading up to the demolition of the Babri Mosque. This chapter provides critical insights into the demolition, which was an important milestone in Hindutva's rise to power. Patwardhan's account gains particular significance because of the way the BJP regime has used the spectacle of the inauguration of the Ram Temple on 22 January 2024 as a propaganda tool. As S. Deb (2024) observes, the inauguration is a step towards realizing the fantasy of Hindu Rashtra (Hindu Nation) and deeply wounding the republic. In recounting the making of the film, Patwardhan documents how history was fabricated to mobilize support for the Ram Temple and its deployment to tear the social fabric. The torn social fabric has allowed the Sangh Parivar to advance its divisive agenda to demonize Muslims and, as several chapters in this volume show, to use it to further corporate interests.

The authors contributing to this collection demonstrate the crucial role played by corporations in first hollowing Indian democracy and then instituting fascism into a hegemonic force. This collection establishes how the state's commitment to the dominance of big business morphed into the freedom for ethnic supremacists and state-sponsored violence on vulnerable populations. We believe that the reluctance among scholars to foreground the role of corporations in the rise of fascism in India is untenable, given the evidence provided in this collection.

The dismissal of fascism as a futile theoretical lens to evaluate contemporary business–state relations is equally counterproductive. While it is correct that Hindutva fascism may not create concentration camps, gas chambers, and imperialist expansions, it shares with the fascisms of Europe chauvinistic nationalism, advancement of corporate interests, annihilation of dissent, propaganda, and stormtroopers to inflict extra-judicial violence both on the street and in private spaces. It also has innovative characteristics and unique religious symbolisms, such as cow vigilantism, razing mosques to build temples, and the use of bulldozers on the houses of Muslims to mobilize popular support.

While acknowledging the central role of capitalism, we agree with Poulantzas (2018) that there is a *relative autonomy* of the political sphere. Relative autonomy means that although a fascist state serves corporate interests, it cannot be completely reduced to it. In essence, fascism acts as the instrument for the resolution of political crises within the bounds of a capitalist framework. Moreover, the rise of fascism in moments of capitalist crises should not be confused with its efficacy in resolving them. History shows that fascism is unable to successfully resolve capitalist crises, and as Desai (2016, 2024) correctly notes, it ends up further exacerbating the problems.

In this conjuncture, however, we should be deeply concerned about the health of Indian democracy. Fascism allows, as Browning (2017) shows in his remarkable book *Ordinary Men*, a widespread receptivity to mass murder. While some part of this violence is directed at the imagined enemies of Hindutva, a more significant part of the violence is directed against the majority Hindu population in a structural form as it is robbed of livelihood, education, health, and environment. To paraphrase Simeon (2016), big business and fascism combine to form a long rope that connects elite interests with mass sentiment, but this rope is marked by a noose at the end of it. And the noose is around the republic and its majority.

The result of the 2024 general elections that has forced the BJP into an alliance with other political parties is undoubtedly a setback to its fascist goals of converting India into a Hindu state conducive to unfettered capitalist exploitation (Desai 2024). It is, however, important to not misinterpret the electoral outcome as a harbinger for the re-establishment of liberal democracy. Recognition of the built-in mechanisms of violent oppression and exploitation, and the permanent threat of their deployment for corporate and fascist ends, should interrupt any celebratory analyses. Moreover, ten years of the Sangh Parivar's near-complete control over institutions have made these mechanisms more sophisticated and aligned with fascist goals (Bal 2024). Indeed, the escalating oppression of minorities and dissenters after the elections is a sobering realization of the resilience of the fascist organizational structure (Mander 2024). If history is an indication, Hindutva tends to emerge after setbacks in an even more virulent form that liberal political formations are ill-equipped to tackle.

In conclusion, the only way to overcome this situation is by recognizing the causes that have contributed to the current conjuncture. As Zetkin (2017, p. 12) reminds us,

> Yes, fascism is surely condemned to decay internally and to fall apart. Only temporarily can it serve the bourgeoisie as a tool of class struggle; only temporarily can it reinforce, whether legally or illegally, the power of the bourgeois state against the proletariat. Still, it would be disastrous for us to fall into the role of clever and refined observers of this process of decay. On the contrary, it is our bounden duty to drive this process forward and hasten it by every possible means.

To effectively counter the rise of fascism in India, it is essential to move beyond neoliberal capitalism, which has hit a dead-end and plunged the world into turmoil (Patnaik 2019). Therefore, to successfully fight against fascism, capitalism has to be resisted through mobilizations that simultaneously challenge corporations and the Sangh Parivar. This will require overcoming the current quagmire of identity politics and revitalizing class politics that consciously rectifies both maldistribution and misrecognition. Such class politics has to also countervail caste and gender inequities as they widely prevail in India if it has to meaningfully challenge fascism. It is perhaps appropriate to conclude the chapter with Arundhati Roy's (2020, p. 10) urgent reminder:

> *What lies ahead*
> *Reimagining the world. Only that.*

Notes

1. Lenin (2020, p. 237) outlines the following key features of monopoly capital: *(a)* the concentration of production and capital has developed to such a high stage that it has created monopolies which play a decisive role in economic life; *(b)* the merging of bank capital with industrial capital, and the creation, on the basis of this 'finance capital', of a financial oligarchy; *(c)* the export of capital as distinguished from the export of commodities acquires exceptional importance; *(d)* the formation of international monopolist capitalist associations which share the world among themselves; and *(e)* the territorial division of the whole world among the biggest capitalist powers is completed. Imperialism is capitalism at that stage of development at which the dominance of monopolies and finance capital is established, in which the export of capital has acquired pronounced importance.

2. The Sangh Parivar frames romantic liaisons between Muslim men and Hindu women as love jihad (Mankekar 2021). Muslim men are accused of seducing Hindu women into falling in love with them with the aim of converting them to Islam. Such accusations result in lynching, murder, and, in some Indian states, legislation that criminalizes inter-religious marriages.
3. See http://vidyabharti.net (accessed 14 March 2025).
4. See https://www.ekal.org/in/our-work/education (accessed 14 March 2025).

References

Ahmad, A. (1993). 'Culture, Community, Nation: On the Ruins of Ayodhya'. *Social Scientist* 21(7–8): 17–48.

Appadurai, A. (2021). 'How to Kill a Democracy'. *Social Anthropology* 29(2): 303–310.

Arendt, H. (1966). *The Origins of Totalitarianism*. London: Penguin.

Azad, R., S. Chakraborty, S. Ramani, D. Sinha (eds.) (2019). *A Quantum Leap in the Wrong Direction*. New Delhi: Orient Blackswan.

Bal, H. S. (2024). 'The Tyranny Will Get Worse'. *The Caravan*, 1 May. https://caravanmagazine.in/politics/tyranny-will-worsen. Accessed 14 March 2025.

Balagopal, K. (2023). *Understanding Fascism: Writings on Caste, Class and the State*. Hyderabad: South Side Press.

Banaji, J. (2016). *Fascism: Essays on Europe and India*. New Delhi: Three Essays Collective.

Banaji, S. (2018). Vigilante publics: Orientalism, modernity and Hindutva fascism in India. Javnost-The Public, 25(4), pp. 333–350.

Baran, P. A., and P. Sweezy (1966). *Monopoly Capital: An Essay on the American Economic and Social Order*. New York: Monthly Review Press.

Basu, T., P. Datta, S. Sarkar, T. Sarkar, and S. Sen (1993). *Khaki Shorts Saffron Flags*. New Delhi: Orient Longman

Benjamin, W. (2008). *The Work of Art in the Age of its Technological Reproducibility, and Other Writings on Media*. New York: Penguin.

Bhatty, K., and N. Sundar (2020). 'Sliding from Majoritarianism toward Fascism: Educating India under the Modi Regime'. *International Sociology* 35(6): 632–650.

Browning, C. (2017). *Ordinary Men*. New York: Harper.

Casolari, M. (2000). 'Hindutva's Foreign Tie-Up in the 1930s: Archival Evidence'. *Economic and Political Weekly* 35(4): 218–228.

Chandrasekhar, C. P. (2019). 'The Political Economy of the Modi Regime'. https://www.macroscan.org/cur/apr19/pdf/Modi_Regime.pdf. Accessed 14 March 2025.

Chandrasekhar, C. P., and J. Ghosh (2012). 'Of Profits and Growth'. https://www.macroscan.org/fet/may12/fet290512Profits_Growth.htm. Accessed 14 March 2025.

Chisti, S. (2023). 'Control + All or Delete: The Draft Broadcast Bill Is a Blueprint for Censorship'. *The Wire*, 7 December. https://thewire.in/government/control-all-or-delete-the-draft-broadcast-bill-is-a-blueprint-for-censorship. Accessed 14 March 2025.

Chowdhury, S. (2023). 'Economics and Politics under Modi Government: A Synoptic View'. *Human Geography* 16(2): 146–161.

Chowdhury, D. R., and J. Keane (2021). *To Kill a Democracy: India's Passage to Democracy*. New Delhi: Macmillan.

Cooper, L. (2021). *Authoritarian Contagian: The Global Threat to Democracy*. Bristol: Bristol University Press.

Das, R. (2020). *The Political Economy of New India*. New Delhi: Aakar.

Deb, A. (2024). 'In Charts: BJP Received More Money from Electoral Bonds than 30 Other Parties Combined'. *Scroll.in*, 15 February. https://scroll.in/article/1063738/in-charts-bjp-received-more-than-50-of-all-electoral-bond-donations-since-its-launch. Accessed 14 March 2025.

Deb, S. (2024). 'Modi's Temple of Lies'. *New York Times*, 18 April. https://www.nytimes.com/2024/04/18/opinion/india-election-modi-religion.html. Accessed 1 May 2024.

Desai, R. (2014). 'A Latter-Day Fascism?' *Economic and Political Weekly* 49(35): 48–58.

———. (2016). 'The Question of Fascism'. In *Making Sense of Modi's India*, edited by H. Suroor, pp. 56–79. New Delhi: HarperCollins.

———. (2024). 'Peak Hindutva'. *New Left Review* 147 (May/June): 89–109.

Dimitrov, G. (1938). *The United Front: The Struggle against Fascism and War*. London: Lawrence & Wishart.

Dutta, A., and K. B. Nielsen (2021). 'Autocratic Environmental Governance in India'. In *Routledge Handbook of Autocratization in South Asia*, pp. 70–80. London: Routledge.

Fromm, E. (1994). *Escape from Freedom*. New York: McMillan

Ghassem-Fachandi, P. (2022). 'Pratikriya, Guilt, and Reactionary Violence'. In *Saffron Republic: Hindu Nationalism and State Power in India*, edited by T. M. Hansen and S. Roy, pp. 284–305. New Delhi: Cambridge University Press.

Giroux, H. A. (1917). 'Trump's Neo-Nazis and the Rise of Illiberal Democracy'. https://truthout.org/articles/neo-nazis-in-charlottesville-and-the-rise-of-illiberal-democracy. Accessed 14 March 2025.

———. (2021). 'Rethinking Neoliberal Fascism, Racist Violence, and the Plague of Inequality'. *Communication Teacher* 35(3): 171–177.

Golwalkar, M. S. (1966). *Bunch of Thoughts*. Bangalore: Sahitya Sindhu Prakashan.

———. (2020 [1939]). *We or Our Nationhood Defined (with A Critique by Shamsul Islam)*. New Delhi: Pharos.

Gopal, G. (2023). 'The Three Criminal Law Bills: Using Criminal Law to Establish Permanent Extra-Constitutional Emergency Powers'. *The Wire*, 1 November. https://thewire.in/law/the-three-criminal-law-bills-using-criminal-law-to-establish-permanent-extra-constitutional-emergency-powers. Accessed 1 April 2024.

Gramsci, A. (1971). *Selections from the Prison Notebooks*. Translated and edited by Quintin Hoare and Geoffrey Nowell Smith. London: Lawrence & Wishart.

Guerin, D. (1973). *Fascism and Big Business*. New York: Monad Press Book.

Hacker, J. S., and P. Pierson (2020). *Let Them Eat Tweets: How the Right Rules in an Age of Extreme Inequality*. New York: Liveright Publishing.

Hansen, T. B., and S. Roy (2022). *Saffron Republic: Hindu Nationalism and State Power in India*. New Delhi: Cambridge University Press.

Hobsbawm, E. (1994). *Age of Extremes: The Short Twentieth Century (1914-1991)*. New Delhi: Viking.

Indian Express (2022). 'Prudent Electoral Trust Gave over Rs 464.8 Cr to Parties; BJP Got Rs 336.5 Crore'. https://indianexpress.com/article/india/prudent-electoral-parties-bjp-8216939. Accessed 14 March 2025.

Jackson, G. (1975). *Blood in My Eye*. London: Penguin.

Jaffrelot, C. (1993). *The Hindu Phenomenon*. New Delhi: Viking.

———. (2021). *Modi's India: Hindu Nationalism and the Rise of Ethnic Democracy*. Chennai: Antxt.

Jha, D. K. (2017). *Shadow Armies: From Yogi Adityanath to Those Charged in the Murder of Gauri Lankesh*. New Delhi: Juggernaut.

Kar, D. (2024). 'The Dark Underbelly of India's Rising Income Inequality'. 24 September, *The Wire*. https://thewire.in/economy/the-dark-underbelly-of-indias-rising-income-inequality. Accessed 14 March 2025.

Karthikeyan, R., A. Mangnale, N. Madhav, and Project Electoral Bond (2024). 'Bharti Group's Rs 150 Crore Bond Donation to BJP Coincided with

Modi Government's Telecom U-Turn'. *Scroll.in*, 27 March. https://scroll.in/article/1065827/bharti-groups-rs-150-crore-bond-donation-to-bjp-coincided-with-modi-governments-telecom-u-turn. Accessed 14 March 2025.

Kasbe, R. (2019). *Decoding the RSS: Its Traditions and Politics*. New Delhi: Leftword Books.

Kershaw, I. (1989). 'The Nazi State: An Exceptional State?' *New Left Review* 1(176) (July–August 1989): 47–67.

Laliwala, S. (2020). 'In the Hindutva Heartland: Bharatiya Janata Party's Superficial Democratization in Gujarat'. *Studies in Indian Politics* 8(2): 247–265.

Landa, I. (2009). *The Apprentice's Sorcerer: Liberal Tradition and Fascism*. Leiden: Brill.

Lenin, V. I. (2020). 'Imperialism, the Highest Stage of Capitalism'. In *Essential Works of Lenin*, edited by H. M. Christman, pp. 177–270, New York: Dover Publications.

Maher, H. (2023). 'Neoliberal Fascism? Fascist Trends in Early Neoliberal Thought and Echoes in the Present'. *Contemporary Political Theory* 23(3): 392–410.

Mander, H. (2024). 'Optimism after Poll Results Dims as Bulldozers Return, Hate Attacks Target Minorities'. *Scroll.in*, 6 July. https://scroll.in/article/1070144/harsh-mander-optimism-after-poll-results-dims-as-bulldozers-return-hate-attacks-target-minorities. Accessed 14 March 2025.

Mankekar, P. (2021). '"Love Jihad". Digital Affect, and Feminist Critique'. *Feminist Media Studies* 21(4): 697–701.

Mann, M. (2004). *Fascists*. Cambridge: Cambridge University Press.

Marcuse, H. (2004). *The New Left and the 1960s: Collected Papers of Herbert Marcuse*, vol. 3. London: Routledge.

Mason, P. (2021). *How to Stop Fascism: History, Ideology, Resistance*. London: Penguin.

Mattei, C. E. (2022). *The Capital Order: How Economists Invented Austerity and Paved the Way to Fascism*. Chicago: Chicago University Press.

Mukherjee, A. (2022). *Political Economy of Colonial and Post-Colonial India*. Delhi: Primus.

Mukhopadhyay, N. (2019). *The RSS: Icons of Indian Right*. Delhi: Tranquebar.

Naqvi, B. (2019), 'How Indian News Channels Are Peddling Hatred against Muslims on Primetime TV'. *Gulf*, 20 October. https://gulfnews.com/world/asia/india/how-indian-news-channels-are-peddling-hatred-against-muslims-on-primetime-tv-1.67265166. Accessed 14 March 2025.

Narayan, K. (2017). 'DRI Authority Cancels Proceedings against Adani Group Companies'. *Indian Express*, 25 August. https://indianexpress.com/article/business/companies/dri-authority-cancels-proceedings-against-adani-group-companies-4813673. Accessed 14 March 2025.

Narrain, A. (2021). *India's Undeclared Emergency: Constitutionalism and the Politics of Resistance*. New Delhi: Westland.

Oxfam (2023). *Survival of the Richest: The India Story*. https://d1ns4ht6ytuzzo.cloudfront.net/oxfamdata/oxfamdatapublic/2023-01/India%20Supplement%202023_digital.pdf?kz3wav0jbhJdvkJ.fK1rj1k1_5ap9FhQ. Accessed 14 March 2025.

Parenti, M. (1997). *Blackshirts and Reds: Rational Fascism and the Overthrow of Communism*. New York: City Lights Books.

Passmore, K. (2014). *Fascism: A Very Short Introduction*. Oxford: Oxford University Press.

Patel, A. (2020). *Our Hindu Rashtra: What It Is, How We Got Here*. Delhi: Penguin.

———. (2022). *Price of the Modi Years*. Delhi: Penguin.

Patnaik, P. (2019). 'Shadow of Fascism'. *Monthly Review*, 8 April. https://mronline.org/2019/04/08/the-modi-years. Accessed 16 July 2024.

———. (2021a). 'The Three Decades of Economic Liberalization'. https://www.macroscan.org/cur/aug21/pdf/Three_Decades.pdf. Accessed 14 March 2025.

———. (2021b). 'The Neo-Liberalism and the Extreme Right'. https://www.macroscan.org/cur/jul21/pdf/Neo_Liberalism.pdf. Accessed 14 March 2025.

———. (2023a). 'Is What We Have Crony Capitalism'. https://www.macroscan.org/cur/jul23/pdf/Crony_Capitalism.pdf. Accessed 14 March 2025.

———. (2023b). 'The Abuse of the Concept of Populism'. https://www.macroscan.org/cur/jan23/pdf/Concept_Populism.pdf. Accessed 14 March 2025.

———. (2023c). 'Fascistic Hostility to Evidence'. https://www.macroscan.org/cur/oct23/pdf/Fascistic_Hostility.pdf. Accessed 14 March 2025.

———. (2024). 'Neo-Liberalism and Neo-Fascism'. YouTube. https://www.youtube.com/watch?v=S6a9ZJp5jHM. Accessed 14 March 2025.

Pauwels, J. R. (2017). *Big Business and Hitler*. London: James Lorimer & Company.

Paxton, R. O. (2005). *The Anatomy of Fascism*. London: Vintage.

Polanyi, K. (2018). *Economy and Society: Selected Writings*. Edited by Michele Cangiani and Claus Thomas Berger. Cambridge: Polity Press.

Poruthiyil, P. V. (2021). 'Big Business and Fascism: A Dangerous Collusion'. *Journal of Business Ethics* 168(1): 121–135.

Poulantzas, N. (2018). *Fascism and Dictatorship: The Third International and the Problem of Fascism*. London: Verso.

Purohit, K. (2023). *H-Pop: The Secretive World of Hindutva Pop Stars*. New Delhi: HarperCollins.

Ramakrishnan, V. (2015). 'The Lynch Mob'. *The Hindu*, 14 October. https://frontline.thehindu.com/cover-story/the-lynch-mob/article23593289.ece. Accessed 14 March 2025.

Reich, W. (1970). *The Mass Psychology of Fascism*. New York: Macmillan.

Rentschler, E. (1996). *Ministry of Illusion: Nazi Cinema and Its Afterlife*. Cambridge, MA: Harvard University Press.

Rockhill, G. (2023) 'Are Fascism and Liberalism Partners in Capitalist Crimes?' YouTube. https://www.youtube.com/watch?v=Vnn_bWDmizw&t=242s. Accessed 14 March 2025.

Rosenberg, A. (2016). 'Fascism as a Mass Movement'. In *Fascism: Essays on Europe and India*, edited by J. Banaji. pp. 19–96. New Delhi: Three Essays Collective.

Roy, A. (2020). *Azaadi: Freedom, Fascism, Fiction*. New Delhi: Penguin Books.

———. (2021). 'We are Witnessing a Crime against Humanity'. *The Guardian*, 28 April. https://www.theguardian.com/news/2021/apr/28/crime-against-humanity-arundhati-roy-india-covid-catastrophe. Accessed 14 March 2025.

———. (2023). 'Modi's Model Is at Last Revealed for What It Is: Violent Hindu Nationalism Underwritten by Big Business'. *The Guardian*, 18 February. https://www.theguardian.com/commentisfree/2023/feb/18/narendra-modi-hindu-nationalism-india-gautam-adani. Accessed 14 March 2025.

Roy, I. (2022). 'India: The Hollowing Out of the World's Largest Democracy'. *Political Insight* 13(2): 26–31.

Roy, S. (2022), 'Hindutva Establishments: Right-Wing Think Tanks and the Mainstreaming of Governmental Hindutva'. In *Saffron Republic: Hindu Nationalism and State Power in India*, edited by T. M. Hansen and S. Roy, 72–106. New Delhi: Cambridge University Press.

Sarkar, S. (2016). 'The Fascism of the Sangh Parivar'. In *Fascism: Essays on Europe and India*, edited by J. Banaji, pp. 135–152. New Delhi: Three Essays Collective.

Sarkar, T. (2022). *Hindu Nationalism in India*. New Delhi: Permanent Black.

Saull, R. (2024). *Capital, Race, and Space: The Far Right from Bonapartism to Fascism*, vol.1. Chicago: Haymarket.

Simeon, D. (2016). 'The Law of Killing: A Brief History of Indian Fascism'. In *Fascism: Essays on Europe and India*, edited by J. Banaji, pp. 153–214. New Delhi: Three Essays Collective.

Stanley, J. (2020). 'How Fascism Works: The Politics of Us and Them'. New York: Random House.

Strohl, D. J. (2019). 'Love Jihad in India's Moral Imaginaries: Religion, Kinship, and Citizenship in Late Liberalism'. *Contemporary South Asia* 27(1): 27–39.

Sud, N. (2022). 'The Actual Gujarat Model: Authoritarianism, Capitalism, Hindu Nationalism and Populism in the Time of Modi'. *Journal of Contemporary Asia* 52(1): 102–126.

Subramanian, A. (2022). 'New Hindutva Timeline: September 2013–October 2020'. In *Saffron Republic: Hindu Nationalism and State Power in India*, edited by T. M. Hansen and S. Roy, 25–58. New Delhi: Cambridge University Press.

Sundar, N. (2016). *The Burning Forest: India's War in Bastar.* New Delhi: Juggernaut Books.

Surendranath, A., and Z. Sikora (2023). 'In Custody Civil Liberties'. *Indian Express*, 14 December, p. 13.

Tiwari, A., and Project Electoral Bond (2024). 'After Rs 170 crore to BJP, Real Estate Firm DLF Got "Clean Chit" in Vadra Deal from Haryana'. *Scroll.in*, 22 March. https://scroll.in/article/1065652/after-rs-170-crore-to-bjp-real-estate-firm-dlf-got-clean-chit-in-vadra-deal-from-haryana. Accessed 14 March 2025.

Toscano, A. (2023). *Late Fascism: Race, Capitalism and the Politics of Crisis*. London: Verso.

Tooze, A. (2006). *The Wages of Destruction: The Making and Breaking of the Nazi Economy*. London: Penguin.

Traverso, E. (2019). *The New Faces of fascism: Populism and the Far Right*. London: Verso.

Vanaik, A. (1994). 'Situating Threat of Hindu Nationalism: Problems with Fascist Paradigm'. *Economic and Political Weekly* 29(28): 1729–1748.

———. (2017). *The Rise of Hindu Authoritarianism: Secular Claims, Communal Realities*. London: Verso.

Varman, R., and D. Vijay (eds.). (2022). *Organizing Resistance and Imagining Alternatives in India*. New Delhi: Cambridge University Press.

Welch, D. (2001). *Propaganda and the German Cinema 1933–1945*. London: I.B. Tauris.

Wiesen, S. J. (2018). 'American Lynching in the Nazi Imagination: Race and Extra-Legal Violence in 1930s Germany'. *German History* 36(1): 38–59.

Zachariah, B. (2020). India has the longest-running fascist movement in the world – the RSS. The Wire, 22 January. https://thewire.in/politics/benjamin-zachariah-fascism-sangh-parivar. Accessed 10 September 2021.

Zetkin, C. (2017). *Fighting Fascism: How to Struggle and How to Win*. New York: Haymarket Books.

2

The Economic Origins of Hindu Supremacism

Marzia Casolari

Hindu–Muslim antagonism is one of the main, if not the main, features of the Sangh Parivar's politics. For a long time, this antagonism was considered merely in religious terms. Despite the presence of extensive literature on the economic features and implications of contemporary Hindutva (Bobbio 2017; Chacko 2019; Desai 2011; Gopalakrishnan 2009, 2006; Iwanek 2014; Karat 2014; Kaul 2017; Kumar 2018; Nanda 2011; Patnaik 2019; Saxena and Sharma 1998; Siddiqui 2017; Sinha and Nayak 2021; Spodek 2010), there is a widespread tendency among scholars to consider the Hindu–Muslim rivalry as connected to identity, religious, or communal factors. This chapter aims to prove that an intimate connection between communal and economic factors existed from the colonial period and that communal strife was not determined by religious but by economic causes. It adds to Gyanendra Pandey's (1999) masterly demonstration of how the British constructed communalism by leveraging economic forces. However, Pandey examines only the economic and social transformations brought about by colonization, but does not consider the interrelation between economic and identity factors as part of the colonial game that I foreground in this chapter.

The chapter explains how the British colonizers deliberately targeted Muslim rulers, who throughout the seventeenth and eighteenth centuries were the main political and economic competitors of the East India Company (EIC), and that, in order to undermine the powers of the Muslim rulers, they implemented both economic and cultural devices, as well as military and political ones. Contrary to the commonly accepted theory according to which the British had a weakness for Indian Muslims, this chapter establishes that the stigmatization of the Muslims was initiated at the hands of the colonial rulers and that the creation of some cultural and religious myths, above all the Ram Janmabhoomi, were adopted to disrupt Muslim political strength and the Hindu–Muslim unity that had prevailed in the early colonial period.

The main objective of the chapter is to demonstrate that the present anti-Muslim stance of the Sangh Parivar is the continuation of colonial practices and that today's discrimination of Indian Muslims is based on economic factors and goals. In order to do so, I will examine the history of the Awadh ('Oudh' for the British) kingdom in early colonial times as a case study to show how the colonizers used many ploys to undermine the Nawab's rule and to extensively exploit the great richness of his state. Introduced by two British officers, the Ram Janmabhoomi issue had the ultimate effect of offering the colonizers a chance to finally annex the state.

Referring to more recent cases, I argue that the three main and most fateful cases of Hindu–Muslim conflicts and violence, namely the Kashmir issue, the Ayodhya demolition and its consequences, and the 2002 anti-Muslim pogrom in Gujarat, the deadliest communal upsurge in this century, all had economic roots. The Ayodhya myth, created by the colonizers and revived by the Sangh Parivar, reproduces a typically colonial hegemonic dynamic. Since fascism should be considered a form of imperialism and colonialism, the Sangh Parivar's approach to the Muslim issue should be, therefore, understood as a fascistic one (Ortiz 2023).

If examined from the economic point of view, ethnic or religious-inspired political violence is provoked by the assumed superiority (or by an inferiority complex) of a majority towards a minority, which can be perceived as a threat or a burden. If the minority is perceived as economically privileged, it is seen as a possible threat: this was the case for the Jews under the fascist and Nazi regimes. If the minority is perceived as economically and socially disadvantaged, it is perceived as a burden: this is the case of the Muslim minority in India under Hindutva supremacy. In both cases, the minority should be crushed.

The origins of the Hindu–Muslim strife: creating myths, rewriting histories

If the Hindu right wing emerged as a powerful political force in the late 1980s, its history is deeply rooted in the Indian colonial past. The economic and social transformations introduced by colonization generally resulted in more favourable conditions for the Hindu right wing. Being the majority, they could leverage the opportunities created, whether intentionally or not, by the colonizers. Despite the belief that the British had a weakness for the Muslims, throughout the early colonial period, Hindus acquired predominant social positions, which gradually developed into hegemony.

Until about twenty-five years ago, the decay of the Muslim community was related to the decline of the Mughal Empire during the eighteenth century. However, this does not seem to be a satisfactory explanation (Casolari 2002). From the crisis of Mughal rule, new powers emerged with a regional dimension, but they were more efficient in managing politics and economic resources. They were the former Mughal provinces of Bengal, Awadh, Hyderabad, Mysore, the Maratha states in central western India, and the Sikh kingdom in the north (Ramusack 2004). It should be unsurprising that four of these six regional states were ruled by Muslim princes since they had an innate privileged position due to their religious and cultural closeness to the Mughals. Some of these Muslim and Hindu princes strenuously opposed the EIC's expansion and increasing power. The first one to challenge the EIC was the Nawab of Bengal, to be defeated at the Battle of Plassey in 1757. With fierce resistance, the Marathas fought three wars against the Company between 1774 and 1819, and, much later, the Sikhs fought two wars, in 1845 and 1849. The Nizam of Hyderabad was the first native ruler to sign a subsidiary treaty with EIC and submit to the British paramountcy in 1798. The Nizam was also forced to do so, but found it convenient to be protected by the British suzerainty against the continuous pressure of the Maratha expansion towards his territories. In the eighteenth century, the Maratha Confederacy was the most powerful state entity in the Indian subcontinent, with the strongest military force. However, despite apparent political cohesion much rivalry took place in the Maratha states, which the EIC could skilfully exploit. The main instrument to disaggregate the Maratha Confederacy was the subsidiary alliance that Peshwa Baji Rao II was forced to accept to overcome the internecine rivalries of the Confederation and to obtain the EIC's protection against his foes at the end of the second Anglo-Maratha War in 1802, with the Treaty of Bassein. Thereafter, other Maratha kings signed separate treaties with the EIC. However, since political pressure was insufficient to bend the power of these rulers, the EIC had to fight three more wars to obtain, in 1843, the capitulation of the Maratha Empire, subsequently dismantling its territories and incorporating them into the Bombay Presidency and the Central Provinces.

Unlike the Marathas, who ultimately became subsidiaries of the EIC, the nawabs of Awadh never surrendered. Although the EIC defeated the Nawab in the Battle of Buxar in 1764, it did not annex Awadh, which extended across the central and lower Doab, the fertile plain between the Yamuna and Ganges rivers. Awadh's prosperous rural economy made the kingdom very attractive to the EIC. Awadh provided India's main grain supplies and was among the most important cotton plantations that, from 1760, represented an essential raw material for the rising British textile industry. At the end of the eighteenth century, British merchants entered the competition with the local producers and traders of *aurang* cotton textiles (Marshall 1975, p. 469). Avoiding direct military action, the EIC pursued a more cunning strategy, aiming to pressure the nawabs to force them to accept the annexation. The EIC resorted to several measures to undermine the stability of the state; in particular, it carried out a war of attrition against the nawabs that had the effect of favouring the rise of the Narayan princes, belonging to the Hindu Bhumiar community. The members of the Narayan family combined military prowess with political ability and diplomatic skills to win the trust of the Mughal emperors and even of the nawabs, some of whom transferred meaningful shares of power to the Narayan kings. In 1740, Balwant Singh declared himself Maharaja of Benares and started a guerrilla war against the Nawab, culminating, in 1750 and 1760, in two major attacks (Bayly 1983, pp. 181–184, 489). In 1775, an exasperated Asaf-ud-Daula signed the Treaty of Benares and exchanged the nawab-ship with the rule of the town, which was ceded to the EIC (Habib and Habib 2014). Thereafter, the EIC had to rely upon the rajas for the administration of the town, despite alternating vicissitudes (Freitag 1989, pp. 10–11).

These shifts in power contributed to a crisis in the economic conditions of *julahas*, the Muslim weavers who traditionally produced and traded the valuable silk saris. *Julahas* were increasingly exposed to the competition of Hindu *gaddidars*, wholesalers who also worked as middlemen between the weavers and the big markets. The economic strength of *gaddidars* grew in parallel to the political power of the Narayan maharajas and other players, such as the *gosains*, Hindu ascetics and 'mendicant traders-soldier' who, as bankers and money lenders, brokered between different political and social groups (Casolari 2002; Cohn 1964; Freitag 1989; Raman 2010). The maharajas and these new economic groups were all involved in the transformation of Benares from a 'mughalizing city' (Freitag 1989, p. 10) into a symbol of Hindu sacredness. The *julahas*, who already occupied the lower ranks of the Muslim society, were permanently affected by these transformations and doomed to a condition of subordination to Hindu economic players. Although, in certain periods, the Muslim weavers could resume their role as traders, their economic competition with Hindu merchants was, until recently, the main reason for the strife between the two communities and communal riots. The recurrent predominance of Hindu commercial players in the Awadh state, and later in the United Provinces and even in present-day Uttar Pradesh, is one of the main causes of Hindu revivalism (Raman 2010).

The transformation of Benares's economic system was just one of the steps by the British that contributed to a gradual erosion of the Awadh state, ending only with its annexation in 1856. Despite the disparaging descriptions of the state's economic conditions and the EIC's recurring assumptions of the political instability of the nawabs' rule or their incapacity to control the army, Awadh was one of the most prosperous Indian states. Cotton and saltpetre were the most attractive resources for the rising British industrial economy, while the state had its own flourishing military industry, able to equip an army of about sixty thousand elements, to which must be added the armed assistants of the *taluqdars*. These industries were crippled after the annexation. In contrast, at the beginning of the British expansion into the state, 'Oudh was practically self-sufficient' (Azmi 1967, pp. 85–86).

Although Awadh's economic history has not been much investigated, the economic importance of this state is a matter of fact. The question is not whether or not and why Awadh, which in those times occupied India's second most fertile area after Bengal, was economically exploited by the EIC; it is why Awadh was not annexed immediately after the Battle of Buxar in 1764. No study has addressed this issue so far. The most compelling argument about the delayed annexation of the state is the necessity for the EIC to maintain a buffer state between the Maratha territories, the surviving possessions of the Mughal Empire, and the ever-impending Durrani conquerors (La Vena 2016–2017, p. 20). However, this territory was vital for British beyond the geopolitical interests. The issue of the annexation of the state was determined by a plurality of factors. Was it the fear of a new military reaction by Awadh's old or possible new allies, namely the emergence of a new coalition of native states and the risk of a long-lasting war of attrition to refrain the EIC from annexing Awadh? Or did the EIC opt for a slow exhaustion that ultimately enabled it to exploit Awadh's resources as much as possible and benefit from the heavy taxation imposed on the nawabs? While the direct rule involved very high costs, the maintenance of the kingdom allowed the EIC to burden the Nawabi state. The EIC's policy in Awadh, swinging between the preservation of 'the autonomy of an Indian ruler' and 'levying demands upon him' is not fully convincing (Marshall 1975, p. 466). Although Marshall acknowledges that the EIC's demands from the Nawab 'severely restricted his freedom of action', he accepts the specious arguments regarding Asaf-ud-Daula's alleged military and financial incapacity (ibid., pp. 466–476). The EIC also used this pretext against Asaf's successors until the last nawab, Wajid-Ali Shah, to justify its designs on Awadh's assets. The point is that most of the evils highlighted by the EIC were caused by its massive intrusions into the affairs of the Nawabi state. For example, it is difficult to deny that the permanent deployment of British troops in Awadh after the Battle of Buxar in 1765 at the Nawab's expense, the appointment of a permanent EIC's resident in Lucknow in 1773, the subsidies imposed to the state in charge for the EIC's 'protection' and 'services', and the annexation in 1801 of a large part of its territory (namely Doab, Rohilkand, and Gorakhpur) were all steps aimed at absorbing as much as possible of Awadh's territory into the EIC's possessions (Bandyopadhyay 2004, p. 5, cited in La Vena 2016–2017, p. 23).[1] Contrary to what Marshall asserts, it does not seem that the EIC tried 'to preserve the autonomy of an Indian ruler' or that, by the end of the 1780s, Hastings and Cornwallis decided to 'significantly reduce their demands upon' the Awadh state, to avoid its collapse (Marshall 1975, pp. 466–467). Instead, the opposite is true because for the EIC, it was more profitable to prolong the agony of the Nawabi state as much as possible. Also, the explanation of the EIC's military interference due to '[t]he Wazir's inability to control his armed forces was threatening to undermine the Company's security in northern India' (ibid., p. 467) is hardly convincing. As Marshall himself acknowledged, when the kingdom passed to Saadat Ali, who was 'a much more capable' nawab than his predecessors, the EIC forced him 'to a major reduction' of his troops in exchange for an increase in the EIC's military forces (ibid., p. 467). It is likely that after exploiting the prosperous Awadh state in any possible way for a century, the EIC sought a pretext to militarily intervene and annex what remained of it at the most convenient occasion for its own economic and political requirements. The occasion was provided by two zealous British officers and amateur scholars.

Robert Montgomery Martin (1801–1868) was an Irish traveller and writer, amateur naturalist, and expert on colonial matters, a founding member of the Colonial Society and the East India Association, and a member of the EIC. He studied the British colonies extensively and published several works, such as *The History, Antiquities, Topography and Statistics of Eastern India*, published in 1838 (Martin 1838). In this book, Martin was the first to state the existence in Ayodhya of ancient Hindu temples, which, according to him, were destroyed by Aurangzeb and not by Babur. Moreover, he mentioned Ram, not as a god, but as a king who ruled in Ayodhya around 775 BCE.

Patrick Carnegy was a little-known figure who served as British Commissioner and Settlement Officer in Faizabad around 1860. He wrote in his book *A Historical Sketch of Tahsil Fyzabad* not only backing the thesis of the destruction of what he defined as 'a fine temple', but also claiming that Ayodhya was Ram's *janmasthan*, the birthplace of the god Ram (Carnegy 1870, p. 21).

Several questions emerge from these stories: the reconstructions by the two officials were merely examples of unscientific, inaccurate, rather naïve early studies on ancient history and archaeology, typical of that period. But were they inspired by political motivations, geared to trigger communal animosity?

The answer lies in the broader perspective of the rising number of Orientalist and Indological studies. From this point of view, Martin's and Carnegy's speculations appear tinged with political intentions. What happened in Ayodhya and the Awadh state was not an isolated case but part of a wider phenomenon: in the same years, another issue, comparable with the *janmasthan* question, was rising around the Somnath Temple, then in the Junagadh sultanate, today in the state of Gujarat. Perhaps the issue concerning the Somnath Temple was less renowned and disruptive than the Ayodhya dispute, though equally capable of producing 'a narrative of communal antagonism' in both the short and long terms (Bobbio 2023, p. 861). The construction of the myth concerning the destruction and plunder of the Somnath Temple at the hands of Mahmud of Ghazni dates to 1842 in the final stages of the First Anglo-Afghan War. At that time Lord Edward Ellenborough, newly appointed as Governor-General of India, ordered General William Nott, who was retreating to Kabul, to retrieve the two gates that embellished Mahmud's tomb in Ghazni and bring them back to Somnath. Ellenborough was convinced, indeed, that the portals originally belonged to the Somnath Temple and were stolen by Mahmud in 1024. It was later discovered that the two gates were never built for the temple and that, in any case, they could not return to the Somnath Temple because it was in ruins. In fact, Ellenborough decided to rebuild it, setting in this way a precedent that went far beyond Somnath, where the temple was rebuilt, and paved the way for further quarrels throughout the country regarding the rebuilding of several other disputed Hindu holy sites besides Ayodhya.[2] The total disregard of Hindu revivalists for the veracity of the alleged discoveries or for the existence of relevant evidence is noteworthy. Once the gates were brought back, the claims about the theft of portals proved to be untrue. Moreover, no references to them were found in any ancient source (ibid., pp. 855, 857).

Something similar happened in Ayodhya, where the existence of an important Hindu temple in the Babri Masjid compound could never be proven, neither on the basis of literature nor archaeology. On the contrary, up to the late 1980s, excavations and inspections conducted by the Archaeological Survey of India in the foundations of the mosque and the adjacent terrain proved unequivocally that no other building had existed on the site (Chadha 2011). When, in the late 1980s to early 1990s, the Sangh Parivar increased its political strength and power, it literally seized the Archaeological Survey of India, with only its sympathizers appointed as administrators and scholars. Since then the consolidated results obtained by the previous research were overturned, although no new proof was provided. What is most striking is that the narrative (and people's beliefs) about Ayodhya and other disputed sites do not take into account authenticity: as Somnath was reconstructed on the basis of the two fake gates, the Ram Temple in Ayodhya is 'rebuilt' under the premises of the unsubstantiated Ram Janmabhoomi. Interestingly, in recent times, the Sangh Parivar revived and adopted these myths, created by the colonizers.

In colonial times, the political manipulation of Indian past, religions, and heritage was always motivated by the political requirements of the British rulers. According to Nilanjan Mukhopadhyay, the revival of old myths about Ram's birthplace in Ayodhya 'came in handy for the British writers, who were modelling the official policy of the time' (Mukhopadhyay 1994, pp. 65–66).[3] It was necessary to promote

> the belief that Mughal emperors had indulged in wanton destruction of Hindu temples and the theory that the two communities were mutual adversaries gained ground and acceptance in official records. (Ibid., p. 66)

Shortly after the publication of Martin's work, tensions started to mount between Hindus and Muslims in Ayodhya/Faizabad over the site of the Babri Masjid, although until then the two communities coexisted without serious disturbance.[4] The first communal riots, in 1855, gave the EIC's garrisons a reason to quell the uprisings and finally gave to the Governor-General Lord Dalhousie a reason, in 1865, to annex the Awadh state. Carnegy's book enshrined the identification of Ayodhya as the site of the *janmasthan*.

While the Ram Janmabhoomi myth was revived when the necessity (and the pretext) to annex the Awadh state became compelling, the story of the stolen gates of Somnath was created just at the end of the First Anglo-Afghan War, when the British troops suffered a huge defeat. As a consequence, the prestige of the EIC had diminished. Above all, in Afghanistan, the British were defeated by Muslims. It was, therefore, necessary to tame India's former rulers and prevent them from following the Afghan example and pose a serious threat to the EIC. The best way to avoid that outcome was to gratify the Hindus. The image of Indian Muslims was permanently affected.

In short, the divisive policy implemented by the EIC had two main goals: first, to drive a wedge between Hindus and Muslims in order to strengthen its own political power while, especially, pursuing its own economic objectives; second, to belittle the image of the Muslims, not only of the Mughal rulers and princes but of the Muslim community as a whole. It is thus possible to assume that the stigmatization of Indian Muslims began in the early colonial period. This assumption is bolstered by other concomitant or subsequent examples repeating similar patterns, even in post-colonial times.

From Kashmir to Ayodhya, or the continuity between past and present

Since the pattern described here was adopted systematically in many contexts, it is possible to trace some remarkable cases of apparently religious conflicts that, in fact, had a non-religious nature, either political (or geopolitical) or economic. One of the most meaningful is the Kashmir issue, the origin of which can be traced back to 1846 when the Treaty of Lahore and the subsequent Treaty of Amritsar settled the first Anglo-Sikh War. The EIC, which won the war, waived the reparation of 10 million rupees that Maharaja Dilip Singh was supposed to pay in exchange for the transfer of the Kashmir Valley and the Hazara province to its possessions. A week after the deal, the EIC sold those territories to Maharaja Gulab Singh of the Dogra family, for the same amount as the reparation (Schofield 2000, pp. 3–13). Ultimately, the Treaty of Lahore was an economic deal in the interests of the EIC, with geopolitical implications: the British feared that Kashmir, like Afghanistan, could fall under Russian influence. In order to preserve the integrity of the British possessions, it was of vital importance to install loyal rulers in power along Indian borders. A Hindu prince in a Muslim-majority state removed the possibility of an alliance between Kashmir and the Afghan emirs. The Maharaja, in turn, had the advantage of being protected by the British.

Kashmir was the largest princely state in British India. The deep rift between the Hindu ruler and his Muslim subjects was certainly not determined by religious differences but by the miserable conditions that the Kashmiri Muslims had to face: heavy taxation, forced unpaid labour, lack of basic rights and discrimination, and the pressure of an emerging Hindu elite, 'pampered' by the Maharaja (Rai 2004; Schofield 2000, pp. 20–22). The narrative promoted by the Sangh Parivar about the unfortunate Kashmiri Pandits expelled from the Valley after independence should be seriously reviewed because, in the pre-independence balance of power, the revenue department of the royal state was dominated by Pandits and Muslim farmers abandoned their land and migrated elsewhere (mainly to Punjab) in response to the harsh living conditions they faced in their own state. The protections enforced in favour of Kashmir by post-independence governments to safeguard the rights of the Muslim majority aimed to prevent the reiteration of similar dynamics in a Hindu-dominated independent India. These protections were eliminated by the cancellation of Article 370 of the Indian Constitution in 2019. This is all in addition to the unspeakable problems raised by the Hindu rule over a Muslim-majority state bordering Pakistan. Kashmir's deep and largely unsolved issues are rooted in its colonial history and originate from long-standing economic, political, and social causes that have little to do with religion.

Perhaps the most divisive issue in modern India and the epitome of the Hindu–Muslim strife, namely the *mandir–masjid* dispute of Ayodhya, was revived in the early 1990s for economic and electoral reasons. The dormant Ayodhya issue reawakened when, on 7 August 1990, Prime Minister V. P. Singh, head of the National Front Government, announced he intended to implement the recommendations of the Mandal Commission report, which had been a dead letter for a decade, and to reserve government jobs for backward castes. The agitations that followed the government's resolution, with self-immolations of students, attacks on public transport, and protests that paralyzed a large part of northern India, overlapped with the Ayodhya issue. The attempt to find a permanent solution to the dispute, initiated at the beginning of the year, was torpedoed as an indirect reaction to the application of the Mandal recommendations. Upper castes, particularly Brahmin students, opposed the resolution, as they believed in and asserted the 'natural' right to occupy public posts since they were better educated. The defence of caste privileges and the related economic status was the real, underlying initial objective of the violent resurgence of the Ayodhya issue. The Sangh Parivar, particularly the Vishva Hindu Parishad (VHP), which was the real actor behind the revival of the Ayodhya quarrel in this phase, took over the protests. The VHP was concerned about the inter-caste character of the disturbances, which opposed young upper- and low-caste Hindus: there was a risk of a fissure within Hindu society. Ayodhya became the catalyst for political upheavals: the function of the Rath Yatra launched by L. K. Advani, which had its epicentre in Ayodhya and led to the first failed attack on the mosque in October 1990, had the function of turning inter-caste into inter-communal tensions, where the Muslims were the scapegoat of economic and social tensions and, ultimately, of electoral games. The results of the 1991 general elections then cemented the rise of the Bharatiya Janata Party (BJP) as the main opposition party (Mukhopadhyay 1994, pp. 270–304).

The economic basis of Indian communalism is not a random factor but a constant trend, so much so that we should talk about an economy of hatred in India. Howard Spodek provided clear evidence of the economic causes of the Hindu–Muslim tension in Ahmedabad that erupted after the 2002 Godhra tragedy (Spodek 2010).[5] Before the rise to power of the BJP, communal violence recurred occasionally; since the BJP's victory in 2014 and its consolidation in 2019, attacks on Muslims and their humiliation have become a constant. What nurtures communal violence is now a widespread and deep-rooted economy of hatred, exacerbated by economic liberalism that erased any form of social solidarity.

Before analysing the economy of hatred in India, it is necessary to introduce political hatred in fascistic contexts, and particularly the comparison between Italian fascism and India's Hindu right wing.

The intimate relation between race and hatred, in a comparative perspective

The renowned Italian historian, Luciano Canfora, opened his book *Fermare l'odio* (Stop the Hate) with a quotation from *Il primo libro del Fascista* (The

First Book of the Fascist) (Canfora 2019, p. 1).[6] Canfora quotes the chapter 'Il catechismo della razza' (The Catechism of the Race) in the 1940 edition. After a brief preface, 'the paragraph La difesa della razza' (the defence of the race) states 'Tutta l'opera del Regime tende a preservare la razza italiana da ogni pericolo e a renderla moralmente e fisicamente forte attraverso la potenza del numero e il continuo miglioramento'.[7] In the wake of the racial laws introduced in Nazi Germany between 1933 and 1935, the fascist regime introduced its own racial laws between 1938 and the early 1940s, aiming to build and protect the Italian 'race'. It was a series of measures such as prohibiting Jews from practising any intellectual and liberal profession, engaging in commercial activities or working in public and private offices, allowing the confiscation of properties, prohibiting intermarriage with non-Jews, and allowing detention and internment in concentration camps. The introduction of these racial laws was announced by Benito Mussolini, during a speech in Trieste on 18 September 1938. The first outcome of these reforms was the so-called Dichiarazione sulla razza (Race Declaration), approved by the Gran Consiglio del Fascismo (Grand Council of Fascism) on 6 October, published on the Foglio d'ordine of the Partito Nazionale Fascista (Order Sheet of the National Fascist Party) on 26 October and enacted as a royal decree on 17 November 1938.

Despite the international outrage provoked by the racial laws, the fascist regime continued to gather consensus outside Italy. It is well known that the British Tories appreciated Mussolini (Casolari 2023, pp. 165–166); at the end of September 1938, after the Munich Agreement, just a few weeks after the enactment of the racial laws (5 and 7 September 1938), Neville Chamberlain praised Mussolini and expressed his gratitude to the *duce* and his foreign minister and son in law, Galeazzo Ciano, for their intercession with Hitler and for convincing him to participate to the negotiations in Munich. International and American press celebrated Mussolini as the saviour of peace, regardless of the newly enforced racist legislation (Canfora 2019, pp. 22–23). After all, the fascist regime had enjoyed the sympathies of the Anglo-American politicians and public opinion since the late 1920s: during his visit to Rome in January 1927 Churchill pronounced the famous sentence 'If I had been an Italian I am sure that I should have been whole-heartedly with you from start to finish in your triumphant struggle against the bestial appetites and passions of Leninism.' A few years later, on the occasion of a meeting of the British anti-socialist, anti-communist Union in London on 18 February 1933, Churchill defined Mussolini as 'the Roman genius' and 'the greatest law-giver among living men. With the fascist regime, Mussolini has established a centre of orientation from which countries which are engaged in a hand-to-hand struggle with socialism must not hesitate to be guided' (ibid., p. 21; *New York Times* 1927).

In 1937, in the United States (US), a survey was conducted where Americans were asked if they preferred fascism or communism: 61 per cent chose fascism. At the end of his European tour in 1937, J. F. Kennedy wrote in his diary that fascism suited Italy and Nazism suited Germany (Canfora 2019, pp. 19–20). The *New York Times* published a detailed and enthusiastic report of Churchill's visit to Rome in 1927 and emphasized his appreciation of Mussolini,[8] while in 1938, after the Munich Agreement, it extolled the role of Mussolini as peacekeeper (ibid., p. 22).

Fascism had, therefore, an international dimension, and the regime's actions had a certain resonance abroad. Indians were acquainted with Italian politics, especially through the British press, which greatly influenced the local one. For instance, Vinayak Damodar Savarkar was well informed about Austria's Anschluss, sending a telegram to President Franklin D. Roosevelt comparing Germany's annexation of Austria with the British occupation of India and asking the American president 'to withdraw her armed domination over Hindustan' (Casolari 2020, p. 226).[9]

If Savarkar was so well informed about the European events, when he quoted Hitler's anti-Jewish policy as an example to be followed to solve the 'Muslim problem in India', he did so with full knowledge of the facts. Savarkar observed, 'A Nation is formed by a majority living therein. What did the Jews do in Germany? They, being in minority, were driven out from Germany' (ibid., p. 90).[10] He further asserted, 'In Germany the movement of the Germans is the national movement but that of the Jews is a communal one' (ibid., p. 91),[11] and 'Just as the land of Germans is Germany ... even so we must have it indelibly impressed on the map of the earth of all times to come "Hindustan"—the land of the Hindus' (Golwalkar 1939, p. 52, cited in ibid.).[12]

Similarly, M. S. Golwalkar's notorious statements mentioning the purges of the Jews in Germany were put forward as a proper treatment for Indian Muslims, and the denial of citizenship rights confirms that even he had a sound knowledge of Germany's racial policy.

> German national pride has now become the topic of the day. To keep up the purity of the nation and its culture, Germany shocked the world by purging the country of the Semitic races – the Jews. National pride at its

> highest has been manifested here. Germany has also shown how well-nigh impossible it is for races and cultures, having differences going to the root, to be assimilated into one united whole, a good lesson for us in Hindustan to learn and profit by. (ibid.)
>
> ...
>
> In a word, they [Muslims] must cease to be foreigners or may stay in the country wholly subordinated to the Hindu nation, claiming nothing, deserving no privileges, far less any preferential treatment, not even citizen's rights. (Bhatt 2001, p. 88; Golwalkar 1939, p. 52, cited in Casolari 2020)

Savarkar and Golwalkar did not ignore the harsh treatment inflicted on German (and Italian) Jews and were ready to adopt the same approach for Indian Muslims.

The close connection between identity and nation, or state, is the core of all past and present fascist and fascistic ideologies, organizations, leaders, and parties, not only in Italy but in any context where far-right-wing groups and movements flourished or still flourish. As Canfora points out, the American neo-Nazis, the hate speech of the Northern League in Italy, the Italian right wing's harsh policy towards migrants (Canfora 2019, p. 4), and, I add, the right-wing extremism that has grown in central Europe since the fall of communism (Abbas et al. 2011) or the Hindu radicalism, which re-emerged in India in the same period, are part of a common trend, namely the (re-) emergence of fascism(s) or fascistic tendencies at the global level. Fascism, indeed, has always been a global phenomenon.[13]

Race has been the core component of all these ideologies, groups, and political parties, in the past and the present. Even when not openly mentioned, race is always implicitly involved in the arguments of the global right wing. For example, a few months before the enactment of the racial laws in Italy, on 14 July 1938, the newspaper *Il Giornale d'Italia* published 'Manifesto degli scienziati razzisti' (Manifesto of Racist Scientists), better known as Manifesto della razza (Manifesto of Race), the ideological and pseudo-scientific basis of the Italian racist policy (Manifesto della razza 1938).[14] The document in ten points was signed by the top Italian scientists. It stated the existence of race on scientific bases, the 'Aryan' lineage of the Italian 'race', and traced a difference between the Mediterranean peoples of Europe and the Afro-Asians. It declared that the Italian race did not include Jews and its purity should be preserved at any cost, especially by avoiding any contamination with people belonging to non-European 'races'. Italians, it said, needed to proclaim themselves 'frankly racist'. Even when 'race' was not directly mentioned, racism was always looming. The obsession for racial purity always referred to the 'Aryan' race.

In India, when Bal Gangadhar Tilak first endeavoured to trace the origin of the 'Aryans', he ultimately shared the prevailing European theory of the Nordic origin of the 'Aryans'.[15] In recent times, the 'Aryan' theory is being revitalized in India by the contemporary right-wing ideology, although slightly differently. The racial theory of Indian civilisation has become 'the "crabgrass" of Indian history', as D. N. Jha (1997, p. 91) pointed out in his review of Thomas Trautmann's famous *Aryans and British India*. This is true today as never before: 'Aryans' and Aryanism have increasingly stepped into the limelight since the political growth of the Hindu right wing and its rise to power. Although the Hindu–Muslim contrast cannot objectively be based on ethnic factors and Muslim diversity is not explicitly related to race issues, the theory of the Indian origin of the 'Aryans', in opposition to the commonly accepted Aryan invasion theory has been used to prove the cultural supremacy of Indo-European Indians since, according to this view, the Indo-European culture is strictly connected to the Hindu culture and religion and with the Indian national language.

In Nazi Germany, race was the ground for repression of the Jewish minority, while in India, with similar mechanisms, the grounds for repression are religious and cultural differences put forward to discriminate against and harass Muslims. The point is not what is different, whether religion, culture, or language, but diversity as such. Racism derives from the fear of the other, as diverse, which turns into hate of the other. However, hatred has to do not only with race but with several other factors. Hate is the lever to impose the hegemony of a group, normally of a majority over a minority. Political and social hegemony, in most cases, is associated with economic predominance. Racial or religious explanations of political hatred often conceal economic factors.

The economics of hate[16]

Economic factors are the most convincing analytical tools to explain an otherwise irrational phenomenon like political hatred. If we analyse political hatred from a materialistic point of view, we discover that its economic motivations in most cases are correlated with the income difference between the haters and the hated. As Edward Glaeser points out, politicians who base their strategies on hatred tend to 'castigate' particularly rich or particularly poor groups. This is the case of Afro-Americans in the US, who are disproportionately poor, or of the Jews in Nazi Germany and fascist Italy, who were perceived as disproportionately rich (Glaeser 2002, p. 4). Indian Muslims can be compared with Afro-Americans in the US, as the most disadvantaged social group: indeed, the economic status of Indian Muslims can be compared to that of Dalits.

The BJP governments adopted pure liberal economic models that, at the social level, resulted in laissez-faire capitalism and, ultimately, social Darwinism. Since coming to power, the BJP has gradually eroded the welfare system, by progressively reducing the budgetary allocations to important social security programmes. For instance, the budgetary allocation to the Mahatma Gandhi National Rural Employment Guarantee Act (MGNREGA), the most important 'safety net' for millions of poor, has declined from 1.85 per cent in 2014–2015 to 1.33 per cent in 2023–2024. Similarly, the allocations to the National Social Assistance Program (NSAP) remained stagnant for the past nine years and declined in real terms from 0.58 per cent of the budget in 2014–2015 to 0.21 per cent in 2023–2024. The National Food Security Act (NFSA), the National Health Mission (NHM), and other anti-poverty schemes followed the same trend. Moreover, the allowances provided under the NSAP remained unchanged since 2007, with INR 200–300 per month for the pensions covered under the programme, a totally inadequate sum to face a constantly increasing cost of living (Sharma and Pathak 2023). In such an environment, for Indian Muslims, as well as for Dalits and the poor in general, the 'survival of the fittest' is the rule. In the competition for economic and social achievement, the frailest subjects, like the minorities and the extremely poor, who nevertheless struggle for their own social redemption or simply for their survival, are considered and treated as enemies.[17] The future perspective is that of a harsh, even violent competition among deprived sectors of Indian society—Dalits, Other Backward Classes (OBC), and Muslims—as an effect of the economic transformations introduced by the adoption of neoliberalism. In this sense, the economic causes of communal riots became particularly evident after the 2002 Ahmedabad anti-Muslim pogrom; if we consider it as a consequence of the race for jobs (between Muslims and low-caste/class labourers) after the closing of the textile mills—the flagships of the town's industrial fabric—created rampant unemployment.[18]

In the fast-growing capitalist economy, Muslims as well as Dalits are a burden for a government that is uninterested in enhancing social protection for the disadvantaged. Violence, intimidation, subjugation, pauperization, and segregation are cost-free, while the implementation of an efficient welfare system requires huge investments.[19] When it is evident that economic growth does not affect the low castes and classes, better to reduce them to the condition of the *Undermenschen* of Nazi Germany.[20] Those who escape the ongoing, untamed, large-scale ethnic cleansing are doomed to invisibility. It is evident that the objective of the Sangh Parivar, now in power in India, is to reduce the emergence of the Muslim population by hindering its socio-economic advancement. Moreover, harassment of non-Hindus goes on unabated.

Hatred justifies mass persecution and even extermination, as pointed out by Glaeser (2002, p. 2). 'Group-level hatred is always fomented by past crimes and future threats'; thus, the Jews' 'notorious misdeeds', invented in the *Protocols of the Elders of Zion*, disseminated prejudices against Jews in Europe, beginning in the middle ages. This, like the myths of the destruction of Hindu monuments by Muslim conquerors and rulers, used to target Muslims in contemporary India, fomented hatred against Jews in Europe.

As far as 'future threats' are concerned, in the case of the European Jews, the menace was represented by Jewish finance, which was feared to dominate the global economy and to prevent the growth of native entrepreneurship. If there was a predominance of Jews among German economic elites, it was not the same in other parts of Europe. In Germany, Jews were just under 1 per cent of the population in 1914, but 25 per cent of the corporate networks were represented by Jewish firms, and the Jews had a prominent role in the banking and financial sectors (Windolf 2011, pp. 4, 11–12). This fuelled the existing anti-Semitic feelings in wider German society. In the troubled waters between the two world wars and with the endless economic crisis of foreign debt, hyperinflation, and widespread unemployment, all exacerbated by the Great Depression of 1929, German Jews became a scapegoat. They were perceived not only as privileged but as the promoters of a so-called international Jewish conspiracy, according to which Jews were taking control of international politics and finance (Mosse 1989).

The stereotype about the pervasive presence of Jews in the Italian economy was widespread in Italy too. According to the census of 1938 (the year when the racial laws were promulgated), Italian Jews were slightly more than

1 per cent of the total population (46,656 against approximately 43,228,000) (Pavan 2003, p. 296). It was true that 43.3 per cent of the Jews in Italy were traders, but 22.9 per cent were street vendors, 51.7 per cent were retailers, and 15.9 per cent were wholesalers. It was also true that only 1.5 per cent of Jews were farmers, compared with 47.7 per cent of the Italian population; 9.4 per cent were professionals, instead of the 0.8 per cent national average; and 11.6 per cent of those employed in the public sector were Jews, compared to 4.4 per cent of Italians. These percentages match with the European averages, with Jews working mainly as traders (especially as small dealers): in Germany, 60 per cent of Jews were traders, while Austria, Czechoslovakia and Hungary had similar proportions. There were 5,782 Jewish owners of companies in Italy: 38.3 per cent in textile factories, 20.7 per cent in the paper and graphic industry, 15.2 per cent in the steel and mechanical industry, and 11.2 per cent in construction. Like other parts of Europe, in Italy, the Jews preferred independent work (44.7 per cent) (ibid., pp. 298–299). Most Jewish companies were small; 64.3 per cent were sole proprietorships (ibid., p. 304). The Italian economic elites amounted to approximately 26,000 subjects, fewer than 0.1 per cent of total employed people aged above 10 years; Jews 868, or 3.3 per cent of the total; and 2.1 per cent of the Italian Jewish community. In percentage, the Jewish economic elite was 21 times larger than the Italian one. Within the Italian Jewish community, the proletarian and peasant classes were almost totally absent (ibid., p. 306). Jewish top managers between the 1920s and 1930s were represented by a few figures of the utmost importance and prestige who held high-ranking positions and, in most cases, were very close to the fascist regime until the promulgation of the race laws. There were slightly more than twenty personalities who acted as heads of banks or chairmen of strategic industries, especially the most important and huge metal, steel, and engineering industries; construction, railways and shipping companies; huge real estate companies; and insurance. In most cases, they held several positions at a time as members of the boards of directors of various companies. All main Italian banks had Jewish directors, managers, members of the boards, and employees. All these personalities were involved with the fascist administration as well, as directors of fascist corporations or units of industrialists (ibid., pp. 307–311). Gino Olivetti, for instance, the founder and owner of the world-famous typewriter company, had been Secretary-General of Confindustria, the Industrial Association, from the early 1920s to the 1930s. Federico Jarach financed the start-up of Mussolini's newspaper, *Il Popolo d'Italia* (ibid., pp. 307–308). Jewish entrepreneurs as councillors of fascist

corporations or trade union federations amounted to 14 per cent of the total (ibid., p. 317). Although the Italian and German Jewish populations were very small compared with those of Eastern European countries,[21] and the Jewish economic elite in Italy represented a narrow minority, they were employed in the most lucrative businesses (ibid., p. 319). From the second half of the 1930s also, in Italy, the perception of a pervasive and hegemonic Jewish presence became widespread. The myth of the Jewish capital and the so-called Jewish octopus also became very popular in Italy.

The rising grudge against Jews and the promulgation of the racial laws are inexplicable if they are not contextualized in the climate of widespread racism. Racist literature and discourse, especially public discourse, spread after 1935 when racism became the common meter to describe and deal with the 'conquered' people (Camera di Commercio Industria Artigianato e Agricoltura, Roma–Unione delle Comunità Ebraiche Italiane 2014, pp. 34–35). Jews, as the most visible Italian minority, were seen as 'alien' non-European people. But this explanation is insufficient; other factors intervened to determine the anti-Jewish frenzy. Economic factors in Italy, as in Germany and elsewhere in Europe, were the main cause of the anti-Jewish hatred. The 1929 economic disaster provoked widespread unemployment among the middle classes, who could not see any opportunities: the small commerce, the craft sector, and liberal professions were saturated, and the Jews were considered as competitors. Jews could better deal with the crisis due to their long-time habit of resisting unfavourable conditions, which enabled them to develop the art of getting by. Moreover, Jews could receive remarkable relief from their own community, which was very cohesive and supportive. On the other hand, when the Italian monopoly capital entered competition with the Jewish financial-speculative capital, Jews were scapegoated, and it was possible to stir up anticapitalistic conflicts (ibid.). The elimination of Jews represented compensation for the economic losses of the Great Recession of 1930, which soon turned into the Great Depression. In this case, the economic side of hatred is represented by the remunerative capacity of hate. Italian capitalists supported fascism as an ideology not only against increasing workers' claims but also against the perceived Jewish menace. The persecutions of the European Jews fall within the category of the 'future threats' described by Glaeser, which are then open to being stigmatized and criminalized as a preamble to ethnic or religious cleansing, as happened during the Second World War in Europe. The psychosis of the so-called

Judeo-masonic conspiracy, widespread in those years, stigmatized Jews, fomenting hatred against them in order to create the excuse to carry out their otherwise inconceivable extermination. The economic significance of this 'solution' was to take their positions and seize their properties and assets. The climate of hate created by Nazism and fascism led to widespread fanaticism, to a destructive and self-destructive rage that ended in a catastrophe and, ultimately, in economic disaster.

Conversely, Indian Muslims fall within Glaeser's category of 'past crimes'. Indeed, the narrative that describes Muslims as plunderers and destroyers of Hindu heritage created a stereotype that goes far beyond the grounds of the Babri Masjid, the Somnath Temple, or other disputed Muslim sites, and nurtures hate justifying the attempt to cancel the identity of Indian Muslims, if not to eliminate Muslims as such. While anti-Semitic feelings in Europe date to the Middle Ages, anti-Muslim feelings in India originate from the British policies described on the preceding pages. At the time of the emergence of Hindu radicalism, between the late 1920s and India's independence, the purpose of the Rashtriya Swayamsevak Sangh (RSS) and the Hindu Mahasabha was to reduce the Muslims' political power that, in pre-partition India, was still strong. It is not surprising that Savarkar and Golwakar compared Indian Muslims to German Jews. However, the anti-Muslim hatred smouldered during the decades of the Congress rule, erupting when the BJP emerged as a political force capable of undermining the hegemony of the Congress in the late 1980s and early 1990s. Anti-Muslim hatred was then exploited for electoral purposes: inter-communal hatred transformed the Muslims into scapegoats for the resentment arising from the application of the Mandal Commission reservations. After the demolition of the Babri Masjid, hatred was transferred from low-caste Hindus to Muslims who, after all, were depicted as 'aliens'. Since the rise to power of the BJP, neoliberalism and the systematic use of violence against Muslims and Dalits have prevented claims for better socio-economic conditions. Violence has been used to suppress dissent and protests against unpopular economic and constitutional changes. Since its rise to power, the BJP has passed controversial laws, such as demonetization and the introduction of the farm laws that have a clear neoliberal approach and adversely affect the lower classes. If the repression of the Punjabi farmers protesting on the outskirts of Delhi in 2020 was relatively less violent, the systematic violence against Muslims and Dalits discourages outcries and protests and limits their social emergence. Anti-Muslim hatred creates the right climate for 'aggression as a defence against threats to man's vital interests' (Glaesar 2002, p. 2): in this case, 'man's vital interest' is not vital at all—just the government's intent to pursue unbridled neoliberalism, with no care for hundreds of millions of Indian poor. Any real or presumed obstacle has to be removed. The bias against Islam and Muslims spread worldwide can only worsen the conditions of Indian Muslims. The elimination of Article 370 brings Kashmiri Muslims back to the subalternity of colonial times since, as we have seen, the BJP is very willing to rely on colonial methods.

Notes

1. These three areas yielded approximately INR 13,523,475 per year.
2. About the dispute regarding temples and mosques in Ayodhya, Varansi and Mathura, Muslim monuments at risk in the BJP's India, and the marginalization of Indian Muslims, see, unfortunately in Italian, Casolari (2022, pp. 51–76).
3. Mukhopadhyay was among the first to recover the memory of Martin's and Carnegy's narrative about the existence of a Hindu temple under the Babri mosque, on the basis of meaningless clues.
4. The twin towns of Ayodhya and Faizabad (originally Fyzabad) are inhabited by the Hindu and Muslim communities, respectively. Faizabad was founded in 1722 near the pre-existing Ayodhya. In May 2017, the Indian government renamed the former Faizabad district into Ayodhya district.
5. A fine analysis of the crisis of the textile industries in Ahmedabad as the cause of the economic and social transformations that led to intercommunal inter-communal violent competition is in Chatterji (1995).
6. Canfora is a scholar of Greek and Roman history with a Marxist background. He can be compared with Romila Thapar for his capacity to use his knowledge of ancient history to explain the present. Besides his works on classical history and historiography, he published several books on the history of Italian and Soviet communism and on contemporary history and politics of Italy, Europe, and Russia. Among his works is *Marx vive a Calcutta* (Marx Lives in Calcutta), published in 1992.
7. 'The regime's task aims to preserve the Italian race from any danger and to strengthen it from the moral and physical point of view, through the might of the number and constant improvement' (translated by the author).

8. Telegram dated 23 April 1938, Nehru Memorial Museum and Library, Savarkar papers, microfilm, roll n. 23, part 2, Miscellaneous Correspondence January 1938–May 1939, quoted by Casolari (2020).
9. Maharashtra State Archives (MSA), Home Special Dept., 60 D(g) Pt. III 1938, cit., 'Translation of the Verbatim Speech Made by V.D. Savarkar at Malegaon on 14.10.1938', in Casolari (2020).
10. MSA, 'A Report on the Meeting Held on 11.12.1938', in Casolari (2020).
11. *Bombay* Chronicle, 29 December 1939, with a summary of Savarkar's speech during the 21st session of the Hindu Mahasabha, in Casolari (2020).
12. On the common ground between the Nazist, Savarkar's and Golwarkar's racist ideas, see also Bhatt (2001).
13. Regarding the aspiration of Italian fascism and the international dimension of fascism, see Casolari (2023); Griffin (1998); Larsen (2001); Griffin, Loh, and Lacqueuri (2006); Hedinger (2013, 2018); Hofmann (2015): Hofmann (2017); Hofmann and Hedinger (2017); Bauerkamper (2010); Bauerkamper and Rossoliński-Liebe (2017); Sluga and Clavin (2017); and Kallis (2021). As far as the expansion of fascism in India is concerned, it is still a rather under-examined topic in international literature.
14. See the document at https://www.osservatoriosulfascismoaroma.org/il-manifesto-della-razza-1938 (accessed 29 March 2025).
15. According to this theory, only the European 'Aryans' had Nordic origins, while Indo–Iranian 'Aryans' originated from central Asia. I put the term 'Aryan' between single quotas because in Europe it does not belong to the common language anymore. I preferably use the term Indo-European or Indo-Aryan, which is commonly used in academic terminology.
16. This title is borrowed from Glaeser (2002) and Cameron (2009), on which this section is largely based.
17. For the sake of brevity and to avoid going off-topic, here I focus only on the hate campaigns and waves of violence against Indian Muslims, but several academic and journalistic works are available on the conditions of Muslims and Dalits and their fate as targets of Hindutva violence.
18. Regarding the connection between the decline of Ahmedabad's textile factories and the 2002 riots, see Breman (2002) and Spodek (2010).
19. Between 2018 and 2023, 189,945 attacks on Dalits were registered (Das 2023). Attacks on Muslims instead are uncountable and uncounted.
20. This parallel is used by Breman (2002, p. 1147).
21. Jews were 5.1 per cent in Hungary, 2.4 per cent in Czechoslovakia, and 9.7 per cent in Poland (Pavan 2003, p. 296).

References

Abbas, M., K. Tvrdá, V. Walach, B. Rydliński, and T. Nociar (2011). 'Right-Wing Extremism in Central Europe: An Overview'. Berlin. https://library.fes.de/pdf-files/id-moe/08840.pdf. Accessed 29 March 2025.

Azmi, A. A. (1967). 'Position of Agriculture in the Economy of Oudh during the Nawabi Regime'. *Proceedings of the Indian History Congress* 29: 85–86.

Bandyopadhyay, S. (2004). *From Plassey to Partition: A History of Modern India*. Hyderabad: Orient Blackswan.

Bauerkamper, A. (2010). 'Interwar Fascism in Europe and Beyond: Toward a Transnational Radical Right'. In *New Perspectives on the Transnational Right*, edited by M. Durham and M. Power, pp. 39–66. New York: Palgrave Macmillan.

Bauerkamper, A., and G. Rossoliński-Liebe (eds.) (2017). *Fascism without Borders: Transnational Connections and Cooperation between Movements and Regimes in Europe from 1918 to 1945*. New York/Oxford: Berghahn Books.

Bayly, C. A. (1983). *Rulers, Townsmen and Bazaars*. Cambridge: Cambridge University Press.

Bhatt, C. (2001). *Hindu Nationalism: Origins, Ideologies and Modern Myths*. Oxford/New York: Berg.

Bobbio, T. (2017). 'Making Gujarat Vibrant: Hindutva, Development and the Rise of Subnationalism in India'. In *Identity, Inequity and Inequality in India and China*, edited by A. Wahlberg. pp. 657–672. London: Routledge.

———. (2023). 'Somnath Mandir in a Play of Mirrors: Heritage, History, and The Search for Identity of the New Nation (1842–1951)'. *Journal of the Royal Asiatic Society* 33(4): 849–869. DOI: https://doi.org/10.1017/S1356186323000287.

Bombay Chronicle (1939). 'Summary of Savarkar's Speech during the 21st Session of the Hindu Mahasabha'. 29 December.

Breman, J. (2002). 'Communal Upheaval as Resurgence of Social Darwinism'. *Economic and Political Weekly* 37(16): 1485–1488.

Camera di Commercio Industria Artigianato e Agricoltura Roma–Unione delle Comunità Ebraiche Italiane (2017). 'Gli effetti delle leggi razziali sulle attività economiche degli ebrei della città di roma (1938–1943)'. Rome.

Cameron, S. (2009). *The Economics of Hate*. Cheltenham: Edward Elgar Publishing.

Canfora, L. (2019). *Fermare l'odio*. Bari: Laterza.

Carnegy, P. (1870). *A Historical Sketch of Tehsil Fyzabad, Including the Former Capitals, Ajudhia and Fyzabad*. Lucknow: Oudh Government Press.

Casolari, M. (2002). 'Role of Benares in Constructing Hindu Political Identity'. *Economic and Political Weekly* 37 (15): 1413–1420.

———. (2020). *In the Shadow of the Swastika: The Relations between Indian Radical Nationalism, Italian Fascism and Nazism*. New York: Routledge.

———. (2022). 'La strumentalizzazione dell'architettura e degli spazi urbani nell'India del BJP'. In *Immagini delle città in asia tra passato epresente*, ed. D. Francavilla, pp. 51–76. Soveria Mannelli: Rubbettino.

———. (2023). *L'asia agli asiatici. la politica 'Indiana' del regime fascista e i rapporti con il nazionalismo radicale*. Città di Castello: Le Monnier Università.

Chadha, A. (2011). 'Conjuring a River, Imagining Civilization: Saraswati, Archaeology and Science India'. *Contributions to Indian Sociology* 45(1): 55–83.

Chacko, P. (2019). 'Marketizing Hindutva: The State, Society, and Markets in Hindu Nationalism'. *Modern Asian Studies* 53(2): 377–410.

Chatterji, P. C. (1995). *Secular Values for Secular India*. New Delhi: Manohar.

Cohn, B. S. (1964). 'The Role of the Gosains in the Economy of the Eighteenth and Nineteenth Century Upper India'. *Indian Economic and Social History Review* 1(4): 175–182.

Das, S. (2023). '189,000 Cases of Attacks on Dalits Registered Since 2018: Govt to Parliament'. *Hindustan Times*, 21 March 2023.

Desai, R. (2011). 'Gujarat's Hindutva of Capitalist Development'. *South Asia: Journal of South Asian Studies* 34(3): 354–381.

Freitag, S. (ed.) (1989). *Culture and Power in Banaras; Community, Performance, and Environment, 1800-1980*. Berkeley: University of California Press.

Glaeser, E. L. (2002). 'The Political Economy of Hatred (Working Paper)'. National Bureau of Economic Research, Cambridge, MA.

Golwalkar, M. S. (1939). *We or Our Nationhood Defined*. Nagpur: Bharat Publications.

Gopalakrishnan, S. (2006). 'Defining, Constructing and Policing a "New India": Relationship between Neoliberalism and Hindutva'. *Economic and Political Weekly* 41(26): 2803–2813.

———. (2009). *Neoliberalism and Hindutva: Fascism, Free Markets, and the Restructuring of Indian Capitalism*. New Delhi: Aakar Books.

Griffin, R. (ed.) (1998). *International Fascism: Theories, Causes, and the New Consensus*. London: Arnold.

Griffin, R., W. Loh, and W. Lacqueur (eds.) (2006). *Fascism Past and Present, West and East: An International Debate on Concepts and Cases in the Comparative Study of the Extreme Right*. Stuttgart: Ibidem-Verlag.

Habib, I., and F. Habib (2014). 'Mapping the Dismemberment of Awadh 1775-1801'. *Proceedings of the Indian History Congress* 75: 455–460.

Hedinger, D. (2013). *Universal Fascism and Its Global Legacy: Italy's and Japan's Entangled History in the Early 1930s*. Leiden: Brill.

———. (2018). 'The Spectacle of Global Fascism: The Italian Blackshirt Mission to Japan's Asian Empire'. *Modern Asian Studies* 51(6): 1999–2034.

Hofmann, R. (2015). *The Fascist Effect: Japan and Italy, 1915-1952*. Ithaca: Cornell University Press.

———. (2017). 'The Fascist New-Old Order'. *Journal of Global History* 12(2): 166–183.

Hofmann, R., and D. Hedinger (2017). 'Axis Empires: Towards a Global History of Fascist Imperialism'. *Journal of Global History* 12(2): 161–165.

Il primo libro del Fascista (2012). 'National Fascist Party: Rome. 1940'. https://bibliotecafascista.blogspot.com/2012/04/il-catechismo-della-razza-1940.html. Accessed 29 March 2025.

Iwanek, K. (2014). 'The Political Economy of Hindu Nationalism: From V.D. Savarkar to Narendra Modi'. *International Journal of Knowledge and Innovation in Business* 1(2): 1–38.

Jha, D. N. 1997. 'Review of Thomas Trautmann, *Aryans and British India*'. *Indian Historical Review* 27(1): 94–97.

Kallis, A. (2021). 'The Transnational Co-Production of Interwar "Fascism": On the Dynamics of Ideational Mobility and Localization'. *European History Quarterly* 51(2). DOI: https://doi.org/10.1177/02656914211006307.

Karat, P. (2014). 'The Rise of Narendra Mori: A Joint Enterprise of Hindutva and Big Business'. *The Marxist*, January–March 2014, pp. 3–15.

Kaul, N. (2017). 'Rise of the Political Right in India: Hindutva-Development Mix, Modi Myth, And Dualities'. *Journal of Labour and Society* 20(4): 523–548.

Kumar, N. (2018). 'Politics of Hindutva in Neoliberal India: Investigating Internal Dynamics'. *International Journal of Research in Engineering, IT and Social Sciences* 8(8): 159–163.

Larsen, S. U. (Ed.) (2001). *Fascism Outside Europe: The European Impulse Against Domestic Conditions in the Diffusion of Global Fascism*. New York: Columbia University Press.

La Vena, P. A. (2016–2017). 'Ayodhya. origine, evoluzione e strumentalizzazione del mito del janmasthan'. BA thesis, University of Turin.

Marshall, P. J. (1975). 'Economic and Political Expansion: The Case of Oudh'. *Modern Asian Studies* 9(4): 465–482.

Martin, R. M. (1838). *The History, Antiquities, Topography and Statistics of Eastern India*. London: W.H. Allen & Co.

Mosse, W. E. (1989). *The German Jewish Economic Elite: 1820–1935: A Socio-Economic Profile*. Oxford: Clarendon Press.

Mukhopadhyay, N. (1994). *The Demolition: India at the Crossroads*. New Delhi: HarperCollins.

Nanda, M. (2011). *The God Market: How Globalisation Is Making India More Hindu*. New York: Monthly Review Press.

New York Times (1927). 'Churchill Extols Fascismo for Italy; He Declares It Has Taught the World the Antidote for Communism. "Charmed " by Mussolini His Conferences in Rome, He Says, Dealt With Improving Condition of the Wage-Earner'. *New York Times*, 21 January. https://www.nytimes.com/1927/01/21/archives/churchill-extols-fascismo-for-italy-he-declares-it-has-taught-the.html. Accessed 29 March 2025.

Ortiz, M. (2023) *Anticolonialism and the Crises of Interwar Fascism*. New York: Bloomsbury.

Pandey, G. (1999). *The Construction of Communalism in Colonial North India*. New Delhi. Oxford University Press.

Patnaik, P. (2019). 'The Ideology of India's Corporate-Financial Oligarchy: A Note'. *Studies in People's History* 6(2): 193–201.

Pavan, I. (2003). 'La presenza ebraica nell'economia italiana alla vigilia delle leggi antiebraiche'. *La Rassegna Mensile di Israel* 69(1): 287–320.

Rai, M. (2004). *Hindu Rulers, Muslim Subjects: Islam, Rights and The History of Kashmir.* London: Hurst & Co.

Raman, V. (2010). 'The Julaha: Momin Ansari of Banaras—A Socio-Historical Trajectory'. *Voice of Dalit* 3(2). DOI: https://doi.org/10.1177/0974354520100208.

Ramusack, B. N. (2004). *The Indian Princes and Their States*. Cambridge/New York: Cambridge University Press.

Roy Burman, B. K. (1997). 'Review of "Aryans and British India"'. *Indian Anthropologist* 27(2): 91–95.

Saxena, K., and P. K. Sharma (1998). 'Hindutva and Economic Liberalization'. *International Review of Sociology* 8(2): 239–251.

Schofield, V. (2000). *Kashmir in Conflict: India, Pakistan and the Unending War* (Italian edition). London: Tauris.

Sharma, A., and N. Pathak (2023). 'Narendra Modi's Decade in Power Has Brought a Shrinking Welfare Landscape to India'. *The Wire*, 27 September.

Siddiqui, K. (2017). 'Hindutva, Neoliberalism and the Reinventing of India'. *Journal of Economic and Social Thought* 4(2): 142–186.

Sinha, G., and B. S. Nayak (2021). 'Rise of Hindutva Politics, Demonetisation, and its Impact on Micro, Small and Medium Enterprises in India'. In

Emerging Markets, edited by V. Bobek and C. H. Quah, pp. 133–144. London. IntechOpen.

Sluga, G., and P. Clavin (eds.). (2017). *Internationalisms: A Twentieth-Century History.* Cambridge: Cambridge University Press.

Spodek, H. (2010). 'In the Hindutva Laboratory: Pogroms and Politics in Gujarat, 2002'. *Modern Asian Studies* 44(2): 349–399.

Windolf, P. (2011). 'The German Jewish Economic Elite (1900–1933)'. Working paper, University of Trier.

3

Fascism Perfected

The Corporate Stage of Hindutva

*Radhika Desai**

That the decade of untrammelled power Narendra Modi enjoyed before losing his majority in his 2024 victory so humiliatingly represented a new phase in the ruinous advance of Hindutva is clear. What is less clear is where the novelty lies. For some, it lies in the Bharatiya Janata Party's (BJP) parliamentary majority, the first for any party since 1984; the centrality of Modi's personality; and the combination of populism, nationalism, majoritarianism, and authoritarianism (Chatterji, Hansen, and Jaffrelot 2019, p. 1). For others, it lies in the Modi regime being a 'governmental formation with considerable institutional heft that converges with wider global currents and enjoys an unprecedented level of mainstream acceptance' (Hansen and Roy 2022, p. 1).

These assessments appear staggeringly placid. Under the Modi regime, minorities—Muslims throughout India, Christians in the north-east and Adivasi lands—and dissident intellectuals are systematically persecuted, often to death; working people are assailed by wilfully brutish experiments—demonetization and draconian COVID-19 lockdowns to take the most egregious—leaving lasting damage. Meanwhile, the topmost corporate capitalist class rejoices in sympathetic legislation, light oversight (if any), and aid in foreign operations. To get power and keep it, the government displays

* I would like to thank Jairus Banaji, Jennifer Ponce De Leon, Gabriel Rockhill, Rohit Varman, and Achin Vanaik for their insightful comments on an earlier draft which greatly improved this chapter. All remaining faults and limitations are, of course, mine.

'unprecedented' and 'sweeping disregard for the constitution', particularly its federalism (Savera 2019), and razes political institutions—the Supreme Court, the Central Vigilance Commission, the Reserve Bank of India (RBI)—with the bulldozer of its parliamentary majority. In cahoots with the police or with their complicity, Hindutva goons systematically attack activists, journalists, and intellectuals and impose near complete censorship on the media and social media. The resulting atmosphere of intimidation is so pervasive that even major capitalists fear speaking openly about the government (*National Herald* 2019).

Most importantly, this majority has been twice acquired through the scandalous alchemy of the first-past-the-post electoral system reacting with corporate money, whose amounts soared in 2019 with the additional obscenity of unconstitutional electoral bonds (Sethi 2019). Indeed, the Modi regime would be impossible without corporate India's munificent backing. Thus, to even begin to capture the novelty of the Modi regime, we need an analysis that focuses on its bond with India's corporate capitalist class, what we may call India Inc. This bond explains the Modi regime's origin and trajectory, constitutes its political raison d'être, and cries out for a properly Marxist and historically nuanced comparison with the relation between classical fascism and monopoly capital.

Most writers on Hindutva, even critical ones, avoid the fascist framework, minimizing the Modi regime's dangers in their sanitized social scientific prose. Meanwhile, the Modi–India Inc. relation is usually examined in the framework of 'crony capitalism' (Guha Thakurta, Ghosh, and Chaudhuri 2014; Bhattacharya and Guha Thakurta 2019; Khatri and Ojha 2016; Crabtree 2018), which entirely misses the radical novelty the relation has come to assume. We analyse this novelty, bringing our analysis of Hindutva as the specifically Indian brand of fascism up to date and demonstrating that the Modi regime represents the third and perfect state of Hindutva fascism in India, making it as uncannily similar to twentieth-century Nazism in Germany (the classical instance of inter-war fascism) as it is possible to get in twenty-first-century India.

In what follows, we provide the historical background that throws the India Inc.–Modi bond into relief as the third phase of Hindutva's advance. Then we outline the 'crony capitalism' analysis, noting its limitations, and refute the major objections against applying the fascist framework to Hindutva. Our analysis follows. It sees the Modi–India Inc. relation as an attempt to preserve and extend corporate capitalist control over the Indian polity in its crisis through the means at hand, which, however, are far from guaranteed to succeed and could easily spin out of the control of the very class that employs them. In laying out this analysis, we show the sobering similarities with Nazism in all key aspects.

Hindutva's advance before Modi

The party of Hindutva is a member of the sprawling Sangh Parivar headed by India's original fascist organization, the Rashtriya Swayamsevak Sangh (RSS). Initially confined to urban small businesspeople in the northern 'cow belt', the story of Hindutva's advance since is ill understood, attributed either to continuous religious mobilization or to Hindutva's 'mainstreaming'.

In reality, India's capitalist class is the key protagonist of Hindutva's rise, which accompanied the expansion and political assertion of that class (Desai 2004a, 2004b, 2011b, 2014), underlining the long-standing Marxist insistence that fascism cannot be understood apart from capitalism.

While the expansion of the capitalist class in India has been examined variously (Patnaik, Chandrashekhar, and Sen 1996; Damodaran 2013; Banaji 2022), given the provenance of most new entrants into India's capitalist classes in the countryside and small provincial towns, this expansion is best seen as the entry of India's provincial propertied classes (PPCs, a term I borrow from Balagopal 1987) into the capitalist class. The emergence of these classes—the originally agrarian dominant- and middle-caste rich peasants and capitalist farmers who diversified into urban and industrial activities as their wealth rose—expanded the capitalist class massively in the last third of the twentieth century.

Inevitably, this expansion had party-political consequences. The agrarian dominant- and middle-caste rich peasants and capitalist farmers were originally contained within the Congress, whose early dominance in India's party system rested on the support of these groups. However, as their wealth and status grew, and the party's predominantly upper-caste leadership failed to acknowledge their growth by giving them greater position and power in the party, they sought political autonomy, promoting their agrarian interests through farmers' movements and their wider business interests through their respective political parties. Generally classed as 'regional parties', these parties are more accurately termed 'parties of the provincial propertied classes' (PPPCs). Through them, the PPCs could, in the first instance, exert control over state capitals.

In the 1980s and early 1990s, it appeared as if, given their history of anti-Brahmanism, the chiefly middle- and dominant-caste PPCs and their parties would have no truck with the BJP. However, on the one hand, enough of them, particularly where capitalist development had narrowed the social distance between the twice-born wealthy and the dominant- and middle-caste wealthy such as in Gujarat (Desai 2011a), proved willing to bury this hatchet and join the BJP directly or through their PPCs to enter coalition with the BJP. On the other hand, the BJP increasingly diluted its Brahmanism to pose as a political force able to unify 'the expanded and more diverse capitalist class, bridging the historically deep divides between the twice-born upper castes and the middle castes and those among its regions and languages' (Desai 2014, p. 2)—to create a pan-Indian, predominantly upper- and middle-caste propertied class. The BJP, now advancing in tandem with the PPCs, could form state governments in coalition with PPPCs and even take power by absorbing PPCs starting in the 1990s (the Janata party state governments had not given the party of Hindutva any chief ministerships) and eventually form the BJP-led coalition governments of 1998–2004 at the centre.

The expansion of the capitalist class had, inevitably, been accompanied by increasingly market-oriented economic policy, and its electoral consequence was that no government had been re-elected after a full term until 2009. The BJP-led National Democratic Alliance's (NDA) defeat in 2004 after its hubristic 'India Shining' electoral campaign followed this pattern. The result was the Congress-led minority United Progressive Alliance (UPA). It was able to win a second term with more votes and seats chiefly because, having been reliant on left parties which parleyed their power into a number of major pro-poor initiatives, including the critically important National Rural Employment Guarantee Act (NREGA), it diluted its neoliberalism (Desai 2011b).

However, the Congress could not reconcile its political desire to remain the Indian capitalist class' party of choice just when that class was entering its corporate phase with its electoral imperative of catering to its social base. Thanks to the BJP's appeal to the upper- and middle-caste wealthy and the exodus of the PPCs from the Congress, it consisted overwhelmingly of lower castes and classes and minorities. Unable to combine electorally necessary welfarism with service to India Inc., the Congress was overwhelmed with corruption scandals in its second term. They, in turn, clogged up normal channels of communication and influence with India Inc. and the latter began complaining about the government's 'policy paralysis'. Anti-corruption movements gained ground and opened an electoral aperture. However, in the throes of its still inconclusive search for a leader to replace the ageing Vajpayee–Advani duo, the BJP seemed ill equipped to step through it.

The ultimate choice of Modi was not the BJP's. As Gujarat's chief minister since late 2001, Modi had demonstrated that he could give the business and corporate elite of a comparatively rich and industrialized state everything it wanted and still win elections as a Hindu strongman who rejected all 'appeasement' of minorities. India Inc. now clamoured for Modi as the man to deliver it from the Congress's 'policy paralysis' by winning elections and expediting matters for it, and, swallowing any misgivings it may have had, the BJP leadership named Modi the party's prime ministerial candidate.

Backed by India Inc., Modi won parliamentary majorities in the next two elections amid the Congress's loss of morale, disunity among the parties opposed to the BJP, stunts like the Balakot strikes, and the aforementioned corporate bankrolling. However, *even with these advantages*, Modi's BJP needed the magic of the first-past-the-post electoral system to win its majorities. It gave Modi's BJP 51.4 per cent and 55.59 per cent of Lok Sabha seats on the strength of the *votes of only 20.6 per cent and 25.2 per cent of the Indian electorate as a whole (including non-voters)* in 2014 and 2019 respectively. That is to say, almost 80 per cent (in 2014) and 75 per cent (in 2019) *did not* vote for Modi's BJP.

Finally, in 2024, the decade's worth of the economic misery that Modi's corporate neoliberalism inflicted on Indians exacted its electoral cost, notwithstanding the lavish Ayodhya consecration and even more corporate money. A united opposition denied Modi a majority, handing him instead a victory that could not have been more humiliating given the hubristic goal of '400 *paar*' (more than 400 parliamentary seats) Modi's BJP set itself. Modi remains the prime minister, but how well he can now serve his India Inc. masters remains to be seen (for a fuller analysis of the 2024 election results, see Desai 2024).

Very little of this understanding is reflected in the crony-capitalism literature on contemporary Indian capitalism.

The crony capitalism analysis

In the late twentieth century, many scholars—Marxist and non-Marxist—tracked the expansion or 'proliferation' of the Indian capitalist class (Patnaik, Chandrashekhar, and Sen 1996; Varma 1998; P. Mishra 1995; Baru 2000; Damodaran 2013), attributing it to market-friendly reforms usually dated to the early 1990s but arguably going back to the late 1960s (Desai 2016). In the new century, a new literature arose, concerned with increasing capital concentration and corporate power. However, uncritical of capitalism and neoliberalism, it assumed that such concentration was an aberration and not the inexorable outcome of capitalism now exacerbated by neoliberalism. Much of this literature also assumed that the solution lay in overcoming India's statist legacy or the myriad compulsions of coalition politics (Guha Thakurta [2002] discusses this problem in the Vajpayee governments of 1998–2004) and implementing consistently neoliberal policies to create a 'level playing field' for firms (Banaji 2022). Despite these limitations, some points in this literature are worth noting.

From concentration to super-concentration

First, already high industrial concentration rose further under Modi. As a share of total investment, private corporate investment rose at the expense of investment in the public and in the small and medium enterprise (SMEs) sectors. Indian billionaires' assets went from 1 per cent of gross domestic product (GDP) in the 1990s to 10 per cent the following decade (Gandhi and Walton 2012), leading the future governor of the RBI, Raghuram Rajan, to ask, 'How long can we resist calling India [an oligarchy]?' given that India was second only to Russia in the number of billionaires in relation to GDP (Rajan 2008). Under Modi, the former deputy governor of the RBI, Viral Acharya, pointed out, certain corporates increased their weight through mergers and acquisitions so fast as to reach 'super-concentration' levels:

> Starting in 2015, the Big-5 started acquiring larger and larger shares within the sectors where they were present.... In particular, their share in total assets of the non-financial sectors rose from 10% in 1991 to nearly 18% in 2021, whereas the share of the next big five (Big 6-10) business groups fell from 18% in 1992 to less than 9%. In other words, the Big-5 grew not just at the expense of the smallest firms, but also of the next largest firms. (Acharya 2023)

Rent-thick concentration

Much of this concentration was occurring, moreover, not in competitive sectors with limited corporate interaction with the state such as information technology/software, engineering sector firms, pharmaceuticals, and finance and banking—these were largely free of the taint of scams—but in 'rent-thick' sectors such as 'real estate, infrastructure, construction, mining, telecom, cement and media' where the 'role of the state in giving licences' was 'pervasive', giving the corporate sector a reputation for illegality and monopolistic practices (Gandhi and Walton 2012, p. 12).

Rising world demand for primary commodities in the twenty-first century, which already pushed many developing countries back into their primary commodity exporting roles, could only exacerbate this tendency in an India plagued with low productivity, low innovation, and low competitiveness in manufacturing. Sure enough, 'the wealth of billionaires shot up most of all in the rent-thick sectors, from mining and property to cement, infrastructure, and telecoms' (Crabtree 2018, pp. 93–94).

Concentration and politics: office, scams, election funding

Inevitably, corporate concentration had political consequences. In the 2000s, wealthy businessmen were increasingly showing up in Parliament, drastically shortening the avenues to political influence for an expanded capitalist class, while corruption and the role of money in elections also rose markedly.

The argument that neoliberal reforms decrease corruption has never been credible and, in India, they only added grand or 'horizontal' corruption involving vast sums changing hands between the wealthy and the powerful in a small number of instances to the already established system of vertical or petty corruption of low-paid state employees—from bureaucrats to policemen—skimming small amounts in a large number of instances from a harassed and irate public (Gupta 2017). Such grand corruption increased the sums involved astronomically and became both cause and consequence of the equally steep rises in the cost of winning elections: counteracting the electoral unpopularity of neoliberal policies among voters afflicted with poverty, inequality, resentment of ill-gotten wealth, mass unemployment, and gloomy prospects required ever more money.

Scandals involving land acquisition, infrastructure projects, sale of public assets, and the awarding of defence contracts (ibid.) rose in the new century. The Indian state's embrace of public–private partnerships (PPPs)—state contracts with private corporations to build infrastructure or run large facilities—became another major hotbed of corruption. Justified, as in the West, as increasing investment without adding to government expenditure, these ventures 'created an entirely new mechanism for astronomical rent extraction', so much so that one observer called India a contractor state—'government of contractors, by contractors, for contractors' (Crabtree 2018, p. 206). Increasing awareness of rentier concentration and corruption led some to hail India's own 'gilded age' resembling late-nineteenth-century United States's 'robber baron' capitalism, allegedly a necessarily violent prelude to a highly efficient form of capitalism. However, India's 'gilded age', if such it was, was headed elsewhere.

House of debt and 'policy paralysis': Modi's moment

For behind these forms of corruption stood another peculiarly Indian one and its crisis became Modi's opportunity.

The crisis was exposed in an August 2012 report by Credit Suisse trying to square the prevailing view that the Indian economy had an easy 2008 crisis with the despondency its author found in conversations with corporate leaders (ibid., p. 227). The explanation lay in a corporate borrowing binge. Historically, corporate business houses in India had privileged access to credit from the banking sector which was nationalised in 1969. By the 2000s, this access was fuelling the exceptional corporate growth and concentration through investment, mergers and acquisitions, and even overseas acquisitions.

This borrowing began to sour after 2008. The ten most indebted corporate groups—Adani, Essar, GMR (named after Grandhi Mallikarjuna Rao), GVK (named after Gunupati Venkata Krishna Reddy), JSW (Jindal South West), Jaypee Group, Lanco, Reliance ADAG (Anil Ambani), Vedanta, and Videocon—saw their loans grow by five times in five years, accounting for 13 per cent of bank loans and 98 per cent of the banking system's net worth: 'Therefore, … in terms of the concentration risk, Indian banks rank higher than most of their Asian and BRIC counterparts' (Gupta and Kumar 2012, p. 3). Given that most Asian economies feature high debt-to-equity ratios compared to their Western counterparts, this was saying something. Not only were they highly leveraged, but they also endangered the solvency of the entire banking sector.

The report caused a sensation. Based on information not usually available thanks to the complex, not to say shady, accounting practices and often private (not publicly listed) ownership structures of the biggest corporations, it revealed that borrower promoters often had little personal stake in the enterprises that they leveraged so highly and often used to acquire assets of questionable value in Europe or Africa. Worse, it also exposed how the little equity they showed one bank was often a loan owed to another. This practice made it even harder to scrutinize their accounts, given that much of this money was channelled through tax havens.

The sensation in business circles soon sparked a full-blown political crisis for the Congress-led UPA government already plagued by several scandals, such as the ones involving coal, 2G, and the Commonwealth Games scams in which it was found avoiding competitive bidding to allocate highly lucrative, risk-free licences and contracts to favoured private firms. In this context, Anna Hazare's anti-corruption movement made political capital from public concern and birthed the Aam Aadmi Party. Not only were the Congress-led UPA government's reputation and electoral prospects severely dented, but India Inc. also washed its hands of the 'paralyzed' UPA government and lighted on Modi as its saviour.

The Modi stage of Hindutva

One would never guess from the crony capitalism literature that the 'policy paralysis' crisis was the key turning point towards the perfection of fascism. The literature assumes an overall continuity of crony capitalism since independence, with 'a blend of "rules" and "deals" alongside a mix of "informal" short- and long-run relationships' between state and business 'with rent-creation and rent-sharing as the explicit or implicit contractual basis' (Chandra and Walton 2020, p. 178). It even credits the Modi government with ending crony capitalism, or at least trying to. Having been elected with 'widespread support from the business community', having 'developed a narrative of anti-corruption', it 'substantially reduced high-level corruption' without hurting big business, we are told. The worst this literature says about the Modi government is that its anti-corruption measures 'have suffered from weak specific designs, administrative burdens (the GST [goods and services tax] reform) or weak implementation (of the IBC [Insolvency and Bankruptcy Code])' and increasing 'uncertainty … over the—potentially discretionary—action on alleged corruption' (ibid., p. 178).

As for India Inc.'s borrowing binge, we are told that Modi was unable (rather than unwilling) to clean up the mess, though there is a suggestion that RBI governor Raghuram Rajan may have been dismissed for trying to do so (Crabtree 2018, pp. 77—78). According to this view, exposés of the UPA government's corruption made Modi so wary of scandals that key corporate leaders like Ambani became 'the unacceptable face of Indian cronyism' and Modi's election was 'complicated' for them as 'the new Prime Minister fearful of accusations of favoritism cut out much of the kind of insider access enjoyed by senior industrialists' (ibid., p. 46).

In reality, Modi did not cut access; he just re-routed it. Rather than cutting deals, Modi functioned by changing 'rules and goalposts ... midgame to help politically connected businessmen'. For instance, 'Adani's rise was aided by a relaxation of prior regulations and veiled threats against business rivals by government investigative agencies' (Bardhan 2023). Mukesh Ambani was similarly helped when, in the face of complaints about Reliance Jio's 'predatory pricing practices... in the telecom sector, the Telecom Regulatory Authority of India hastily amended the previous rules: no foul, no harm' (ibid.).

In short, under Modi, India Inc. enjoys efficient and frictionless access to the government. With scrutiny, whether by coalition partners, parliament, or the media curtailed, rather than corruption scandals, we see laws and institutional practices changed to suit India Inc. while the interests of the wider Indian economy and the overwhelming majority of Indians get short shrift.

The Modi governments have fundamentally transformed relations between India Inc. and the Indian state, making them closer, more secure, and more secret than ever. With India Inc.'s bankrolling transforming Modi's slim pluralities into brute parliamentary majorities that block parliamentary scrutiny and dispense with interfering coalition partners, Modi enjoyed almost complete media control and freedom from public scrutiny and power over bureaucrats and judges. Though electoral bonds are now declared unconstitutional, for two elections they extended India Inc.'s bankrolling even further, as corporates not yet funding Modi's BJP were threatened or enticed into doing so. The organization of repression in favour of India Inc. was complete and nearly watertight. The Sangh Parivar's goons were now needed, if at all, only to engage in the retail intimidation of opponents, who still stubbornly crop up here and there, and to spread a pall of insecurity and fear.

Applying the fascist framework

While it is true that the term 'fascism' gets bandied about, or used instrumentally, the question of Hindutva's fascist character will not go away. The RSS's fascist inspiration has been well documented (Casolari 2020) and quite openly avowed. During and after the assault on the Babri Masjid in 1989 and then again in 1992, numerous left-wing writers (Ahmad 1993; Patnaik 1993; Sarkar 1993) noted the striking similarities between Hindutva's methods, whether staging spectacles or mobilizing the lumpen, and those of the fascisms of inter-war Europe.

Among those who have considered and rejected the fascist framework for Hindutva, liberal approaches that ignore fascism's capitalist character are not much use. They focus, haphazardly, on incidentals—in the Nazi case, on Hitler's personality and role and Nazism's ideological aspects, particularly its anti-Semitism—and fall prey to the Cold War equation of fascism and socialism as forms of 'totalitarianism', disregarding their contrasting class-characters.

Thus, Christophe Jaffrelot has been unconvincing. Writing in the early 1990s, he argued that the Sangh Parivar focused on society, not race, that it was not 'putschist', and that it emphasized organization over a supreme leader (Jaffrelot 1999 [1993], pp. 61–62). However, while Nazism may have focused on race, any generic 'other' can serve as the 'enemy within' to build the authoritarian unity of the rest of the 'nation'. Given that the first-past-the-post system allows fascist parties to take power in coalition (as between 1998 and 2004 and again in 2024), or win strong parliamentary majorities (as in 2014 and 2019) through corporate munificence, it has so far been quite unnecessary for Hindutva to be 'putschist', though we cannot discount that a putsch may be attempted if circumstances change. Finally, while organization, particularly of para-state violence, has always been central to all fascist movements, the RSS has never flagged in its efforts to promote its various personalities, no matter how lacklustre, while the personality cult around Modi, complete with well-compensated public relations firms practically manufacturing charisma and the cooperation of a pliant media, can hardly be denied. Marxist approaches situate fascism in its capitalist historical and material context. Though most classical Marxist writings on fascism were written in the heat of the battle against it in inter-war Europe, it is possible to extend and update them in light of historiography since.

This is precisely what Nicos Poulantzas's *Fascism and Dictatorship* (1974) did, though later research revealed two major limitations. First, while

Marxists rightly emphasized that ruling classes took the fascist option to resolve the crisis of their rule, they did not consider that fascism could fail to do so and simply constitute a new phase of the same crisis. Second, while Marxists rightly argued that capital, specifically monopoly capital, brought fascism to power, they did not account for the autonomy that fascist movements could and would acquire from corporate capital. Below we flesh out our case for understanding how closely the Modi–India Inc. relation resembles Hitler's relations with the German corporate capitalist class on the basis of this corpus of work.

Before proceeding, however, we must deal with Marxist objections to applying the fascist label to Hindutva. Achin Vanaik's are the most comprehensive. Also writing in the early 1990s, while he conceded that the RSS and European fascist movements were similar, he also argued that the fascist label applies not to movements but to the 'situation': 'It is the fascist situation that "matures", not the fascist entity' (Vanaik 1994, p. 1739). Eight differences between the Indian situation and the inter-war European one made the fascist framework inapplicable: (*a*) the scale of the dislocation caused by the First World War, (*b*) the sense of civilizational decline and elite and popular disillusion with the liberal order, (*c*) the greater receptivity to anti-liberalism and lack of confidence in bourgeois democracy, (*d*) the depth of the inter-war crisis of European capitalism, (*e*) the acuity of the subjective experience of that crisis by the capitalist class, (*f*) the strength of the economic compulsions driving external expansionism of capitalist countries as theorised by the classical theories of imperialism, (*g*) the much greater 'actuality of the revolution' given the greater strength and organization of the working-classes, and, finally, (*h*) the squeezing of the middle classes. These differences meant that while fascism may formally be a generic phenomenon, it was for all practical purposes 'confined spatially and temporally to inter-war Europe'.

As we see subsequently, however, the two decades that separate that judgement from Modi's first election victory have arguably reversed all these or made them matters of degree, not quality.

The perfection of fascism in India

For Poulantzas, bourgeois rule was normally exercised through liberal representative systems, more or less democratic, depending on the extent of the franchise and the fairness of the elections, in which competing, conflicting, and colluding bourgeois interests are brokered in parliaments (Poulantzas 2018 [1974]). Fascism was one of three exceptional forms of bourgeois rule, along with dictatorship and Bonapartism.

Fascism, involving an extraordinary level of repression that extended beyond the bounds of constitutionality and of the normal repressive apparatus of the state, is a constant temptation in capitalism, and in monopoly capitalism, it is all the stronger. The interests of the smaller number of corporations dominating the economy are at once more strongly opposed to those of working people and even small and medium capital, and more privileged over and above them. This gap between the needs of accumulation and legitimation (Habermas 1974) became abruptly wide in the Weimar Republic as decades-long trends towards monopolization encountered a wider franchise and greater powers to a parliament with a large working-class presence.

Of the three exceptional forms, while dictatorship involves the abolition of democracy outright, Bonapartism and fascism can emerge within apparently functioning liberal representative institutions. Bonapartism involves balancing the opposed interests of capital and the popular classes through concessions to both, while fascism is focused on organizing repression to preserve monopoly capital's power. Both have been known to deploy non- or para-state organizations of force. They mobilize middle, lower middle, and lumpen working classes by arousing resentment against relevant 'others' and through irrationalist ideologies offering easy 'final' solutions to society's multiplying problems. The aim is to impose 'order' through violence and intimidation (Marx's discussion of the activities of the 'Society of December 10' under Louis Napoleon best illustrates how even Bonapartism can deploy such force; see Marx 1963 [1853]) supplementing state repression.

This para-state organization of violence makes fascism a dangerous choice for capitalist classes. Attractive as it may seem to re-impose order or resolve some other real or apparent crisis, the para-state organization forms a social base from which a fascist regime can act independently of the will of the ruling classes that brought it to power, much as Hitler did (Kershaw 1989).

We are now ready to appreciate the parallels between Hitler's relation to the inter-war German corporate-capitalist class and the Modi–India Inc. link.

Like Nazism, Hindutva fascism emerges at a time when the right is emboldened and the left is weak. The most common Marxist objection to applying the fascist framework today is that fascism was responding to a powerful mass working-class left organization in inter-war Europe and no such challenge is visible today in the West or India. This Comintern interpretation and the related 'Bonapartist' understanding of figures like Gramsci and Trotsky—that fascism was the outcome of an 'equilibrium' of social power between the capitalist and the working class—has since been challenged: 'The beginning of the rise of fascism presupposes a significant series of working-class defeats' (Poulantzas 2018 [1974], p. 139).

While working-class organization and combativeness were then at a historical peak not seen since—with the Russian Revolution and revolutionary waves in Western Europe after the Great War—ultimately, these forces were quelled in a Europe-wide resurgence of the right, which included old-fashioned authoritarians like Horthy, Pilsudski, and Franco, conservatives, large phalanxes of clerical forces, as well as fascism. If fascism constituted the cutting edge of this resurgence (Hobsbawm 1994, pp. 112–114), this was because it was the form of right-wing politics adapted to organizing on the new political terrain of mass working-class enfranchisement to sustain the rule of capital in its monopoly phase. That is why it often projected itself as democratic and even socialist and as speaking for the common man. While the right threatened the inherited liberal order already in crisis, the left was divided and weak. After the initial post-war revolutionary wave, it threatened no government in Western Europe.

Left weakness also rules out the Bonapartist diagnosis. Fascism balanced the capitalist and working classes neither in Germany nor in Italy and, 'throughout the rise of fascism, the bourgeoisie remained the principal aspect of the principal contradiction' (Poulantzas 2018 [1974], p. 61). In sum, by the time Hitler came to power, 'the one political force which had the potential to combat Nazism—organized labour—had for years been disastrously split and had long since ceased to play any significant role in determining the struggle for power' (Kershaw 1989, p. 58). So the contemporary Indian, and indeed the world, situation of a resurgent right and a discouraged, not to say devastated, left has more in common with the situation in which Nazism rose than the common Marxist objection allows.

The context of mass politics is also the same. It required Hitler to be a 'talented demagogue' (Pauwels 2017, p. 29), engaging fulsomely in democratic and even socialist rhetoric and projecting himself as a man of the people: 'I have the ambition to make the German people rich and Germany beautiful. I want to see the living standard of the individual raised.', Hitler said (Tooze

2006, p. 135). Modi's projection of himself as a 'backward caste' man from a poor, uneducated family for popular consumption is of this ilk. Nevertheless, while it was impossible for Hitler to advance electorally without some working-class support, the elites and the petty bourgeois supported him disproportionately (Fritz 1987).

Like Hitler, Modi accompanies his demotic face with an elite one. 'When dealing with industrialists, bankers, large landowners, high-ranking military men, and other rich and powerful Germans who, like himself, loathed socialism, [Hitler] made it very clear that the objective of his party was nothing other than "the destruction and eradication of the Marxist worldview"' (Pauwels 2017, p. 29). While we do not have records yet of Modi's conversations with the high and mighty of India Inc., the only reason they may not contain quite such open disavowals of socialism or the popular interest is that Modi and his corporate cronies are so agreed, and Modi's record in Gujarat speaks such volumes, that little needs to be said.

Fascism is the choice of corporate capital looking for a resolution in a time of crisis. Post-war political and intellectual compromises with fascism obscure the central role of big business and aristocratic conservatives in its rise. A distinction, even an opposition, is drawn between conservatism—elite, cultured, and refined—and plebeian forms of mass right politics, pre-eminently fascism. However, while undoubtedly elitist establishments disdained fascists in general, and Hitler in particular, for their rough social origins, in a crisis, determined to retain political purchase, they came around to relying on these despised forces everywhere in inter-war Europe (Blinkhorn 1990). Only this turnaround brought fascism to power.

Pauwels (2017) has persuasively demonstrated, more specifically, how most scholarship on fascism systematically underestimates the critical role of big business in bringing fascism to power, particularly helped by Henry Ashby Turner's *German Big Business and the Rise of Hitler* (1985).

Weimar Germany's ruling classes began to see Hitler as the solution to their complex political crisis as the liberal and conservative parties that hitherto formed coalition governments lost ground, instability threatened and legislation was stalled in a fractured parliament. Capitalists sought a leader capable of winning elections and implementing unpopular measures. Hitler submitted his application, as it were, by making electoral gains at the expense of liberal and conservative parties in campaigns blaming the crisis on Jews rather than on capitalism. As corporate leaders cultivated him, he also promised them a very lucrative rearmament programme, increases in labour discipline as well as a war to colonize Eastern Europe to make up for Germany's lack of colonies, and even to destroy the Soviet Union. German big business now backed Hitler with the money and the media support to bring him to power (Pauwels 2017, pp. 36–44).

Hitler explained his true programme in a meeting of several hundred businesspeople his early corporate supporter, Thyssen, organised to win over the remaining doubters. Denying any working-class or socialist objectives, declaring his belief in the sanctity of private property, he proposed to erase the normal public–private distinction in capitalist societies and make the public sphere as authoritarian as one of their firms:

> ... the authoritarian principle of submission to the leader (*Führerprinzip*), which he enforced in his party and which the members of his audience applied as much as possible to their firms: [was] the same principle he proposed to apply to the state. Just as the direction of a firm should not be entrusted to the workers, Hitler added, the direction of a state should not be entrusted to the popular masses.... Democracy in politics ... corresponded to common ownership of enterprises in the economy, ... to communism; conversely, private property ... harmonised with an authoritarian political system. Consequently, ... the democratic system of Weimar had to be wiped out in favour of a dictatorship ... for the good of industry and finance, of course. (Ibid., p. 42)

Modi's bond with India Inc. was formed in circumstances which, accounting for differences in historical context, including the longer existence of fascist forces in India and internationally, are uncannily similar.

When India Inc. lighted on Modi as its strongman saviour, he was a much better-known quantity, having been tried and tested in Gujarat for more than a decade. In 2001, the Gujarat BJP government's difficulties—a long-running crisis caused by the rivalry of the Patidar and Kshatriya factions compounded by a botched response to the 2001 Kutch earthquake and allegations of corruption—were mounting. Local elections and state assembly by-elections were being lost. When the chief minister resigned ostensibly for health reasons, Modi's long lobbying for the job to the BJP central leadership paid off despite his lack of legislative or governmental experience. His chief contribution to date had been confined to the mobilizations that culminated in the destruction of the Babri Masjid in 1992. While it paid electoral dividends, they were not enough to give the BJP an absolute majority, permitting only coalition government in 1998.

Modi became Gujarat's chief minister on 7 October 2001, the day the war in Afghanistan began. With the 13 December terrorist attack on the Indian parliament, Indian Islamophobia, aided by the rampant Western version, mounted towards a fever pitch and Modi now proceeded to orchestrate, in early 2002, the genocide of Muslims on the pretext of the (never investigated) deaths of some Sangh Parivar 'volunteers' at Godhra railway station. The purposes were to rally a divided state BJP, consolidate electoral support among the state's upper- and middle-class/caste Hindus, intimidate the rest, and project himself as a strong and resolute leader for state elections scheduled for December 2002. Unopposed by all but the most valiant and scattered civil society forces, Modi succeeded, winning a thumping majority with close to 50 per cent of the popular vote.

The first element of his rule—the ideology of authoritarian social unity reinforced by the intense repression of minorities which not infrequently burst into violence by Hindutva goons and created a pervasive and persisting atmosphere of fear and dread (Sud 2022)—was now in place. The second, the bond with Gujarat's and India's corporate capitalist class, would now be forged over the bodies of its victims.

Corporate leaders initially reacted to the Godhra 'riots' with fury. After all, the damage was estimated at INR 20 billion (USD 409 million); frightened international investors had ceased new investment in Gujarat and Indian corporate leaders worried about further eruptions of violence. Many also expressed revulsion at the open communalism on display, complaining about India losing face as a secular country, expressing shame and condemnation and one even calling it what it was, a 'genocide', a strong word for a CEO, even on a bad day (Jose 2012).

After his December electoral victory, Modi organized a meeting with the Confederation of Indian Industry (CII) in New Delhi in January 2003 to attempt a 'reconciliation'. Things did not go as planned. Though Jamshed Godrej and Rahul Bajaj, scions of two leading industrial families, and the director-general, Tarun Das, joined Modi on the stage, they berated him, one after another, for not ensuring 'the safety and security of all Gujaratis', for making 2002 a 'lost year' for Gujarat, creating insecurity, and scaring away investment, and much else besides. Modi could only listen and fume: 'You and your pseudo-secular friends can come to Gujarat if you want an answer. Talk to my people. Gujarat is the most peaceful state in the country' (ibid.).

However, Modi, long adept at mobilizing street muscle, now showed he could also mobilize corporate muscle. Soon, sympathetic Gujarati businessmen, led by Gautam Adani, formed the Resurgent Group of Gujarat (RGG) and threatened to withdraw from the CII *en masse*. If this was not already a problem given Gujarat's industrial importance, Modi began to restrict the CII's access to the BJP-led union government. The pincer action worked. Das, the CII's director-general, apologized publicly, and soon the CII was organizing international meetings with investors for Modi.

Tough love having achieved its purpose, Modi turned on the charm, and the freebies. Now capitalists began receiving unstinting regulatory cooperation and extravagant giveaways from the Gujarat government. This was the essence of the much-hyped 'Gujarat model', the other prong in Modi's strategy.

The truth of Gujarat's allegedly exceptional development under Modi has been amply exposed. Its human development indices were deplorable (Hensman 2014; Hirway, Shah, and Shah 2014). If there was growth, it was for the better off, the urban, the biggest companies, and the most capital-intensive activities, while working people suffered some of the lowest wages in the country and appalling human development indicators (Jaffrelot 2015). Claims about poverty reduction could not stand up to evidence of low wages, increasing inequality, reduced employment, neglect of small and marginal farmers, the plight of agricultural labour, persisting malnutrition, and agriculture's declining share of state GDP, even as more than half the workforce remained dependent on it. Even the aggregate growth rate was less than stellar: higher than the national average but not higher than other economically dynamic states, including Maharashtra and Karnataka.

The 'Gujarat model' had no development strategy, only a fawning subservience to big corporations that handed them control over the pace and pattern of growth through quantum increases in 'infrastructure to facilitate the inflow of corporate investment, ... [and changes] in governance to address the requirements of corporate units... [along with] incentives and subsidies on investments to the corporate sector to attract investments' (Hirway 2017).

Land-use laws went from protecting small and medium farmers to easing land acquisition for real estate and industrial uses. State subsidies for private infrastructure investment reduced state expenditure on welfare, health, and education. Indulging the corporate preference for developing greenfield rather than brownfield sites devastated the environment. Captive port facilities and power generation capacities for corporations met their transport and electricity needs while hundreds of villages awaited both. Private generators sold surplus power at exorbitant prices to the state-owned Gujarat Urja Vikas Nigam, putting it in the red (Sood 2012).

Thus, Modi had demonstrated his utility to India Inc. for a decade before the Congress-led UPA government entered its 'policy paralysis'. Initially, the BJP seemed unable to capitalize on it. In electoral doldrums, immobilized by strategic exhaustion, its urgent leadership transition to replace the ageing Vajpayee–Advani duo was stalled as serious leadership contenders like Pramod Mahajan died untimely deaths.

This was when India Inc. began clamouring for Modi to be made BJP prime ministerial candidate, the strong leader capable of overcoming 'policy paralysis'. For a corporate capitalist class reliant on government contracts and favours, the 'policy paralysis' was nothing short of a major crisis. Modi had already demonstrated his ability to expedite matters for Gujarat Inc., and now he was invited to repeat the performance on the giant scale of India. India Inc. got its way with the Sangh Parivar and went on to bankroll Modi's campaign, pulling off 'the biggest corporate heist in history' (*Economic and Political Weekly* 2014, p. 7).

Thus began a new stage in Hindutva's relation to India's propertied classes: Hindutva 3.0, if you will. During 1.0, in the early decades of independence, Hindutva was confined to northern cow-belt petty capital. In 2.0, it rode the waves of Hindutva's Ram Temple mobilizations and capitalist class expansion as the PPCs joined its ranks and their parties entered into coalition arrangements, finally forming the 1998–2004 Vajpayee coalition governments. They would have remained the peak of what the BJP could expect. Only the crisis of the Congress policy paralysis created the opening for Hindutva 3.0, the Modi–India Inc. bond (the earlier phases are analysed in Desai 2004b, 2011b, 2014).

Fascism serves corporate capital against not only the working class but also small and medium capital. Once in power, Hitler proceeded to solve German big business's biggest problem—insufficient demand—through a cornucopia of state orders, including a large-scale rearmament programme. With corporate profits rising rapidly from 1933, these were first 'used to undo the damage done by the Depression. Then, from the late 1930s onwards, they financed an extraordinary investment boom such as had never before been seen in German industrial history.' They also enabled the 'high pressure development of certain key technologies: the technologies necessary to achieve the regime's twin objectives of increased self-sufficiency (autarchy) and rearmament' (Tooze 2006, p. 114). State largesse towards big capital was financed through deficit spending, cuts in social expenditure, and large-scale borrowing benefitting financial capital. Aryanization also helped: confiscated Jewish property ended up with corporates close to the Nazi Party.

Meanwhile, small capital was shafted, paying higher taxes to service-debt owed to big capital and finding retail prices frozen while big business set wholesale prices (Pauwels 2017, p. 81). Not surprisingly, self-employment went from 20 per cent to 16 per cent of the active population between 1933 and 1939, while wage workers rose from 52 per cent to 53.6 per cent. 'Tragically, for all too many members of the *mittelstand*, the "proletarianization" they had feared so much, and which had prompted them to join the ranks of the Nazis, became a reality after the same Nazis had come to power' (ibid.).

Daniel Guerin's distinction between big and small business attitudes to labour sheds much light on the fate of working people. With lower fixed costs and awareness that low wages reduce purchasing power for their products, small and light industries pursue a policy of '"class collaboration", "industrial peace", and other "insidious" ways of taming, and corrupting, the proletariat' (Guerin 1973, p. 30). Big business, however, takes a 'tough boss' stance. Partly rooted in their economic weight and political influence, the higher organic composition of their capital—the ratio of capital spent on fixed capital and inputs compared to that spent on hiring labour—is key. It narrows the limits within which production is profitable. Whenever the steel makers, for instance, are unable to run their works at a sufficiently high capacity, the 'fixed charges' (interest, depreciation) on their plants are distributed over an insufficiently large quantity of products, and profits are impaired. When a strike breaks out, the least stoppage of production means losses mounting into the millions. If the economic crisis sharpens, they are unable to cut their fixed costs and must reduce their wage bill; brutal wage cuts are for them an imperious necessity (ibid.).

Hitler's demagoguery never won elections in a proportional representation system and nor did it translate into material benefits for working people. While rearmament indeed mopped up unemployment, German workers lost rights and later also lives and limbs in the war. Although wages increased from the depression era depths, they remained low, were subject to deductions and contributions to Nazi organizations, and were devalued by inflation and deterioration in the quality of consumer goods. While wages declined as a percentage of national income, working hours rose. 'Clearly, in Hitler's Germany only a small minority of the population lived in circumstances which we today would describe as comfortable' (Tooze 2006, p. 143). Destitution reached heights that prompted a working-class man, distressed by his own and his compatriots' condition and fearful of war, to try to assassinate Hitler in 1939 (Kershaw 2009).

Hitler's response could not have anticipated what passes for the 'welfare' policies of the Modi regime more closely: Nazi authorities 'responded primarily with symbolic gestures, accompanied by much propagandistic fanfare'. Winter aid, for instance, which gave some assistance to the 'Aryan' poor, consisted of private donations, highly visible public collections of money, clothing, food, and so on; and, once again, wage deductions, voluntary only in theory. The German public suspected that a considerable part of the revenues was appropriated by Nazi bigwigs and organizations and/or diverted to help finance the armament programme. Generally speaking, the level of social assistance in the Third Reich remained below the level of 1928 (Pauwels 2017, p. 79).The Modi regime makes much of how in contrast to the UPA's doles and handouts, it provides 'entitlements' and 'empowerment' (Aiyar 2019, p. 83). In reality, it offers paltry gains and squeezes each one for propaganda and electoral advantage. A bizarre and varied range of benefits—cooking stoves, toilets, small houses, liquid petroleum gas (LPG) connections, bank accounts, and whatnot—are offered under schemes connected with great fanfare to the figure of the prime minister. The centralization of information under the Aadhaar card system permits local BJP workers to know who the *labharthi*s (beneficiaries) of these schemes in each constituency are and, at election time, they are gathered in meetings or visited at home to remind them of what they owe Modi (Mehta 2022, pp. 62–80; V. Mishra 2019). While '[t]here is little credible evidence regarding the effectiveness of these schemes and their [beneficial] socioeconomic impact … there is a high correlation between receiving welfare benefits and voting for the BJP' (Aiyar 2019, p. 82).

Although Modi did not rescue India Inc. from a Great Depression but from the 'policy paralysis' crisis, the services rendered are remarkable. Rather than ending corruption, Modi simply found ways of doing the same favours to India Inc. either by changing laws and procedures so that the illegal became legal or, failing that, by ensuring that neither parliamentary nor media scrutiny could expose the resulting corruption.

Under Modi, public sector banks forgave 'enormous debts, and many large "wilful defaulters" … essentially robbed these banks with impunity' of an estimated INR 12,000 billion (Sircar 2023). The 2016 IBC, hailed as 'transformational legislation', has been toothless in making corporates accountable. Corporate accounting and transparency standards were already lax and the government proceeded to undermine its own IBC through 'selective regulatory forbearance'. Not only has loan recovery been 'absurdly low, but also the entire system has been brazenly gamed by the politically connected. Delayed court judgments are often due to evasive action by defaulting borrowers, even as they continue to strip assets' (Bardhan 2023). The real aim may well have been to permit capital centralization.[1]

With the domestic press incapable of any criticism of Modi or his corporate cronies, accounting problems were exposed by international actors. Though not without sympathy with India Inc., the discovery of malpractices that could harm foreign investors has forced them to be quite damning as in the case of the Hindenburg revelations about Adani and Deloitte's refusal to audit important companies such as Adani Ports Special Economic Zone (APSEZ) and earlier BYJU'S (Cornish 2023).

Under Modi, therefore, partial resolution of the corporate debt crisis has occurred at the expense of small capital, who face tight credit conditions while the big firms of India Inc., whose reckless borrowing created problems in the first place, get off more or less scot-free (Sircar 2023) and even continue borrowing abroad almost without limit since lenders assume such borrowers enjoy a 'sovereign guarantee' (Bardhan 2023).

More broadly, Modi has run the economy disastrously for Indian workers, peasants, and small capital and in favour not only of big capital but, reportedly, of half a dozen of its top conglomerates—above all Adani, Ambani, Tata, and Birla (Mandhana and Purnell 2023). The rest of the country has not only suffered from the pro-corporate policy paradigm but has been additionally assailed by a series of disastrous experiments, from demonetization to the implementation of GST (so burdensome to small businesses) to the draconian COVID-19 lockdown in 2020, all of which set back the economy massively.

Economic growth under Modi is much hyped domestically and in the West, which needs India as a counterweight to China. It is, however, a statistical construct (Subramanian 2019; Mody 2023). In reality, aggregate growth has been lacklustre and economic policy bias towards the growth of a handful of the biggest corporations has increased inequality and introduced a disastrous new dualism in India's economy in which the vast majority fares badly while India Inc. prospers and even invests abroad. Given the rentier bias of India Inc., it is no wonder that Modi's much-touted 'Make in India' campaign, which aimed to increase foreign direct investment (FDI), has failed, with foreign capital showing little interest and the share of manufacturing in the economy declining.

Fascism's resolution to the crisis of big capital proves illusory. For all the favour Modi has shown India Inc., he has failed to resolve its crisis. The economy's miserable growth and employment performance, with a spate of suicides among the unemployed poor (Trivedi 2022), has reduced demand and investment (Chandra 2020). By favouring a handful of corporations, it has left most of India Inc. out. As the big players' dominance grows, so do the barriers to entry for others: 'People don't see a point in entering any space where these big corporations are already.... You don't want just a small group of companies winning everything over and over again' (Rohit Chandra in *The Economist* 2019). That is not all. As the unresolved banking crisis continues, businesses, not only start-ups and SMEs but also larger firms, find it hard to raise credit. Finally, many big-business people complain that, given its penchant for dealing with a few big firms, the government appears to prefer dealing with foreign capital rather than serving the domestic capitalist class (Chandra 2020).

Surprising though this may be, it is par for the fascist course. The assumption made by many Marxists, including Poulantzas, that fascism would provide a lasting solution or stabilization is not validated by the historical record: 'The fascist period in Germany was *part of, rather than a resolution to,* the political crisis of representation of the early 1930s' (Caplan 1977, p. 94, emphasis original). Fascism's

> essential contradiction ... derives from [its] being a type of coercive structure in which the control of the extraction of surplus value is displaced from the labour process to the political process, in a vast enhancement of the state's political role.... As a system, it cannot be other than permanently fraught with its own downfall, for politically it has forfeited (by exceeding) the state's brief under capitalism: to act as *the guarantor of the conditions for the reproduction* of the conditions of production of surplus value—the rest being up to capital. This delicately distanced relationship of the political and the economic is explosively compressed under fascism, and the political is enthroned in a threatening autonomy. (Ibid., pp. 95–96, emphasis original)

The politicization of everything can only lead to ever greater instability which can be addressed with ever greater politicization in a self-propelling cycle.

Instability can also arise elsewhere. For example, German big business did not put Hitler in power on its own: other social forces—large landowners, the military elite, and the church—contributed. Moreover, the disproportionately petty bourgeois masses whose votes brought Hitler close enough to power to be shoved into it by a constitutional impropriety were also part of the equation. Inevitably, 'the hopes of some often conflicted with the expectations of others' (Pauwels 2017, p. 116).

Modi is no different, not least given India's vastly greater scale and diversity. He too must pay his dues to groups other than India Inc. While there is no longer a substantial class of large landlords, competing members of the upper- and middle-caste/class coalition of the propertied that the BJP had secured already in the twentieth century continue to cause difficulties. Modi has also had to advance the BJP's politicization of the military by creating the department of military affairs and the post of chief of defence staff to head it so that the military becomes more capable of joint, coherent, and coordinated action across the services, plays a greater role in Indian foreign policy, and, ultimately, emerges from the firm civilian control established over it since independence (Mukherjee 2021). Though this process is far from complete, it cannot advance far without fomenting unease in the rest of the country, not to mention within India Inc.

Modi must also be attentive to the other main element of his own power cartel, the RSS, and he must keep a wary eye on electability. While all liberal democracies must reconcile the irreconcilable—preserve class power amid mass politics—fascisms face this difficulty most acutely, imparting paradoxical aspects to its public face. Like Hitler, Modi combines the appearance of strength and decisiveness with often mystifying inaction and aloofness:

> Hitler's approach to government was in many ways remarkably non-interventionist. Access to him, even for government ministers, was difficult, for some impossible. Pinning him down to a clear decision was often a hopeless task. (Kershaw 1989, p. 63)

Modi is remarkably similar: witness his long and unexplained disappearances at critical moments, such as the COVID-19 crisis or the Manipur crisis.

The purpose is to preserve 'charismatic authority': 'To protect his exalted "charismatic" image, built around national unity, Hitler could not afford to be involved in the day-to-day disputes of divisive politics' (ibid.) nor with any failing or failed policy. Kershaw further explains that Hitler's 'lack of intervention was a reflection of his Darwinist principle of struggle—letting the stronger in a dispute emerge through competition. It matched his wholly unbureaucratic style, aloofness from all routine administration, and disinterest in legislative niceties. And it was also a direct product of the type of leadership Hitler embodied' (ibid.).

German big business in the 1930s, like Indian industry today, was also far from a unified bloc, and if, on the whole, Hitler did the bidding of German big business, he 'did it in his way, that is, in an authoritarian, crude, brutal way' (Pauwels 2017, p. 118); this would also be true of Modi and the more refined elements of the coalition backing Modi will continue to feel ambivalence, if not distaste.

Fascism acquires a dangerous autonomy from the ruling classes. The very need of ruling classes to summon an outside force to resolve its crisis of rule makes fascism pregnant with the possibility of that force acquiring an unacceptable and dangerous autonomy.

> ... exceptionally, the weakness of the traditional ruling class relative to the charismatic leadership of the fascist mass movement means that the autonomy of that leadership expands rather than contracts,... Instead of restoring their own control, the traditional elites then find themselves outflanked. (Kershaw 1989, pp. 57–58)

The irrationalism necessary to fascism, if it is to create mass support without making material concessions to working people, makes this autonomy particularly dangerous. While it can muster electoral support with its heady mix of nationalism, hate, prejudice, and spectacles, irrationalism can overpower any rational calculation of capitalist interests. Hitler's irrationality, inter alia, elevated the persecution of Jews and other despised minorities to new heights and escalated the war to levels at which Germany could not possibly hope to prevail when he declared war against Russia and then another against the US (ibid., p. 64).

Will Modi's and the RSS's irrationalism—of which there is plenty of evidence, with Modi's claims about plastic surgeons in ancient India or

COVID-19 treatments or the parade of 'holy men' asked to comment on the recent success of the Indian Space Research Organisation's (ISRO) moon landing across India's Modi-manic mainstream media—affect the conduct of policy, whether on the matter of the repression of minorities or in the case of policy towards Pakistan and China? How much further damage will it do? What dangers will it lead India into?

It eliminates opposition and popular forces. Though no longer threatened by the left, on coming to power, Hitler still eliminated the left and eventually all opposition parties. First came the *Kommunistische Partei Deutschlands* (KPD), blamed in May 1933 for the staged Reichstag fire, which also became an excuse for the *Ermächtungsgesetz*, the enabling legislation that permitted Hitler to pass laws without parliamentary or presidential consent. The trade unions, the Social Democratic Party of Germany (SPD), and then, in July 1933, all other parties followed.

Modi may not have abolished opposition parties and, for the most part, given their weakness and disunity, particularly costly in the first-past-the-post electoral system, he did not have to. However, he did go so far as to imprison key opposition leaders and freeze Congress finances during the 2024 campaign. More generally, he has consolidated his and Hindutva's presence in the media and social and cultural institutions to an extent as to eliminate all other forces.

There remains the popular element of fascism. The 'night of long knives' eliminated the plebeian and therefore potentially radical brown shirts of the *Strumabteilung*, or the SA. It was replaced by the *Schutzstaffel*, or the SS, a more elite formation with many aristocratic members (and much smarter uniforms, designed by Hugo Boss; Pauwels 2017, p. 55). In India, the closest parallel to that has been the sidelining of the RSS and its key figures as Modi and his lieutenant, Amit Shah, have established their dominance (Deshpande 2022). Whether they can replace the RSS with another organization, perhaps their party organization, remains unclear and they may yet have to eat a humble pie before the RSS.

Even if ousted, fascism remains an ever-present temptation. Inter-war European fascisms are believed to have perished in the war, though the solicitude shown to surviving fascists by Western powers anxious to keep Europe capitalist meant that fascism lived on and enabled the fascist resurgence of our time.

If in the early post-war decades, the fascist temptation was resisted in the imperial homelands, it was thanks to the empowerment of working people worldwide that took the form of class compromise in the First

World with its Keynesian welfare states, industrial regulation, and financial repression, essentially borrowing from the socialist toolkit, communist regimes stretching from Prague to Pyongyang, and distinctly left-leaning developmentalism in the Third World. With the onset of neoliberalism, itself based on the defeat of working people and poor countries worldwide, the fascist temptation is, unsurprisingly, back.

How great is the possibility of Hindutva fascism perfected by Modi ending in war? Prabhat Patnaik rejected this possibility in 2020 (Patnaik 2020). For him, whereas the 'finance capital' of the early twentieth century 'was *nation-based* and interested in acquiring or defending "economic territory" vis-a-vis other rival nation-based finance capitals, today [it] is *international* and hence opposed to any partitioning of the world whatsoever' (emphasis original). Moreover, given that today's finance capital is averse to both taxation of capitalists and borrowing, even fascist regimes will fight shy of any large-scale militarist drive and so 'are unlikely to engage in large-scale wars' as opposed to 'localized ones'.

However, not only was Patnaik writing before the US-led proxy war against Russia, the intensification of the new Cold War against China, and the current conflict in Gaza, but his distinction between 'national' and 'international' 'finance capital' is questionable. Monopoly capital continues and remains tied to nation states (not least the US), cracks in the imperial block are widening, and today it is fighting to preserve what remains of its international or imperial power against its accelerating decline, particularly vis-à-vis socialist China.

US pressure on India to side with it against China is intensifying and the possibility that a Modi government might lead India into a militarist misadventure is not negligible. Nor is the possibility that wars—such as one an increasingly irrationalist Modi government might seek to launch against Pakistan—may be intended as limited but may spin out of control and lead to a larger conflagration. The US-led West's inability to launch a 'large scale militarist drive' did not stop it from provoking the conflict over Ukraine and is not stopping it from encouraging Israel or provoking China. The likelihood that India will lose these wars only makes the homology with Nazi Germany stronger.

Patnaik also envisaged the possibility that, in the absence of a world war that ends fascism, Modi may be defeated in elections and may even accept defeat. However, this will put Hindutva fascism under Modi or some other leader only an India Inc.-bankrolled election away from returning to power because the underlying crisis of India Inc.'s rule will remain unresolved. In these circumstances, only a resolute turn towards popular power in India can end fascism.

Note

1. Jairus Banaji, personal communication (September 2023).

References

Acharya, V. V. (2023). 'India at 75: Replete with Contradictions, Brimming with Opportunities, Saddled with Challenges'. 27th March draft for Brookings Papers on Economic Activity (BPEA), 1–33. https://pages.stern.nyu.edu/~sternfin/vacharya/public_html/pdfs/Brookings_India_piece_Acharya_March_2023_v14.pdf.

Ahmad, A. (1993). 'Culture, Community, Nation: On the Ruins of Ayodhya'. *Social Scientist* 21(7–8) (July–August): 17–48. DOI: https://doi.org/10.2307/3520344.

Aiyar, Y. (2019). 'Modi Consolidates Power: Leveraging Welfare Politics'. *Journal of Democracy* 30(4) (October): 78–88. DOI: 10.1353/jod.2019.0070.

Balagopal, K. (1987). 'An Ideology for the Provincial Propertied Class'. *Economic and Political Weekly* 22(36–37): 1544–1546.

Banaji, J. (2022). 'Indian Big Business: The Evolution of India's Corporate Sector from 2000 to 2020'. Phenomenal World, 20 December. https://www.phenomenalworld.org/analysis/family-business. Accessed 31 March 2025.

Bardhan, P. (2023). 'Unmasking India's Crony Capitalist Oligarchy'. Project Syndicate, 13 February. https://www.project-syndicate.org/commentary/gautam-adani-scandal-india-crony-captalism-by-pranab-bardhan-2023-02. Accessed 31 March 2025.

Baru, S. (2000). 'Economic Policy and the Development of Capitalism in India: The Role of Regional Capitalists and Political Parties'. In *Transforming India*, edited by F. E. A. Frankel, 207–230. New Delhi: Oxford University Press.

Bhattacharya, A. K., and P. Guha Thakurta (2019). 'Contours of Crony Capitalism in the Modi Raj'. In *Majoritarian State: How Hindu Nationalism Is Changing India*, edited by H. T. B. Chatterji, P. Angana, and C. Jaffrelot, pp. 193–214. New Delhi: Oxford University Press. DOI: https://doi.org/10.1093/oso/9780190078171.003.0011.

Blinkhorn, M. (ed.) (1990). *Fascists and Conservatives: The Radical Right and the Establishment in Twentieth-Century Europe.* London: Routledge.

Caplan, J. (1977). 'Theories of Fascism: Nicos Poulantzas as Historian'. *Editorial Collective* 3(1): 83–100. DOI: https://doi.org/10.1093/hwj/3.1.83.

Casolari, M. (2020). *In the Shadow of the Swastika: The Relationships Between Indian Radical Nationalism, Italian Fascism and Nazism.* London: Routledge.

Chandra, R. (2020). 'CFOs to Bankers to SME Owners, What India's Business Class Says About Modi Govt'. *The Print*, 1 October. https://theprint.in/opinion/cfos-bankers-msme-india-business-class-modi-govt/514275. Accessed 31 March 2025.

Chandra, R., and M. Walton (2020). 'Big Potential, Big Risks? Indian Capitalism, Economic Reform and Populism in the BJP Era'. *India Review* 19(2): 176–205. DOI: 10.1080/14736489.2020.1744997.

Chatterji, A. P., T. B. Hansen, and C. Jaffrelot (eds.). (2019). *Majoritarian State: How Hindu Nationalism Is Changing India.* New Delhi: Oxford University Press. DOI: https://doi.org/10.1093/oso/9780190078171.001.0001.

Cornish, C. (2023). 'Deloitte Resigns from Adani Ports as Auditor'. *Financial Times*, 13 August. https://www.ft.com/content/5b0cafdb-52ec-404e-9efc-a9630acc9315. Accessed 31 March 2025.

Crabtree, J. (2018). *The Billionaire Raj: A Journey through India's New Gilded Age.* New York: Crown Publishing Group.

Damodaran, H. (2013). *India's New Capitalists: Caste, Business and Industry in a Modern Nation.* New Delhi: Permanent Black.

Desai, R. (2004a). 'The Cast(e) of Anti-Secularism'. In *Will Secular India Survive?* edited by M. Hasan, pp. 175–209. New Delhi: Imprint One.

———. (2004b). *Slouching towards Ayodhya: From Congress to Hindutva in Indian Politics* (2nd revised edition). New Delhi: Three Essays.

———. (2011a). 'Gujarat's Hindutva of Capitalist Development'. *South Asia: Journal of South Asian Studies* 34(3): 354–381. DOI: 10.1080/00856401.2011.620551

———. (2011b). 'Hindutva's Ebbing Tide?' In *Understanding India's New Political Economy*, pp. 172–185. Routledge. DOI: https://doi.org/10.4324/9780203829608.

———. (2014). 'A Latter-Day Fascism?' *Economic and Political Weekly* 49(35) (30 August): 48–58.

——— (2016). 'The Slow-Motion Counterrevolution: Developmental Contradictions and the Emergence of Neoliberalism'. In *Social Movements and the State in India: Deepening Democracy*, edited by K. B. Nielsen and A. G. Nilsen, pp. 25–51. London: Palgrave. DOI: 10.1057/978-1-137-59133-3_2.

———. (2024). 'Peak Hindutva?' *New Left Review* 147 (May–June): 89–109.

Deshpande, V. (2022). 'BJP's Organizational Reshuffle Shows That Modi Has Effectively Pushed the RSS to the Background'. *Scroll.in*, 21 August. https://scroll.in/article/1030936/bjps-organization al-reshuffle-shows-that-modi-has-effectively-relegated-the-rss-to-the-background. Accessed 31 March 2025.

Economic and Political Weekly (2014), 'Editorial: Anger, Aspiration, Apprehension'. *Economic and Political Weekly* 49(21) (May), p. 7.

The Economist (2019). 'India Inc. Is Growing Disenchanted with Narendra Modi'. 17 August. https://www.economist.com/business/2019/08/17/india-Inc.-is-growing-disenchanted-with-narendra-modi. Accessed 31 March 2025.

Fritz, S. G. (1987). 'The NSDPA as Volkspartei? A Look at the Social Basis of the Nazi Voter'. *History Teacher* 20(3) (May): 379–399. DOI: https://doi.org/10.2307/493126.

Gandhi, A., and M. Walton (2012). 'Where Do India's Billionaires Get Their Wealth?' *Economic and Political Weekly* 47(40) (6 October): 10–14.

Guerin, D. (1973). *Fascism and Big Business*. New York: Pathfinder Press.

Guha Thakurta, P. (2002). 'Ideological Contradictions in an Era of Coalitions: Economic Policy Confusion in the Vajpayee Government'. *Global Business Review* 3(2): 201–223. DOI: https://doi.org/10.1177/097215090200300203.

Guha Thakurta, P., S. Ghosh, and J. Chaudhuri (2014). *Gas Wars: Crony Capitalism and the Ambanis*. Self-published.

Gupta, A. (2017). 'Changing Forms of Corruption in India'. *Modern Asian Studies* 51(6): 1862–1890. DOI: https://doi.org/10.1017/S0026749X17000580.

Gupta, A., and P. Kumar (2012). 'India Financial Sector'. *Credit Suisse: Equity Research* (2 August). https://docslib.org/doc/668870/india-financial-sector-house-of-debt. Accessed 31 March 2025.

Habermas, J. (1974). *Legitimation Crisis*. Boston, MA: Beacon Press.

Hansen, T. B., and S. Roy (2022). *Saffron Republic: Hindu Nationalism and State Power in India*. Cambridge: Cambridge University Press.

Hensman, R. (2014). 'The Gujarat Model of Development'. *Economic and Political Weekly* 49(11) (15 March).

Hirway, I. (2017). 'The Truth behind the Gujarat Growth Model'. *The Wire*, 8 December. https://thewire.in/economy/the-truth-behind-the-gujarat-growth-model. Accessed 31 March 2025.

Hirway, I., A. Shah, and G. Shah (2014). *Growth or Development; Which Way Is Gujarat Going?* New Delhi: Oxford University Press.

Hobsbawm, E. J. (1994). *Age of Extremes: The Short Twentieth Century 1914–1991*. London: Michael Joseph; Viking.

Jaffrelot, C. (1999 [1993]). *The Hindu Nationalist Movement and Indian Politics: 1925 to the 1990s.* India: Penguin Books.

———. (2015). 'What "Gujarat Model"?—Growth without Development—and with Socio-Political Polarisation'. *South Asia: Journal of South Asian Studies* 38(4): 820–838. DOI:10.1080/00856401.2015.1087456.

Jose, V. K. (2012). 'The Emperor Uncrowned'. *The Caravan*, 29 February. https://caravanmagazine.in/reportage/emperor-uncrowned-narendra-modi-profile. Accessed 31 March 2025.

Kershaw, I. (1989). 'The Nazi State: An Exceptional State?' *New Left Review* (I/176) (July–August). https://newleftreview.org/issues/i176/articles/ian-kershaw-the-nazi-state-an-exceptional-state. Accessed 31 March 2025.

———. (2009). *Hitler.* London: Penguin.

Khatri, N., and A. Ojha (2016). *Crony Capitalism in India: Establishing Robust Counteractive Institutional Frameworks.* London: Palgrave.

Mandhana, N., and N. Purnell (2023). 'Modi's Vision for India Rests on Six Giant Companies'. *Wall Street Journal,* 21 June. https://www.wsj.com/articles/modi-india-economy-reliance-industries-adani-group-tata-d2c4f89e. Accessed 31 March 2025.

Marx, K. (1963 [1852]). *The Eighteenth Brumaire of Louis Bonaparte.* New York: International Publishers.

Mehta, N. (2022). *The new BJP: Modi and the Making of the World's Largest Political Party.* Chennai: Westland.

Mishra, P. (1995). *Butter Chicken in Ludhiana.* New Delhi: Penguin.

Mishra, V. (2019). 'Lok Sabha Elections 2019: Arid Chitrakoot Fertile for "Superman, Saviour"'. *Indian Express*, 7 May. https://indianexpress.com/elections/chitrakoot-bundelkhand-elections-2019-modi-bjp-bsp-5711871. Accessed 31 March 2025.

Mody, A. (2023). 'India's Boom is a Dangerous Myth'. Project Syndicate, 29 March. https://www.project-syndicate.org/commentary/india-economy-boom-is-a-myth-actually-failing-most-people-by-ashoka-mody-2023-03?barrier=accesspaylog. Accessed 31 March 2025.

Mukherjee, A. (2021). 'The Great Churning: Modi's Transformation of the Indian Military'. War on the Rocks, 5 May. https://warontherocks.com/2021/05/the-great-churning-modis-transformation-of-the-indian-military. Accessed 31 March 2025.

National Herald (2019). 'Rahul Bajaj: We Are Scared to Criticise Modi Govt'. 1 December. https://www.nationalheraldindia.com/india/rahul-bajaj-we-are-scared-to-criticise-modi-govt. Accessed 31 March 2025.

Patnaik, P. (1993). 'The Fascism of Our Times'. *Social Scientist* 21(3–4) (March/April): 69–77. DOI: https://doi.org/10.2307/3517631.

———. (2020). 'Neoliberalism and Fascism'. *Agrarian South: Journal of Political Economy* 9(1): 33–49.

Patnaik, P., C. P. Chandrashekhar, and A. Sen (1996). 'The Proliferation of the Bourgeoisie and Economic Policy'. In *Class Formation and Political Transformation in Post-Colonial India,* edited by T. V. Sathyamurthy, 55–79. Oxford: Oxford University Press. DOI: https://doi.org/10.5860/choice.35-1772.

Pauwels, J. (2017). *Big Business and Hitler.* Toronto: Lorimer.

Poulantzas, N. (2018 [1974]). *Fascism and Dictatorship: The Third International and the Problem of Fascism.* London: Verso.

Rajan, R. (2008). 'Is There a Threat of Oligarchy in India?' Speech to the Bombay Chamber of Commerce on its Founders Day celebration, 10 September. https://faculty.chicagobooth.edu/-/media/faculty/raghuram-rajan/research/papers/is-there-a-threat-of-oligarchy-in-india.pdf

Sarkar, Sumit. 'The Fascism of the Sangh Parivar'. *Economic and Political Weekly,* 30 January 1993.

Savera (2019). 'The Constitution Under Attack at 69: Why Modi Govt. Has So Little Respect for the Constitution'. Communist Party of India (Marxist). https://cpim.org/views/constitution-under-attack-69-part-1-why-modi-govt-has-so-little-respect-constitution. Accessed 31 March 2025.

Sethi, N. (2019). 'Electoral Bonds: Seeking Secretive Funds, Modi Govt. Overruled RBI'. *Huffpost,* 17 November. https://www.huffpost.com/archive/in/entry/rbi-warned-electoral-bonds-arun-jaitley-black-money-modi-government_in_5dcbde68e4b0d43931ccd200. Accessed 31 March 2025.

Sircar, J. (2023). 'The Modi Govt. Used Ordinary Indians' Money to Square the Accounts of Wilful Defaulters, Fraudsters'. *The Wire,* 4 August. https://thewire.in/banking/the-modi-govt-used-ordinary-indians-money-to-square-the-accounts-of-wilful-defaulters-fraudsters. Accessed 31 March 2025.

Sood, Atul. 2012. *Poverty amidst Prosperity: Essays on the Trajectory of Development in Gujarat.* New Delhi: Aakar Books.

Subramanian, A. (2019). 'India's GDP Mis-Estimation: Likelihood, Magnitudes, Mechanisms, and Implications'. CID Faculty Working Paper No. 354, Centre for International Development, Harvard University, Cambridge, MA. https://www.hks.harvard.edu/centers/cid/publications/faculty-working-papers/india-gdp-overestimate. Accessed 31 March 2025.

Sud, N. (2022). 'The Actual Gujarat Model: Authoritarianism, Capitalism, Hindu Nationalism and Populism in the Time of Modi'. *Journal of Contemporary Asia* 52(1): 102–126. DOI: https://doi.org/10.1080/00472336.2020.1846205.

Tooze, A. (2006). *Wages of Destruction: The Making and Breaking of the Nazi Economy.* London: Viking.

Trivedi, D. (2022). 'NCRB 2021 Report: Dying Young and Jobless in India'. *Frontline*, 22 September.

Turner, H. A. (1985). *German Big Business and the Rise of Hitler.* New York: Oxford University Press.

Vanaik, A. (1994). 'Situating Threat of Hindu Nationalism: Problems with Fascist Paradigm'. *Economic and Political Weekly* 29(28) (9 July): 1729–1748.

Varma, P. (1998). *The Great Indian Middle Class.* New Delhi: Viking.

4

Finance Capital, Neoliberalism, and Neo-Fascism*

Prabhat Patnaik

Writing over a century ago, Vladimir Lenin had talked of finance capital as the 'coalescence of bank and industrial capital' and of a financial oligarchy presiding over this capital that sat on the boards of directors of both banks and industrial establishments. But Lenin's concepts were located in the context of an inter-imperialist rivalry, where the finance capitals and financial oligarchies of different advanced capitalist countries were both country-based and engaged in conflict with their counterparts in other advanced capitalist countries over the acquisition of 'economic territory' (Lenin 1976).

Contemporary capitalism, however, is characterized by a muting of inter-imperialist rivalry. This muting is rooted, not in any agreement among capitalist powers to divide the world peacefully (as Karl Kautsky had visualized in what is called 'ultra-imperialism') but in the formation of an *international* finance capital, which is not essentially country-based and which, far from wanting to divide the world into different spheres of influence, actually wants to remove all such divisions so that it can move freely across the globe. Contemporary finance capital, therefore, is *globalized* (that is, *international*); it is not part of any *national* imperialist strategy, as it had been in Lenin's time; and it is employed not just in industrial production but also in rampant speculation that has given rise to several asset-price bubbles.

* An earlier version of this chapter was published as Prabhat Patnaik, 'Finance Capital and Contemporary Imperialism', *Social Scientist* 50, nos. 11–12 (November–December 2022): 33–42.

What is more, contemporary finance capital is not just itself globalized, but actually creates the condition for the 'globalization of production', that is, to relocate productive activities from the metropolis to the Global South where wages are lower, by imposing so-called discipline on these countries, by forcing them to pursue neoliberal policies, with the help of global financial institutions like the International Monetary Fund (IMF) and the World Bank.

The imposition of the neoliberal order

The imposition of the neoliberal order, the widespread adoption of the neoliberal strategy, and, by implication, the decimation of the earlier dirigiste strategy are brought about under the hegemony of international finance capital; it reflects this hegemony and is in turn an instrument for the assertion of this hegemony. Behind contemporary imperialism, which is exercised through the neoliberal order, stands the hegemony of international finance capital. Imperialism had been weakened by the two world wars and the crisis of the Great Depression of the inter-war period. The process of decolonization, the introduction of universal adult franchise in the metropolis, the adoption of welfare state measures in the metropolis, and the acceptance of Keynesian 'demand management' to maintain a high level of economic activity were all concessions made by imperialism to cope with the existential threat that it faced at the end of the Second World War with the spread of the socialist camp.

When imperialism was coping with this challenge and consolidating its position, huge agglomerations of finance were occurring in American and European banks, which wanted to go global in search of profitable opportunities. The international monetary system that existed at the time, the Bretton Woods system, was, however, a hurdle against such globalization, since it allowed countries to impose trade and capital controls, and they did. But the Bretton Woods system, which had decreed the dollar to be 'as good as gold' (officially convertible at USD 35 per ounce of gold) was undermined by the same process that had led to the formation of such huge blocks of finance in the hands of the banks, namely, the massive outpouring of dollars from the United States (US).

The contradictions of the dirigiste regime, which in the metropolis had taken the form of rapid inflation, were used by these agglomerations of finance to discredit post-war dirigisme and impose on the world the neoliberal order that entailed in many ways the revival of the old, uncontrolled, 'spontaneous' capitalism. What we see in this period of neoliberalism is a reversal of many of the achievements of the dirigiste period, which in the metropolis had taken the form of several benefits for the working class, and which, in the Global South, had consisted of national control over natural resources, food grain self-sufficiency, and the use of the public sector as a bulwark against metropolitan capital and as an instrument for building up the technological base of the economy.

The neoliberal regime entails, above all, relatively unrestricted flows of goods and services and of capital, including finance, across country borders. What this means is that globalized or *international* capital confronts the *nation* state, a confrontation that can have only one outcome, that is, the nation state must always accede to the demands of globalized finance capital (to retain the 'confidence of the investors'), so that there is no massive capital outflow from the country precipitating a financial crisis. This amounts to a loss of sovereignty of the state, a narrowing of the class orientation of the state, and an abridgement of democracy.

The loss of sovereignty of the state follows from the fact that it necessarily obeys the dictates of international finance capital, and these dictates, completely unrelated to the country of origin of finance capital, are summarized in the neoliberal agenda. Likewise, the abridgement of democracy follows from the fact that since all political formations that dare not break from the vortex of global financial flows pursue the same economic agenda (which means in effect all political formations other than the Marxist left), the people have no real choice between alternative economic agendas; and the denial of choice between alternatives makes a mockery of popular sovereignty. The sovereignty of the people, in other words, which democracy upholds, is replaced in effect by the sovereignty of globalized finance capital. It is the change in the class orientation of the state under neoliberalism, however, that needs a detailed discussion.

Implications of neoliberalism in the Global South

Instead of standing apparently above classes and intervening in favour of particular classes whenever the need arises, as even the bourgeois state had done earlier, the state under neoliberalism intervenes almost exclusively in favour of the domestic corporate–financial oligarchy that is integrated with globalized capital. This means a withdrawal of whatever measures of support and protection for the 'working people' (that is, workers, peasants, and petty producers) that had been in place under the dirigiste regime. True, this withdrawal does not happen all of a sudden; it occurs over time, often camouflaged by holding out false hopes and promises, but it represents an inescapable tendency under a neoliberal regime.

For instance, the withdrawal of price support for foodgrain production in India has not yet occurred, though it has for cash crops; when it was tried for foodgrains by the Modi government through its three famous farm laws, the government had to retreat temporarily in the face of determined peasant resistance. The subservience of peasant agriculture to the domination of international agri-business, and of petty production in general to the encroachment of big capital, is an inescapable tendency under neoliberalism; but its full implementation in India has taken time and is not yet completed. (The Modi government's attempt to cut down what it calls 'freebies' is another blatant effort to further the agenda of subverting peasant agriculture.)

But even when the subversion of peasant agriculture is not yet completed, the very process of carrying it out, through measures like the withdrawal of input subsidy and of price support for cash crops, and through the privatization of services like education and health, exposes the peasantry to acute hardship by squeezing its real incomes. One consequence of this, visible in India, is the mass suicides of peasants. The other is the migration of distressed peasants to towns in search of employment: between the 1991 and 2011 censuses, the number the census calls 'cultivators' has declined by fifteen million; some may have been pushed into the ranks of agricultural labourers, but others have migrated to towns and cities in search of jobs.

At the same time, because of the phenomenon of relatively unrestricted imports, the rate of technological change gets accelerated in domestic production, which raises the rate of growth of labour productivity in the capitalist sector. Hence, even when the rate of growth of gross domestic product (GDP) increases under neoliberalism compared to the earlier dirigiste period, as is supposed to have happened in India, the rate of growth of labour productivity increases to such an extent that the rate of growth of employment, which is the difference between the two, actually slows down. This appears to have happened in India, where the rate of growth of employment in the neoliberal period is even below the natural rate of growth of the workforce. This means that, let alone absorbing migrants from the countryside, the urban economy cannot even absorb the natural increase in the workforce already employed by it.

The net result of neoliberal economic policies, therefore, is an increase in the relative size of the reserve army of labour in the total workforce, though it manifests itself not through a rise in open unemployment but through distributing a given amount of work among more workers, each earning less. The subversion of petty production (including peasant agriculture) under neoliberalism in a situation where the capitalist sector's capacity to absorb labour slows down and the relative size of the reserve army of labour increases has the effect not just of increasing income inequality, but of lowering the average real income of the working population.

This lowering of the average real income shows itself in a rise in the poverty ratio. The percentage of the rural population unable to access 2,200 calories per person per day (the original official definition of poverty in rural India) went up from fifty-eight in 1993–1994 to sixty-eight in 2011–2012; the percentage of urban population unable to access 2,100 calories per person per day (the original official definition of poverty in urban India) went up from fifty-seven to sixty-five over the same period (U. Patnaik 2019). The average real income of the working population has declined, while labour productivity has increased in the economy as a whole, and the proportion of economic surplus in total output has obviously increased. Because of this, the income inequality has widened, as is clear from a study by Chancel and Piketty (2017).

Such a widening of income inequality in turn changes the pattern of demand, away from the goods demanded by the working people towards goods demanded by the surplus earners. The latter being less employment-intensive than the former, this further restricts the rate of growth of employment and further strengthens the tendency towards a swelling of the reserve army of labour. This is not just a phenomenon specific to India; it is a worldwide phenomenon and arises from the logic of neoliberal capitalism.

This phenomenon needs to be located in its historical context. The anti-colonial struggle had been a multi-class struggle in which not only the workers and peasants but even the bourgeoisie and the urban middle class had participated. The dirigiste economic strategy, even as it tried to build capitalism in India and elsewhere, had tried to do so in relative autonomy from imperialism (its building up of the public sector and its pursuit of non-alignment in foreign policy testify to this effort; Kalecki 1972a); it had thus retained the support of this class bloc in this endeavour.

Neoliberalism, which entails a reassertion of imperialism upon the working people of the country, though of a new phase of imperialism, breaks this class bloc. It enlists the support not just of the big bourgeoisie (that is, the corporate–financial oligarchy) but even of a segment of the middle class that lives off the surplus. Thus, imperialism in its new phase not only breaks the class bloc that had fought the imperialism of the earlier phase but creates an immense and growing divide within society. On one side of this divide are those who get integrated with international finance capital, that is, the corporate–financial oligarchy and the upper segment of the urban middle class (apart from the landlords, who had remained substantially aloof from the earlier anti-imperialist struggle and who insulate themselves from the current agrarian distress under neoliberalism by diversifying their activities away from agriculture into other avenues). And on the other side of the divide are working people, that is, the urban workers, construction workers, agricultural labourers, the mass of the peasantry, petty producers, artisans, craftsmen, fishermen, and others.

This particular divide within the nation is a new and specific feature of contemporary imperialism. During colonial times, it was only the landlords and a few comprador capitalists (whose weight in India was quite marginal) who were on the other side of the divide, and the bulk of the nation was united against imperialism. Now, however, a significant accretion of strength is occurring in the pro-imperialist camp, that is, the camp on the side of international finance capital, the one supporting neoliberalism. This camp includes not just the corporate–financial oligarchy but a big chunk of the articulate urban middle class. This latter class is a beneficiary of the neoliberal regime, and of whatever relocation of activities from the metropolis to the Global South occurs in this regime.

The crisis of neoliberalism

Ironically, while the neoliberal regime widens the gap *within* societies of the Global South between the working people and the oligarchy (and the urban upper middle class), it imposes a restraint upon any widening of the gap between the workers in the metropolis and those in the Global South. This is because of the mobility of capital-in-production from high-wage to low-wage economies; such mobility does not *equalize* wages between the metropolis and the Global South; but it does keep their divergence in check. Historically, as labour productivity had increased in the metropolis, real wages too had risen there, while in the Global South, the massive labour reserves created by colonial deindustrialization had kept wages tied to a subsistence level so that the real wages in the two regions had diverged over time.

Such divergence had been possible because labour was not allowed to move from the 'south' to the 'north', while capital, though allowed to move in the opposite direction, never actually did move *to set up industries to meet global demand* (as distinct from meeting local demand or as distinct from promoting primary production). Under neoliberalism however, while labour from the 'south' is still not allowed to move freely to the 'north', capital from the 'north' has started relocating itself to the 'south'. This ensures that 'northern' wages cannot rise any more relative to 'southern' wages, which means that 'northern' wages too are now subject to the baneful effects of the massive 'southern' labour reserves. In other words, the wages in *no* segment of the world economy rise, even as labour productivity rises everywhere, which means that the share of economic surplus rises everywhere, not just within countries but also for the world economy as a whole.

This phenomenon has prompted many to argue that the world economy should now be seen in terms of the antagonism between the capitalists of the world and the workers of the world, rather than the antagonism between the metropolis and the Global South. The concept of imperialism is no longer relevant, since big bourgeoisie in the Global South now makes common cause with its counterpart in the metropolis, while the workers in the metropolis share the same fate as the workers in the Global South.

This, however, would be an erroneous conclusion to draw, a conclusion that would cripple revolutionary praxis. While a worker–peasant alliance *within* a Global South economy is possible and meaningful, a global alliance of workers belonging both to the 'north' and the 'south' is nowhere on the horizon. Waiting for such an alliance, as the 'global-capital-versus-global-workers' view would recommend, would mean waiting ad infinitum. Imperialism, in short, does not necessarily always mean one country exploiting another. It also covers the case where metropolitan capital, together with the capital of a Global South country, exploits the working people of that Global South country, and that too so intensively that their average real incomes are lowered (for example, metropolitan capital's exploiting workers within the metropolis itself so intensively that their real incomes too are lowered or stagnant is not germane to the issue of identifying imperialism).

The rise in the share of economic surplus in output, both within countries and at the global level, entails a tendency towards overproduction. Since a rupee accruing to the working people is more or less fully spent on consumption while a rupee accruing to surplus earners is spent only partly on consumption, a shift from wages to surplus implies, other things remaining the same, a reduction in overall consumption. Such a reduction would also bring down investment over time, so that aggregate demand would come down, slowing the rate of growth of the economy. Any such slowing down then produces a cumulative downward movement of GDP compared to its original time path.

It may be thought that such a tendency towards overproduction can be counteracted through state intervention, as the English economist John Maynard Keynes had suggested. If the reduction in consumption expenditure because of the shift from wages to surplus can be offset by an equivalent increase in state expenditure, then there need be no *actual* overproduction. This, however, requires that such state expenditure should be financed through either a fiscal deficit or a tax on the capitalists (or the rich in general). If it is financed by a tax on working people who more or less consume their entire income, then state expenditure simply replaces working people's expenditure on consumption, without causing any net addition to aggregate demand. But if it is financed by a fiscal deficit or taxes on the rich, then state expenditure would add to aggregate demand. Neoliberalism, however, frowns not just on any taxation of the rich, but also on any increase in the fiscal deficit *incurred to raise economic activity and employment.*

A fiscal deficit for financing state expenditure to raise the level of activity and employment, even though it would also raise capitalists' profits, is opposed by finance capital because it *delegitimizes* capitalism by projecting that the system is incapable of functioning without state intervention. This is why fiscal responsibility legislation, limiting the size of the fiscal deficit relative to GDP to a minuscule 3 per cent, is passed in most countries (except the US).

The ability of the capitalist state to stem the tendency towards overproduction therefore is nullified under a neoliberal regime. The US, despite not having fiscal responsibility legislation, is hamstrung for a different reason. Since a good deal of demand generated within the US 'leaks' out abroad in the form of import demand, an enlarged fiscal deficit on its part within a neoliberal regime generates greater demand and hence employment and output *abroad*, while saddling the US with greater external debt, a situation not acceptable to the US. It follows that a neoliberal regime necessarily and inevitably gets overtaken by a crisis of overproduction, as the world economy has been since 2008.

The reason the crisis had been averted before 2008 was the formation of asset-price 'bubbles'—first the 'dot-com bubble' and then the 'housing bubble' in the US that had artificially boosted demand in the US economy, and hence in the world economy as a whole; but with the collapse of the 'housing bubble', world capitalism has sunk into a prolonged and protracted crisis from which there seems to be no way out within the confines of neoliberalism.

The rise of neo-fascism

It is in this context that neofascist tendencies have been in the ascendancy all over the capitalist world. Fascist elements exist in all modern societies, but usually as fringe phenomena. They move centre stage only when supported by big business, and this happens when the economy gets submerged in a protracted and insurmountable crisis that poses a threat to the existence of the system. In such a situation, fascist elements become useful to big business for several reasons. First, their ruthless commitment to authoritarianism comes in handy for suppressing working-class organizations and workers' struggles. Second, they target some hapless religious, ethnic, or linguistic minorities, and foment hatred against them within the majority group, to completely move the discourse away from material living conditions towards obtaining revenge for some imagined wrongs committed by these minority groups against the majority in the past. Third, this very campaign divides the working people and helps prevent any united struggles on issues of material deprivation generated by the crisis.

Big business forms an alliance with the fascist elements because of the 'benefits' these elements bring to it in a period of insurmountable crisis (in fact the crisis itself is often blamed on such a vilified minority group, for example, unemployment being blamed on immigrants). It promotes these elements through financial and media support and helps them come to power in exchange, not just for general security against working-class militancy in the face of the crisis but for tangible gains for enrichment which become otherwise elusive in a period of crisis.

We are witnessing such trends in contemporary India, where there is a corporate–Hindutva alliance which has led to the creation of an authoritarian regime and growing fascistic trends. The features of the Hindutva–corporate regime are (*a*) an authoritarian suppression of dissent, (*b*) the fomenting of hatred against a hapless minority group, (*c*) the conferring of massive benefits on big business generally and on certain favoured elements within it in particular, and (*d*) the combination of reliance on state institutions with the use of fascist thugs, for unleashing repression.

As long as neoliberalism had ushered in high growth, even though this growth was accompanied, as we have seen, by an increase in absolute poverty of the working people, it still enjoyed a degree of general support, as it held out the hope that it would eventually bring benefits to the suffering people, that the fruits of this growth would eventually 'trickle down' even to those experiencing material deprivation at the moment. With the onset of the crisis, however, this hope disappears; the system requires a new prop for its viability and this is provided by neo-fascism (P. Patnaik 2021).

There is a tendency among liberals to see the ascendancy of Hindutva–fascistic trends entirely in sociopolitical terms, such as the use of religious symbolism by the liberal bourgeois political formations, the lack of any concerted fight against 'communalism', and so on. This sees the Hindutva agenda of the fascist RSS in complete isolation from neoliberalism. Marxism alone links the two, which is why it can also see the connection between the emergence of neo-fascism in India and similar tendencies in other parts of the world. While the ascendancy of neo-fascism is extremely dangerous for the working people, it is also indicative of the *weakness* of neoliberal capitalism, the fact that it can no longer proceed in its old ways. This ascendancy in short is the potential harbinger of a fundamental change.

There is a crucial difference between the old fascism of the 1930s and contemporary neo-fascism. Unlike the earlier cases, the crisis cannot be overcome even by neo-fascism today. The old fascism had got the countries where it had come to power out of the Great Depression, as soon as it came to power, through borrowing-financed military expenditure that it undertook in preparation for war. Japan was the first country to come out of the Great Depression in 1931, followed by Germany after the coming to power of the Nazis in 1933 (Kalecki 1972b). There was even a brief period when unemployment had been overcome but the full horrors of the war had not yet been unleashed, during which the fascists had acquired a degree of popularity in the countries where they held power.

Neo-fascism, however, is incapable of overcoming mass unemployment, because the same constraint that hampers liberal bourgeois governments, namely the dictate of international finance capital to refrain from either taxing the rich or resorting to a fiscal deficit for garnering resources that can raise government expenditure to stimulate aggregate demand, also holds for a neo-fascist government. Such a government, therefore, cannot expand aggregate demand, unlike the old fascist governments in whose case finance capital was basically *national* and hence amenable to state persuasion.

This means that the neo-fascist government could conceivably be voted out of office: its incapacity to overcome the crisis will at some point affect its popularity, and it also retains the shell of democratic practices like elections despite making democracy hollow. But even if it is voted out of office, since the succeeding liberal government too cannot overcome the crisis within the confines of neoliberalism and would earn public disapproval for this, neo-fascism will soon make a comeback. Neo-fascism, in other words, will be with us for a long time because of the lingering crisis of neoliberalism, vitiating the atmosphere and causing, over time, a progressive 'fascification' of society.

To overcome neo-fascism, it follows, we have to overcome the conjuncture that produces it, the conjuncture of the crisis of neoliberal capitalism. Since this crisis cannot be overcome within the confines of neoliberal capitalism itself, its resolution requires going beyond neoliberal capitalism. And since neoliberal capitalism represents the very latest stage that capitalism has reached, a world beyond which even bourgeois theorists cannot imagine, going beyond it must entail a transition, through stages, towards socialism.

In other words, unlike what the liberal thinkers imagine, the struggle against neo-fascism is not just a matter of forming a united front with other political forces to restore the status quo ante; that would only bring neo-fascism back to office after a short while. The struggle against neo-fascism can succeed only if it puts an end to the crisis unleashed by neoliberalism, and the measures for doing so will necessarily set up a dialectic that will carry us beyond capitalism, not immediately, of course, but through stages.

The dead end of neoliberalism constitutes historically the potential harbinger of a socialist order. Progress towards such an order would be complex, drawn out, and fraught with difficulties, but a theoretical awareness of this historic potential is essential for praxis.

References

Chancel, L., and T. Piketty (2017). 'Indian Income Inequality 1922–2015: From British Raj to Billionaire Raj?' (Tech. Rep. No. 2017/11). World Working Paper Series, World Inequality Database. https://wid.world/document/chancelpiketty2017widworld. Accessed 28 March 2025.

Kalecki, M. (1972a). 'Intermediate Regimes'. In *Selected Essays on Economic Growth in Socialist and Mixed Economies*, pp. 162–169. Cambridge: Cambridge University Press.

———. (1972b). 'Stimulating Business Upswing in Nazi Germany'. In *Last Stage in the Transformation of Capitalism*, 65–73. New York: Monthly Review Press.

Lenin, V. I. (1976). 'Imperialism, the Highest Stage of Capitalism'. In *Selected Works (3 Volumes)*, vol. 1, pp. 634–731. Moscow: Progress Publishers.

Patnaik, P. (2021). 'Why Neo-Liberalism Needs Neo-Fascists'. *Boston Review*, July 19.

———. (2019). *Exploring the Poverty Question* (Technical Report). New Delhi: Indian Council of Social Science Research.

5

Communalization, Fascization, and Business Nexus

Anand Teltumbde

> The ideal subject of totalitarian rule is not the convinced Nazi or the convinced Communist, but people for whom the distinction between fact and fiction (i.e., the reality of experience) and the distinction between true and false (i.e., the standards of thought) no longer exist.
>
> —Hannah Arendt, *The Origins of Totalitarianism*

From the mid-eighties of the last century, the neoliberal economic model, devised by the anti-collectivist theorists,[1] which conceptually elevates competition as a high principle, has been favoured by the ruling classes. It remains nothing but a social Darwinist contrivance for accumulation by dispossession (Harvey 2004). Since the collapse of the Soviet system, it has become almost the default model sans alternative. The endemic crises it entails and the alienation it engenders necessitate increasingly authoritative responses and demagogic strategies from the rulers, using existing social divisions in the form of castes, religions, ethnicities, and so on, which lead to the fascization of societies.

While this trend is visible everywhere today, some countries have congenial ideological resources for the fascization of their societies. India, with a hegemonic Brahminist ideology (with its hierarchical ethos and the organizational dominance of its hegemons in the state apparatus as well as in civil society) is uniquely positioned. While fascization has been discernible since the 1990s in the overt majoritarian communalism whipped up by the Bharatiya Janata Party (BJP), it was somewhat muted by the lack of political consensus and the moral scruples of constitutional decencies. The current dispensation under Narendra Modi, the conscious choice of the big business in India and global capital that have withdrawn their long-standing support of the Congress Party, lacks these constraints. Modi, with his fascist model perfected in the Hindutva laboratory of Gujarat over a decade, has nearly accomplished the fascization of the country. He is close to the ultimate goal of the 'Hindu Rashtra'—the ultra-fascist–Brahminist paradigm that reinforces the hierarchical social structure and creates a totalitarian state under the control of upper-caste elites. The role of market and business in fascization is evident: they are the drivers as well as the beneficiaries.

Communalism in history

Communalism is a politically constructed belief that people belonging to a particular religion have common social, political, and economic interests and that they constitute separate 'organic wholes' or homogenous and cohesive communities (Chandra 2008). Implicit in the process of organizing such exclusive communities is hostility to one or another community. This hostility becomes intense when such communities live together and share common economic, political, and other resources—particularly, if the resources happen to be inadequate for the development of society as a whole. Hostility is further amplified and made explicit in organizations like the Rashtriya Swayamsevak Sangh (RSS) and the Muslim League (Mukhia 1972).

In India, communalism mainly refers to the hostility between Hindus and Muslims engineered by these organizations. The term was coined by the British colonial government as the strategic 'divide-and-rule' ploy to manage its colonies. The British constructed religious or ethnic identities with ethnographic accounts and distorted histories, and incited strife between people (Horowitz 1985) leading to serious inter-communal violence (Graff and Galonnier 2013; Horowitz 1985; Jones 1981). While certain exclusiveness of religious and sectarian outlook has always existed in Indian history as part of the tradition and economic and social life, its transformation into communalism is a modern phenomenon associated with the colonial emergence of a middle class and economic stagnation. Economic stagnation led to the collapse of traditional status systems, loss of identity, and competition for scarce resources, resulting in frustration, identity confusion, and a sense of relative deprivation. It led to a volatile climate in which minor issues like killing a cow or playing music near a mosque provoked extreme violence, eclipsing the real issues of government jobs, political positions, and educational opportunities (Hasan 1982).

When the British started taking control of the subcontinent from the Mughal Empire, the Brahmins saw an opportunity to take revenge on Muslims who had kept them subdued for over six centuries. In Bengal, the seat of British rule, there had been incipient attempts at mobilizing masses through 'Hindu Melas' in the late 1860s with the idea of rallying Hindus, particularly the educated youth, behind the concept of reviving the glories of the Hindu past. In this, they were supported by prominent Bengalis such as the Tagore family and others of their ilk. The process generated ecumenical articulations about a Hindu identity that was further strengthened by the activities of the educated middle class, which expressed itself in discursive as well as organizational forms to disseminate the ideas about 'Hindu-ness' (Sengupta 1993, p. 32).

The transformation of this identity into a militant one against the Muslim 'other' is reflected in *Anandmath*, an influential novel written by Bankim Chandra Chattopadhyay (1838–1894), a quintessential representative of the Bengali middle class. It preached cleansing of Muslims and hailed British rule, which remained the behavioural theme of the Sangh Parivar all through colonial rule (Islam 2017). The battle of the Santans (the rebel Hindu monks) in *Anandmath* is stated in terms of a crusade: 'We do not want a kingdom—we only want to finish off the Muslims and their clans because they despise god.'

The cult of emaciated Bharat Mata as a symbol of Hindu victimhood, which is at the root of Hindu militancy, also was started in the Hindu Mela and was propagated in the literature, such as in *Anandmath*, as the goddess to be worshipped (*Vande mataram*, or 'I bow to thee mother'). *Anandmath* was so influential that militant nationalist groups like the Dacca Anushilan Samiti emulated initiation rites given in it for the Santans. The universalist dimension of this self-defining Hindu discourse was later presented on an international platform by Swami Vivekananda (1863–1902) (J. Sharma 2013).[2]

These ideas for the self-definition of Hindus were paradoxically sourced from the European orientalist construction of Hinduism and what it regarded as the heritage of Hindu culture. It involved transcending from earlier segmented identities to one based on religion, which then had to be refashioned to provide an ideology which would bind the group (Thapar 1989; Thapar, Mukhia, and Chandra 1969).

Negotiating an identity in terms of a common cultural heritage also served the interests of the Hindu landlords in north Bengal, by silencing the peasants and marginalizing the Muslim community. These moves precipitated the foundation of the Central National Mohammedan Association in 1878 with the avowed aim of morally reviving the Muslims by working in harmony with Western culture (Banglapedia 2021). Interestingly, neither the Hindu nor the Muslim organization had any quarrel with the British masters.

Earlier, also in reaction to the conquest of India by the British and their modern ideas (liberty, equality, fraternity, democracy, and justice), a movement for reforms in Hindu society had sprouted, pioneered by Raja Rammohan Roy (1772–1833) with the founding of the discussion circle, Atmiya Sabha, in 1814. It discussed important social and political questions of the time. In 1828, it became the Brahmo Sabha, which was later renamed Brahmo Samaj. The Brahmo Samaj influenced the Bengal Renaissance of the nineteenth century, pioneering all religious, social, and educational advances of the Hindu community and inspiring the launch of similar reform movements outside Bengal, such as the Parmahans Mandali and the Prarthana Samaj, founded respectively in 1840 and 1867 in Bombay. The last and perhaps the most influential movement in the reformist *samaj* series was the Arya Samaj founded by Dayanand Saraswati (1824–1883) in 1875 in Bombay, which, however, gained strength in Punjab.

The Arya Samaj gave educated Hindus a political orientation and an impetus to carry on political work. From 1899, its members began to participate in (and finally dominate) the Punjab Congress. Though these reform movements promoted principles of reason (rationalism) and humanism, along with reliance on faith and traditional authority to support their appeal, and criticized ritualistic, superstitious, illogical, and obscurantist aspects of Indian religion, they contributed to Hindu militancy and aggravated Hindu–Muslim relations (Barrier 1967). In response, Muslims founded their own organization, the All India Muslim League, in 1906 in Dhaka. After the 1907 disturbances, however, the Arya Samaj played a crucial role in the shift from nationalist to communal organizations (ibid.). Subsequently, it gained strength and catalysed the formation of Hindu Sabhas in Punjab, which became the precursor of the Hindu Mahasabha, founded in 1915.

These reform movements reinforced the Hindu discourse and identity. However, despite their efforts to communalize Hindus, they could not overcome the segmented identities of a people divided into numerous castes, regions, sects, and languages. Even the Hindu communal organizations, the Hindu Mahasabha and the RSS (founded in 1925) and its political outfit, the Bharatiya Jan Sangh (BJS) (which became the BJP in 1980), remained ineffectual until the 1990s when India adopted neoliberal reforms, giving impetus to economic growth and the growing middle class.

Communalism and fascization

After the incipient efforts in Bengal, Maharashtrian Brahmins took charge of shaping political Hindu identity, giving it a lasting ideological and organizational form by borrowing from European fascism. The motivational genesis of it lay in the defeat in the 1818 battle of Bhima Koregaon of Peshwas, the Brahmins who had usurped the Maratha kingdom of Shivaji after his death. Initially, this identity manifested as individual rebellions (by Vasudeo Balwant Phadke, Chaphekar Brothers, and others) against the British, but after realizing its futility, they settled with Hindu nationalism and trained their violence instead on Muslims. It is leaders from the Maharashtrian Brahmins who largely led and are still leading communalist movements threatening the pluralism of Indian society.

Communalism and fascization are intimately related. While communalism of the minority leads to separatism, communalism of the majority leads to fascism. Communalism induced in the Muslim minority by the persistent anti-Muslim rhetoric of the Hindus during the colonial times ultimately resulted in the partition of the country. The Hindutva forces have been at work since the establishment of British sovereignty in India but were curtailed by the inclusivist societal ethos and then Nehruvian consensus, neither conducive to nurturing communalism.[3] Nonetheless, underneath the façade of secularism, communalism was able to thrive silently in society. It would wait for an opportune time to raise its ugly head, which it did in 2014, simultaneously driving the process of fascization of state and society.

Fascism is a leader-centric cult and hence the definition of his (the fascist leader is always a 'he') politics, ideology, and conduct decide the character of the government/state over which he presides. A short definition of fascism is 'fascism is a cult of the leader' (Stanley 2018). It involves the leader setting the rules about what is true and false. 'So, any kind of expertise and even reality is a challenge to the authority of the leader' (ibid.). Even institutions that teach multiple perspectives on history in all its complexity threaten the fascist leader. The fascist leader, observes Stanley, promises national restoration in the face of humiliation—supposed humiliation—by liberals, homosexuals, immigrants, and minorities. He also promises that he will gain revenge for this humiliation and restore a glorious previously lost order.

All these attributes strongly resonate in Modi, a prototypical fascist leader. Right from his stint as the chief minister of Gujarat, he displayed fascist characteristics, which have grown to an alarming magnitude after 2014, when he took over total control of the country as the prime minister. Ashish Nandy (2002), an Indian political psychologist, recalls his encounter with Modi when he was

> a small-time Rashtriya Swayamsevak Sangh pracharak trying to make it as a small-time Bharatiya Janata Party functionary ... but it [the interaction] left me in no doubt that here was a classic, clinical case of a fascist.... Modi ... met virtually all the criteria that psychiatrists, psychoanalysts and psychologists had set up after years of empirical work on the authoritarian personality. He had the same mix of puritanical rigidity, narrow emotional life, massive use of projection, denial and fear of his own passions combined with fantasies of violence—all set within the matrix of clear paranoid and obsessive personality traits.

Let us test Modi out on some additional features. Stanley (2018) gave three essential features of fascism:

1. *Fascists conjure a 'mythic past' that has supposedly been destroyed.* As Benito Mussolini had Rome, Turkey's Recep Tayyip Erdoğan had the Ottoman Empire, and Hungary's Viktor Orban rewrote the country's constitution with the aim of 'making Hungary great again', Modi sees glorious, mythical, ancient India not only spiritually great but also superior in sciences and technology. He celebrates an exalted status of a self-proclaimed *vishvaguru* (teacher of the world), which he promises his 'new India' will soon regain. Hindu civilization, his Sangh Parivar claims with no credible evidence, was the greatest of all the nations but was destroyed by the Muslims and thereafter by the British. Fascist leaders, as Stanley states, 'position themselves as father figures and strongmen', *à la* Modi who boasts of a '56-inch

chest', a 'Hindu Hriday Samrat', who alone can restore the lost greatness of India.

2. *Fascist leaders sow division.* They succeed by 'turning groups against each other', inflaming historical antagonisms and ancient hatreds for their own advantage. Social divisions in themselves—between castes, classes, religions, ethnic groups, and so on —are what we might call pre-existing conditions. Fascists may not invent the hatred, but they cynically instrumentalize it: demonizing outgroups, normalizing, and naturalizing bigotry, stoking violence to justify repressive law and order policies, curtailing civil rights, instituting mass imprisonment, and murdering manufactured enemies. The Sangh Parivar's enemies, as Golwalkar declared, were Muslims, Christians, and Communists. Modi transformed the polarization of society into an art form. It is this core strategy which lies behind his spectacular rise and his becoming one of the most powerful leaders in the world.
3. *Fascists are against truths.* Fascists 'attack the truth' with propaganda, in particular 'a kind of anti-intellectualism' that 'creates a petri dish for conspiracy theories'. For fascists, truth does not matter at all. Modi's disdain for intellectualism, reflected by his 'Harvard versus hard work' comment, is well known. Also, equally well known is his trait to lie with a Goebbelesque flourish. In reality, Modi fits Hannah Arendt's description in that '[b]efore mass leaders seize the power to fit reality to their lies, their propaganda is marked by its extreme contempt for facts as such, for in their opinion fact depends entirely on the power of a man who can fabricate it' (1958, p. 358). The best testimony for this came in the form of the people who suffered most from Modi's irrational 'demonetization' of 86 per cent of the currency notes with a few hours' notice, which was justified by repeating a fraudulent line: what if one bore a little pain for the sake of the nation!

The biggest force behind Modi is the Sangh Parivar and the myriad outfits it has launched in every segment of society. The fascist proclivities of its progenitors—Tilak, Moonje, Savarkar, Hedgewar, Golwalkar—have since been established (Teltumbde 2020). For almost a century, the Sangh Parivar has been concertedly working towards its aim—to establish a Hindu Rashtra—but remained ineffectual until India adopted neoliberal economic policies.

Neoliberal push for Hindutva

Pushed to the brink of economic collapse by 1990, India adopted the World Bank and International Monetary Fund (IMF)-sponsored neoliberal reforms—a euphemism for the counter-revolutionary strategy to shift the power from workers to the owners of capital by weakening the state and expanding the ideals of free market. In reality, neoliberalism shifts the orientation of the state to protecting the interests of large capital by placing markets above any social contract. Neoliberalism has decimated labour rights, denuded people of their civil liberties, imposed rigid limits on fiscal deficits, given massive tax breaks and bailouts to big capital, sacrificed local production for multinational supply chains, and privatized public sector assets at throwaway prices. Under neoliberalism, governments must obey the dictates of finance capital, lest it leave the country *en masse* and precipitate an acute financial crisis undermining confidence in a country. The sovereignty of the people is thus replaced by the sovereignty of global finance and the domestic corporations within it (Patnaik 2021). This abridgement of democracy is justified by political and economic elites on the grounds that neoliberal economic policies usher in higher gross domestic product (GDP) growth. However, even IMF economists have conceded that neoliberal policies are responsible for growing income inequality rather than GDP growth (ibid.).

These reforms were initially sold to the public with trickle-down prospects. The global financial crisis of 2008–2009 and stagnation in the world economy disproved them. As economist Prabhat Patnaik succinctly explained, the old prop of trickle-down economics having lost its credibility had needed to be replaced by 'an alliance between globally integrated corporate capital and local neofascist elements' (ibid.).[4]

Although the Congress Party brought in neoliberalism, it suited the right-wing BJP better, notwithstanding the nationalistic rhetoric its sibling Swadeshi Jagran Manch fabricated to politically oppose the Congress. Neoliberal policies soon manifested in severe crises among the lower strata in the form of farmers' suicides, rising unemployment, inflation, environmental destruction, and so on. This came in handy for the BJP as they could convert people's vulnerability into a sense of confidence by mobilizing them to reach for the imagined glory of their heritage, symbolized in the religious–cultural supremacist icon of 'Ram' and demonizing Muslims as the enemy. It was politically necessary, too, to counter the potential threat of the Other

Backward Classes (OBCs) being lured away because of the creation of Mandal reservations for them. The television series *Ramayana*, broadcast on the national channel, Doordarshan, from 1987 to 1989—one blunder of the Congress regime among many—was instrumental in whipping up nationalist politics around cultural motifs of Hindutva.

On the surface, Hindutva politics appears contradictory to neoliberalism, as communalism is not attuned to a 'free' market. But, in reality, the forces of Hindutva and neoliberalism have consolidated each other's positions in society, politics, and the economy. Modi, unabashedly neoliberal and pro-big capital, has provided enough proof over his tenure as the chief minister of Gujarat that he could simultaneously practise his Hindutva politics of hatred and pursue a neoliberal economic agenda. After all, people hardly understand the complexity of the economy; what matters is their perception, which could be shaped by propaganda.

Modi perfected propaganda following the Goebbelsque dictum of telling 'big enough lies' and making the media repeat it incessantly, while starving the contrary voices of resources and even smothering them. It was a perfect following of the fascist playbook. None of his claims, whether made in respect to Gujarat or now about India, have come true, but people perceive them to be true. Any statistical system that mirrors reality has thus been anathema to his government. Making people believe that the economy is doing well or that the adverse outcomes are not the result of policies tames the resentment of the poor and serves the neoliberal agenda of further concentration of wealth. Indeed, Modi provided enough proof for the complementarity of Hindutva and neoliberalism during his fascist rule in Gujarat.

Similarities between neoliberalism and Hinduism abound. For instance, both neoliberalism and Hinduism place no value on liberty, equality, and fraternity, the radical principles upheld in favour of people. Liberty, like every other thing in Hinduism, is metred as per the social hierarchy: the Brahmins having it all, and the Dalits none. Neoliberalism upholds it in principle for all, but in reality it entails the negation of itself, and inequality is considered natural, divinely ordained (in the case of Hinduism), and a catalyst of human progress. Fraternity cannot be a value in neoliberalism, which privileges unbridled competition between people, and, likewise, it cannot be a value in Hinduism, which ordains brutalization through caste.

These astounding ideological affinities between the two accentuate the existential orientation of people towards the occult of Hindutva and social

Darwinism. This compatibility of Hindutva and neoliberalism serves business interests.

Hindutva fascism and business

The post-colonial regime, contrary to the profession of the political class and the façade of the republican constitution they created, continues to be committed to serving the interests of the capitalists and propertied classes. It, however, carried the burden of promises to the masses made during the freedom struggle and had to camouflage this with the rhetoric of welfarism. The eight big capitalists of the country, well before the actual transfer of power (in January 1944), had prepared a plan entitled *A Brief Memorandum Outlining a Plan of Economic Development for India*, which came to be known as the Bombay Plan. Its second edition (part 2) was published the following year. The key theme of the Bombay Plan was the inability of fledgling Indian industry to undertake requisite investments, and therefore government intervention in industrial development through the public sector with deficit financing was necessary to transform the society from agrarian to industrialized (Anstey 1945).

Although Jawaharlal Nehru, the first prime minister of India, did not officially accept the plan, 'the Nehruvian era witnessed [what was effectively] the implementation of the Bombay Plan; a substantially interventionist state and an economy with a sizeable public sector' (Krishna 2005). The next significant policy intervention the state undertook was land reforms in the garb of fulfilling the Congress commitment made during the freedom struggle, but actually to create a class of landowners out of the most populous Shudra band of castes in vast rural areas as an ally of the Congress. Whatever little land redistribution took place under these reforms benefitted the Shudra tenants, leaving many actual cultivators of Dalit castes high and dry with an alibi that they were not found in records. The Green Revolution, a capitalist strategy to increase agricultural output, enriched this landowning class, transforming part of it into a class of rich farmers. Though not adequately noted, these two policy interventions radically changed the social relations in the countryside. While the Green Revolution brought in money, economy, and markets for input (seeds, fertilizer, pesticide, insecticide, electricity, water, and so on) and output (farm produce), credit, implements, services, and so on, characterizing capitalist relations, the rich farmers, who had taken over the social reins of power from the displaced Brahmins, would, however, not let go of the caste relations, with serious implications to Dalits, who became victims of both caste feudalism as well as of the emergent capitalist system. The tax-free accumulated agricultural surplus of the rich farmers found its way into many petty businesses (rice mills, flour mills, *daal* mills, contracting, transport services, and so on), bringing them face to face with the prowess of politics and thereby kindling political aspirations in them. The Congress could satiate them to some extent, but when this failed, they manifested into rival blocks or parties.

The late 1960s saw a multi-stranded crisis of capitalism, just as it passed its golden period of two decades and began manifesting social conflicts predominantly characterized by popular rebellions against state militaries and bureaucracies in most parts of the globe.[5] In India, this took the form of various movements, like Naxalite and Dalit Panthers. It strangely coincided with the fading of the halo of the Congress Party as the vanguard of the freedom movement and consequently made electoral politics competitive. The primordial identities of castes and communities were eyed as valuable sources of vote blocs for the electoral market, and a way to enhance the role of big money from businesses to fund casteist and communal strategies. This social unrest and political turmoil culminated in prime minister Indira Gandhi declaring an emergency in 1975, inaugurating her full-throated authoritarian rule. The RSS, the fountainhead of majority communalism and its political outfit, the BJS, donned the halo of victimhood of having suffered with other opposition parties during the emergency and skilfully exploited the opportunity by joining the united front of all opposition parties against the Congress in the form of the Janata Party, which came to power by defeating the Congress in the 1977 elections. Identified until then as an offshoot of the Brahminical RSS and treated mostly as a political pariah in an environment dominated by the ethos of socialism and secularism, the BJS successfully mainstreamed itself and even tasted power in the Janata Party government.

The Janata Party collapsed under the burden of its contradictions within two years and BJS reorganized itself as the Bharatiya Janata Party. It could make no headway electorally in the next two elections even after racking up the contentious Ram Mandir issue. In the 1984 election, the party touched the trough with just two members of parliament (MPs) in Lok Sabha. It was greatly helped by the political blunders of the Congress's prime minister,

Rajiv Gandhi, in 1985–1986, when he amended the Indian Constitution and weighed in with the *maulvis* to overturn the reformist Supreme Court judgment in the *Shah Bano* case[6] and opened the locks of the Babri Masjid to assuage Hindus, enraged by his decision to appease orthodox Muslims (Hasan 1993). Also, as mentioned earlier, the decision by his government to broadcast Ramanand Sagar's *Ramayana* through Doordarshan was a blunder too, as it severely dented the secular tradition of the institution and paved the way for the ambitious run of the Hindutva forces.[7] When the Vishwanath Pratap Singh government, embroiled in political uncertainty, decided to implement the recommendations of the Mandal Commission report granting reservations to the OBCs, the BJP intensified the Ram Mandir movement by taking up the Rath Yatra in 1989 and catapulted itself as the challenger to the Congress party, actually grabbing the power in 1996 for sixteen days, and then in 1998 for a full term.

Driven to desperation by the debacle in the 1984 election, the BJP adopted a pronounced communal stance, albeit under the control of prime minister Atal Bihari Bajpai, mainly due to the fear of alienating the BJP's alliance partners, on whose support its political fortune was hinged. But when, in 2001, Modi, the *pracharak* of the RSS, turned BJP politician sans popular base and took over the chief ministership of Gujarat, he went whole hog using majority communalism as the BJP's electoral plank. He endeared himself to the majority Hindus by exploiting the controversial Godhra incident on 27 February 2002 (in which 59 *kar sevaks*, or religious volunteers, including women and children, were burnt alive in a fire in a bogie of Sabarmati Express) to engineer unprecedented pogrom of Muslims in the state.

Securing a firm electoral grip on the state, he assumed fascist control and embarked on neoliberal development, which, with his well-oiled propaganda machine, further tightened his grip on power. It greatly helped the entrenched social and economic classes/castes. He overcame the intrinsic contradiction between communalism and neoliberalism, in that, whereas communalism may enthuse the masses, neoliberal development appeals to the middle class upwards but not to the lower classes (who bear the burden of crises created by neoliberal development). For the first time, Modi, riding on the wave of communalism, transformed Gujarat into the most neoliberal state in India. Economist Jayati Ghosh aptly observed that the Modi government, which is now more openly declaring its Hindu majoritarian and Hindu nationalist instincts, is also unabashedly neoliberal and pro–big capital, including global capital (Ghosh 2020).

The fallout of communalism was the ghettoization of Muslims in Ahmedabad and other cities. Muslims sold out their dwellings cheap and moved to Muslim areas, bringing good business opportunities to real-estate sharks. Ghettoization also helped many Hindus grab Muslim businesses. The biggest beneficiary, of course, was Modi himself who consolidated a majoritarian constituency of Hindus. Towards expansion of the market, Hindutva gave a fillip to the commoditization of many products and services, including cow dung and urine-based products and godly tourism and rituals. Likewise, while big businesses hugely supported Modi and reaped rich dividends from this munificence, some of them attracting even the charge of cronyism, small and medium businesses suffered from his policies like demonetization, goods and services tax (GST), and pandemic handling (Dharshini, Kajla, and Bhattacharya 2021).

Modi ran the state like his fiefdom, ignoring the institutionalized processes. The Comptroller and Auditor General (CAG) revealed, many years later, a number of 'irregularities' from this period. The CAG accused the Gujarat government of causing huge losses to the exchequer by bestowing 'undue' favours to large companies, including Reliance Industries, Essar, the Adani Group, Larsen & Toubro, and Ford. Land allotment was the main issue, but not the only one: 'During the last five years, the audit reports have highlighted cases of non/short levy, non/short realisation, underassessment/ loss of revenue, incorrect exemption, concealment of turnover, application of incorrect rate of income tax, incorrect computation, etc., worth Rs 5,287.48 crore (Rs 52.8748 Billion)' (Comptroller and Auditor General of India 2012). This indictment came after the CAG asked more than 5,000 queries and made 15,100 audit observations (Jaffrelot 2019). None of these interventions made any difference, and the aforementioned Gujarat-based companies have continued to register good results. Consider some more examples.

It is said that just a simple SMS 'welcome' from Modi to Ratan Tata brought Tata's Nano car project from Singur in West Bengal to Sanand in Gujarat. The terms agreed to by the government can only be called a largesse: a soft loan of INR 9,570 crores (INR 95.7 billion) at 330 per cent of the first-phase investment of INR 2,900 crores (INR 29 billion), including relocation charges, with no interest for the first twenty years; single interest on it at 0.01 per cent payable monthly after twenty years; loan amount to be disbursed on monthly basis in the form of refund of gross value added tax (VAT); originally the refund was to be calculated at 330 per cent of the VAT paid, but later it was negotiated down to 230 per cent, reducing the loan amount to INR

6,669.99 crores (INR 66.6999 billion); payment for government land to be made in eight equal annual instalments with compound interest at 8 per cent per year; 1.100 acres of land allotted with all requisite permissions; exemption from stamp duty (4.9 per cent of total sale price), electricity duty, registration charges (1 per cent of the sale price), and transfer charges for conversion of land status from agriculture to non-agriculture; and 14,000 cubic meters per day water, permission to draw ground water for immediate needs (Dave and Damodar 2015). Tata was not the only one to be so favoured.

Similarly, the conglomerate Larsen & Toubro was allotted 800,000 square metres of prime land in the industrial zone of Hazira, Surat, without auction, at the rate of INR 1 per square meter, thereby costing the state exchequer a few hundred crore rupees (Jaffrelot 2024). The Essar Group was allotted 208,000 square metres of disputed land for a steel plant on the CRZ (Coastal Regulation Zone) and forest land that could not be allotted as per Supreme Court guidelines (ibid.). The occupier is unauthorized, but no action has been taken by the state machinery (ibid.).

In Mundra, Adani acquired up to 7,350 hectares of land on the 30-year, renewable leases 'for as little as one U.S. cent a square meter (the rate maxed out at 45 cents a square meter). He in turn has sublet this land to other companies, including state-owned Indian Oil Co., for as much as $11 a square meter. Between 2005 and 2007 at least 1,200 hectares of grazing land was taken away from villagers' (Bahree 2014).

As a result of these doles, the market capitalization of the Adani Group has allegedly increased by 8,615 per cent between 2002 and 2012, that of Essar by 4,507 per cent, and that of Reliance Industries by 1,357 per cent. In light of these numbers, it is not surprising that the corporate 'who's who' of the country had profuse praise for Modi during 'Vibrant Gujarat', a biannual forum to showcase Gujarat to the investor community. For example, Ratan Tata stated, 'Narendra Modi is an extremely easy person to deal with—very informal, compatible and pleasant, and capable as well. It is very difficult not to feel comfortable with him.' In 2007, Mukesh Ambani declared, 'Narendrabhai is a leader with a grand vision ... amazing clarity of purpose with determination... strong ethos with a modern outlook, dynamism and passion.' In 2013, Anil Ambani, who had already projected Modi as the next prime minister of India, likened him to Mahatma Gandhi, Sardar Patel, Dhirubhai Ambani (his father), and Arjuna, the hero of the Mahabharata, before calling him 'king of kings'. Surely, Gujarat made notable progress in attracting investment, though not as much as claimed. Hundreds of companies were attracted to

'Vibrant Gujarat', and promises of investment worth hundreds of thousands of crores were secured. The realization of promised investments declined steadily over the years, but by the middle of the first decade of the century, investment in Gujarat had risen significantly and Modi had become one of the favourite chief ministers of Indian businessmen.

Modi, who had squirmed his way to the seat of power, was greatly helped by the religious polarization of the Gujarati society and by big capitalists in successive elections and paved the way for his elevation to the highest post of prime minister of the country. His election campaign in 2014, promising *achchhe din* (good times) reminded one of Ronald Reagan's now-famous 1984 presidential slogan: 'Morning in America'. Indeed, many people likened Modi to Reagan and Margaret Thatcher, who had ruthlessly furthered the neoliberal agenda in their countries. In anticipation of his victory, the stock market had surged; the foreign investors put in huge money in Indian stocks and bonds, reflecting the overall business sentiment. He continued to cheer up big business, often to the detriment of the small and medium firms. He effected changes in foreign direct investment rules, opening many sectors for foreign investment, from coal mining to space exploration and from defence production to steel and luring deep-pocketed multinational companies (MNCs) to eventually take over these crucial sectors. These changes, coupled with the ambitious programme of privatization of public sector assets, have opened huge opportunities for investors.

Modi enacted the Insolvency and Bankruptcy Code (IBC), a system to quickly declare companies insolvent or bankrupt, allowing bigger corporate houses to buy them at low prices, while banks and other creditors (mostly public money) would lose huge amounts on their loans. One of the much-celebrated measures of Modi is the implementation of the goods and services tax (GST), which centralized virtually all taxation powers that had earlier resided with states. In his characteristic style of big-bang imposition of GST in 2017, Modi destroyed thousands of small and medium enterprises (SMEs), rendering their workforce unemployed. He sought to impose three farm laws and an amendment to the Electricity Act in 2020 in the midst of the deadly COVID-19 pandemic. It was a naked attempt to deliver the country's agricultural production and trade system into the greedy jaws of the corporate sector. The farmers had a unique demonstration of resistance, overcoming all kinds of odds created by the fascist government, and compelled Modi to eat a humble pie and take back the farm laws. Given its pro-big business stance, one cannot be sure a Modi-led government would respect peoples' will and not bring them back surreptitiously.

The Modi government scrapped twenty-nine existing labour laws and merged them into four labour codes between 2019 and 2020. These codes deal with wages, industrial relations, social security and occupational safety, and health and working conditions. Together, the codes destroy whatever meagre protection was offered by earlier labour laws against exploitation, low wages, dismissal from service, detrimental working conditions, and so on. The new codes enshrine a hire-and-fire right for employers, provide for fixed-term employment, change the way minimum wages are fixed, allow increased working hours, make it difficult to organize, and almost finish off the labour law implementation machinery. All of these were longstanding demands of the corporate sector and the Modi government fulfilled them, ignoring the concerns of the working-class movement. Even before these codes were fully defined, they have been implemented. This has led to huge insecurity in jobs, stagnant wages, deteriorating work conditions, and increased workloads. Meanwhile, profits in industrial houses and other companies have soared in the past few years as they threw workers out during the pandemic to maintain their profit margins.

The Modi government has also used its full fiscal and financial powers to provide enormous largesse to the corporate sector. In 2019, it affected a cut in the corporate tax rate from 30 per cent to 22 per cent (35 per cent to 26 per cent if surcharges, and so on, are included). This amounted to a grant of INR 1,450 billion to the corporate sector. The logic that this would lead to more investment and more jobs has proved to be faulty. Between 2014–2015 and 2020–2021, the Modi government gave various rebates, concessions, and waivers worth INR 6,150 billion to corporate taxpayers, according to union budget documents. These are distinct from concessions given to non-corporate entities and individuals and do not include revenue foregone due to customs duty rebates.

Since Modi came to power eight years ago, INR 10,720 billion worth of loans have been written off by banks, mostly public sector banks (PSBs), which act on the directives of the government. Most of these loan write-offs benefitted the corporate sector. The government wrote off an aggregate amount of INR 8,160 billion for PSBs and INR 11,180 billion for scheduled commercial banks (SCBs) during the last six financial years, from 2015–2016 through 2021–2022. This is largely public money, and it has gone into the coffers of big sharks who wilfully defrauded the people.

Between 2014–2015 and 2021–2022, the government sold off various public sector enterprises for a whopping INR 4,860 billion to various private bidders. As these disinvestments did not go as planned, the Modi government came up with a programme of leasing out INR 60 billion worth of public assets such as railway lines and stations, telecom systems, power transmission lines, oil and gas pipelines, roads, bridges, ports, and so on, to private entities, under the National Monetisation Pipeline. These so-called leases will run for up to forty years, making them, in effect, disguised sales.

Big businesses reaped benefits from their massive support to Modi. Their continued support is revealed through the controversial financial tool, electoral bonds notified by the Modi government on 2 January 2018. These bonds, issued by the State Bank of India (SBI), could be purchased by any individual or corporate entity and donated to any registered political party with at least 1 per cent of the vote share. There are nineteen such parties today, but of all the electoral bonds issued between March 2018 and 2022, the BJP received more than half of all of them. Between March 2018 and 2022, Election Commission data have shown that the BJP received INR 52.7 billion, or 57 per cent, of the total (NDTV 2023). To implement the Election Bond Scheme, major amendments were made to India's election law, the Companies Act, and the Income Tax Act through the Finance Act of 2017. This scheme effectively legitimated corruption through bribery by the corporates and extortion by the ruling parties. It may prove to be the biggest ever scam in history. It is evidenced by the fact that the government has unleashed genocide of Adivasis (indigenous people) in the name of rooting out Maoism, but basically to hand over their lands, containing trillions of rupees worth of minerals, to corporations. The military campaign against Adivasis started in 1991 as per neoliberal dictums, but Modi's fascist rule has stepped it up to a genocidal scale. Even those who spoke for them are not spared and are incarcerated as urban Naxals, an ingenious oxymoron.[8] The campaign was also designed to send terror waves across the country so as to silence dissent. With the brute legislative majority, complete subjugation of state apparatus and media, and the saffron gangs in civil society, the playbook of fascism had completely supplanted the Constitution.

The market and business are primarily propelled by profit and not by ideology. However, they would certainly favour an ideology that promises profit, as demonstrated under the present ruling dispensation in India.

Conclusion

Communalism in India, in its incipient form, is birthed by the middle class belonging to the Brahminic castes, born during colonial rule and with aspirations to regain their hegemonic hold over the subcontinent, which they had largely lost under Muslim rulers for nearly 600 years. This loss was accentuated by a stagnant economy and, later, by the colonial rulers' 'divide-and-rule' policy. Communalism is never natural. It needs singular identities that overcome the multitude of naturally formed identities that people have. In India, castes, tribes, sects, languages, and ethnicities were the primary identities of people, but they were forced into a neat division of two religions: Hindu and Muslim. Communalism may begin with a constructed majority—for example, Hindus—resenting the presence of people unlike them and who are perceived to be unjustly partaking what belonged to the majority. Once achieved, this resentment induces the same in the minority group. The minority's communalism leads to separatism while the majority's to fascism.

The communal politics that played out in the context of and with the encouragement of colonial rule led to a horrific partition of the country, which benefitted only the ruling classes on both sides. It certainly did not solve any problem and rather aggravated it, providing necessarily for the fascization of both societies, at the cost of their people. The lessons, however, were never learnt because the new rulers made use of those very divisive (nationalistic) sentiments for their political sustenance.

In India, the communal organization of the Hindus is uniquely represented by a hydra-headed Sangh Parivar with fascist proclivities (Islam 2018), but it could not make headway until the neoliberal reforms that needed fascist forces for their sustenance came into the country. Although the Congress Party brought in these reforms, it could not compete with the BJP, backed by its 'parivar', an ideological stance and a fascist infrastructure. Although the fall of the Congress may be attributable to a combination of multiple factors, the fascist resource base of the BJP has certainly been a major one. The BJP under a proven fascist leader with complete control of the entire institutional structure of the state, including media, and using India's market muscle to manage international opinion, has moved a fascist juggernaut with full force towards its goal of Hindu Rashtra, which would be the restoration of the Brahminic hierarchical structure duly adapted for modern times. Hindutva, communalism, fascism, and neoliberalism are the complementary ideologies of the right wing that both consolidate and in turn get consolidated by the market and business.

Notes

1. The term 'neoliberalism' was first coined in 1938 at the Walter Lippmann Colloquium by noted economists in Paris, including Walter Lippmann, Friedrich Hayek, and Ludwig von Mises.
2. According to Jyotirmaya Sharma, Vivekananda was 'the father and preceptor of Hindutva', a Hindu chauvinist who favoured the existing caste system, denigrated non-Hindu religions, and deviated from his guru Sri Ramakrishna's more liberal and egalitarian teachings.
3. Nehru created a system of governance that eschewed left and right extremism. It is this system that is popularly known as Nehruvian Consensus (see C. Sharma 2013).
4. Patnaik (2021) called post-globalization fascists as neo-fascists. I used just 'fascist' for simplicity (as implied in 'fascization', although I agree with him).
5. In the United States, a series of protests and revolutionary movements like the Black Panthers took place. In reaction to the Tet Offensive, protests had sparked a broad movement in opposition to the Vietnam War all over the United States as well as in London, Paris, Berlin, and Rome. In most Western European countries, the protest movement was dominated by students. The most spectacular manifestation of these was the May 1968 protests in France, in which students linked up with wildcat strikes of up to ten million workers, and for a few days, the movement seemed capable of overthrowing the government. In many other countries, struggles against dictatorships, political tensions, and authoritarian rule were also marked by protests in 1968, such as the beginning of the Troubles in Northern Ireland, the Tlatelolco massacre in Mexico City, and the escalation of guerrilla warfare against the military dictatorship in Brazil. In Central and Eastern Europe, there were widespread protests that escalated, particularly in the Prague Spring in Czechoslovakia; in Warsaw, Poland; and in Yugoslavia.
6. The *Shah Bano* judgment was pronounced on 25 April 1985, and Rajiv Gandhi got an act—the Muslim Women (Protection of Rights on Divorce) Act, 1986—passed by Parliament in 1986.

7. The series was telecast from January 1987 to August 1989, by the Rajiv Gandhi government, perhaps to gain goodwill with the Hindus, but it proved a boon to the BJP in its Ram Mandir movement (see Prince 2018).
8. Elgar Parishad, or the *Bhima Koregaon* case, in which sixteen activists, scholars, professors, and lawyers from all over the country were arrested and put in jails for allegedly planting fabricated documents in computers of some of the accused, is an illustrative case. Notwithstanding the forensic investigation by an independent agency of international repute that termed it as the worst case of tampering of evidence in the world, which the courts have not yet taken cognizance of, the bail verdicts coming from the courts one after the other have observed that prosecution failed to present any credible evidence for a prima facie crime.

References

Anstey, V. (1945). 'Review: A Brief Memorandum Outlining a Plan of Economic Development for India'. *International Affairs* 21(4): 555–557.

Arendt, H. (1958). *The Origins of Totalitarianism*. Cleveland: World Publishing Company.

Bahree, M. (2014). 'Doing Big Business in Modi's Gujarat'. *Forbes*, 12 March. https://www.forbes.com/sites/meghabahree/2014/03/12/doing-big-business-in-modis-gujarat. Accessed 28 March 2025.

Banglapedia (2021). 'Central National Muhamedan Association'. https://en.banglapedia.org/index.php/Central_National_Muhamedan_Association. Accessed 26 January 2023.

Barrier, N. G. (1967). 'The Arya Samaj and Congress Politics in the Punjab, 1894-1908'. *Journal of Asian Studies* 26(3): 363–379.

Chandra, B. (2008). *Communalism in Modern India*. New Delhi: Har Anand Publications.

Comptroller and Auditor General of India (2012). 'Report of 2011: Performance Audit on Revenue of Government of Gujarat'. https://cag.gov.in/uploads/download_audit_report/2012/Gujarat_Revenue_2011_Chap_5.pdf. Accessed 29 January 2023.

Dave, K., and K. Damodar (2015). 'After GM Exit, Nano Gives Gujarat Big Scare'. *Times of India*. https://timesofindia.indiatimes.com/business/india-business/after-gm-exit-nano-gives-gujarat-big-scare/articleshow/48907604.cms?from=mdr. Accessed 29 January 2023.

Dharshini, P., A. Kajla, and A. Bhattacharya (2021). 'Demonetisation, GST and Lockdown: How the Modi Government Has Wrecked India's Small Businesses'. *Scroll.in.* https://scroll.in/article/1011509/demonetisation-gst-and-lockdown-how-the-modi-government-has-wrecked-indias-small-businesses. Accessed 29 January 2023.

Ghosh, J. (2020). 'Hindutva, Economic Neoliberalism and the Abuse of Economic Statistics in India'. *South Asia Multidisciplinary Academic Journal.* DOI: 10.4000/samaj.6882.

Graff, V., and J. Galonnier (2013). 'Hindu–Muslim Communal Riots In India (1986–2011)'. SciencesPo. https://www.sciencespo.fr/mass-violence-war-massacre-resistance/en/document/hindu-muslim-communal-riots-india-ii-1986-2011.html. Accessed 29 January 2023.

Harvey, D. (2004). 'The 'New' Imperialism: Accumulation by Dispossession'. *The Socialist Register* 40: 63–87.

Hasan, Z. (1993). 'Communalism, State Policy, and the Question of Women's Rights in Contemporary India'. *Bulletin of Concerned Asian Scholars* 25(4): 5–15.

Hasan, Z. K. (1982). 'Communalism and Communal Violence in India'. *Social Scientist* 10(2): 25–39.

Horowitz, D. (1985). *Ethnic Groups in Conflict.* Oakland: University of California Press.

Islam, S. (2017). 'Adityanath Hailed as Anandmath Sanyasi: Anandmath Preached Cleansing of Muslims and Hailed British Rule'. https://www.academia.edu/33034154/UP_Chief_Minister_Hailed_As_Anandmath_Sanyasi_Anandmath_Preached_Cleansing_of_Muslims_and_Hailed_the_British_Rule?uc-g-sw=32176675. Accessed 26 January 2023.

———. (2018). *RSS: Marketing Fascism as Hindu Nationalism.* Delhi: Pharos Media.

Jaffrelot, C. (2019). 'How Narendra Modi Brought Industrialists to Gujarat (and Cut Many Corners in the Process)'. *Scroll.in.* https://scroll.in/article/907850/how-narendra-modi-brought-industrialists-to-gujarat-and-cut-many-corners-in-the-process. Accessed 29 January 2023.

———. (2024). *Gujarat under Modi: Laboratory of Today's India.* London: Hurst & Company.

Jones, K. W. (1981). 'Religious Identity and the Indian Census'. In *The Census in British India: New Perspectives*, edited by N. G. Barrier, pp. 73–101. Delhi: Manohar.

Krishna, A. V. (2005). 'Globalization and Communalism: Locating Contemporary Political Discourse in the Context of Liberalization'. In *Religion, Power and Violence: Expression of Politics in Contemporary Times*, edited by R. Puniyani, pp. 44–67. New Delhi: Sage Publications.

Mukhia, H. (1972). 'Communalism: A Study in Its Socio-Historical Perspective'. *Social Scientist* 1(1): 45–57.

Nandy, A. (2002). 'Obituary of a Culture'. https://www.india-seminar.com/2002/513/513%20ashis%20nandy.htm. Accessed 14 March 2025.

NDTV (2023). 'BJP Secured 57% of Electoral Bonds between 201–2022; Congress Got 10%'. 18 January. https://www.ndtv.com/video/news/news/bjp-secured-57-of-electoral-bonds-between-2018-2022-congress-got-10-677373. Accessed 29 January 2023.

Patnaik, P. (2021). 'Why Neoliberalism Needs Neofascists'. *Boston Review*, 19 July. https://www.bostonreview.net/articles/why-neoliberalism-needs-neofascists. Accessed 14 March 2025.

Prince, V. P. (2018). 'Appropriation of Puranic Narratives in Indian Socio-political Discourse'. *Literary Herald* 4(3): 78–83.

Sengupta, I. C. (1993). 'Colonialism and Cultural Identity: The Making of a Hindu Discourse, Bengal 1867-1905'. Unpublished PhD thesis, Department of History, School of Oriental and African Studies, London. https://eprints.soas.ac.uk/28888/1/10673058.pdf. Accessed 26 January 2023.

Sharma, C. K. (2013). 'Rise and Demise of Nehruvian Consensus: A Historical Review'. Munich Personal RePEc Archive. https://mpra.ub.uni-muenchen.de/61434/1/MPRA_paper_61434.pdf. Accessed 26 January 2023.

Sharma, J. (2013). *A Restatement of Religion: Swami Vivekananda and the Making of Hindu Nationalism*. Connecticut: Yale University Press.

Stanley, J. (2018). 'Yale Professor Jason Stanley Identifies Three Essential Features of Fascism'. https://www.openculture.com/2018/10/yale-professor-jason-stanley-identifies-three-essential-features-of-fascism.html. Accessed 26 January 2023.

Teltumbde, A. (2020). *Hindutva and Dalits*. New Delhi: Samya; SAGE Publications.

Thapar, R. (1989). 'Imagined Religious Communities? Ancient History and the Modern Search for a Hindu Identity'. *Modern Asian Studies* 23(2): 209–231.

Thapar, R., H. Mukhia, and B. Chandra (1969). *Communalism and the Writing of Indian History*. New Delhi: Peoples' Publishing House.

6

Populism, Fascism, Neoliberalism*

Ajay Gudavarthy and Vijay Gudavarthy

Analysing fascism in India has been rather unnecessarily polarized, both by Marxist approaches overemphasizing economic causality and by non-Marxist approaches overemphasizing ideology, politics, organizational aspects, and social psychology.[1] This difference is important in the historical condition and context in which an analysis of the current regime in India is being made. Whereas Antonio Gramsci defined fascism on an international scale as 'an attempt to resolve problems of production and exchange with machine-guns and pistol shots', in India, the rise of an authoritarian regime with fascist tendencies is certainly not a result of the nation being caught up in an international war. It could be more significant to examine the social reality that lends consent to the authoritarian model of politics and governance and how the forms in which it surfaces exhibit fascist tendencies (Gramsci 1984).[2] The fascist regimes during the Second World War were different from the post-war ones, specifically with reference to the experience of developing nations like India. In this context, the distinction between fascist movements and fascist regimes is important, and there seems to have been a right-wing

* An earlier version of this chapter was published as Ajay Gudavarthy and Vijay Gudavarthy, 'Populism, Fascism, Neoliberalism: Theorizing Contemporary India', in *Spectres of Fascism: Historical, Theoretical, and International Perspectives*, ed. Samir Gandesha, pp. 223–240 (London: Pluto Press, 2020). A shorter version of the chapter was also previously published as Ajay Gudavarthy, 'How BJP Appropriated the Idea of Equality to Create a Divided India', *Economic and Political Weekly* 53, no. 17 (28 April 2018).

extremist movement pushing for the rise of a regime in India (Dimitrov 1984; Reich 1980; Koves and Mazumdar 2005). If Narendra Modi's regime cannot be characterized as a fascist regime, it certainly has been an authoritarian one with fascist tendencies, and what needs to be explained is how such a regime manages to manufacture popular consent. This chapter first explores the underlying developmental processes which contextualize right-wing populism and then analyses the modes through which right-wing populism has managed to usher in a regime in which its fascist tendencies have popular consent.[3]

Neoliberal development, social crisis, and right-wing populism

In India, the rise of an authoritarian state preceded the rise of fascist tendencies. The ideal liberal constitutional state has been displaced by pragmatic authoritarianism associated with the use of force to address the need for capital as part of the neoliberal development model (Lerche 2007; Levien 2011). In many ways, the current condition is diametrically opposite to the assessment made by Michal Kalecki with reference to the functional role that Nazism served in the economic development of Germany. The role of force is in making the citizens accept the denials and deprivations following the withdrawal of the state. The challenge for analysis, however, is to explain its manufacture of consent for such force.[4]

This authoritarian state associated with the neoliberal development process has acquired a new political legitimacy given by the Sangh Parivar forces in the name of clean governance, which attempts to reconcile the neoliberal development project with the cultural nationalism agenda addressing the deepening social crisis neoliberalism has produced.

The rural agrarian crisis resulting from the neoliberal development project with an extremely skewed land ownership structure has resulted in absentee landlords seeking to continue social hegemony without being part of the rural economy. This leaves aspirational groups taking tenancy operating within a set of patronage relations to cope with the risks and uncertainties, and is an important space for cultural revivalism seeking social unity (R. Vijay 2012; Murali and Vijay 2017). These aspirational groups have exposed themselves to enormous risks associated with the agrarian crisis. As the nation transitions from self-cultivating farmers to tenants, it encounters a process associated with the social origins of authoritarian regimes (McCormick

2000; Moore 1993; Vanaik 1994).[5] It is well known that reinforcing traditional customary hegemonies and consent for domination have a significant role in uneven development in a vulnerable nation state (Aijaz 1993; Morton 2007).

In India, social groups and classes that fail to cope with the crisis-ridden rural economy end up experiencing distress and being displaced from the rural economy. Such social groups and classes end up joining the ranks of the millions of temporary, seasonal, circular migrants in search of employment in other areas, predominantly through inter-state mobility. Such workers have insecure, unstable and precarious work, unwritten contracts, and conditions of employment in which they lack the proof of identity that would make them recognized employees. They are denied minimum legal social protections and exposed to overexploitation in sweatshops that employ them. As informal labour, they are disorganized, lack trade unions, and are rendered voiceless as they are displaced from their social niche in their places of origin only to surface as outsiders and migrants in search of work and are disenfranchised and disconnected from local communities even if they find work (Breman 2003).

The right-wing populist majoritarian view provides a surrogate assimilation into the imagined unified 'Hindu society' and a surrogate emancipation of these migrants, carving the cultural–nationalist idea of an outsider. This transforms the outsiders of development into the insiders of the cultural–national narrative. Additionally, such workers, who see employment as a survival strategy, face abuse and physical violence which is normalized as management and control of the labour process. The nature of labour relations in such informal employment has been characterized multiple times as un-free, neo-bondage, and modern slavery (Breman 2008; Mishra 2011). This type of labour relations, accentuated by neoliberal policy, supplies all the micro-elements and manipulations that could easily lend legitimacy to the rise of an authoritarian regime (G. Vijay 2003, 2009).

Vulnerability and insecurity generate predatory modes of relations between competing networks for survival far from generating solidarity amongst those experiencing poverty and deprivation. This does not help such populations to distinguish a democratic regime from an authoritarian one. From the vantage point of these workers, eulogies of liberal democracy fall flat. They are a distant elite privilege denied to them. While this society operates on its own norms, for it to wrap its normative frames in liberal political values and modern social rationalities would be far-fetched (Sengupta and Vijay 2017).

Meanwhile, the micro, small, and medium enterprises (whether carrying on their activity by employing wage labour or as self-employed enterprises) play a significant role in the economy but are similarly threatened by the rise of big capital (Banerjee 2010). This segment of the economy also depends on social networks embedded in traditional social identities based on caste, community, and regional and linguistic identities, both to derive protections against legal regulation and to carry out their economic activities. Social closures and exclusions generated by the aforementioned structures get innately built into these networks. These networks are preserved through institutionalized cultural practices, customs, and rituals in a space that could easily be subverted by right-wing political agents (Gorter 1996). The neoliberal development processes have thus generated socially mediated markets on the one hand and market-necessitated patronages on the other (Thorat and Newman 2010; White 2003).

The social transformation interventions by the welfare state have failed (an experience which has many similarities with the failure of the Weimar Republic) (Balderston 2002; Hong 1955). The failure of several policy interventions needs to be understood in terms of their ability to address the aspirations raised through, for example, the promises made in land reforms, the 'Garibi Hatao' (End Poverty) programme, modernization, a rights-based approach, and so on. These failures have led to a condition of social impatience amongst the aspiring social groups and classes seeking substantive mobility, who find that their democratic representation seems to be engaged in subverting development (G. Vijay 2016). The risk that democratic institutions are dumped by the vulnerable social constituencies under such conditions and their inclination to support authoritarian regimes has been noted by Georg Lukacs.[6] The second dimension of the development process underway is the threat faced by petty capital to the challenges posed by neoliberal reforms and competitive pressures from the penetration of big capital, which sees people's constitutional rights and legal protections as constraints to growth and development. Petty capital and big capital, thus, both use the rhetoric of national unity to obscure widespread violations of civil and political rights as well as the dismantling of institutions.

Yet another important structural contributor to the rise of the current regime has been the role of financial capital. Financial capital, which has long operated in the black economy, has had a major role to play in several economic activities, notably the extraction sector, realty, and the credit markets. Apart from a significantly large role in the economy operating unaccounted for, financial capital has brought illegal mining, 'encroachments', and 'settlements', and is associated with the mafia as a credible force to enforce contracts. While lack of enforcement of the law was common in the informal economy, the successful enforcement of illegality through the systematic use of the mafia has become the hallmark of the rise of financial capital and its influence on the state machinery. This phenomenon has been attributed to the rise of the business of private protection when the state fails (Gambetta 1993). The massive state failure and normalization of illegalities and crimes as part of economic transactions have become commonplace, and yet another important source legitimizing the 'strongman' and authoritarianism.

There are several instances cutting across classes, social groups, and regions, in which finance capital has 'dispossessed' the livelihoods of communities. For example, it is common knowledge that the rural agrarian economy depends predominantly on informal money lenders. While as per law, operating unregistered informal lending at usurious interest rates is illegal, this illegality has been normalized. These interest rates have ranged from 10 per cent per month, compounding every six months, to up to 10 per cent per day. In addition, financial capital perpetrates illegalities in the urban and peri-urban realty sectors. Realty markets are based on speculation, which causes massive appreciation of land prices based on scarcity owing to the perfect inelasticity of the supply of land. Speculation is both an economic activity and a cultural, social mode, both in the enormous risk and rents that it relies on and the disconnects that finance capital's valuations have with the real economy. David Harvey (2006) calls this a problem of overaccumulation in the form of fictitious capital. Interest-bearing capital promotes a variety of illegalities. These illegalities have diabolical outcomes: the working poor space (due to pressure on and rivalry for urban basic amenities) gets precarious survivability in the otherwise socially hostile and economically unviable urban space; they also cause dispossession of entitlements of the poor and vulnerable groups and transfer assets to profitable uses. Some otherwise marginalized sectors also benefit financially from speculative appreciation of land prices.

Those adversely affected by these processes are generally the landless poor, who become tenants aspiring for socio-economic mobility but do not have collaterals to pledge for formal credit or who squat or encroach on urban lands for lack of accommodation. They also include, for instance, distressed poor belonging to extremely backward areas such as the KBK (Kalahandi Balangir Koraput) region of Odisha or the greenfield manufacturing industrial migrant informal workers from eastern Uttar Pradesh, Bihar, Jharkhand, or Chhattisgarh working in Telangana, as well as self-employed individuals living on the margins of urban areas. These sections of society comprise the Scheduled Castes (for national level analysis pertaining to land, see Nancharaiah 2022) and the Scheduled Tribes in the case of distressed migrants from the KBK region; and in the case of greenfield industries, it is predominantly Other Backward Classes (OBCs), while the urban self-employed in the informal activities are constituted, in addition to the social groups already mentioned, in sections of the so-called upper castes. They are subjected to open and brazen violations of legal regulations, as well as arbitrariness of the regulatory mechanisms, and this creates a fertile ground for the delegitimization of formal institutions. This delegitimization is used by the neoliberal narrative of rent-seeking for legal regulations, with allocational efficiency being left, therefore, to unregulated markets. The neoliberal model, however, has a problem of being seen as catering to the rich and the elites. It is, therefore, also employed by the right wing, not to make institutions effective or efficient as an alternative to the neoliberal model, but to erode institutions and, in various sections of society, to mobilize righteous anger.

This righteous anger against ineffective, inefficient, and arbitrary governance is combined with cultural and social narratives involving socially constructed threats and risks seen through the prism of the binary of majority–minority on the grounds of changing demography. Sociocultural cohorts suffer unacceptable injustice and injuries, lose opportunities, and experience exploitation, deprivation, and immiseration. These conditions are employed as a weapon against selected vulnerable minority groups (towards mobilizing the majority constituency) whose accommodation gets seen as undue patronage. All liberal and natural justice-based interventions of affirmative action are seen as appeasement, short-sighted political gimmickry, or discrimination. The vulnerable minorities are then projected as the elites and some super-rich beneficiaries are celebrated as success stories belonging to the majority. The conflict condition is thus converted into an ideal context for accentuating neoliberal reforms and reinforcing retrogressive sociocultural hegemonic reordering of social, cultural, and political power.

A transformation of the economic crisis into a sociocultural conflict using majoritarian mobilization as a strategy works much more readily in regions with histories of existing conflicts (partition-related atrocities; ethnic, linguistic, regional, and caste conflicts; and so on). Thus, like venture financial capital, which seeks opportunities through exploration and extractions, Hindutva venture politics explores and extracts sociocultural conflicts (buried yet brewing in the annals of history due to its complicated nature and the hesitancy of the liberal left to face this complexity, head-on, for fear of being found to be politically incorrect). Hindutva processes them as raw materials for the production and development of majoritarianism, depleting and degrading the social, cultural, and political ecology of the republic. Paradoxically, we therefore see that alongside rising violence, social animosity, shrinking democratic space and freedoms, there is an appreciation of the value of financial assets.

It is against the backdrop of these conditions that the production of consent for the right-wing populism-based authoritarian regime with fascist tendencies needs to be understood. In what follows, the modes through which right-wing populism has managed to expand itself are presented.

From moral rejection to 'political intervention'

Contemporary populism in India has changed the nature of public–political discourse by inaugurating new meanings and effects through an over-determination of significations that has foregrounded the limits of what we have generally understood as 'progressive' politics.

India has had other moments of populism. In the 1970s, for instance, it witnessed 'agrarian populism' that succeeded in bringing various agrarian classes under the leadership of the rich peasantry. In 2014, however, it introduced a range of new populist features. Indian polity moved away from its centrist character. There was no longer a balancing act between agriculture and industry, culture, and civilizational discourses. Instead, it managed to recalibrate the place and role of local and regional identities, the national trumped the local, and, finally, latent emotions and everyday ethics were effectively mobilized. The old distinctions between left and right are being replaced by a new kind of meta-narrative of 'us' versus 'them.' The process of creating the other is achieved not merely through physical violence, coercion, and intimidation; rather, it is achieved through a sustained process of gaining consent in a moral discourse that combines old narratives and replacing given or prevalent moral and normative structures with new aspirations, anxieties, and social imaginaries.

It carefully sutures the old with the new and shifts between two ends of the spectrum, sometimes claiming what we had earlier was mutually exclusive practices. It fuses the polar opposites and produces new kinds of 'de-binarised' discourses. It replaces ideas of antagonism and contradiction with continuity and social harmony; it replaces the emphasis on rights and liberty with fraternity and community. It is therefore imperative to decode what is old and what is new in this discourse, what is populist and what is authoritarian, and what the social narrative is behind the more visible modes of exclusion, violence, and the criminalization of politics.

Chantall Mouffe (2005, p. 72) has argued against a moral rejection or refutation of right-wing populism:

> The response of traditional parties to the rise of right-wing populism has clearly contributed to exacerbating the problem.... This is why moral condemnation and the setting up of a 'cordon sanitaire' have so often constituted the answer to the rise of right-wing populist movements.

Instead, we need to analyse 'its specificity and its causes'. 'Moral condemnation' of the right has to be replaced by an analysis of the 'moral structure' on which it builds its politics.

As Jan-Werner Müller (2015, p. 83) puts it, 'Populism, I suggest, is a particular moralistic imagination of politics, a way of perceiving the political world which places in opposition a morally pure and fully unified people against small minorities, elites in particular, who are placed outside the authentic people.'

This idea of a 'fully unified people' in India refers to a unified Hindu society. While it excludes the minorities in the first instance, it also must create a palpable unity within a diversified majority. This diversity, internal to the authentic majority, needs to be recast into a unity. Differences in social location, conflict of interests, and structural contradictions must be re-imbricated to promote social harmony, community, fraternity, and continuity with change: a glorious past with an aspirational future. It needs to aim for a change that is non-disruptive.

The 'authentic majority' is a social imaginary that can be replaced. Sought to be actualized through 'performance' and 'narrative' (Alexander 2006), it is intriguing to find that it has taken a more socially concrete and institutionalized shape in the industrialized state of Gujarat in the west and Uttar Pradesh in the north that have got locked into a de-industrialized phase and remained primarily agrarian. The social imaginary of an 'authentic majority' can cut across regional histories of growth and development but remain intricately connected to 'local histories'.

Much of the analysis on populism has focused on the larger narrative of 'us' versus 'them,' largely ignoring how right-wing populism attempts to maintain the unity of 'us' and how it produces an authentic majority which is essentially divided across caste, region, language, culture, and lifestyles. Right-wing populism has introduced a new set of political discourses and practices, the tenability of which will inform us of the future of right-wing populism in India.

Indian right-wing populism: what is making it thrive?

We will attempt to map these new sets of practices and how they have worked themselves in India. We develop a political, rather than a moral, critique of right-wing populism.

Undermining institutions

Right-wing populism has managed to turn traditional progressive political practices on their head. Critique is absorbed or re-signified, often in opposition to its original meaning. For instance, the reason for the defeat of the Congress, as is largely argued, has been poor implementation of welfare policies such as the National Rural Employment Guarantee Act (NREGA). The Bharatiya Janata Party (BJP) began with a critique of poor implementation through a discourse on corruption, but gradually resignified it into a critique of welfare itself. The BJP was able to place anger against growing economic inequalities, paradoxically, in the service of its own pro-corporate politics.

Similarly, a critique of institutional crises and the non-responsive character of the institutions lead to strategies that further undermine institutions. It does not lead in a progressive and linear manner to a demand for more accountability, but to further insularity. For instance, a critique against the slow judiciary and corrupt police in India leads to the legitimization of a strategy, or, rather, a policy of 'encounters', as recently announced by Uttar Pradesh's chief minister, Yogi Adityanath.

Here, it is instructive to observe how the left-liberal critique of the class character of democratic institutions is usurped to legitimize an aggressive state that, in fact, makes institutions further dysfunctional to the peril of the socially and economically weak and religious minorities. Further, the right-wing critique of Pakistan being a dysfunctional democracy—because it targets its minorities and is ruled by the army—is used to build exactly the same kind of governance model in India (this is especially the case after the revocation by executive decree of Article 370, a constitutional provision granting special status to Kashmir). Moral critique reverses itself into a moral justification of the same set of practices it condemns.

Old with the new

The old structure of politics is stitched to a new imagery, while in essence it remains the same. The rise of right-wing populism also emerged as a critique against technocratic liberalism and governance based on experts. The reasoning behind such a critique was that the dominance of a small elite blocks mass participation, thereby undermining the very essence of democracy. However, the rule of technocrats is being replaced by demagoguery and the strongman phenomenon, which only further undermines the democratic ethos, as Mouffe (2005, p. 65) observes:

> Liberal theorists looked for other explanations to fit their rationalist approach, insisting for instance on the role of uneducated, lower-class voters, susceptible to being attracted by demagogues.

However, this susceptibility is prevalent in other sections of the society too, including the middle class.[7] They perceive the dynasty rule of the Congress as an obstacle to be removed to pave the way for mass participation. The strongman phenomenon is justified as a response against the rule of the elites. The strongman becomes a symbol against 'consensus elites', ushering in an extra-institutional mobilization. One justifies the other and one cannot continue without the other.

Street violence, mass rioting, and public lynching are seen as modes of mass participation and conflict with the overbearing insularity of authoritarian rule. In such scenarios, it symbolizes order, discipline, and control of the old elites and religious minorities and implies public sanction, patronage, and impunity for the authentic majority. It also fuses the polar opposites—authoritarian rulers and extra-institutional mobilizations.

In doing this, the old structure of patronage politics and the rule of a few elites is re-signified without changing the essence (by not opening any new avenues for democratic participation). Here, it stitches the critique built by left-liberal discourses to the new kinds of extra-institutional mobilization. It builds on the fact that, in India, the discourse of formal equality has spread without commensurate change in the social and material conditions.[8] This inaugurates a different kind of social psychology.

Mobilizing culture

Right-wing populists mobilize culture and passions and have a grasp over the social psychology of many social groups that are aspirational about the legitimacy of equal treatment, but are engaged in a concrete struggle against routine incivility. Further, right-wing populists also sympathize with the declining social power of dominant social groups. The outbursts by Jats, Patidars, Marathas, Kapus, Kshatriyas, and other dominant castes are symptomatic of the anxieties that dominant castes experience during social transformation.

Left-liberals offer no alternative political agenda to any of these groups. Further, there are economically weak among the dominant castes. Their conflicting interests are replaced by mobility and unity. Reservations based on an economic criterion, instead of caste, is a case in point. It allows for mobility without the stigma of caste. Right-wing populism offers alternative ideas of social harmony, fraternal feelings, and community fellow-feeling that ostensibly allow mobility for the subordinate groups and also empathize with the dominant groups and their declining social power. This is yet again an instance of attempting to fuse polar opposites into continuity. It partly recognizes that the economically poor among the dominant castes are also socially stigmatized.

For instance, the poor among the Brahmins are not elites in the traditional sense of the term. The right sees a possibility of forging a unity based on a social experience of poverty. Economic elites are, therefore, pitched against cultural subalterns. They could be referred to as 'mezzanine elites' (Atanda and Cojocaru 2021).

How these differences at one level are going to play out against a certain kind of commonality at another level is a continuing challenge for right-wing populism in India. The right has to stitch the 'hurt pride' of the dominant castes with the social stigma of the subaltern castes. The difficulty of such a mode or the socially conservative aspect of such an experiment is visible in the recent conflicts between Dalits and Marathas in Bhima Koregaon.

At another level, this seems to be a feasible experiment with the emergence of new cultural subalterns across castes, classes, and regions. They are marked by a common opposition to modernity, liberal institutionalism, the role of experts and technocrats, difficulty in coping with global cosmopolitanism and secular ethos, and the dominance of English and its accompanying cultural valuation, and more. Right-wing populism is articulating this common nodal point, at times overcoming the sharp divisions between the various social groups. David Goodhart (2017, p. 3), in his recent book, sums this up:

> The old distinctions of class and economic interest have not disappeared but are increasingly overlaid by a larger and looser one, between the people who see the world from Anywhere and the people who see it from Somewhere.

New political fault lines

The new political fault line is between 'open' and 'somewhere'. The 'open' people are 'portable' and have 'achieved' identities based on educational and career success which make them generally comfortable and confident with new places and people (ibid., p. 3).

The 'somewheres' are more rooted and usually have 'ascribed' identities, which is why they often find rapid change more unsettling (ibid.). Finally, Goodhart observes that even an advanced capitalist country like Britain remains the 'gold standard', having introduced this dual process of generating an aspirational class alongside social groups that perceive their declining social status. Goodhart (2017, p. 3) argues,

> The helter-skelter expansion of higher education in the past twenty-five years—and the elevation of educational success into the gold standard of social esteem—has been one of the most important, and least understood, developments in British society. It has been a liberation for many and for others a symptom of their declining status.

This partly explains the unrest among the dominant castes in India, mentioned earlier in this article, who perceive their decline and have a sense of anxiety as to how castes lower down the order are moving ahead through affirmative action policies.

Marathas arguing against reservations for Dalits and wanting to move out of the agrarian sector to the formal job market is a clear point highlighting this tension. Further, the carefully choreographed controversy around the educational qualifications of Modi, who has claimed to belong to a lesser privileged class and caste status, and of Smriti Irani, a female public representative, precisely played out this tension. Any critique or suspicion around their degrees becomes symbolic of the elites' denial of mobility to newly asserting social groups such as the lower castes and women.

Similarly, the crisis in various institutions of higher education, including Jawaharlal Nehru University (JNU), the University of Hyderabad (UoH), the Indian Institutes of Technology (IITs), and the Film and Television Institute of India (FTII), among others, is representative of breaking the hold of the social elite and their hegemony over public institutions. The controversy surrounding JNU, under the current political regime, again represents a palpable critique against the privileged spaces occupied by an elite and marked by the life of the mind and the aspiration to question everything instead of expressing solidarity and loyalty. This is then linked to the discourse of nationalism.

Nationalism, in other words, is a political mode of representing those left out of this process, those suffering anxieties due to the spread of higher education. JNU, despite having a progressive admission policy, becomes an elite space, while the current regime's mode of changing the policy frame of admission, in spite of excluding the majority, becomes a step that is against divisive politics and symbolic of nationalist assertions.

'Political emotions' and proto-fascism

In all of this, subaltern castes remain torn between a cultural identification against elite/open spaces, where they perceive a commonality with the nationalist discourse, and the need for a more inclusive policy frame. Dalit and OBC politics, in its back-and-forth movement between identifying with the right and also generating a counter-narrative, has been a visible trend under the current populist regime.

While the dominant castes suffer from the anxiety of decline, subaltern castes suffer from the insecurity of losing hard-earned benefits; both need different modes of coping with the situation that cannot be strictly realistic but need a gloss of self-valorization. The slogans of 'New India' or 'achchhe din' are more of what one desires than what is real. De Sousa and Morton (2002, p. 265) explain:

> My approach to accuracy goes via an account of what makes a story accurate. Stories can be accurate but not true, and emotions can be accurate whether or not they are true. The capacity for emotional accuracy, for emotions that fit a person's situation, is an aspect of emotional intelligence, which is as important an aspect of rational human agency as the intelligent formation of beliefs and desires.

Instincts, gut feelings, and perceptions allow for an articulation of what may not be otherwise considered legitimate in a hierarchal context such as that of India.

The emergence of new cultural subalterns has, in effect, recast the old 'Bharat versus India' conundrum, with the old kind of class orientation around issues of economic inequality being refashioned around a conflict between economic elites and cultural subalterns. This undoubtedly tunes into the fact that caste groups are unevenly placed across economic, political, and social indicators. While the rhetoric against the high-end and invisible economic elites creates one kind of commonality, common social stigma creates another possibility.

The drama around demonetization pitched it against economic elites, while the combination of nationalism and a mounting crisis in institutions of higher education strives for a commonality of cultural subalterns. This allows for a discourse that is pro-corporate but anti-modernity; it helps to push for high-end capitalist growth marked by bullet trains and urbanization and also addresses the community anxieties that capitalist modernity introduces; it allows to claim a legacy of a pure past to be enjoined with claims for a radically altered future; it sympathizes with preservation of community identities, including control of their women and property, yet it can lay a claim to a politics that is beyond caste and religious considerations. It is in such combinatory postulations that right-wing populism strikes and mobilizes a new kind of 'common sense'.

The current round of populism has been emerging in India since 2014. Indian democracy had a populist turn from the days of Indira Gandhi with her 'Garibi Hatao' slogan. However, the current mode of populism is not restricted merely to electoral purposes but has also begun to dictate the policy frame (demonetization is a clear instance of this).

Indian democracy has moved beyond the 'Congress system' and is entering a post-Bahujan phase where large categories such as Dalit and OBCs are giving way to smaller sub-categories articulating and claiming independent identities and moving between various political parties. This has allowed the BJP to strategize by drawing up a new coalition between the dominant castes at one end and Dalits and OBCs on the other. They are fragmenting the polity on the one hand and conjoining them with a unified Hindutva narrative on the other. In doing this, a populist narrative works as a glue, creating a new kind of discourse of 'us' and 'them', in some instances vis-à-vis the economic elites, while in others it could be the Muslims.

It could well be asked how the formation of a 'post-Bahujan' phase that refers to breaking down Dalit and OBC identities into smaller sub-castes being actively mobilized can be connected to the neoliberal phase of capitalism. The Multidimensional Poverty Index of the United Nations Development Programme (UNDP) released in 2019 observed that between 2006 and 2016, India managed to lift 271 million out of 'abject poverty'. However, the World Bank's *Poverty and Shared Prosperity* report of 2020 argued that in middle-income countries, many non-poor households may be one shock away from falling back into poverty. This perpetual sense of precarity combined with growing democratic aspirations for mobility have managed to create, as noted earlier, new forms of political subjectivity. While the possibility and imagination of aspirations have created new avenues for post-patron relations leading to a post-Bahujan phase, it has simultaneously entrenched new vulnerabilities and anxieties that can also explain the 'rightward shift' in Bahujan politics.

As Prashant Jha (2017, p. 178) notes in his study of the BJP's electoral strategy,

> It was meant to make the Hindu bitter at what he was not getting; it was meant to make him feel resentful of the Muslim for being pampered; it was meant to bracket all other parties as pandering to specific interests based on religion. In the name of a common citizenry and an unbiased state, it was meant to divide communities.

Populism has foregrounded what Carl Schmitt refers to as the irreducibility of multiplicity. While in the immediate context, it seems to have undermined institutions and democratic ethos, it also carries with it the possibility of further democratizing the polity by highlighting the multiple voices that inhabit it. This, however, remains one possibility, while the continued assertion of the populist mode may permanently alter the contours of democracy providing new justifications to extra-institutional discourses.

Notes

1. Dimitrov defines fascism as the open terrorist dictatorship of the most reactionary, most chauvinistic, and most imperialist elements of finance capital. Others hold that fascism need not represent the interests of finance capital alone but could be understood as a process wherein financial capital plays the dominant role within a combination of various sections of the ruling classes. Fascism could therefore be seen also as representing the general interests of monopoly capital rather than specific sections of financial capital. Some scholars have held that the terrorist dictatorship of the general interests of monopoly capital must come in the form of a mass movement to qualify as a fascist regimes; others have held that irrespective of the mass movement and the social composition underlying the terrorist dictatorship, it must be seen as a variant form of fascist regimes (Koves and Mazumdar 2005).
2. Gramsci argues that the normalization of brutality in the civil society is the source that manufactures the hegemony for decomposed consent to the fascist state:

   > [T]o understand the full force of these assertions, it is enough to recall; that Italy holds first place for murders and bloodshed; that Italy is the country where mothers educated their infant children by hitting them on the head with clogs—it is the country where the younger generations are least respected and protected; that in certain Italian regions, it seemed natural until a few years ago to put muzzles on grape pickers, so that they could not eat the grapes; and that in certain regions the landowners locked their labourers up in sheds when the working was over, to prevent meetings or attendance at evening classes. (Gramsci 1984, p. 82)

   According to the founding members of Voice of India (VoI), a Hindu extremist organization, 'Secularists of every hue keep proclaiming the RSS to be a radical militant Hindu organisation. But conscious perceptive Hindus cannot but see that RSS has proved to be a paper tiger.... On issue after issue RSS starts with a roar, then shrinks into a whisper, then grovels and gives up, defeated but careful to save its face by inventing excuses' (Nanda 2009).

3. 'One of the basic functions of Nazism was to overcome the reluctance of big business to large scale government economic intervention. German big business agreed to a deviation from the principles of laissez-faire and to a radical increase of the role of the government in the national economy – on conditions that the government machine would submit to direct control in their partnership with the Nazi leaders' (Kalecki 1972, p. 100).
4. Barrinigton Moore Jr insists that fascism protected the interests of big agriculture in Italy at the expense of agricultural labourers and small peasant. The number of owner-operators dropped by 500,000 between 1921 and 1931 while the number of 'cash-and- share' tenants rose by 400,000. In Germany, says Moore, Nazism in power junked its pseuedo-radical agrarian populism since building a strong war economy could only occur on the basis of industry (Moore 1993, p. 592).
5. 'The situation today however is such that this exposure of the betrayal of democratic reforms, the democratic disguise of the fascistoid state machinery—based on the consent of all bourgeois parties, including social democracy—is becoming evident to the broad masses ... the nihilism among the workers about bourgeois democracy as a result of disillusionment with the politics of the Social Democratic Party has to be combated' (Lukacs 1971).
6. One of the approaches analyses fascism as a movement of the petty bourgeoisie. Fascism, according to this approach, represents the rebellion of the middle classes who see their economic security and social status threatened alike by big business and organized working-class movement expressing opposition to capitalism and socialism—identifying with assertions about reviving the glorious past (Koves and Mazumdar 2005).
7. [I]n its new guise, the state is openly partisan to the interests of monopoly capital, of big business, which is today busily engaged with state support in carrying on 'fusions' and 'mergers' and rapidly advancing the process of centralization of capital. This shift to a state that is blatantly partisan to big business has brought in its trail increasing privatizations for the working people everywhere (Patnaik 1997, pp. 195–200).
8. This idea has been developed in A. Gudavarthy (2023).

References

Alexander, J. C. (2006). *The Civil Sphere*. New York: Oxford University Press.

Aijaz, A. (1993). 'Fascism and National Culture; Reading Gramsci in the Days of Hindutva'. *Social Scientist* 21(3–4): 272.

Atanda, K., and A. Cojocaru (2021). 'Shocks and Vulnerability to Poverty in Middle-Income Countries'. World Bank Blogs: Let's Talk Development. https://blogs.worldbank.org/developmenttalk/shocks-and-vulnerability-poverty-middle-income-countries. Accessed 22 July 2029.

Balderston, T. (2002). *Economics and Politics in the Weimar Republic*. Cambridge: Cambridge University Press.

Banerjee, G. S. (ed.) (2010). *Accumulation by Dispossession: Transformative Cities in the New Global Order*. New Delhi: Sage Publications.

Breman, J. (2003). *The Labouring Poor in India*. New Delhi: Oxford University Press.

———. (2008). *The Jan Breman Omnibus*. New Delhi: Oxford University Press.

De Sousa, R., and A. Morton (2002). 'Emotional Truth'. *Aristotelian Society Supplementary* 76(1): 247–275.

Dimitrov, G. (1984). 'The Working Class against Fascism'. In *Marxists in Face of Fascism: Writings by Marxists on Fascism from the Inter-War Period*, edited by D. Beetham, pp. 179–186. New Jersey: Barnes and Noble.

Gambetta, D. (1996). *The Sicilian Mafia: The Business of Private Protection*. Cambridge: Harvard University Press.

Goodhart, D. (2017). *A Road to Somewhere: The Populist Revolt and the Future of Politics*. London: C. Hurst & Co.

Gorter, P. (1996). *Small Industrialists, Big Ambitions: Economic and Political Networks on a Large Industrial Estate in West India*. New Delhi: Oxford University Press.

Gramsci, A. (1984). 'On Fascism'. In *Marxists in Face of Fascism: Writings by Marxists on Fascism from the Inter-War Period*, edited by D. Beetham, pp. 82–87. New Jersey: Barnes and Noble.

Gudavarthy, A. (2018). 'How BJP appropriated the Idea of Equality to Create a Divided India'. *Economic and Political Weekly* 53(17) (28 April): 1–11.

———. (2023). 'How India's New "Mezzanine Elite" Classes Enable Majoritarian Politics'. *The Wire*, 6 April. https://thewire.in/caste/how-indias-new-mezzanine-elite-classes-enable-majoritarian-politics. Accessed 23 July 2023.

Harvey, D. (2006). *The Limits to Capital*. London: Verso.

Hong, Y. S. (1955). *Welfare, Modernity and the Weimar State 1919–1933*. New Jersey: Princeton University Press.

Jha, P. (2017). *How the BJP Wins: Inside India's Greatest Election Machine*. New Delhi: Juggernaut Books.

Kalecki, M. (1972). 'Fascism of Our Times'. In *The Last Phase in the Transformation of Capitalism*, pp. 99–106. New York: Monthly Review Press.

Koves, M., and S. Mazumdar (2005). *Resistible Rise: A Fascism Reader*. New Delhi: Left Word Books.

Lerche, J. (2007). 'A Global Alliance against Forced Labour? Unfree Labour, Neo-Liberal Globalization and the International Labour Organization'. *Journal of Agrarian Change* 7(4): 425–452.

Levien, M. (2011). 'Special Economic Zones and Accumulation by Dispossession in India'. *Journal of Agrarian Change* 11(4): 454–483.

Lukacs, G. (2005). 'Blum Thesis'. In *Resistible Rise: A Fascism Reader*, edited by M. Koves and S. Mazumdar, pp. 226–240. New Delhi: Left Word Books.

McCormick, B. L. (2000). 'Modernization, Democracy, and Morality: The Work of Barrington Moore, Jr'. *International Journal of Politics, Culture and Society* 13(4): 591–601.

Mishra, L. (2011). *Human Bondage: Tracing its Roots in India*. New Delhi: Sage Publications.

Moore, B. (1993). *Social Origins of Dictatorship and Democracy: Lord and Peasant in the Making of the Modern World*. Boston: Beacon Press.

Morton, D. (2007). *Hegemony and Passive Revolution: Unraveling Gramsci*. London: Pluto Press.

Mouffe, C. (2005). *On the Political*. London: Verso.

Müller, J. W. (2015). 'Parsing Populism: Who Is and Who Is Not a Populist These Days?' *Juncture* 22: 80–89. DOI: https://doi.org/10.1111/j.2050-5876.2015.00842.x.

Murali, D. A., and R. Vijay (2017). 'Revival of Agriculture Sector and Increasing Tenancy in India'. *Economic and Political Weekly* 52(31): 18–21.

Nancharaiah, G. (2022). *B. R. Ambedkar, Economic Development and Dalits in Post-Independence India*. Abingdon and New York: Routledge.

Nanda, M. (2009). 'Hindu Triumphalism and the Clash of Civilizations'. *Economic and Political Weekly* 44(28): 106–114.

Patnaik, P. (1997). 'A Note on the Political Economy of the "Retreat of the State"'. In *Whatever Happened to Imperialism and Other Essays*, pp. 194–210. New Delhi: Tulika Books.

Reich, W. (1980). *The Mass Psychology of Fascism*. New York: Orgone Institute Press.

Sengupta, T., and G. Vijay (2017). 'The Uncivil and De-Institutionalizing Labor Relations of Accumulation through Disuse: The Case of the Brick Kiln Industry in Telangana'. In *Rural Labor Mobility in Times of Structural Transformation*, edited by D. N. Reddy and K. Sarap, pp. 327–345. Singapore: Springer Publications.

Thorat, S., and K. Newman (2010). *Blocked by Caste*. New Delhi: Oxford University Press.

Vanaik, A. (1994). 'Situating threat of Hindu Nationalism'. *Economic and Political Weekly* 29(28): 1729–1748.

Vijay, G. (2003). 'Migration, Vulnerability and Insecurity in New Industrial Labor Market'. *Economic and Political Weekly* 40(23): 2304–2312.

———. (2009). 'De-Fragmenting "Disintegration of Value Creation": From Value Chains to Value Cycles'. *Economic and Political Weekly* 44(22): 85–94.

———. (2016). 'Subsistence Economy in a Subverted Development: Re-Rethinking Development Concretely'. In *Marginalisation, Development and Resistance: Essays in Honour of S. R. Sankaran*, vol. 2, edited by J. Saxena and G. Haragopal, pp. 298–324. New Delhi: Aakar Publishers.

Vijay, R. (2012). 'Structural Retrogression and Rise of "New Landlords" in Indian Agriculture: An Empirical Exercise'. *Economic and Political Weekly* 47(5): 18–21.

White, B. H. (2003). 'The Workforce and Its Social Structures'. In *India Working: Essays on Society and Economy*. New York: Cambridge University Press.

7

The Challenge of Combating Fascism in India*

Arvind Narrain

One of the difficulties we face is how to characterize the current regime headed by Narendra Modi, which has won back-to-back victories in three elections (2014–2024). The terminology within which we understand the regime is important, as what to expect from the regime flows from its nature and how to resist it will emerge from an understanding of its character. What is apparent about the regime is its pronounced authoritarianism, with the regime increasingly unaccountable to any constitutional authority.

The Spanish political scientist Juan Linz called such regimes, in which the leader has arbitrary and unlimited discretion, 'sultanist' and a species of authoritarianism. Linz (2000, p. 259) defines an authoritarian regime as 'ruler-centred' where the

> ruler exercises his power without restraint at his own discretion and above all unencumbered by rules or by any commitment to an ideology or value system. The binding norms and relations of bureaucratic administration are constantly subverted by personal arbitrary decisions of the ruler, which he feels no need to justify in ideological terms.

---

* This chapter draws from and updates some of the arguments from my book: Arvind Narrain, *India's Undeclared Emergency: Constitutionalism and the Politics of Resistance* (Westland Publications Private Limited, 2021).

What 'sultanism' implies is captured indelibly by Girish Karnad in his play *Tughlaq*. Karnad captures Mohammad Bin Tughlaq, who embodied this form of arbitrary and whimsical decision-making, be it the decision to issue currency in brass or the decision to shift the capital to Daulatabad. Clearly, the Modi regime has 'sultanist' characteristics, based on the personalized and arbitrary decision-making which characterizes the regime. Both the decision to impose a nationwide lockdown with four hours' notice and the decision to withdraw currency notes have more than a whiff of Mohammed Bin Tughlaq!

However, the question is whether this is a sufficient descriptor of the regime or if its features go beyond being an authoritarian regime.

When one calls a regime authoritarian, the understanding is that the regime may be unpopular, but maintains itself through force. The military dictatorships in Latin America in the twentieth century, the current rule of the generals in Myanmar, as well as the rule of General Sisi in Egypt are just three paradigmatic examples of regimes based on force.

However, fascist rule, counterintuitively, does not perceive force to be its primary instrument of rule. In fact, Hitler in *Mein Kampf* argues:

> The first foundation for the creation of authority is always provided by popularity.... With this support in hand, political leadership must then employ force, 'the second foundation of all authority', to stabilize its power. Political power established through popularity and stabilized with force, however, cannot endure until supported by social tradition, the final cornerstone of power. A popular authority, stabilized by force and aligned with popular traditions, may be regarded as unshakable. (Stoltzfus 1996, p. 4)

This popular character of fascism was also foregrounded by Arthur Rosenberg, writing during the Nazi era, when he characterized fascism as a 'mass movement'. According to Jairus Banaji, Rosenberg's insight is vindicated by later thinkers. For instance, Clara Zetkin, in 1923, warned that it would be an error to 'see fascism only as a military terrorist movement, not as a mass movement with deep social roots' (Rosenberg 2016, p. 39). Radhika Desai also agrees with Banaji's insight, noting that

> Rosenberg's analysis was distinctive among the Marxist analyses of his time in emphasising fascism's mass base, its ideological and social

> mobilisation, the connivance of state authority in its rise to power, and the use of 'Stormtroopers.' Rather than a movement of the petty-bourgeoisie, interwar fascisms were mass movements (that is to say, cross-class) movements. (Desai 2016, p. 21)

Apart from having the character of a mass movement, what are the characteristics of a fascist regime?

Fascism is rooted in an ideology of ethnic superiority and especially works through lawless vigilante forces. The ideology of superiority of an ethnic grouping is also oriented towards the promise of future greatness based on past glory. As John Foot (2022, p. 93) in his analysis of Italian fascism puts it, 'Italian fascism was neither exclusively nostalgic nor exclusively modern … it was also a march back towards ancient greatness, to a place which symbolized a former magnificent empire: the past was being revived and reinvented, fascism claimed through a new and glorious future.' Fascism, while seemingly about the construction of a united people, is also committed to protecting the interests of the owners of capital and allowing for the growth of capital at the expense of both labour and the environment.

Fascism, thus understood, is a force which challenges the basic ideology of the Indian Constitution of the equality of all persons regardless of race or religion, the supremacy of the rule of law, as well as the injunction of the Directive Principles of State Policy, under Article 39(c) that the 'operation of the economic system does not result in the concentration of wealth and means of production to the common detriment'.

This chapter examines these three dimensions of fascism—ethnic superiority, mob violence, and protection of private capital—in the Indian context and what fascism means for Indian constitutionalism.

The notion of ethnic superiority: violence and Hindutva

In contemporary India, the lynching of Muslims under the pretext of cow slaughter protection has become all too common. However, that violence, though seemingly arbitrary, draws its inspiration from an ideological framework which motivates and legitimizes it and its actions. In fact, participants in mob violence who believe in Hindutva see themselves as noble warriors protecting the national interest, and it is this ideology of nationalism which allows them to transmute what are in fact crimes into *seva* (selfless service) for the nation.

The ideology that animates mob violence finds articulation in the works of V. D. Savarkar and M. S. Golwalkar—key ideologues of Hindutva. At its core, the doctrine strives to unite and strengthen the Hindu community and assert the superior (if not exclusive) claim of the Hindus to live in the territory of India.

Savarkar, as political philosopher Jyotirmaya Sharma writes in *Hindutva: Exploring the Idea of Hindu Nationalism*, believed Hindus to be the 'bedrock on which an Indian independent state could be built. India's freedom from colonial rule was inextricably linked to the independence of our people, our race, our nation, so Hindus had to be masters in our own house' (J. Sharma 2003, p. 156). In his essay 'What Is Hindutva?', Savarkar lays down the conditions for minority communities to be considered part of the nation:

> Ye who by race, by blood, by culture, by nationality possess almost all the essentials of Hindutva, and has been forcibly snatched out of our ancestral home by the hand of violence—ye have only to render wholehearted love to our common Mother and recognise her not only as Fatherland (pitribhumi) but even as Holy land (punyabhumi); and ye would be most welcome to the Hindu fold. (Quoted in Jaffrelot 2007, p. 96)

If minority communities were to belong to the country, Savarkar wanted them to give up their religious faith and 'return' to the Hindu fold as he considered India to be a land for only Hindus.

For Golwalkar, the essence of Hindutva lay in the dissolution of the individual within the collective, be it an organization, society, or nation. As Sharma writes in *Terrifying Vision*, 'Addressing the Sangh in 1954, he [Golwalkar] likened the annihilation of individuality in favour of the nation to a piece of salt falling into water and dissolving. What remains of the salt is just the taste … but the physical form withers away completely.' For Golwalkar, the 'dissolution of individuality was the true indicator of a nation's welfare and progress' and ultimately 'the individual becomes the nation itself' (J. Sharma 2007, pp. 4–5).

The most frightening part of the 'terrifying vision' that Sharma highlights is its intolerance of diversity and the effort to shape human beings in one mould. In essence, this production of conformity attacks human individuality, the very basis of freedom.

What is this collective in which the individual is to be subsumed? Golwalkar, like Savarkar, believed that the essence of India was 'the Hindu race with its Hindu Religion, Hindu Culture and Hindu Language (the natural family of Sanskrit and her offsprings)' as he writes in *A Bunch of Thoughts*. He goes on to say that 'in Hindustan exists and must needs exist the ancient Hindu nation and nought else but the Hindu Nation. All those not belonging to the national i.e. Hindu Race, Religion, Culture and Language, naturally fall out of the pale of real "National" life' (Jaffrelot 2007, pp. 116–117).

The Hindu nation in Golwalkar's rendering is reliant on a common language, preferably Sanskrit or its offspring, Hindi. This of course creates a vast divide as the southern Indian languages do not have a Sanskrit origin. On the question of caste, Hindutva leaders, like Golwalkar, believe in perpetuating the caste system, and the 'Hindu Rashtra' (polity) has, of course, shown no inclination to tackle the problem of caste head-on.

Not being able to address the questions of caste and language that stood in the way of building a Hindu Rashtra, Golwalkar instead focused on his other obsession, the three 'internal threats' to the Hindu nation—Muslims, Christians, and communists. (Golwalkar 1966; see Islam 2017). On what was to be done with those designated as 'threats', Golwalkar was unambiguous in his book *We or Our Nationhood Defined*:

> To keep up the purity of the race and its culture, Germany shocked the world by her purging the country of the Semitic races—the Jews. Race pride at its highest has been manifested here. Germany has also shown how impossible it is for races and cultures, having differences going to the root, to be assimilated into one united whole, a good lesson for us in Hindustan to learn and profit by. (Quoted in Islam 2017, p. 22)

The thoughts of Golwalkar and Savarkar provide the foundational ideology which justifies Hindutva mob action in the country today, based as it is on the elimination of internal differences, construction of a militarized and unified Hindu community, as well as the purging of those seen to be outsiders in the Hindu nation. Hindutva is not only based on the notion of the collective's supremacy over the individual but is also a fundamental challenge to the idea of territorial nationalism. Not all inhabitants of a nation, according to Hindutva, get equal rights, going against the very basis of the Indian Constitution. Those who are not Hindu, the doctrine propagates, should either be assimilated into Hinduism or live as second-class citizens or be eliminated.

The ideology of ethnic superiority has played itself out over a period of time, with devastating consequences for the Muslim community, especially after the Modi government came to power. From hate crimes against Muslims including murders for the fact of being Muslim (Desai and Jesani 2023) to demolitions of Muslim homes and shops[1] (People's Union for Civil Liberties [PUCL] 2023), the de facto disenfranchisement of Muslims is a reality in India today.

Even members of parliament (MPs) are not spared from its ugly consequences. As recently as 22 September 2023, a Bharatiya Janata Party (BJP) parliamentarian (Ramesh Bidhuri) coarsely abused his fellow MP, Danish Ali, calling him 'pimp', 'terrorist', and 'militant' and also using the words 'mullah' and 'katwa' (an ethnic slur for a Muslim man) on the floor of Parliament in the new Parliament building. The abusive language used by the MP is unfortunately common on social media as well as in election speeches by leaders associated with the BJP. This is the first time, however, that hate speech of this nature meant to demean, ostracize, and isolate the entire Muslim community has been hurled in Parliament itself.

This should not be seen as a one-off incident, especially given that the Speaker is yet to take action against Ramesh Bidhuri for openly challenging the core constitutional principles of fraternity, dignity, and equality. It should rather be seen as an attempt to call into question whether Muslims are entitled to the status of being human and enjoying rights. The speech attacks the fundamental basis of our constitutional order, namely our shared humanity, or what the Constitution characterizes as fraternity. Bidhuri is stigmatizing Muslims as less than human and signalling from the highest forum of the country that Muslims are not deserving of equal respect as fellow citizens of India. Such dehumanization reduces the social standing and acceptance within the society of Muslims and goes beyond causing individual distress; it has a social impact. In the long run, such dehumanization paves the way for even more consequential crimes against the Muslim community. In short, the gravest crimes that international law contemplates, namely genocide, as well as crimes against humanity, have their sociopolitical roots in ideologies of dehumanization. As the Indian Supreme Court in *Pravasi Bhalai Sanghatan v. Union of India* observed,

> Hate speech lays the ground-work for later, broad attacks on vulnerable groups that can range from discrimination, to ostracism, segregation, deportation, violence and, in the most extreme cases, to genocide. Hate

> speech also impacts on a protected group's ability to respond to the substantive ideas under debate, thereby placing a serious barrier to their full participation in our democracy. (*Pravasi Bhalai Sangathan vs U.O.I. and Ors*, AIR 2014 SC 1591, 2014)

A grim forecast of where adherence to this ideology of Hindutva will lead was made by Asaduddin Owaisi, MP from Hyderabad, speaking in reference to the Bidhuri hate speech against Danish Ali, when he remarked that the day Muslims will be lynched in parliament is not far off (ABP News 2023).

This prognosis may not be an exaggeration if one takes seriously the similarities between Hindutva in India and fascism in Italy. Communist and socialist MPs were physically attacked in the Italian parliament for their political beliefs when fascists took power. In 1921, Italy's first fascist deputies brought violence into the parliament itself. The target of their ire was an elected communist MP, Misiano, who was attacked in the parliament by fascist deputies and ejected from the House. As Antonio Gramsci put it, 'the first action of the fascists in Parliament is an act of pure and simple criminality, not one which can be assigned any political significance, not even with the most mind-bending thought processes' (Foot 2022, p. 93). This unremitting violence against communists and socialists resulted in the intimidation and torture of a number of them and the murder of one of the outspoken anti-fascists, Matteotti, in 'broad daylight by fascists in the centre of Italy's capital city' (ibid., p. 151).

The mob as an integral part of the Indian polity

Ever since the Modi government has come to power, mob lynchings have intensified. As many as 90 per cent of religious hate crimes since 2009 occurred after Modi led the BJP to power in 2014, as shown by data compiled by the India Spend media group (Mander 2018).

From the murder of Mohammed Akhlaq for supposedly having beef in his house in 2015, to the lynching of Pehlu Khan on the 'suspicion of smuggling cattle' and the knifing of Junaid Khan over an argument on seat-sharing in a train in 2017 (Mander 2017), to the burning alive of Nasir Hussain and Junaid Khan in 2023 by Monu Manesar and his band of state-sanctioned cow vigilantes (Khanna 2023), India has witnessed the rise of the lawless mob, which has, with impunity, attacked Muslims, Dalits, and Adivasis.

While the mob inflicts mindless brutal violence on persons who have committed no crime, the crimes of the mob are often documented by the perpetrators themselves and forwarded as WhatsApp videos (Shih and Verma 2023). They often take place in broad daylight, indicating that the mob does not fear law enforcement authorities. Lynchings are also characterized by a sexualized form of brutality in which the public seems to not only participate but also revel.

These lynchings, combined with the brutal violence which the mob perpetrates, are deeply concerning. The police are indifferent to what are after all crimes committed in the public view. The perpetrators exhibit neither shame nor guilt but rather take pride in their illegal deeds. Very often, pictures of lynchings are taken and posted on social media as though the perpetrators were heroes. All of this results in a turning of the moral order on its very head.

The impunity the vigilantes enjoy owes much to biased investigations which makes conviction a distant possibility. Investigations by the police, Human Rights Watch found in their study titled *Violent Cow Protection in India* (2019), were deeply biased and filled with delays in filing FIRs (first information reports). In nearly a 'third of the cow-related vigilante killings since 2015', the police filed 'cases against victims or witnesses. In some cases, witnesses turned hostile because of threats from the police or from the accused and their supporters' (Human Rights Watch 2019, p. 7).

The police, in short, toe the line of the political executive of the day. Human Rights Watch quotes Meeran Borwankar, a former police commissioner of Pune, Maharashtra, who said that 'the unprofessional conduct of the police in such cases may come from their personal beliefs and bias, as well as what they perceive to be the message from the political leadership'. She also added, 'The general atmosphere in the country is that it is our holy duty to save the cow' (Human Rights Watch 2019, p. 27).

The biased police action has a cascading effect with judges being presented with insufficient evidence linking the accused to the crime, making an acquittal more likely and cementing the impunity enjoyed by vigilantes.

In India, mobs are driven to act within what Ravish Kumar describes as 'the cloak of religious fervour'. For the mob, the cow is the symbol of a Hindu nation, and it justifies its brutal acts as defending the same. As Hannah Arendt put it, the mob becomes a direct agent of nationalism (Arendt 1973). In Kumar's (2024, p. 60) analysis, the perverse logic of 'inciting mobs' to fulfil the so-called nationalist agendas is that 'if democracy is the will of the majority, is not a mob the majority?' The mobs represent the ethnic nation based on the rejection of a constitutional idea of India. Similarly, in Hitler's Germany, the mobs claimed to represent the Aryan nation and targeted those who did not conform to that model of nationhood, be it Jews, homosexuals, or other minorities. In India, those outside the (upper-caste) nation are lower castes and religious minorities who are the targets of mob violence.

The mob, as a representative of the majoritarian nation, challenges the norms of a liberal democracy. The mobs are defined by 'lawlessness' and attack liberal democracy as an effete and outmoded form of governance which does not recognize the rightful place of the majority. When liberal democracy is challenged as non-representative of the majority, the emerging parallel to Hitler's Germany and Mussolini's Italy is chilling. As Kumar presciently notes, 'to become a mob, at any place, at any time, is to become Hitler's Germany' (ibid., p. 87).

It is those who stand excluded from society and the benefits of the economy who were the recruits to the mobs of Hitler's Germany. A similar analysis of who comprised the mob in Tsarist Russia was put forward by Leon Trotsky:

> Now, this man without shoes has become king. An hour ago he was a trembling slave hounded by the police and by hunger. Now he feels like an absolute despot, he can do anything he likes, everything will pass, he is master of life and death. If he feels the urge to do so, he throws an old woman from the window of the third floor to the pavements below, he smashes the skull of a baby with a chair, he rapes a small girl in front of a crowd of people. He shrinks from none of the tortures which only a brain driven mad with liquor and frenzy could contrive. For he can do anything he likes, everything will pass. God bless the Tsar. (Quoted in Rosenberg 2016, p. 39)

What Trotsky is gesturing towards is 'the sense of freedom when in a crowd, or a sense of having been given "permission" by one's leaders to act, to hit and to abuse', which in effect is the 'permission' to act without constraints and moral injunctions[2] (Hansen 2021, p. 38).

One account of who comprises the mob in India today is provided by the Karnataka unit of the PUCL in a report on the infamous vigilante attack on girls in a Mangalore pub in 2009. The report excavates the background of the members of the right-wing Hindutva group Sri Ram Sene who carried out the attack.

> Those who are part of the Sri Ram Sene and attacked the pub are poor, they have no visible future, no pocket money; they can't go to Coffee Day, for example. They also cannot go out with or even talk to the girls whom they attacked. The fact that these girls don't even look at them but only talk to certain boys increases their anger. They have a lot of anger that they cannot enjoy holidays, that they cannot go to hotels and that they have to carry their own lunch boxes. While on the outside, the attacks seem to be motivated by Hindutva, on the inside, it is anger. (PUCL, Karnataka, 2009, p. 51)

While the members of a vigilante force may suffer from feelings of exclusion and impotence, being a part of a vigilante mob gives them a sense of 'power, fraternity and freedom' (Hansen, 2021, p. 38). What being part of such a mob offers is 'a sense of being involved in something bigger than oneself, of being protected and acting with impunity, the enjoyment of the strange suspension of norms during riots and pogroms' (ibid. p. 38).

In Arendt's (1973, p. 356) analysis, being part of a totalitarian movement in Nazi Germany 'gave the masses of atomized, undefinable, unstable and futile individuals a means of self-definition and identification' which 'restored some of the self-respect they had formerly derived from their function in society' and 'created a kind of spurious stability'. The totalitarian movement's propaganda was able to 'rationalize the essentially futile feelings of self-importance and hysterical security that it offered to the isolated individuals of an atomized society' (ibid.).

The mob in contemporary India is a significant actor, as it was in Nazi Germany and fascist Italy. There is no better indicator of India's slide towards fascism than the threatening presence of the mob as an integral part of its polity. It also bears noting that the mob is not totally disorganized. Its lawlessness is organized through multiple organizations owing fidelity to the ideology of Hindutva.

The way this vast network of organizations come together to achieve the Rashtriya Swayamsevak Sangh's (RSS) goals is best described by Justice Manmohan Singh Liberhan in his 2009 commission report on the destruction of the Babri Masjid, for which he pinned the responsibility on the leaders of this family of organizations, the Sangh Parivar:

> These organizations are collectively an immense and awesome entity with a shrewd brain, a wide encompassing sweep and the crushing strength

> of the mob. The leadership provided by the RSS, BJP, VHP and the other mutating and constantly transforming organisations like the Hindu Mahasabha and the Jan Sangh, in furtherance of the suspect theories of the founders of these organisations was consistent and unabashed. The ends are all that matter to the core group of thinkers and the destruction of the disputed structure was only one victorious battle in their ongoing campaign against secularism and the multicultural society, clothed in the garb of religion. (Liberhan Ayodhya Commission 2009, p. 924)

'Mutating and constantly transforming organisations' gestures to the various organizational forms, right from local-level cow protection committees to state-level so-called voluntary organizations to finally what Liberhan refers to as the 'the leadership provided by the RSS, BJP, VHP'. Even as their forms may vary, these groups take forward the claim that Hindus have a superior, if not exclusive stake, in the Indian nation. At its heart, this idea of ethnic superiority is based on the work of Golwalkar and Savarkar and the motivating ideology behind the loose multiplicity of organizations that enforce a form of mob justice.

Unconditional defence of private capital

Much as there is a social project underlying fascism, there is an economic one as well. The noise surrounding the social project, often proclaimed from the rooftops, does not surround the economic project. The economic policy adopted by fascism is often disguised and one needs to look at what is being done rather than what is being said. Clearly, 'fascist regimes rarely disturb the power of corporations that have caused many of the inequalities and much of the discontent' in society (Poruthiyil 2021, p. 122). Rather, once in power (regardless of having railed against the elites when fascism was still a movement), fascists give that form of politics a quiet burial and move to the next stage which is a merger with plutocracy (Pierson 2017).

This dimension of fascism was explained by Rosenberg in his writing on Nazi Germany. Acutely conscious of and citing the example of fascist Italy, he wrote:

> In November, 1921, at the third congress of his party, Mussolini assured them [capitalists] that while he was of course opposed to liberalism

> in the political sense, he was unconditionally in favour of economic liberalism: 'If possible, I would be even inclined to hand over railways and post and telegraph back to private enterprise in order to relieve the state of economic functions that are really quite uneconomical.' In this way fascism returned to an unconditional defence of private capitalism. (Rosenberg 2016, p. 61)

What aids fascist regimes in merging 'populism with plutocracy' are disasters, both natural and manmade. Coups, terrorist attacks, and earthquakes, according to Naomi Klein, induce a 'shock', which disorients and distracts people. It is precisely this moment of shock which is used to push through far-reaching economic changes which further the interests of capitalists, disadvantage labour, and set back climate change and environmental justice (Klein 2007). In recent times, the natural disaster which produced precisely this kind of shock was the COVID-19 pandemic. It 'disoriented the public' and allowed for the introduction of measures which in normal times would have met with tremendous pushback. The singularity of the shock produced by COVID-19, apart from the stress on the health system, is that the key institutions of democracy were put in a state of suspended animation. The imposition of lockdown by countries around the world as a public health measure has meant that the normal functioning of the institutions of democracy, such as parliament, courts, and media, not to mention the right to assembly through protests and demonstrations, and the expression of opinion by student activism, and so on, was affected.

Despite demands from opposition members to allow online functioning of the various parliamentary committees (Nair 2020) and in spite of this being a global practice during the pandemic, India alone among the democracies decided to completely suspend the working of parliamentary committees. The functioning of Parliament during the pandemic was a shadow of its normal self, thereby obscuring executive actions from any effective scrutiny (Verma 2020). Other important actors in a democracy, whether civil society or political parties, have also been seriously hobbled and have been unable to play the watchdog role crucial to upholding democratic values. Protests and demonstrations, which are a way to express public opinion in a democracy, stood suspended, especially during the lockdown.

The Supreme Court, which could have adapted itself to the changed circumstances and played its role in ensuring that the executive functioned within the limits of the Constitution, unfortunately abdicated its responsibility, especially during the first wave of COVID-19, as seen in the lack of response to the migrant crisis.

At this time, the current regime in India has carried out far-reaching changes in the areas of social, economic, and political life, which would not have been possible if the institutions of democracy had been able to function. Three policy shifts that favour private capital, related to environment, labour, and agriculture, are presented and analysed here.

Weakening environment protections

The government rolled out a draft proposal in March 2020 to amend the environment impact assessment procedures, placing many projects beyond the purview of public hearings, effectively rendering local communities voiceless in such decisions (Kapoor and Dinesh 2021). The timing of this decision was widely criticized. As the Centre for Policy Research, Delhi, noted in a letter to the government,

> The EIA notification is an important regulation through which the impacts of land use change, water extraction, tree felling, pollution, waste and effluent management for industrial and infrastructure projects are to be studied and used in developmental decision making. Any change in this law has a direct bearing on the living and working conditions of people and the ecology. The EIA notification elicited a strong response in spite of the restrictions during the lockdown with 'over two million comments, most asking to retract the draft. (Ibid., p. 2)

In September 2020, the Karnataka High Court issued a stay order prohibiting the Ministry of Environment, Forest, and Climate Change from publishing the final notification. However, as environmental activists Meenakshi Kapoor and Krithika A. Dinesh argue in an article in *The Wire*, the government is operationalizing the draft notification by making piecemeal amendments to the environment impact assessment notification, 2006, removing crucial environmental safeguards (ibid.).

As a report by Pinto and Van Adhikar Media Team (2020, p. 1) noted,

> During the nationwide lockdown from 24 March to 30 June 2020, the Forest and Expert Appraisal Committees within the Ministry of

> Environment, Forests and Climate Change went on a project-clearing spree for large-scale industrial, mining, hydropower, road, and highway construction projects, without any due diligence and in absolute disregard of environmental laws and the FRA [Forest Rights Act, 2006].

The consent of *gram sabhas* was not taken (as mandated by the FRA) in the prime minister's auction of forty-one coal blocks across five states in central India announced in June 2020. Specifically, an amendment made to section 8A of the Mines and Minerals (Regulation and Development) Act, 1956, said that a successful bidder for an existing mining lease near its expiration does not need the otherwise mandatory *gram sabha* consent, since the modification to the Act deems the new lessee able to 'grandfather' mandatory *gram sabha* consent (ibid.).

An analysis of the Expert Appraisal Committee (a centre-appointed committee which evaluates coal, hydro and river valley, thermal, non-coal mining, infrastructure, coastal regulations zones, and industrial projects) and the Forest Advisory Committee meeting minutes during the lockdown—about forty of them, some as short as ten minutes and others up to five hours—reveal that approximately 120 projects were recommended, ninety were deferred, thirty were returned for reconsideration, and only two were rejected. A quarter of the recommended projects were in Fifth Schedule districts, where land transfer can be restricted keeping in mind the interests of scheduled tribes.

Weakening labour protections

The pandemic has also been used by several state governments to suspend labour laws, in the garb of protecting businesses. For instance, Uttar Pradesh and Madhya Pradesh, both BJP-ruled states, promulgated ordinances to relax certain aspects of existing labour laws. The Uttar Pradesh Temporary Exemption from Certain Labour Laws Ordinance, 2020, states, 'All factories and establishments engaged in manufacturing process shall be exempted from the operation of all Labour laws for a period of three years', with the relaxation specifically allowing for the working day to be extended to twelve hours. Another notification, dated 8 May 2020, specifically exempts all factories registered under the Factories Act, 1948, from provisions regulating weekly hours, daily hours, overtime, intervals of rest, and so on, of all adult workers. Thus, Uttar Pradesh has, in effect, suspended thirty-five of the thirty-eight labour laws for three years, including laws related to industrial disputes, trade unions, and contract workers (Narrain, Krishnan, and Rozario 2020).

Further, BJP-ruled Gujarat, Haryana, Uttarakhand, Himachal Pradesh, Assam, Goa, Uttar Pradesh, and Madhya Pradesh, as well as Congress-ruled Rajasthan, have given notices that the length of the work can increase to twelve hours a day (Ram 2020). As recently as July 2020, Karnataka, another BJP-ruled state, approved a labour ordinance which aimed at 'improving the ease of doing business' by increasing the labour threshold for key labour legislations such as the Industrial Disputes Act, 1947; Contract Labour Regulation and Abolition Act, 1970; and Factories Act, 1948, before they began to even apply. Thus, under section 25K of the Industrial Disputes Act, the worker threshold was increased from 100 to 300. This means that only establishments employing 300 or more persons will have to seek government permission for closure, retrenchment, or layoff. With the increase in the threshold from twenty employees to fifty employees, the Contract Labour Act will now apply only to establishments with more than fifty employees (Mohammed, 2020).[3]

As Maitreyi Krishnan, Clifton D' Rozario (both lawyers and trade union activists), and I wrote for Firstpost,

> While the history of the neo-liberal era is about the progressive whittling down of labour law protections, these amendments in one fell swoop attempt to take Indian labour back to the unregulated laissez-faire days of 19th-century European capitalism. These ordinances are not only illegal and unconstitutional but also starkly indicative of the larger designs of a state determined to take advantage of the pandemic to push the working class to the situation of rightlessness. (Narrain, Krishnan, and Rozario 2020, p. 4)

The central government has also used the cover of the pandemic to push through four new labour codes, bringing about fundamental changes to labour law and further weakening the rights of organized labour. The reorganizing of a century of labour jurisprudence began with the passing of the Code on Wage in 2019. In September 2020, three more codes, namely the Social Security Code, the Industrial Relations Code, and the Occupational Safety, Health, and Working Conditions Code, were passed with little debate in Parliament. 'The Rajya Sabha passed all three within two hours,' said an article in *Seminar* by well-known trade union leader and labour law jurist, Babu Mathew, and co-author, Kavya Bharadkar (Bharadkar and Mathew 2021, p. 1).

Under the Industrial Relations Code, if workers want to go on strike against the employer, they must serve strike notice to the employer at least fourteen days in advance. On the other hand, if, within the period, the labour commissioner calls a meeting with the employer/management and the workers' union to find a solution to the problem, then strikes cannot be held for sixty days. This law makes it highly difficult, if not impossible, for workers to strike. If workers do not give the notice to strike fourteen days in advance, the strike will be declared illegal (Karmakar 2020).

Under the Occupational Safety Code, the threshold for application of the code is the employment of ten or more workers. As Bharadkar and Mathew (2021, p. 6) note, 'a very small minority of Indian establishments cross this threshold'. If there was one important labour context in which reforms were passed, it was really the mass migration of thousands of labourers, sometimes on foot, when the unplanned lockdown was declared. Migrant labour suffered during the lockdown due to non-payment of wages, non-availability of food and rations, and lack of medical care. However, the code, rather than increasing the protections for migrant labourers, further dilutes the existing ones by increasing the threshold for applicability of the code from five migrant workers in an establishment (according to the Inter-State Migrant Workers Act, 1979) to ten.

The Social Security Code replaces nine social security laws, including the Employees' Provident Fund Act, 1952; the Maternity Benefit Act, 1961; and the Unorganized Workers Social Security Act, 2008. Under the new code, the central government may notify various social security schemes for the benefit of workers. These include an Employees' Provident Fund Scheme, an Employees' Pension Scheme, and an Employees' State Insurance Scheme. However, as Bharadkar and Mathew (2021, p. 3) note, this code is voluntary and, at best, creates 'enabling provisions' for 'progressive extension of better social security measures to the working class—it is neither guaranteed, nor can be demanded legally'.

What the passing of the labour codes during the pandemic shows is that the government was neither prepared to debate such far-reaching changes to labour law nor concerned about the impact of the pandemic on the working class. In fact, as Bharadkar and Mathew (2021, p. 6) observe, 'post-pandemic, the working class requires stronger legal protection—not more neglect and precarity'. However, the labour codes demonstrate a striking indifference to the needs of 90 per cent of India's labourers who are in the unorganized sector and weaken legal protections for the working class as a whole.

Opening agriculture to private capital

The central government has also utilized the pandemic to push through what has come to be known as the farm laws, even though, constitutionally, the central government does not have the legislative competence to do so as agriculture is a state subject. This is the centre's most drastic effort yet to fundamentally alter the relationship between the individual and the state, with the farmer being abandoned, in effect, to the full strength of market forces (Narayanan 2020). The effect of the laws as apprehended by farmers is that the state will move towards dismantling the Agricultural Produce Marketing Committees as well as the minimum procurement price, leaving small farmers in an uneven bargaining position because they must negotiate the sale of their produce with larger corporations (Yadav 2020). Farmers see this as an unmitigated disaster that will only increase corporate control over Indian agriculture. While farmers have been demanding changes in agricultural laws and policies in line with the recommendations of the M. S. Swaminathan Commission of 2006 (providing minimum support price to all crops), the government has been dismantling any state support to the agricultural sector (Sainath 2020).

Though the central government chose the time of the pandemic to introduce these laws, calculating that farmers would be silent due to the pandemic, it was proven wrong by the massive organized protests against these laws under the banner of the Samyukta Kisan Morcha, which began in November2020 and continued through 2021 (H. Sharma 2021).[4]

The changes briefly discussed thus far are to some fundamental laws of the land. Some of these are the outcome of determined and long-term struggles by labour, farmers, Adivasis, forest dwellers, and the rural poor. Klein's perceptive analysis that capitalism thrives on disaster provides a good pointer to understand why the government chose to undertake such extreme measures during a global health crisis: capitalism remakes the world to benefit capital owners while further attenuating the rights to health, food, clean air, and water, as well as diluting the rights of labour.

The three instances demonstrate that the benefits to the owners of capitalists during the pandemic were clear. According to an Oxfam (2021) report on the 'inequality virus', during the lockdown the wealth of (Indian) billionaires increased by 35 per cent. Their study showed that what 'Ambani earned during the pandemic would keep the 40 crore informal workers at risk of falling into poverty due to COVID-19 above the poverty line for at least 5 months' (*The Wire* 2021, p. 1). The changes to labour, land, and environmental laws, as well as the increase in wealth of the already wealthy, only illustrate Rosenberg's point that in a time of crisis, 'fascism returned to an unconditional defence of private capitalism' (Rosenberg 2016, p. 169).

Conclusion: what is to be done?

There are four ideas which are important to combat a fascist polity. First, the defence of constitutionalism should be a counterpoint to fascism. Second, support can be built for a project of inclusive nationalism. Third, the rise of inequality must be addressed. Finally, all those who are existentially threatened by fascist politics come together.

In a time when fascism is on the rampage, it is vitally important to keep alive the constitutional state. This would include work that generates a popular consciousness familiar with constitutional texts, important decisions of the Supreme Court, as well as a history of the many strands of the freedom struggle which resulted in the Indian Constitution (Narrain and Ravishankar 2021). Keeping constitutionalism alive, even if institutions abdicate their constitutional responsibility, is vital. As Gautam Bhatia puts it,

> it remains important at all times to articulate and defend the rule of law as an independent value, and to record and demonstrate how the actions of the Court fall short in that respect; in other words, there must at all times be an active struggle to preserve the idea of the rule of law, despite—or even because of—what happens in the Courts. (Bhatia 2020, p. 10)[5]

The constitutional vision of inclusive nationalism must be put forward to counter the fascist imaginings of a nationalism built on excluding the other. An inclusive idea of nation based on the 'ability to see full and equal humanity in another person' must replace the aggressive, xenophobic, and exclusive idea of the nation (Nussbaum 2013, p. 3). This is no pipe dream.

In recent Indian history, the anti-Citizenship (Amendment) Act (CAA) protest did precisely this by invoking the symbolism of the nation as an inclusive entity. The protest sites had protestors energetically waving the national flag even as they carried posters with images of Gandhi and Ambedkar. The events had speeches which harked back to the history of the Indian national movement as well as songs and poetry from India's radical literary traditions and spoke of liberty, equality, and fraternity. Thus, the deeply felt identification with the nation was channelled towards a critical, humanist, and inclusive sense of belonging. This became an important counterpoint to the exclusivist understanding of the nation.

And yet, while the defence of constitutional values is an important starting point, by itself it may be unable to address the scale of challenges to be faced. In particular, the Constitution has not been a bulwark against the deeply unequal world created by neoliberal globalization. This form of globalization is, in fact, putting the Constitution under threat. The human rights regime inaugurated by the Universal Declaration of Human Rights is being supplanted by a framework of trade-related market-friendly human 'rights' (Baxi 2008).

The Constitution as the source of the normative values of both law and public policy is slowly being supplanted not by any one law but by a policy framework with its roots in adherence to the Washington Consensus (Pellissery et al. 2020). It is this policy consensus which must be forcefully challenged.

In Thomas Piketty's (2020) analysis, the crisis the world is facing (social, economic, and environmental) is due to the socially unsustainable levels of inequality:

> The top decile's share [of income] has risen almost everywhere. Take for example, India, the United States and Russia, China, and Europe. The share of the top decile in each of these five regions stood at around 25-35 percent in 1980 but by 2018 had risen to between 35-55 percent.... In India the change from 1980 to 2018 is among the largest, moving from 32 to 55% with 10% of the population now earning over 55% of all income. (Ibid., p. 21)

Piketty argues that these levels of inequality are unsustainable and the ideology of 'neo-proprietarianism', which demands absolute respect for the right to private property, should be forcefully challenged. There have to be new forms of social ownership of property that replace the idea of permanent ownership with temporary private ownership of property (ibid.).

Finally, to take forward an effective resistance against fascism, one must first recognize the existential threat posed by the fascist regime to all forms of diversity, be it on grounds of religion, caste, class, language, sexuality, or political opinion and ideology. The recognition of the existential threat has to be followed by all those who are threatened by the new regime coming together in a broad front. However, as history has taught us, those in the middle of the furious flow of history are sometimes blind to the contours of the emerging beast. The present is solely analysed through the lens of the immediate past, which fails to account for the emergence of something unprecedented. It is not easy to recognize the nature of fascism, and it is very difficult, for even those who face an existential threat, to come together until it is too late. But that is the imperative.

In a historical analogy, when the American freedom fighters signed the Declaration of Independence, it was clear that this was an act of war and if they did not win the war, they would be killed. As Benjamin Franklin is reputed to have said, 'We must all hang together, or assuredly we shall all hang separately' (cited by Campbell 2015, p. 789). Similarly, if at this moment, political movements, political parties, civil society groups, social movements, and individuals who are existentially threatened by the fascist project do not act in unison, the project will succeed.

The famous poem by Pastor Niemoller has never seemed more urgent and appropriate:

> First they came for the socialists, and I did not speak out—because I was not a socialist.
>
> Then, they came for the trade unionists, and I did not speak out—because I was not a trade unionist.
>
> Then they came for the Jews, and I did not speak out—because I was not a Jew.
>
> Then they came for me—and there was no one left to speak for me. (United States Holocaust Memorial Museum 2023)

Notes

1. The state's response of bulldozing only the homes of Muslims in Nuh elicited a sharp response from the Punjab and Haryana High Court, which labelled

it a 'form of ethnic cleansing'. This practice of employing bulldozers in Uttar Pradesh, Madhya Pradesh, Delhi, and Haryana degrades Indian democracy. When the state begins to act outside the rule of law, then the state itself becomes an instrumentality of terror. What is terrorism if not the employment of means of violence outside the rule of law meant in particular to induce fear in the minority community? Unless this unconscionable practice of the state deploying the bulldozer is stamped out, the Indian state will metastasize itself from a constitutional state owing allegiance to the rule of law to a rogue state.

2. As Thomas Blom Hansen points out, according to Sigmund Freud, this permission to act without constraints is 'one of the conditions driving the support for fascism'.
3. These changes are based on recommendations made by the Ministry of Labour and Employment, and 'prior instruction' was issued by the president of India through a letter by the Ministry of Home, Government of India.
4. Although it should be noted that the sustained protests of over a year resulted in the government withdrawing the farm laws.
5. See also the work of Vinay Kumar (2024) on generating a constitutional consciousness through postcards which capture the original artwork of the Constitution as well as the debates in the Constituent Assembly on key concepts.

References

ABP News (2023). '"Day Not Far When a Muslim MP Is Lynched...": Owaisi Slams PM Modi over Bidhuri's Speech'. 25 September. https://news.abplive.com/news/india/asaduddin-owaisi-slams-pm-modi-over-ramesh-bidhuri-speech-danish-ali-day-not-far-when-muslim-mp-lynched-in-parliament-1631712. Accessed 24 April 2024.

Arendt, H. (1973). *The Origins of Totalitarianism*. London: Harcourt Brace Jovanovich.

Baxi, U. (2008). *The Future of Human Rights*. New Delhi: Oxford University Press.

Banaji, J. (2016). *Fascism: Essays on Europe and India* (Enlarged and Updated). New Delhi: Three Essays Collective.

Bharadkar, K., and B. Mathew (2021). '738 Kavya Bharadkar and Babu Mathew: The Journey of Labour Regulation'. https://india-seminar.com/2021/738/738_kavya_and_babu.htm. Accessed 24 April 2024.

Bhatia, G. (2020). 'ICLP Turns 7: A Constitutionalism Without the Court'. Constitutional Law and Philosophy, 1 August. https://indconlawphil.word

press.com/2020/08/01/iclp-turns-7-a-constitutionalism-without-the-court. Accessed 5 April 2025.

Campbell, J. (1995). 'The Pragmatism of Benjamin Franklin'. *Transactions of the Charles S. Peirce Society* 31(4): 745–792.

Desai, R. (2016). 'Hindutva and Fascism'. *Economic and Political Weekly*, 30 December. https://www.epw.in/journal/2016/53/review-article/hindutva-and-fascism.html. Accessed 24 April 2024.

Desai, M., and L. Jesani (2023). 'Alarm Bells Must Set Off in the Country on the Hate Killings by RPF Constable Chetan Singh!' https://pucl.org/manage-press-stateme/alarm-bells-must-set-off-in-the-country-on-the-hate-killings-by-rpf-constable-chetan-singh. Accessed 5 March 2025.

Foot, J. (2022). *Blood and Power: The Rise and Fall of Italian Fascism*. London: Bloomsbury Publishing.

Golwalkar, M. S. (1966). *Bunch Of Thoughts*. Bangalore: Sahitya Sindhu Prakashana.

Hansen, T. B. (2021). *The Law of Force: The Violent Heart of Indian Politics*. New Delhi: Aleph Book Company.

Human Rights Watch (2019). 'India: Vigilante "Cow Protection" Groups Attack Minorities'. 18 February. https://www.hrw.org/news/2019/02/19/india-vigilante-cow-protection-groups-attack-minorities. Accessed 5 April 2025.

Islam, S. (2017). *Golwalkar's 'We or Our Nationhood Defined': A Critique*. New Delhi: Pharos Media & Pub.

Jaffrelot, C. (2007). *Hindu Nationalism*. Princeton: Princeton University Press.

Karmakar, N. (2020). 'The New Labour Codes: Depriving Workers of Rights'. 12 October. https://www.cpimlnd.org/the-new-labour-codes-depriving-workers-of-rights. Accessed 5 March 2025.

Kapoor, M., and K. Dinesh (2021). 'Throughout the Pandemic, Environmental Clearance Law Has Been under the Chopping Block'. *The Wire*, 13 May. http://thewire.in/environment/throughout-the-pandemic-environmental-clearance-law-has-been-under-the-chopping-block. Accessed 24 April 2024.

Klein, N. (2007). *The Shock Doctrine: The Rise of Disaster Capitalism*. New York: Alfred A. Knopf.

Khanna, R. (2023). 'Was Monu Manesar a Part of BJP's "Use and Throw" Charade or Something More?' *The Wire*, 18 September. https://thewire.in/communalism/was-monu-manesar-a-part-of-bjps-use-and-throw-charade-or-something-more. Accessed 24 April 2024.

Kumar, R. (2024). *The Free Voice*. New Delhi: Speaking Tiger Books.

Kumar, V. (2024). 'Constitution Is a Thread That Connects Us to the Freedom Struggle'. https://creativemornings.com/talks/vinay-kumar. Accessed 5 April 2025.

Liberhan Ayodhya Commission (2009). 'Report'. https://www.mha.gov.in/en/about-us/commissions-committees/liberhan-ayodhya-commission. Accessed 24 April 2024.

Linz, J. J. (2000). *Totalitarian and Authoritarian Regimes*. London: Lynne Rienner Publishers.

Mander, H. (2017). 'Junaid, My Son'. *Indian Express*, 1 July. https://indianexpress.com/article/opinion/columns/junaid-my-son-4729828. Accessed 5 March 2025.

———. (2018). 'Hate Crimes in India: New Tracker Finds Victims Are Predominantly Muslims, Perpetrators Hindus'. *Scroll.in*, 13 November. https://scroll.in/article/901206/new-hate-crime-tracker-in-india-finds-victims-are-predominantly-muslims-perpetrators-hindus. Accessed 24 April 2024.

Mohammed, A. (2020). 'Karnataka Government Tweaks Three Laws, Approves Labour Ordinance'. *Deccan Herald*, 24 July. https://www.deccanherald.com/india/karnataka/karnataka-government-tweaks-three-laws-approves-labour-ordinance-864859.html. Accessed 24 April 2024.

Nair, S. K. (2020). 'Govt. against Virtual Meetings of Parliamentary Standing Committees, Citing Confidentiality'. *The Hindu*, 12 July. https://www.thehindu.com/news/national/govt-against-virtual-meetings-of-parliamentary-standing-committees-citing-confidentiality/article32059764.ece. Accessed 5 March 2025.

Narayanan, S. (2020). 'The Three Farm Bills'. 28 September. https://www.theindiaforum.in/article/three-farm-bills. Accessed 24 April 2024.

Narrain, A., and P. Ravishankar (2021). *Preamble: A Brief Introduction—The Constitution of India*. Bengaluru: Alternative Law Forum.

Narrain, A., M. Krishnan, and C. D. Rozario (2020). 'COVID-19 Lockdown: Uttar Pradesh and Madhya Pradesh Watering Down Labour Laws Is a Body Blow to the Working Class'. Firstpost, 11 May. https://www.firstpost.com/india/covid-19-lockdown-uttar-pradesh-and-madhya-pradesh-watering-down-labour-laws-is-a-body-blow-to-the-working-class-8355791.html. Accessed 24 April 2024.

Narrain, A. (2021). *India's Undeclared Emergency: Constitutionalism and the Politics of Resistance*. Chennai: Westland Publications Private Limited.

Nussbaum, M. C. (2013). *Political Emotions: Why Love Matters for Justice.* Cambridge, MA: Harvard University Press.

Oxfam (2021). 'The Inequality Virus'. https://www.oxfamindia.org/knowledge hub/workingpaper/inequality-virus-india-supplement-2021. Accessed 5 March 2025.

Pellissery, S., B. Mathew, A. Govindjee, and A. Narrain (2020). 'Transformative Law and Public Policy'. New Delhi: Routledge.

People's Union for Civil Liberties (PUCL) (2009). 'Cultural Policing in Dakshina Kannada: Vigilante Attacks on Women and Minorities, 2008-09'. 1 March. https://sabrangindia.in/document/cultural-policing-dakshina-kannada-vigilante-attacks-women-and-minorities-2008-09. Accessed 24 April 2024.

——— (2023). 'Manipur, Nuh and the Criminal Law Amendments: Terror outside the Law and the Injustices of the Law'. 31 August. https://pucl.org/manage-writings/manipur-nuh-and-the-criminal-law-amendments-terror-outside-the-law-and-the-injustices-of-the-law. Accessed 5 March 2025.

Pierson, P. (2017). 'American Hybrid: Donald Trump and the Strange Merger of Populism and Plutocracy'. *British Journal of Sociology* 68(5): 105–S119.

Piketty, T. (2020). *Capital and Ideology.* Cambridge, MA: Harvard University Press.

Pinto, A., and Van Adhikar Media Team (2020). 'How the Government Diluted Forest Rights of Adivasis during Lockdown'. Behanbox, 20 July. https://behanbox.com/2020/07/20/how-the-government-of-india-used-the-lockdown-to-dilute-the-forest-rights-of-communities-voices-of-the-people-affected-by-coal-mining-projects. Accessed 5 March 2025.

Poruthiyil, P. V. (2021). 'Big Business and Fascism: A Dangerous Collusion'. *Journal of Business Ethics* 168(1): 121–135.

Pravasi Bhalai Sangathan vs U.O.I. and Ors, AIR 2014 SC 1591 (2014). https://indiankanoon.org/doc/194770087. Accessed 24 April 2024.

Ram, A. B. (2020). 'Relaxation of Labour Laws across States'. PRS Legislative Research, 12 May. https://prsindia.org/theprsblog/relaxation-of-labour-laws-across-states. Accessed 24 April 2024.

Rosenberg, A. (2016). 'Fascism as a Mass-Movement (1934)'. In *Fascism: Essays on Europe and India*, edited by J. Banaji. New Delhi: Three Essays Collective.

Sainath, P. (2020). 'All About the New Farm Laws and Farmers Protest'. https://www.youtube.com/watch?v=16Dmm34vK5g. Accessed 5 March 2025.

Sharma, H. (2021). 'Explained: Why PM Modi Withdrew the Three Farm Laws—and the Precedent from Six Years Ago'. *Indian Express*, 19 November. https://

indianexpress.com/article/explained/narendra-modi-farm-laws-repealed-explained-7630834. Accessed 5 March 2025.

Sharma, J. (2003). *Hindutva: Exploring the Idea of Hindu Nationalism*. New Delhi: Viking.

———. (2007). *Terrifying Vision: M. S. Golwalkar, the RSS, and India*. New Delhi: Penguin Books India.

Shih, G., and P. Verma (2023). 'He Live-Streamed His Attacks on Indian Muslims. YouTube Gave Him an Award'. *Washington Post*, 27 September. https://www.washingtonpost.com/world/2023/09/26/india-monu-manesar-viligante-social-media. Accessed 24 April 2024.

Stoltzfus, N. (1996). *Resistance of the Heart: Intermarriage and the Rosenstrasse Protest in Nazi Germany*. New York and London: W.W. Norton.

The Wire (2021). 'COVID-19 Sharpened Inequalities in India, Billionaires' Wealth Increased by 35%: Report'. https://thewire.in/rights/covid-19-sharpened-inequalities-in-india-billionaires-wealth-increased-by-35-report. Accessed 24 April 2024.

United States Holocaust Memorial Museum (2023). 'Martin Niemöller: "First They Came for the Socialists..."'. 11 April. https://encyclopedia.ushmm.org/content/en/article/martin-niemoeller-first-they-came-for-the-socialists. Accessed 24 April 2024.

Verma, M. (2020). 'Parliaments in the Time of the Pandemic'. *Economic and Political Weekly*, 13 June. https://www.epw.in/journal/2020/24/commentary/parliaments-time-pandemic.html. Accessed 24 April 2024.

'We Must Hand Together or Surely We Shall Hang Separately' (2015). https://www.youtube.com/watch?v=4xIRIa7vz0M. Accessed 5 March 2025.

Yadav, A. (2020). 'Why Landless and Marginal Farmers Are the Backbone of Farmer Protests'. Newslaundry, 4 December. https://www.newslaundry.com/2020/12/04/why-landless-and-marginal-farmers-are-the-backbone-of-farmer-protests. Accessed 24 April 2024.

8

One-Dimensional Mania

Unmasking the Nexus of Brahmanical Hindutva, Corporate Dispossession, and State Violence in India

Ashok Kumbamu

The ascent of the Bharatiya Janata Party (BJP) to power in 2014 marked a significant transformation in India's sociopolitical landscape. The BJP, as the political wing of the Sangh Parivar, a network of Hindu supremacist organizations, strategically utilized the full spectrum of politico-legal systems and socio-economic institutions in its attempt to shape India into a Hindu Rashtra (Hindu Nation). This effort has gained remarkable momentum, particularly following the BJP and its alliances' successive electoral victories and firm control over the Indian parliament. For building Hindutva (Hindu nationhood) politics, the BJP adopts a primordial perspective, defining a nation through socio-biological links or socially constructed cultural connectivity, such as language, religion, territory, and kinship (de Souza 2022; Kumbamu 2020; Shani 2021). Deeply immersed in such primordialism, the Sangh Parivar defines the nation based on the idea of oneness (one law, one culture, one religion, and one language), which aims to promote Hindu supremacy, stigmatizing and labelling those who diverge from its definition as 'enemies' or 'anti-nationals' (Banaji 2018; Chacko 2023; Frykenberg 2008; Siddiqui 2017). As a result, there is an increasing criminalization of various forms of political dissent. This includes actions ranging from targeted 'legal' assaults on opposition political parties and ideologies to overt threats and 'conspiracy' cases against activists, academics, journalists, writers, and artists.

In this political context, deep-seated concerns have emerged regarding the state of democracy, civil liberties, and the functioning of constitutional institutions. Furthermore, the concept of secularism, once proclaimed as a cornerstone of India's democratic ethos, has undergone a complex transformation, sparking debates and many interpretations. Historically, secularism has been weaponized in Indian politics, often employed as a strategic tool to achieve political objectives. While the Indian Constitution ostensibly champions secularism, critical scholars like Pritam Singh (2005) contend that it always carries a subtle 'Hindu-tainted' essence. This contention is based on specific provisions that seemingly reflect a Hindu-centric perspective. Notable examples include the inclusion of 'Bharat' in Article 1, subtly aligning the constitutional nomenclature with Hindu cultural identity, and Article 48 advocating for cow protection, which is associated with Hindu religious sentiments. In addition, Article 25(2)(B) expresses the state's special interest in promoting 'social welfare and reform' within the Hindu religion (ibid.). However, the BJP systematically dismantled the concept of secularism and constructed it as a challenge to the dominant Hindu identity, leading to the coining of the derogatory term 'sickular' by the Sangh Parivar forces (Acharya 2020; Sato 2023; Shani 2021). This pejorative label seeks to undermine the defence of religious and ethnic minorities, framing it as a sign of weakness. This calculated rebranding is part of a broader campaign aimed at eroding some of the key principles of the Indian Constitution such as justice, equality, liberty, and freedom.

In its efforts to get a grip over social and political institutions, the Sangh Parivar has exerted its influence across multiple fields, including the media (Manchanda 2002; Mehta and Kaye 2021), the judicial system (Sundar 2023), and education (Bhatty and Sundar 2020; Flåten 2017; Kadiwal et al. 2022; Sundar 2004; Visweswaran et al. 2009; Anand and Lall 2022). These efforts towards establishing a Hindu state not only dispossess historically marginalized communities but also undermine the essence and functionality of the democratic system itself. This growing apprehension has ignited a rallying cry among oppositional (liberal and left) political parties and various civil society organizations: 'save the constitution, save the nation' (Raja 2022). This call holds a dual significance.

First, it creates a condition for a role reversal, calling upon the people to assume the role of guardians of the Constitution to prevent potential abandonment. This shift in roles underscores the urgent concern that the instrument conceived to shield the citizens now needs protection. The implications of the endangered Constitution extend far beyond mere rhetoric. They encompass the attrition of democratic checks and balances, creating an environment in which authority becomes increasingly concentrated within the Hindutva political faction. This concentration of power poses a direct challenge to the delicate equilibrium that forms the foundation of a functional democracy—a vision enshrined in the Constitution but, unfortunately, one that has struggled to materialize since its inception. Second, it underscores the urgency of preserving India's rich diversity and pluralistic identity against the encroachment of parochial, exclusionary Hindutva ideology (P. Chatterjee 1997).

The convergence of centralized authority, the suppression of all forms of dissent, and the gradual destruction of democratic institutions and values have raised an urgent and compelling inquiry into whether India's current trajectory exhibits similarities with the defining features of a fascist state. The discourse surrounding the characterization of contemporary India and its potential evolution into a fascist state is notably nuanced and multifaceted. It encompasses a spectrum of viewpoints, reflecting a wide array of interpretations and analytical perspectives. Considering this multidimensionality, this chapter explores politico-economic and sociocultural dynamics surrounding fascist tendencies and their broader and deeper implications for Indian society and politics. It also delves into the symbiotic alliance that has emerged between Brahmanical Hindutva forces, corporate entities, and the state apparatus, analyzing their collaborative strategies and modus operandi.

Weaponizing nationalism for reproducing a Hindutva narrative

Hindutva is not solely about Hindu religion; it is a complex narrative that intertwines religion, 'sacred' territory, shared racial and ethnic characteristics, and a common language to construct an ethnonationalist identity (Savarkar 1989 [1923]). The architect of Hindutva, V. D. Savarkar, drew inspiration from Western theories of nationalism, highlighting these elements as critical components of identity (Burak 2020). By emphasizing these complex dimensions of identity, Hindutva forces aim to foster a sense of unity, belonging, and security among Hindus, uniting them under a broader cultural and national identity (Ahmad 2022; Anand 2016; Anderson and Jaffrelot 2018; Jaffrelot 2011; Shani 2021; Thapar 2009; Visweswaran et al. 2009).

In the development of classical fascism, the concept of nationalism played a pivotal role, catalysing the mobilization of the masses through the exploitation of societal divisions. Roger Griffin (2013) underscores this by asserting that political actors of fascism strategically accentuate existing fault lines—whether based on ethnicity, religion, or culture—constructing a narrative that positions one dominant group as the rightful custodian of the national identity and superior to others. In doing so, this narrative inherently designates others as outsiders, creating a divisive 'us' versus 'them' paradigm. This intentional manipulation of societal divisions becomes a mechanism for mobilizing support and fostering a sense of collective identity and belonging that aligns with the tenets of nationalism (Brubaker 2017; Griffin 2013). Rogers Brubaker (2017) expands on this understanding, highlighting the critical role of threat perception in the mobilization of support for fascist and right-wing populist ideologies. According to Brubaker, fascist leaders frame issues in a way that resonates with the fears and aspirations embedded in the collective identity of their target audience—that is, 'us'. Simultaneously, they construct a discourse projecting the so-called outsiders (them) as a potential threat to national integrity. By emphasizing manufactured threats to the nation, fascist leaders can effectively evoke the emotional aspects of national identity. Anthony Smith (1991) and John Breuilly (1993) provide similar insights into the complex interplay between nationalism and the development of fascism. Smith argues that the construction of national identity involves both highlighting commonalities within a group and distinguishing them from others. This process creates a foundation for religious or ethnic identity politics and a sense of belonging, a key element in the mobilization strategies of fascist movements.

In a similar vein, Griffin (2013) argues that the development and spread of fascist ideologies entail a deliberate construction of an idealized and exaggerated national identity by political actors associated with fascism. In this process, such actors create a narrative that glorifies and amplifies specific aspects of the nation's identity, often emphasizing selective historical achievements, cultural attributes, ethnic or religious heritage, or a discourse of exceptionalism. This idealized version serves as a tool to garner support and cultivate a fervent sense of national pride among the people. By idealizing the national identity, fascist political actors forge a powerful symbol representing strength, superiority, and a unique destiny. This exaggerated symbol becomes a focal point for mobilization and a means to nurture a collective identity that transcends individual differences. The romanticization of the nation plays a crucial role in fascists' efforts to make a shift from nationalism to ultra-nationalism. It is crucial to recognize that this shift is not a reflection of objective reality but rather a social construction by fascist forces to consolidate power, manipulate public sentiment, and foster loyalty to their political agenda.

Griffin (2013) also emphasizes the role of charismatic or populist leadership in fascist movements. Fascist leaders often present themselves as charismatic figures who embody the ideals of the nation. A key historical strategy is their ability to connect emotionally with the masses and convey a vision of a resurgent, 'powerful', and great nation. This charismatic leadership style contributes to the creation of a strong personal connection between the leader and the followers, facilitating the propagation of ultra-nationalist ideologies. Robert Paxton (2004) delves into the analysis of classical fascism, highlighting the significance of the construction of negation, especially its rejection of liberalism, socialism, and rationalism. This rejection forms a core strength of fascism. The process involves initially creating a void through negation and subsequently attempting to fill it by incorporating local beliefs, rituals, and symbols that emotionally resonate with the local populations. This unique sociocultural process, influenced by local factors, distinguishes Italian and German fascisms from each other and other iterations such as Romanian and Japanese. Despite the diverse local contexts, fascists consistently chose to self-identify as such.

In India, the Sangh Parivar adeptly deploys nationalist narratives and symbols to advance its sociopolitical agenda. By emphasizing the concept of 'one nation', the Sangh Parivar promotes a unified national identity deeply rooted in Hindu culture (Jaffrelot 2005). They strategically align their identity with national symbols such as the flag, anthem, and Bharat Mata, projecting an image of patriotism and linking their objectives with the broader national narrative. In doing so, they aim to present themselves as a legitimate and integral part of the national fabric, reinforcing the perception that their ideology is not only compatible with but is synonymous with the values encapsulated in these symbols (Noorani 2000).

This association enables the Sangh Parivar to tap into the emotional and cultural resonance these symbols hold for the public. It creates a narrative wherein the Sangh Parivar is portrayed as a defender of the nation's cultural and historical identity, fostering a sense of ownership and guardianship over what is deemed quintessentially national. This strategic alignment also aids in mobilizing support by appealing to the sentiments associated with these symbols, thereby strengthening the ideological connection between the Sangh Parivar and its followers. To justify their ideological imposition on national symbols and history, they have undertaken the project of historical revisionism, involving the selective interpretation of historical events and figures and the reconstruction of a narrative aligned with their ideological objectives. This historical revisionism is presented as an endeavour to revive and safeguard India's ancient heritage. Moreover, this is framed as a nationalist duty, positioning the preservation of the nation's cultural identity as paramount (Jaffrelot 2007; Sharma 2019).

In addition, the Sangh Parivar strategically uses patriotic sentiments to gather support and propagate a specific vision of the nation. One of the recent key strategies, for example, is the promotion of the Uniform Civil Code (UCC) as a nationalist endeavour. Proponents of the UCC argue that its implementation would contribute to the development of a cohesive national identity by unifying personal laws across diverse religious communities. This perspective of 'one nation, one law' emphasizes the UCC as a mechanism for promoting equality and common citizenship by transcending religious distinctions (Suman and Sahu 2023). However, critics contend that the imposition of a uniform code encroaches upon religious freedoms and traditions deeply embedded in personal laws (Menon 2005; Sur 2018). It is seen as a tool to enforce the Sangh Parivar's vision of a homogeneous Hindu identity as the ideal for the nation (Ramachandran 2020; Shani 2021).

Another instance of nationalist rhetoric can be observed in the context of anti-cow slaughter legislation. Legislation and campaigns against cow slaughter are often couched in terms of protecting the sacredness of the cow, an animal revered in Hinduism. The Sangh Parivar presents this as a nationalist cause, aligning with the cultural values of a significant section of the population (Gundimeda 2023; Parveen 2020; Reddy 2021). These examples illustrate how the Sangh Parivar strategically deploys nationalist narratives and symbols to further its sociopolitical objectives.

The deliberate distortion of historical narratives goes beyond intellectual manipulation; it is a calculated effort to reshape collective memory and forge a narrative that aligns with the Hindutva ideological framework. This intentional reinterpretation serves to establish a historical continuum that supports the narrative of Hindus as victims and portrays perceived adversaries as the 'other', threatening the nation's identity and security. Historian Ramachandra Guha (2007) notes that mobilizing nationalist feelings serves as a powerful legitimizing tool for Hindutva policies. This mobilization is not just about historical accuracy but a strategic maneuvering of collective memory to suppress dissent and consolidate political power. It fosters a narrative where any opposition to Hindutva ideology is portrayed as an act against the nation's interests.

Manipulated seriality, propaganda machinery, and the propagation of fear

Historically, to create conducive conditions for fascism, mass propaganda methods were employed as major tools for manipulating public opinion. In addition to fostering a climate of conformity, fascists also use surveillance and violence to construct a culture of fear and insecurity, leading to the breakdown of communal bonds and the alienation of individuals from society (Neocleous 2005; Stanley 2020). Hannah Arendt (1973) refers to this phenomenon as the 'atomization' of society. This deliberate 'atomization' and dehumanization of individuals facilitate the fascist regime's control and manipulation of the populace (ibid.). Furthermore, the political polarization of society based on divisive rhetoric (such as race, ethnicity, language, and religion) and economic disparities can contribute to a condition of hopelessness and anomie that would be attractive to 'solutions' offered by fascists (Balta, Rovira Kaltwasser and Yagci 2022; Stanley 2020). Those individuals who are attracted to fascist manipulations, as Arendt also contends, might involve themselves in or support the machinery of fascist regimes. Their involvements in fascist propaganda and in committing heinous crimes do not necessarily arise out of inherent malice, but rather due to their conformity to the system and a lack of critical thinking.

Arendt's seminal work, *Eichmann in Jerusalem: A Report on the Banality of Evil* (1964), delves into the trial of Adolf Eichmann, a high-ranking Nazi official responsible for orchestrating the logistics of the Holocaust. Arendt argues that Eichmann's actions were characterized by a disturbing ordinariness, a bureaucratic mindset that blindly followed orders without any critical reflection. According to Arendt, Eichmann exemplified a type of evil that arises not from a malevolent nature, but from a failure to think independently and critically about one's actions. Thus, authoritarianism or fascism fosters a societal condition in which individuals become manipulated subjects and appendages to structural processes.

For understanding the mobilization of the masses and the crippling of critical thinking, Jean-Paul Sartre (1960) provides a unique lens through the concept of 'manipulated seriality', shedding light on the passive consumption of fascist ideology. This framework introduces a dichotomy between organized groups and unorganized masses, labelled as 'seriality.' Sartre argues that organized groups possess coherence, structure, and agency, while unorganized masses lack inherent connections, rendering them susceptible to manipulation by fascist movements (ibid.). Sartre's analogy of individuals waiting for a bus aptly captures the essence of seriality—a superficial unity based on a shared goal but lacking intrinsic relationships. In this scenario, individuals may stand together momentarily with a common objective, akin to how unorganized masses might align temporarily with fascist movements due to shared sentiments, a sense of belonging, or perceived common goals. Sartre's concept underscores the vulnerability of alienated and unorganized masses to manipulation, as their lack of inherent connections makes them more malleable to the influence of organized fascist ideologies seeking to exploit their collective passivity.

The concept of manipulated seriality helps us understand Hindutva's strategic mass mobilization. This mobilization is not grounded in genuine inclusivity, as Hindus are divided based on castes and sociocultural practices (see, for example, Ilaiah 2005). Instead, it relies on the calculated manipulation of collective sentiments. This highlights the importance of the critical examination of how Hindutva forces construct narratives to manipulate seriality, fabricating unity while advancing its political objectives. Examples include the exploitation of communal tensions, propagation of anti-minority sentiments, engagement in cultural nationalism, divisive rhetoric in political campaigns, associating patriotism with specific norms, and the revisionist interpretation of history.

In the construction of manipulated seriality, the widespread use of digital technologies and media serves as instrumental tools in the arsenal of the Hindutva fascist machinery (Udupa 2018). The Modi government has also extended its surveillance apparatus to monitor individuals expressing dissenting views on social media against the Hindutva ideology. This expansion of state surveillance raises concerns about the potential misuse of governmental mechanisms and agencies, including the National Investigation Agency and the Directorate of Enforcement, to threaten and oppress voices critical of Hindutva politics. The BJP government has also adopted various undemocratic methods, including media censorship, legal actions against critics, and the imposition of stringent online regulations, creating an environment of fear and restricting the space for opposing viewpoints (S. Ghosh 2023; Yilmaz and Saleem 2023). This orchestrated control over digital spaces and media not only manipulates public opinion but also stifles dissent, reinforcing the manipulated seriality that Hindutva seeks to create and exploit for its political advancement (Basu and Sen 2023).

The *vishvaguru* of fascism: is Hindutva fascism exported, or is Western fascism imported?

At the core of Hindutva, Brahmanical hegemony plays a pivotal role in shaping a specific interpretation of Hinduism (Jaffrelot 2005; 2007). Proponents of Hindutva often advocate for ideals and norms traditionally associated with Brahminism, including hierarchical social structures, gender norms, and cultural practices (Frykenberg 2008; Gray 2020). While Hindutva politics emphasizes Hindu identity, it selectively interprets Hindu culture and history, glorifying and justifying oppressive elements while downplaying those associated with 'lower' castes, religious, and sexual minorities (Frykenberg 2008). Brahmanical Hindutva domination extends beyond cultural and religious spheres, permeating into political and social domains, including education, media, law, and governance (Jaffrelot 2007). B.R. Ambedkar rightfully criticizes Brahmanism, asserting that the core ideal of Hinduism is not focused on individuals or society at large but rather revolves around a specific caste—the Brahmin, whom he categorizes as the caste of 'Supermen' (Ambedkar 1987). Ambedkar highlights a distinctive principle within Hinduism wherein the definition of what is considered right and good is tied to serving the interests of the Brahmin caste. He writes, 'Hinduism is the gospel of the superman, and it teaches that what is right for the superman is the only thing which is called morally right and morally good' (ibid., p. 74). This contradicts liberal principles of justice and social utility, highlighting the inherent inequality and domination within the Hindu social order (ibid., p. 72).

Ambedkar's exploration gains additional depth as he examines Friedrich Nietzsche's references to the Manusmriti (The Laws of Manu) in his philosophical discourse. This analysis offers a pathway to investigate potential connections between Nietzsche's ideas and the Hindu societal structure, particularly the caste system outlined in the Manusmriti. Nietzsche's engagement with Manu suggests an intellectual intersection between Western philosophical thought and Hindu socio-religious frameworks, which holds historical significance. This connection becomes particularly relevant when considering Adolf Hitler's selective interpretation of Nietzsche's philosophy. Hitler's use of Nietzschean concepts, such as the 'superman' and the 'will to power', to justify the supremacist ideology of Nazi Germany adds complexity to the discussion. This interpretation highlights the adaptability of philosophical concepts when wielded by political figures for ideological justifications. According to Ambedkar, 'Nietzsche's thought is Hitler in action and that Nietzsche was the foremost pioneer of the Nazi accession to power' (ibid., p. 75). Nietzsche himself has openly declared that in developing his philosophy he merely followed the scheme of Manu. Nietzsche regarded the Manusmriti as 'an incomparably intellectual and superior work' (quoted in Ambedkar 2000, p. 2). As per Ambedkar (1987, p. 76),

> If there is any difference between Manu and Nietzsche, it lies in this. Nietzsche was genuinely interested in creating a new race of men which will be a race of supermen as compared with the existing race of men. Manu, on the other hand, was interested in maintaining the privileges of a class who had come to arrogate to itself the claim of being supermen. Nietzsche's supermen were supermen by reason of their worth. Manu's supermen were supermen by reason of their birth. Nietzsche was a genuine disinterested philosopher. Manu, on the contrary, was a hireling engaged to propound a philosophy which served the interests of a class born in a group and whose title to being supermen was not to be lost even if they lost their virtue.

Nietzsche's concept of supermen, as mentioned by Ambedkar, is depicted as a product of intrinsic qualities and accomplishments, suggesting a meritocratic ideal where individuals rise to a superior status based on their achievements. On the contrary, Manu's supermen are ascribed their elevated status solely due to their birth into a privileged caste, irrespective of their virtues.

Ambedkar argues that Manu's philosophy is tailored to maintain the status and privileges of this class/caste, even if they deviate from virtuous conduct. This interpretation lends support to the notion that the essence of fascism, characterized by a hierarchical social order and the notion of a superior class, could have been transmitted from Hinduism through Nietzsche's admiration for Manu.

Ambedkar further posits that the denial of freedom within the Hindu social order is a severe injustice, causing significant harm by mutilating and emasculating individuals from 'lower' castes. Despite using inhumane methods, the Hindu social order is paradoxically credited with effectively preserving itself while maintaining a reputation for being humane. In a provocative assertion, Ambedkar suggests that the Nazis could have taken lessons from the Hindus on suppressing dissent without resorting to overt cruelty, thereby presenting themselves as humane masters in the process. As Ambedkar says, 'The Nazis had indeed a great deal to learn from the Hindus. If they had adopted the technique of suppressing the masses devised by the Hindus, they would have been able to crush the Jews without overt cruelty and would have also exhibited themselves as humane masters' (ibid., p. 127).

The Hindu 'humane masters' are now projecting a global image as *vishvaguru*, or 'world teacher,' aspiring for India to assume a role as a global teacher or spiritual guide. Despite concealing its eternal (Sanatana) inhumane character, Brahmanical Hindutva forces assert the title of *vishvaguru*, emphasizing their potential to impart universally relevant wisdom, knowledge, and values. This brand represents a desire to share the profound insights of India's sages and thinkers worldwide and to advocate for principles of peace, tolerance, and spiritual harmony (Hall 2017). However, the concept of *vishvaguru* selectively highlights Hinduism from the Brahmanical perspective while diminishing contributions from other religions and marginalized philosophical traditions within the country, potentially leading to a skewed portrayal of India's cultural and spiritual diversity (Mannathukkaren and MacEachern 2023). Furthermore, the *vishvaguru* concept is susceptible to political instrumentalization, used by political leaders to evoke nationalist sentiments, divert attention from domestic issues, or assert India's global dominance (de Estrada 2023). Consequently, the spiritual and philosophical dimensions are exploited for political gain. Drawing on Ambedkar's interpretation of the influence of Manu on the ideological growth of Nazism, one could argue that Brahmanical Hindutva is indeed the *vishvaguru* of fascism.

Fascist democracy: bulldozing constitutional institutions and building the state of impunity

In the late twentieth and early twenty-first centuries, right-wing populist governments paved the way to fascism within parliamentary systems (Payne 1996). This phenomenon aligns with what Fareed Zakaria termed 'illiberal democracy' to describe a political system that employs elections to choose leaders including presidents, prime ministers, or legislators, while simultaneously infringing upon fundamental rights and freedoms (Zakaria 1997). In parliamentary democracy, the exercise of majority rule through electoral processes, whether authentic or a façade, introduces the potential risk of the tyranny of the majority, raising concerns about the potential infringement on individual freedom and rights (Dahl 1971). Constitutional liberalism emerges as a critical safeguard against the excesses of democratic majoritarianism, prioritizing individual liberties, equality, and the rule of law (Rawls 1993). Liberal thinkers contend that, without a robust liberal framework, democracy may degrade into a mere procedural exercise, neglecting substantive elements vital for inclusivity and the protection of diverse voices and rights (Diamond and Morlino 2005; Lijphart 2012; Mill 1861).

On the contrary, Marxists argue that liberal democracies, while ostensibly promoting political equality, fundamentally serve the interests of the bourgeoisie or capitalist class, perpetuating class-based inequalities. The Marxist critique asserts that the state, functioning as an instrument of the ruling class, utilizes democracy to legitimize and sustain capitalist relations and exploitation (Bottomore 1983). Moreover, Marxists argue that the illusion of choice in the political landscape masks the underlying continuity in policies favouring the capitalist class. They argue further that the influence of capitalism on the political process in the so-called vibrant democracies is profound with financial interests, lobbying, and corporate power shaping political decisions and diluting the ideals of equal value and participation (Wood 1999).

The Indian Constitution reflects liberal principles through the inclusion of fundamental rights, such as equal protection under the law in Article 14 and the right to freedom of speech and expression in Article 19. Additionally, Article 21 safeguards the right to life and personal liberty, underscoring the importance of individual freedoms. These provisions are designed to shield individuals from potential abuses of majority power (Austin 2013). Beyond these fundamental rights, the Directive Principles of State Policy in the Constitution, outlined in Part IV (Articles 36–51), constitute a distinctive feature extending beyond political liberalism into the social and economic domains. While not legally enforceable, the Directive Principles serve as guidelines for the government in formulating policies and laws. However, ambiguity surrounds their interpretation and implementation due to their non-justiciable nature, potential conflicts with fundamental rights, vague language, and discretionary powers vested in political authorities (Austin 1966; Baxi 1982).

Another salient liberal feature within the constitutional tapestry is the formidable presence of judicial review—a mechanism endowing the judiciary, notably the Supreme Court of India, with the authority to scrutinize and potentially invalidate governmental actions inconsistent with constitutional tenets (Austin 1966). This mechanism assumes a pivotal role in upholding liberal principles, functioning as a check on governmental authority and particularly safeguarding fundamental rights. This characteristic contributes to the delicate equilibrium between democratic governance and the preservation of liberal principles, engendering a dynamic interplay within the constitutional framework. Landmark Supreme Court decisions, such as *Kesavananda Bharati v. State of Kerala*, underscore the pivotal role of judicial review in upholding constitutional supremacy and reinforcing India's allegiance to a liberal democratic order (ibid.). However, it is important to note that the Constitution does not explicitly assert its liberal character in the discussions of the Drafting Committee, within the text itself or in its interpretations.

The Indian Constitution, while embodying liberal principles, also exhibits certain illiberal elements that warrant scholarly scrutiny. One notable instance is the imposition of emergency provisions, specifically Article 352, which grants the president the authority to proclaim a state of emergency in the event of perceived threats to the nation. The misuse of this provision during the twenty-one-month emergency (June 1975–March 1977) under prime minister Indira Gandhi's regime raised concerns about its potential for illiberal exploitation (Ganguly 2002). During this period, fundamental rights were suspended and political dissent was suppressed, signalling a departure from liberal democratic norms. Furthermore, the sedition laws embodied in section 124A of the Indian Penal Code have been a subject of critique for their illiberal implications. The broad interpretation and application of these laws to curtail freedom of expression have been challenged because they stifle dissent and are inconsistent with liberal democratic values (Chakrabarti and Chakrabarti 2012). The sedition laws have been utilized at times to penalize criticism of the government, raising concerns about their compatibility with the spirit of a liberal constitutional order.

During Modi's tenure, India has witnessed a significant deterioration in the norms and practices that underpin its democratic framework, despite the formal preservation of key democratic institutions. This informal decline contrasts sharply with the emergency period under Indira Gandhi, when democratic institutions were formally dismantled. Presently, concerns about illiberal tendencies have emerged, marked by the erosion of institutional independence, particularly within the judiciary and regulatory bodies, questioning the robustness of checks and balances strategically designed to prevent the concentration of power (Varshney 2019). Key positions in major government agencies have been filled with individuals closely aligned with Hindutva ideology. This trend extends to pivotal institutions, including universities, vigilance and criminal investigation agencies, election commissions, and the judiciary, raising concerns about the compromised independence of these entities. Such actions not only risk tilting the delicate balance of power but also pose a significant challenge to the democratic underpinnings of the Indian political system (Hansen and Roy 2022; Siddiqui 2017).

However, labelling the faltering democratic system in Modi's India as an illiberal democracy is inappropriate, as neither liberal nor democratic values were deeply ingrained in society and the political landscape due to the historically oppressive social structure. Instead, given the pervasive influence of Brahmanical dominance, characterized as fascist, across various sociopolitical realms, it is more appropriate to call it a 'fascist democracy' (Roy 2023). In the Indian context, this term captures the Brahmanical domination and oppression shaping the sociopolitical structure, enabling hierarchical and exclusionary practices. It is crucial to note that the term 'fascist democracy' appears as an oxymoron, highlighting the incongruity between true democracy and fascist ideologies associated with authoritarianism, suppression of dissent, and the rejection of pluralistic values. This characterization underscores not only the absence of liberal values but also the deliberate promotion of the Brahmanical sociopolitical order aligned with fascist principles.

Modi's India: crony capitalism and the crooked political system

Crony capitalism is a politico-economic phenomenon characterized by the close relationships between business leaders and governments, resulting in preferential treatment, resource allocation, and regulatory advantages for well-connected individuals or corporations (Shleifer and Vishny 1994). This symbiotic relationship often leads to a lack of transparency, as the government's economic policy decisions are influenced by political connections rather than economic rationality or considerations of social justice (Djankov et al. 2002). Consequently, crony capitalism has negative impacts, such as resource misallocation, corruption, and nepotism (Leff 1964; Olson 2000). It can also affect democratic institutions, weakening the rule of law and eroding public trust (Keefer and Stasavage 2003). Moreover, crony capitalism deviates from the principles of classical capitalism, which are meant to promote a free and competitive market, foster innovation, and reward risk-takers. This process, akin to what Joseph Schumpeter (1942) called 'creative destruction', is assumed to drive progress and economic growth. In stark contrast to classical capitalism, crony capitalism obstructs competition, stifles innovation, and eliminates opportunities. Cronies engage in rent-seeking activities (aimed at obtaining economic benefits or 'rents' without creating new wealth or contributing any value to society) within the market, completely disregarding the foundational principles of capitalism (Aligica and Tarko 2014; Mukherjee 2019).

Although the idealized notion of capitalism emphasizes fair competition and merit, cronyism is intrinsic to the capitalist system, manifesting in various forms from laissez-faire to neoliberalism (Coyne and Hall 2019; Patnaik 2023). George Joseph Stigler (1971), a proponent of the free market, argues that regulatory agencies within capitalism can be susceptible to capture, a phenomenon he terms 'regulatory capture', by powerful corporations, highlighting an inherent vulnerability to cronyism. The Marxist critique, as articulated by Thomas Bottomore (1983), suggests it is not merely a regulatory aspect but a structural link between capitalism and the perpetuation of class-based inequalities. They further assert that the very nature of capitalism creates conditions conducive to crony capitalism. The Marxist critique of crony capitalism also posits that the democratic façade serves to veil the underlying continuity in policies that consistently favour the capitalist class (Miliband 1969; Wood 1999).

In the Indian context, the phenomenon of crony capitalism transcends political affiliations, affecting both the Congress and BJP regimes. During the Congress era, the Licence Raj, spanning from the 1950s to the early 1990s, served as a breeding ground for crony capitalism. This regulatory framework, characterized by extensive government control over various industries, created an environment where businesses with political connections could flourish. The Licence Raj's regulations, licences, and permits provided fertile ground for the establishment of crony relationships. Big businesses sought political affiliations to navigate this complex system, influencing policies to secure their interests within the framework of state control over industries

(Mazumdar 2008). In the early 1990s, the Congress adopted neoliberal economic policies dictated by the World Bank and the International Monitory Fund, aiming to dismantle the regulatory Licence Raj system and foster a more open and competitive economic environment (Sen 2017). The government asserted that these policies would promote growth and development and attract foreign investment by reducing regulations and encouraging private sector participation. As the government shifted away from a heavily regulated economy, new sectors and industries opened to private players. The rapid and transformative nature of economic liberalization created a dynamic environment where the rules of engagement were evolving. In this transitional phase, the absence of robust regulatory and oversight mechanisms made it easier for businesses to engage in crony practices (Khatri 2016). This also led to a significant increase in corruption, with several scandals coming to light (Chacko 2018; Hassan 2018; Sen 2017).

It is crucial to acknowledge that there is no evidence supporting the notion that neoliberal policies have weakened crony activities; instead, indications suggest that these policies have fuelled an increase in such practices (Reinsberg, Kentikelenis, and Stubbs 2021). In the Indian context, neither the implementation of free-market neoliberalism nor the change in the ruling-class regime has led to a decrease in the growth of crony capitalism; in fact, there is evidence of its escalation, particularly in Modi's India (Bardhan 2022; Khatri and Varma 2019). According to the Crony Capitalism Index, India was ranked tenth among countries with high levels of crony capitalism. From 2014 to 2023, the wealth generated by crony-capitalist sectors increased from 5 per cent to nearly 8 per cent of the country's gross domestic product (GDP) (*The Economist* 2023). Notably, this accumulation of wealth is concentrated in the hands of a specific group of individuals and families, transforming crony capitalism into a manifestation of oligarchic capitalism (E. Chatterjee 2023; Siddiqui 2023).

On 11 August 2014, Raghuram Rajan, the former Reserve Bank of India governor, during the Twentieth Lalit Doshi Memorial Lecture in Mumbai, made a significant statement:

> The crooked politician needs the businessman to provide the funds that allow him to supply patronage to the poor and fight elections. The corrupt businessman needs the crooked politician to get public resources and contracts cheaply. And the politician needs the votes of the poor and the underprivileged. Every constituency is tied to the other

in a cycle of dependence, which ensures that the status quo prevails. (Rajan 2014)

This symbiotic relationship is starkly exemplified by the association between the BJP and a select group of corporations, such as Adani Group and Ambani's Reliance Industries. For a detailed account of how the BJP promoted its crony partner, Adani, as exposed by the Hindenburg report, and its implications for the Indian economy, see Siddiqui (2023).

While aggressively promoting neoliberal economic policies that the Congress government initiated, Hindutva forces facilitated the growth of their crony partners to build corporate loyalty to the BJP and secure their financial support (Poruthiyil 2021; Sud 2022). This allegiance is crucial in securing vital resources for political campaigns and other activities. A notable tool in the landscape of political funding is the introduction of electoral bonds, a unique financial instrument rolled out by the BJP government in 2018. Electoral bonds allow donors to contribute to political parties while keeping their identities confidential from the public. While the anonymity feature aims to shield donors from potential backlash or intimidation, it has triggered debates surrounding transparency and accountability in political financing (D'Costa 2020; Khaitan 2020). Within six years, the State Bank of India sold USD 22.3 billion worth of bonds, with the BJP receiving the highest share of 57 per cent. However, on 15 February 2024, the Supreme Court struck down the electoral bonds scheme, declaring it 'unconstitutional' (BBC 2024).

The reciprocal relationship between the BJP and big corporations, particularly Adani and Ambani's Reliance and their media outlets, helps Hindutva forces to exert indirect control over public narratives and suppress dissent in alignment with their ideological agenda (Oxford Analytica 2022; T. Singh 2023). Simultaneously, allegations of crony capitalism within the banking sector, exemplified by cases like Vijay Mallya's departure and the Nirav Modi fraud, expose a compromised regulatory environment, raising concerns about the impartial functioning of economic governance (Swain 2020; Yadav 2022).

When Modi became the prime minister, the corporate world saw him as the 'neoliberalizer-in-chief for the world's largest democracy' (E. Chatterjee 2023, p. 123). The idea of a 'New India' propagated by the BJP primarily focuses on economic growth, privatization, and corporate expansion as the primary indicators of success (Ahmed 2022; Sundar 2022). This concept of Modi's 'New India' sidelines the importance of social welfare and equitable development, portraying India's path to becoming a global economic superpower as the ultimate goal. Such discourses serve to legitimize policies that prioritize the interests of corporations, the economic elite, and imperial forces while downplaying the concerns and needs of disadvantaged communities. Like classical fascists, Hindutva fascism lacks a specific economic policy but aims to strengthen and expand the capitalist system by adeptly navigating the apparent contradiction between neoliberalism and crony capitalism, all while proclaiming the so-called *swadeshi* (self-reliance) agenda (J. Ghosh 2020).

The BJP's policies for dispossession and violence

Since 2014, the BJP-implemented policies that underscore a narrative of 'oneness', potentially overshadowing the richness of diversity and plurality within the country. As mentioned earlier, while propagating their Brahmanical agenda, Hindutva forces have created an environment conducive to corporate growth. At the core of their economic strategy lies the 'Make in India' campaign, designed to propel domestic manufacturing and position India as a global economic hub. Despite the purported aim of stimulating economic growth, the implementation of policies associated with economic liberalization, deregulation, and corporate expansion has had significant implications for marginalized communities. A major concern has been the widespread dispossession of land by industrial and infrastructural projects (Chacko 2019; Chhachhi 2020; Gopalakrishnan 2006; Siddiqui 2017). Land acquisition has frequently resulted in the forced displacement of farmers, indigenous populations, and other vulnerable groups, with these communities often inadequately compensated and provided with insufficient rehabilitation and resettlement support (Mukerji 2017; S. R. Singh 2021; Sundar 2020).

For the realization of their vision of 'New India', the BJP government has implemented a range of social, political, and economic policies. An overview of these policies is presented in Table 8.1. These policies collectively underscore how the Modi government employs constitutional mechanisms to promote and legitimize neoliberal Hindutva politics of dispossession and violence.

The Modi government's economic policies, driven by a clear agenda to provide a secure politico-economic environment for corporations, have had diverse impacts on various sectors. For instance, the Pradhan Mantri Jan Dhan Yojana (PMJDY) of 2014 significantly influenced big businesses,

Table 8.1 Policies and legislation implemented by the Modi government to advance the interests of Hindutva and corporations

Category	Policy/Law	Year	Proclaimed objective	Shortcoming
Social policies	Pradhan Mantri Awas Yojana (PMAY)	2015	Housing for economically weaker sections	Unsustainable urban planning, funding constraints, and ambitious targets
	Pradhan Mantri Kaushal Vikas Yojana (PMKVY)	2015	Enhancement of employability skills	Poor alignment with the needs of the industrial sector and inefficient assessment of outcomes
	Ayushman Bharat Yojana	2018	Improves access to healthcare services	Inadequacy of coverage and effectiveness of the healthcare model
	One Nation, One Ration Card (ONORC)	2019	Enables access to subsidized food across states	Inefficient implementation strategies, exclusion errors, and inadequate technological infrastructure
	New Education Policy (NEP)	2020	Intended long-term impact on education: 'one nation, one student id, one curriculum, and one exam'	Can exacerbate existing inequalities and saffronize education by propagating the Sangh Parivar agenda; simultaneously aiming to align education with the interests of corporations
Economic reforms	Pradhan Mantri Jan Dhan Yojana (PMJDY)	2014	Increases banking accessibility	Dormant accounts, financial literacy, and the need for complementary policies, among other challenges

(Cont.)

Table 8.1 (*Cont.*)

Category	Policy/Law	Year	Proclaimed objective	Shortcoming
	Demonetization	2016	Intended to curb black money	Disastrous impact on the informal economy and created economic disruption for the general public
	Goods and services tax (GST)	2017	Streamlines tax structure: 'one nation, one tax'	Complexity, compliance challenges, and a negative impact on small businesses
	Labour code reforms	2019	Facilitates ease of doing business	Concerns about potential exploitation of labour, erosion of workers' rights, and lack of consultation with labour unions
	Atmanirbhar Bharat Rojgar Yojana	2020	Aims to boost job creation	Lack of a holistic approach and limited implementation
	Farm Laws	2020	Intended to liberalize agricultural trade	Laws made in favour of corporate interests and did not consider addressing farmers' concerns
Citizenship and identity	Citizenship Amendment Act (CAA)	2019	Amends criteria for Indian citizenship	Has become a tool to legalize discrimination against religious minorities; exclusionary nature challenges constitutional values
	Abrogation of Articles 370 and 35A (Jammu and Kashmir's status)	2019	Recreation of a new status for Jammu and Kashmir; creation of 'one nation, one constitution'	Concerns about democracy, human rights violations, and a lack of local consultation

(*Cont.*)

Table 8.1 *(Cont.)*

Category	Policy/Law	Year	Proclaimed objective	Shortcoming
	National Register of Citizens (NRC)	2021	Aims to identify Indian citizens	Accusations of discrimination, exclusion, and concerns about potential statelessness among marginalized communities
Legal and regulatory	Electricity (Amendment) Bill	2022	Aims to reform the power sector	Potential impact on consumers, privatization, and challenges in the power sector
	Personal Data Protection Bill	2023	Legislation to safeguard personal data	Potential infringement of privacy, possible misuse, and government surveillance
	Uniform Civil Code (UCC)	2023	Establishes standardized laws for all citizens, irrespective of religions	Can encroach upon religious freedoms and traditions, potentially imposing a homogenous Hindu identity
Security and surveillance	Unlawful Activities (Prevention) Amendment Bill	2019	Amendments to strengthen counter-terrorism measures	Concerns about misuse against activists, stifling dissent and impacting democratic freedoms

Source: Collated by the author.

particularly in banking and financial technology (fintech). Geared towards financial inclusion, the policy expanded the customer base for banks and financial technology companies, fostering innovation and growth within these industries. Demonetization in 2016, aimed at curbing black money and promoting a digital economy, presented mixed consequences for big businesses. While digital payment platforms and fintech companies thrived, traditional or small businesses faced disruptions due to cash shortages

(Chacko 2019; Kaul 2017). The goods and services tax (GST) introduced in 2017 aimed to streamline the tax structure, benefitting larger corporations but posing challenges for smaller enterprises and the informal sector in adapting to the new system (P. Singh 2023). Labour code reforms in 2019 aimed to enhance the ease of doing business, providing greater flexibility for corporations while enabling labour exploitation and erosion of workers' rights (Upadhyay 2021). The farm laws of 2020 were introduced to further liberalize agricultural trade and promote contract farming. These changes have the potential to enable a significant corporate influence over various stages of agriculture, ranging from seeding to grain trading (Baviskar and Levien 2021; Singh, Singh, and Dhanda 2021).

Similar to economic policies, the Modi government also introduced several controversial social policies aiming at constructing a hegemonic discourse of neoliberalism and Hindutva politics (Lall and Anand 2022). For example, the New Education Policy (NEP) of 2020 was intended to create a 'one nation, one curriculum, one exam' system. The hidden agenda of this policy is to create a uniform and standardized educational system across the country. This approach can undermine the diversity of India's cultural and educational landscape. India is a country with rich linguistic, cultural, and regional variations, and imposing a singular curriculum will undermine the unique needs and identities of different regions and communities. Moreover, the NEP strongly emphasizes cultivating the so-called traditional Indian values such as 'truth (*satya*), righteous conduct (*dharma*), peace (*shanti*), love (*prem*), and non-violence (*ahimsa*)'. However, it conspicuously remains silent on crucial issues such as equality and equity, women and transgender rights, caste discrimination, and secularism. This sectarian approach undermines the democratic essence of educational systems (Kidwai 2021). In addition, there are concerns about the privatization of education under the NEP. The policy encourages public–private partnerships in education, raising questions about accessibility, affordability, and the potential commercialization of the education sector. Increased privatization can exacerbate existing educational inequalities, creating a divide between well-funded private institutions and under-resourced public schools. Furthermore, the NEP facilitates the Hinduization of education by introducing Hindu mythology into Indian history and the marginalization of regional languages (A. Singh 2023).

In the domain of security laws, the Congress government initially enacted the Unlawful Activities Prevention Act (UAPA) in 1967. Subsequently, in 2004, it underwent significant amendments, solidifying its position as the primary counter-terrorism law by enhancing its provisions. The primary objective was to prevent 'unlawful' activities deemed as a threat to the nation. However, the Congress misused it to target activists challenging the legitimacy of oppressed ruling classes (Singh, Mishra, and Pandey 2022; A. Singh 2012). Following the Congress's footsteps, the BJP government further amended the UAPA in 2019 to make it even more draconian, often misusing it to stifle all forms of political dissent under the guise of national security (Nair 2020; Saxena 2021). Originally enacted to counter 'terrorism' and unlawful activities, the UAPA has been applied more expansively, prompting questions about its use as a mechanism to target political adversaries and quell civic dissent. In recent years, there has been a trend of an increasing number of UAPA cases (Suresh 2019). For instance, between 2015 and 2020, 5,924 cases were registered, leading to the arrest of 8,371 individuals under the UAPA. This suggests a growing reliance on this law to restrict activities perceived as threats by the government (People's Union for Civil Liberties [PUCL] 2022).

The UAPA has been employed against activists, public intellectuals, academics, artists, and journalists expressing dissent towards the government's policies. These individuals, detained and accused under the UAPA, have been labelled as 'urban Naxals' or 'anti-nationals'. The alarming concern is not only about the number of UAPA cases but also about the broad and ambiguous definitions within the law. The UAPA's vague language can be used to criminalize a wide range of activities, making it a powerful instrument in the hands of the government. The increased use of the UAPA and its potential for misuse raises fundamental questions about the subversion of legal frameworks for political ends, curtailing democratic principles and freedoms (PUCL 2022; Singh, Mishra, and Pandey 2022).

In response to the politics of dispossession and violence, various forms of resistance have emerged across India. Grassroots movements and activist networks have mobilized to resist the BJP's policies, employing strategies ranging from legal challenges to public protests. For instance, the Citizenship Amendment Act (CAA) sparked nationwide protests in 2019, as individuals and groups expressing concern about its potential exclusionary impact on religious minorities. This resistance, often led by civil society organizations, human rights activists, students, and affected communities, has played a crucial role in amplifying voices against perceived injustices and discriminatory practices (Ahmed 2020; Bhushan 2021). The National Register of Citizens (NRC) policy has encountered vehement opposition, particularly for its potential to render religious minorities stateless. Activists and advocacy groups have leveraged legal avenues and public awareness campaigns to challenge the policy's discriminatory aspects. Similarly, the Unlawful Activities (Prevention) Amendment Bill has faced legal and discursive resistance from various quarters, including legal experts and civil and human rights activists concerned about threats to civil liberties (Bhatia 2021; Varshney 2019).

The farmers' movement in India, which unfolded in response to the contentious farm laws introduced in 2020, has carved a historic chapter in the nation's people's struggle narrative. The protests, marked by massive demonstrations, tractor rallies, and an enduring sit-in at Delhi's borders, garnered widespread national and international attention. After months of negotiations and sustained protests, the Indian government, recognizing the intensity and persistence of the movement, took the unprecedented step of repealing the controversial farm laws in November 2021. This remarkable turnaround underscored the potency of grassroots movements in influencing governmental decisions and emphasized the role of public mobilization in shaping policy outcomes. The farmers' victory serves as a compelling testament to the resilience and collective power of marginalized communities in safeguarding their rights and challenging policies that threaten their well-being (Lerche 2021; Krishnamurthy 2021; Singh, Singh, and Dhanda 2021).

The Adivasis (indigenous communities) in the regions of Odisha, Bastar, and Jharkhand have been steadfastly resisting the twin challenges of displacement and militarization imposed on their territories. These communities, often residing in resource-rich areas, find themselves at the intersection of development projects and security concerns. The government's push for industrialization, mining, and infrastructure development frequently results in the displacement of Adivasi communities from their ancestral lands. This forced displacement not only disrupts their traditional ways of life but also poses a threat to their cultural identity and social cohesion (Das and Pattnaik 2022; Jairath 2021; Subramaniam and Rokde 2021).

Simultaneously, these regions often witness significant militarization, with the deployment of security forces to counter the armed revolutionary movement or perceived threats. The militarization exacerbates tensions, leading to human rights violations, displacement, and an atmosphere of fear and insecurity among the Adivasi populations. In response to these challenges, Adivasis have organized and mobilized to protect their land, livelihoods, and cultural heritage. They engage in peaceful protests, advocacy, and legal battles to resist the encroachment on their territories and assert their right to self-determination. These resistance movements reflect the Adivasis' determination to safeguard their way of life and challenge the impositions that threaten their existence. The dynamics of these resistance movements underscore the significance of civic engagement and collective action in defending democratic values and protecting the rights of the dispossessed (Kapoor 2022; Varshney 2019).

Conclusion

A critical examination of the Hindutva strategies employed by the BJP government exposes a deliberate political agenda aimed at reshaping India's sociopolitical landscape into a one-dimensional nation, suppressing the diversity of thoughts and expressions. The weaponization of nationalism emerges as a central strategy, using its influence to foster a sense of belonging among the populace. However, this belonging often comes at the expense of marginalizing dissent, promoting a singular Hindutva narrative. The BJP government strategically exploits nationalist sentiments to craft a dominant discourse that fortifies its Hindutva agenda, stigmatizing alternative perspectives as unpatriotic.

In conjunction with the weaponization of nationalism, the manipulation of seriality stands out as another crucial strategy. This manipulation involves the careful orchestration of events and narratives, contributing to the construction of a collective memory aligned with the ruling party's ideological goals. By controlling the narrative and selectively emphasizing historical events or cultural symbols, Hindutva forces seek to shape public consciousness and foster a shared identity within the Brahmanical Hindutva ideology. This approach not only solidifies a specific historical interpretation but also excludes alternative narratives challenging the dominant ideology.

The intertwining of crony capitalism with the Hindutva political system raises concerns, prompting scrutiny about the alignment of policies with the broader public interest. This problematic relationship invites questions about the extent to which political decisions are influenced by the interests of dominant corporations, potentially compromising fairness and equitable representation. In addition, the BJP government's policies designed for dispossession cast a shadow over marginalized communities, showcasing a governance model that prioritizes the interests of oppressive castes and classes at the expense of inclusivity, social justice, and human rights.

The essence of Hindutva lies in the preservation of Brahmanical domination and oppression, permeating various aspects of the cultural and social fabric of Hindu society. Even in the face of potential electoral defeat for the BJP, dismantling Hindutva fascism necessitates a profound cultural revolution, challenging and uprooting the domination of Brahmanical ideology by championing equity, inclusivity, and social justice, and rejecting hierarchical caste structures.

Fascism in India is not just a regime; it is a political, sociocultural, and economic process that operates at discursive as well as practical levels. It operates at the structural, institutional, interpersonal, and individual levels. However, Brahmanical Hindutva, functioning in symbiosis with corporations and operating as a form of fascist democracy, is not immune to resistance. It faces opposition from democratic, secular, and progressive forces emanating from diverse political orientations. The one-dimensional ideology propagated by Hindutva is fundamentally at odds with the rich tapestry of pluralism and diversity that characterizes India's history and collective experiences.

References

Acharya, A. (2020). 'From Secular to Sickular'. In *Religion and Politics in South Asia* (2nd ed.), edited by A. Riaz, pp. 101–123. New Delhi: Routledge.

Ahmad, A. (2022). *New Dimensions of Indian Historiography: Historical Facts and Hindutva Interpretation*. New Delhi: KK Publications.

Ahmed, H. (2020). 'Making Sense of India's Citizenship Amendment Act 2019: Process, Politics, Protests'. *IFRI: Institut Français des Relations Internationales. Asie. Visions*, No.114. https://www.ifri.org/en/publications/notes-de-lifri/asie-visions/making-sense-indias-citizenship-amendment-act-2019-process. Accessed 15 November 2023.

———. (2022). 'New India, Hindutva Constitutionalism, and Muslim Political Attitudes'. *Studies in Indian Politics* 10(1): 62–78.

Aligica, P. D., and V. Tarko (2014). 'Crony Capitalism: Rent Seeking, Institutions and Ideology'. *Kyklos* 67(2): 156–176.

Ambedkar, B. R. (1987). *Dr. Babasaheb Ambedkar: Writings and Speeches*, vol. 3. Bombay: Government of Maharashtra.

———. (2000). 'Hinduism, Thy Name Is Inequality!' *Communicalism Combat*. https://www.sabrang.com/cc/comold/may00/history.htm. Accessed 10 June 2022.

Anand, D. (2016). *Hindu Nationalism in India and the Politics of Fear.* New York: Springer.

Anand, K., and M. Lall (2022). 'The Debate between Secularism and Hindu Nationalism–How India's Textbooks Have Become the Government's Medium for Political Communication'. *India Review* 21(1): 77–107.

Anderson, E., and C. Jaffrelot (2018). 'Hindu Nationalism and the "Saffronisation of the Public Sphere": An Interview with Christophe Jaffrelot'. *Contemporary South Asia* 26(4): 468–482.

Arendt, H. (1964). *Eichmann in Jerusalem: A Report on the Banality of Evil.* New York: Viking Press.

———. (1973). *The Origins of Totalitarianism.* Boston: Houghton Mifflin Harcourt.

Austin, G. (1966). *The Indian Constitution: Cornerstone of a Nation.* Bombay: Oxford University Press.

———. (2013). *Working a Democratic Constitution: A History of the Indian Experience.* Bombay: Oxford University Press.

Balta, E., C. Rovira Kaltwasser, and Alper H. Yagci (2022). 'Populist Attitudes and Conspiratorial Thinking'. *Party Politics* 28(4): 625–637.

Banaji, S. (2018). 'Vigilante Publics: Orientalism, Modernity and Hindutva Fascism in India'. *Javnost: The Public* 25(4): 333–350.

Bardhan, P. (2022). 'Inequality and Capitalism in India'. *Studies in Indian Politics* 10(2): 176–184.

Basu, S., and S. Sen (2023). 'Silenced Voices: Unraveling India's Dissent Crisis through Historical and Contemporary Analysis of Free Speech and Suppression'. *Information and Communications Technology Law.* DOI: 10.1080/13600834.2023.2249780.

Baviskar, A., and M. Levien (2021). 'Farmers' Protests in India: Introduction to the JPS Forum'. *Journal of Peasant Studies* 48(7): 1341–1355.

Baxi, U. (1982). *The Crisis of the Indian Legal System.* New Delhi: Vikas.

BBC (2024). 'Electoral Bonds: India's Supreme Court Scraps Anonymous Election Funding.' 15 February. https://www.bbc.com/news/world-asia-india-68302442. Accessed 15 February 2024.

Bhatia, M. (2021). 'State Violence in India: From Border Killings to the National Register of Citizens and the Citizenship Amendment Act'. In *Stealing Time: Migration, Temporalities and State Violence*, pp. 171–196. Cham: Springer International Publishing.

Bhatty, K., and N. Sundar (2020). 'Sliding from Majoritarianism toward Fascism: Educating India under the Modi Regime'. *International Sociology* 35: 632–650.

Bhushan, B. (2021). 'Citizens, Infiltrators, and Others: The Nature of Protests against the Citizenship Amendment Act'. *South Atlantic Quarterly* 120(1): 201–208.

Bottomore, T. (1983). *A Dictionary of Marxist Thought*. Cambridge, MA: Harvard University Press.

———. (1991). *Classes in Modern Society*. London: Allen and Unwin.

Breuilly, J. (1993). *Nationalism and the State*. Chicago: University of Chicago Press.

Brubaker, R. (2017). 'Why Populism?' *Theory and Society* 46(5): 357–385.

Burak, B. (2022). 'Teaching Nation-Building and Nationalism: A Critical Perspective of Turkish Academia'. *Journal of Applied Learning and Teaching* 5(1): 89–98.

Chacko, P. (2018). 'The Right Turn in India: Authoritarianism, Populism and Neoliberalisation'. *Journal of Contemporary Asia* 48(4): 541–565.

———. (2019). 'Marketizing Hindutva: The State, Society, and Markets in Hindu Nationalism'. *Modern Asian Studies* 53(2): 377–410.

———. (2023). 'Disciplining India: Paternalism, Neo-liberalism and Hindutva Civilisationalism'. *International Affairs* 99(2): 551–565.

Chakrabarti, S., and S. Chakrabarti (2012). 'Sedition: A Comparative Analysis'. *NUJS Law Review* 5: 49–50.

Chatterjee, E. (2023). 'India's Oligarchic State Capitalism'. *Current History* 122(843): 123–130.

Chatterjee, P. (1997). *The Nation and Its Fragments: Colonial and Postcolonial Histories*. Princeton: Princeton University Press.

Chhachhi, A. 'Neoliberalism, Hindutva and Gender: Convergence and Contradictions in the Provision of Welfare'. *Feminist Dissent* 5 (2020): 50–93.

Coyne, C. J., and A. R. Hall (2019). 'Cronyism: Necessary for the Minimal, Protective State'. *Independent Review* 23(3): 399–410.

Dahl, R. A. (1971). *Polyarchy: Participation and Opposition*. New Haven: Yale University Press.

Das, M., and B. K. Pattnaik (2022). 'Understanding Anti-POSCO Movement in Odisha: Through the Politics of Development'. *Oriental Anthropologist* 22(1): 67–92.

D'Costa, O. (2020). 'Opacity, Democracy and Political Funding-An Overview of the Indian Electoral Bond System. System'. *International Journal of Law, Management, and Humanities* 3(4): 913–926.

de Estrada, K. S. (2023). 'What Is a Vishwaguru? Indian Civilisational Pedagogy as a Transformative Global Imperative'. *International Affairs* 99(2): 433–455.

de Souza, R. (2022). 'Hindutva and Ethnonationalism in the Indian American Diaspora'. *Oxford Research Encyclopedia of Communication*. https://oxfordre.com/communication/view/10.1093/acrefore/9780190228613.001.0001/acrefore-9780190228613-e-1254. Accessed 15 November 2023.

Diamond, L., and L. Morlino (2005). *Assessing the Quality of Democracy*. Baltimre: Johns Hopkins University Press.

Djankov, S., R. La Porta, F. Lopez-de-Silanes, and A. Shleifer (2002). 'The Regulation of Entry'. *Quarterly Journal of Economics* 117(1): 1–37.

Flåten, L. T. (2017). 'Spreading Hindutva through Education: Still a Priority for the BJP?' *India Review* 16(4): 377–400.

Frykenberg, R. E. (2008). 'Hindutva as a Political Religion: An Historical Perspective'. In *The Sacred in Twentieth-Century Politics*, pp. 178–220. London: Palgrave Macmillan.

Ganguly, S. (2002). 'The State of Human Rights in India'. *Political Science Quarterly* 117(1): 141–142.

Ghosh, J. (2020). 'Hindutva, Economic Neoliberalism and the Abuse of Economic Statistics in India'. *South Asia Multidisciplinary Academic Journal* 24: 1–7.

Ghosh, S. (2023). 'India and the Pandemic: Democratic Governance at Crossroads'. *International Journal of Asian Studies* 20(1): 217–236.

Gopalkrishnan, S. (2006). 'Defining, Constructing and Policing a "New India": Relationship between Neoliberalism and Hindutva'. *Economic and Political Weekly* (2006): 2803–2813.

———. (2023). 'New Education Policy 2020 in India: Future Rewinds to the Past'. *International Journal of Inclusive Education*: 1–18. DOI: https://doi.org/10.1080/13603116.2023.2215785.

Gray, S. (2020). 'History, the Hindu Right, and Subversion of Brahmanical-Hindu Political Thought'. In *The Oxford Handbook of Comparative Political Theory*, edited by Leigh K. Jenco, Murad Idris, and Megan C. Thomas, pp. 240–260. New York: Oxford University Press.

Griffin, R. (2013). *The Nature of Fascism*. New Delhi: Routledge.

Guha, R. (2007). *India After Gandhi: The History of the World's Largest Democracy*. New Delhi: HarperCollins.

Gundimeda, S. (2023). 'Debating Cow-Slaughter: The Making of Article 48 in the Constituent Assembly of India'. *India Review* 22(1): 1–27.

Hall, I. (2017). 'Narendra Modi and India's Normative Power'. *International Affairs* 93(1): 113–131.

Hansen, T. B., and S. Roy (ed.) (2022). 'What Is New about "New Hindutva"?' In *Saffron Republic: Hindu Nationalism and State Power in India.* Cambridge: Cambridge University Press.

Hassan, Z. (2018). 'Collapse of the Congress Party'. In *Rise of Saffron Power, Reflections on Indian Politics,* edited by M. Rehman. pp. 154–67. New York: Routledge.

Ilaiah, K. (2005). *Why I Am Not a Hindu: A Sudra Critique of Hindutva Philosophy, Culture and Political Economy.* Kolkata: Samya Books.

Jaffrelot, C. (2005). *The Sangh Parivar: A Reader.* New Delhi: Oxford University Press.

———. (2007). *Hindu Nationalism: A Reader.* Princeton: Princeton University Press.

———. (2011). 'The Invention of an Ethnic Nationalism'. In *Religion, Caste and Politics in India*, pp. 38–53. Delhi: Primus Books.

Jairath, V. (2021). 'Environment as Land: Understanding Anti-Displacement Politics in Jharkhand'. *Journal of Developing Societies* 37(2): 216–231.

Kadiwal, L. A., L. O. Singha, S. W. Kamble, and K. E. Dandare (2022). 'India and Me: Education for Critical Consciousness in India'. In *Education in Troubled Times: A Global Pluralist Response*, pp. 213–236. Newcastle-upon-Tyne: Cambridge Scholars Publishing.

Kapoor, D. (2022). 'Rural Dispossession and Resistance in Asia and Africa'. In *The Essential Guide to Critical Development Studies*, edited by Henry Veltmeyer and Paul Bowles, pp. 341–349. New Delhi: Routledge.

Kaul, N. (2017). 'Rise of the Political Right in India: Hindutva-Development Mix, Modi Myth, and Dualities'. *Journal of Labor and Society* 20(4): 523–548.

Keefer, P., and D. Stasavage (2003). 'The Limits of Delegation: Veto Players, Centralized Bargains, and the Survival of Democracies'. *American Political Science Review* 97(3): 387–396.

Khaitan, T. (2020). 'Killing a Constitution with a Thousand Cuts: Executive Aggrandizement and Party–State Fusion in India'. *Law and Ethics of Human Rights* 14(1): 49–95.

Khatri, N. (2016). 'Definitions of Cronyism, Corruption, and Crony Capitalism'. In *Crony Capitalism in India: Establishing Robust Counteractive Institutional Frameworks*, pp. 3–7. London: Palgrave Macmillan.

Khatri, N., and A. Varma (2019). 'Dynamics of Corruption and Cronyism in India'. In *Indian Business*, edited by P. Budhwar, A. Varma, and R. Kumar, 61–71. London: Routledge.

Kidwai, A. (2021). 'Towards Inequality'. *Postcolonial Studies* 24(1): 33–39.

Krishnamurthy, M. (2021). 'Agricultural Market Law, Regulation and Resistance: A Reflection on India's New "Farm Laws" and Farmers' Protests'. *Journal of Peasant Studies* 48(7): 1409–1418.

Kumbamu, A. (2020). 'Saffron Fascism: The Conflux of Hindutva Ultra-Nationalism, Neoliberal Extractivism, and the Rise of Authoritarian Populism in Modi's India'. In *The Global Rise of Authoritarianism in the 21st Century*, edited by Berch Berberoglu, 161–177. London: Routledge.

Lall, M., and K. Anand (2022). *Bridging Neoliberalism and Hindu Nationalism: The Role of Education in Bringing about Contemporary India*. Bristol, UK: Policy Press.

Leff, N. H. (1964). 'Economic Development through Bureaucratic Corruption'. *American Behavioral Scientist* 8(3): 8–14.

Lerche, J. (2021). 'The Farm Laws Struggle 2020–2021: Class–Caste Alliances and Bypassed Agrarian Transition in Neoliberal India'. *Journal of Peasant Studies* 48(7): 1380–1396.

Lijphart, A. (2012). *Patterns of Democracy: Government Forms and Performance in Thirty- Six Countries*. New Haven: Yale University Press.

Manchanda, R. (2002). 'Militarised Hindu Nationalism and the Mass Media: Shaping a Hindutva Public Discourse'. *South Asia: Journal of South Asian Studies* 25(3) (2002): 301–320.

Mannathukkaren, N., and D. MacEachern (2023). 'Constructing a Vishwaguru (World Teacher): Hindu Nationalism, Populism and the Domestic Consumption of Narendra Modi's Global Image'. *Third World Quarterly* 44(11): 2370–2390.

Mazumdar, S. (2008). 'Crony Capitalism and India: Before and After Liberalisation'. MPRA Paper No. 19627. http://mpra.ub.uni-muenchen.de/19627. Accessed 2 January 2024.

Mehta, D. S., and B. V. Kaye (2021). 'Media Censorship: Obscuring Autocracy and Hindutva-Ideology in Indian Governance'. *Communication, Culture and Critique* 14(3): 524–528.

Menon, N. (2005). *Recovering Subversion: Feminist Politics Beyond the Law*. Champagne: Universty of Illinios Press.

Miliband, R. (1974). *The State in Capitalist Society*. London: Quartet.

Mill, J. S. (1861). *Considerations on Representative Government*. London: Parker, Son & Bourn.

Mukerji, S. (2017). 'Land Acquisition in Contemporary India: The Growth Agenda, Legislation and Resistance'. *Indian Journal of Public Administration* 63(1): 85–103.

Mukherjee, C. (2019). 'On Crony Capitalism'. *Decision* 46: 35–39.

Nair, T. (2020). 'Weaponization of Sedition and the UAPA to Curb Free Speech in India'. *International Journal of Law, Management, and Humanities* 3(6): 1132–1137.

Neocleous, M. (2005). 'Gothic Fascism'. *Journal for Cultural Research* 9(2): 133–149.

Noorani, A. G. (2000). *The RSS and the BJP: A Division of Labour.* New Delhi: LeftWord Books.

Olson, M. (2000). *Power and Prosperity: Outgrowing Communist and Capitalist Dictatorships.* New York: Basic Books.

Oxford Analytica (2022). 'Concern over Media Freedom Will Grow in India'. *ExpertBriefings*. DOI: https://doi.org/10.1108/OXAN-DB272755.

Parveen, N. (2020). 'In the Name of Cow: Legal–Constitutional Discourse and the Contours of Contemporary Indian Politics'. *Studies in Indian Politics* 8(2): 214–229.

Patnaik, P. (2023). 'Is What We Have "Crony Capitalism?"' https://peoples democracy.in/2023/0709_pd/what-we-have-"crony-capitalism. Accessed 5 December 2023.

Payne, S. G. (1996). *A History of Fascism, 1914–1945.* Madison, WI: University of Wisconsin Press.

Paxton, R. O. (2004). *The Anatomy of Fascism.* New York: Knopf.

People's Union for Civil Liberties (PUCL) (2022). 'UAPA: Criminalizing Dissent and State Terror—Study of UAPA Abuse in India, 2009-2022'. New Delhi. https://pucl.org/wp-content/uploads/2023/05/PUCL-28.09.2022.pdf. Accessed 8 March 2023.

Poruthiyil, P. V. (2021). 'Big Business and Fascism: A Dangerous Collusion'. *Journal of Business Ethics* 168: 121–135.

Raja, D. (2022). 'Save the Constitution, Save the Nation'. *New Indian Express*, 30 August. https://www.newindianexpress.com/opinions/2022/aug/30/save-the-constitution-save-the-nation-2492820.html. Accessed 30 August 2022.

Ramachandran, S. (2020). 'Hindutva Violence in India'. *Counter Terrorist Trends and Analyses* 12(4): 15–20.

Rajan, R. (2014). 'Finance and Opportunity in India'. Twentieth Lalit Doshi Memorial Lecture. RBI Speech, 11 August. https://www.rbi.org.in/scripts/BS_SpeechesView.aspx?Id=908. Accessed 10 April 2023.

Rawls, J. (1993). *Political Liberalism*. Columbia: Columbia University Press.

Reddy, R. N. (2021). 'Of Holy Cows and Unholy Politics: Dalits, Annihilation and More- than-Human Urban Abolition Ecologies'. *International Journal of Urban and Regional Research* 45(4): 643–657.

Reinsberg, B., A. Kentikelenis, and T. Stubbs (2021) 'Creating Crony Capitalism: Neoliberal Globalisation and the Fueling of Corruption'. *Socio-Economic Review* 19(2): 607–634.

Roy, I. (2023). 'India's Fascist Democracy'. In *The Rise of the Radical Right in the Global South*, edited by R. Machado-Pinheiro and T. Maia-Vargas, pp. 36–57. London: Routledge.

Sartre, J. P. (2004). *Critique of Dialectical Reason*, vol. 1. Translated by Alan Sheridan-Smith. London: Verso.

Sato, H (2023). 'Sickular' and 'Povertarian': Politics and Economics of Hindu Supremacy, 1992–2022'. Discussion Paper 900, IDE (Institute of Developing Economies), Chiba, Japan.

Savarkar, V. D. (1989 [1923]). *Hindutva*. Bombay: Veer Savarkar Prakashan.

Saxena, S. (2021). 'Crushing Dissent Under the Veil of National Security: A Critical Analysis of the Provisions of the UAPA and the NSA'. *Indian Politics and Law* 6: 243–254.

Schumpeter, J. A. (1942). *Capitalism, Socialism and Democracy*. New York and London: Harper and Brothers (HarperCollins).

Sen, C. (2017). 'Curbing Crony Capitalism in India'. Working paper. https://azimpremjiuniversity.edu.in/SitePages/pdf/APU-Working-Paper-Series-5-curbing-crony-capitalism-in-India.pdf. Accessed 4 July 2019.

Shani, G. (2021). 'Towards a Hindu Rashtra: Hindutva, Religion, and Nationalism in India'. *Religion, State and Society* 49(3): 264–280.

Sharma, J. (2019). *Hindutva: Exploring the Idea of Hindu Nationalism*. New Delhi: Aleph Book Company.

Shleifer, A., and R. W. Vishny (1994). 'Politicians and Firms'. *Quarterly Journal of Economics* 109(4): 995–1025.

Siddiqui, K. (2017). 'Hindutva, Neoliberalism and the Reinventing of India'. *Journal of Economic and Social Thought* 4(2): 142–186.

———. (2023). 'From Rapid Growth to Cronyism: Explaining India's Economic Development'. *Asian Profile* 51(4): 313–328.

Singh, A. (2012). 'Criminalising Dissent: Consequences of UAPA'. *Economic and Political Weekly* 47(38): 14–18.

Singh, A. (2023). '"Decolonizing" the NCERT Social Science Textbooks: Hinduisation of History and Issues of Gender and Caste'. In *Great Transition in India: Issues and Debates*, edited by C. Kim, and M. Kim, pp. 33–55.

Singh, P. (2005). 'Hindu Bias in India's "Secular Constitution": Probing Flaws in the Instruments of Governance'. *Third World Quarterly* 26(6): 909–926.

——. (2023). 'The Economic Consequences of Authoritarian Neoliberalism in India'. *World Review of Political Economy* 14(2), pp. 263–292.

Singh, P., S. Mishra, and S. Pandey (2022). 'A Weapon to Stifle Dissent: Unlawful Activities (Prevention) Act, 1967'. *Journal of Positive School Psychology* 6(3): 9896–9902.

Singh, T. (2023). 'The Authoritarian Roots of India's Democracy'. *Journal of Democracy* 34(3): 133–143.

Singh, S. R. (2021). *Land Acquisition and Resource Development in Contemporary India*. Cambridge: Cambridge University Press.

Singh, T., P. Singh, and M. Dhanda (2021). 'Resisting a "Digital Green Revolution": Agri-logistics, India's New Farm Laws and the Regional Politics of Protest'. *Capitalism Nature Socialism* 32(2): 1–21.

Smith, A. D. (1991). *National Identity*. Reno: University of Nevada Press.

Stanley, J. (2020). *How Fascism Works: The Politics of Us and Them*. New Delhi: Penguin Random House.

Stigler, G. J. (2021). 'The Theory of Economic Regulation'. In *The Political Economy: Readings in the Politics and Economics of American Public Policy*, edited by T. Ferguson and J. Rogers, pp. 67–81. New Delhi: Routledge.

Subramaniam, M., and P. Rokde (2021). 'Silger Protest Taps into Wider Anger in Bastar over Security Camps Coming Up in the Name of Roads'. *Scroll.in*, 18 June. https://scroll.in/article/997617/silger-protest-taps-into-wider-anger-in-bastar-over-security-camps-coming-up-in-the-name-of-roads. Accessed 20 July 2021.

Suman, S., and R. K. Sahu (2023). 'Arguments for and against Implementation of Uniform Civil Code in India'. *Indian JL and Legal Research* 5(2). https://heinonline.org/HOL/LandingPage?handle=hein.journals/injlolw11&div=106&id=&page=. Accessed 23 February 2024.

Sundar, A. (2022). 'Modi's New India: Hatred, Dispossession, Desperation'. In *The Radical Right: Politics of Hate on the Margins of Global Capital*, pp. 64–92. Netherlands: Brill.

Sundar, N. (2004). 'Teaching to Hate: The RSS's Pedagogical Program'. *Economic and Political Weekly* 39(16): 1605–1612.

——. (2020). 'Bastar, Maoism and Salwa Judum'. In *The Maoist Movement in India*, pp. 235–248. New Delhi: Routledge India.

——. (2023). 'The Supreme Court in Modi's India'. *Journal of Right-Wing Studies* 1(1). DOI: https://doi.org/10.5070/RW3.1499.

Sud, N. (2022). 'The Actual Gujarat Model: Authoritarianism, Capitalism, Hindu Nationalism and Populism in the Time of Modi'. *Journal of Contemporary Asia* 52(1): 102–126.

Sur, E. (2018). 'Triple Talaq Bill in India: Muslim Women as Political Subjects or Victims?' *Space and Culture* 5(3): 5–12.

Suresh, M. (2019). 'The Slow Erosion of Fundamental Rights: How Romila Thapar v. Union of India Highlights What Is Wrong with the UAPA'. *Indian Law Review* 3(2): 212–223.

Swain, S. (2020). *The Great Indian Fraud: Serious Frauds Which Shook the Economy.* London: Bloomsbury Publishing.

Thapar, R. (2009). 'The History Debate and School Textbooks in India: A Personal Memoir'. *History Workshop Journal* 67(1): 87–98.

The Economist (2023). 'The 2023 Crony-Capitalism Index'. https://www.economist.com/international/2023/05/02/the-2023-crony-capitalism-index. Accessed 2 November 2023.

Udupa, S. (2018). 'Enterprise Hindutva and Social Media in Urban India'. *Contemporary South Asia* 26(4): 453–467.

Upadhyay, S. (2021). 'Organized Labor and the Politics of Right-Wing Hegemony in India'. Dissertation, Johns Hopkins University, Baltimore.

Varshney, A. (2019). 'Modi Consolidates Power: Electoral Vibrancy, Mounting Liberal Deficits'. *Journal of Democracy* 30(4): 63–77.

Visweswaran, K., M. Witzel, N. Manjrekar, D. Bhog, and U. Chakravarti (2009). 'The Hindutva View of History: Rewriting Textbooks in India and the United States'. *Georgetown Journal of International Affairs*: 101–112.

Wood, E. M. (1999). *The Origins of Capitalism*. New York: Monthly Review Press.

Yadav, H. (2022). 'An Analysis of Recent Corporate Frauds in India and USA and Their Nexus with Corporate Governance'. *International Journal of Law Management and Humanities* 5(1): 337–360.

Yilmaz, I., and R. M. A. Saleem (2023). 'Hindu Nationalism and Digital Surveillance in India'. In *Digital Authoritarianism and its Religious Legitimization: The Cases of Turkey, Indonesia, Malaysia, Pakistan, and India*, edited by I. Yilmaz, pp. 131–149. Singapore: Springer Nature.

Zakaria, F. (1997). 'The Rise of Illiberal Democracy'. *Foreign Affairs* 76(6): 21–43.

9

The Political Challenges Hindutva May Face in the Years to Come

Amit Shrivastava

With the rise of the Bharatiya Janata Party (BJP) to power in India in 2014, and over the following years, questions around the nature of this regime and its increasingly close links to large Indian corporates have drawn attention. That these links exist is beyond dispute. However, their specific nature and what they can tell us about the RSS (Rashtriya Swayamsevak Sangh)–BJP combine, the Sangh Parivar (the family of organizations led by the RSS, including the BJP), is less clear, as in what they might mean for its future trajectory and for the future trajectory of Indian politics.

This chapter, a preliminary exploration of these questions, is largely confined to specific aspects of this government's economic policies. In this context, it will argue that these links are embedded within a specific political trajectory and that this trajectory may lead to eventual possibilities that are neither easy to predict nor necessarily in line with intuitive expectations. Indeed, I will argue that, instead of the apparent stability and supposed strength of the corporate–BJP–state nexus that currently exists, the years to come are likely to see more challenges to this nexus than are usually expected—and a key reason for this is the dynamic produced by this nexus itself.

The historical relationship between the Sangh Parivar and Indian big capital

The relationship between Indian big business and the Sangh Parivar is not a recent one, but arguably such a relationship also did not characterize the RSS's history for most of its existence. It is important here to note that the RSS's claims of economic ideology have always been nebulous and were perhaps best articulated in Deendayal Upadhyaya's 'integral humanism' (Upadhyaya 1979), a broad, corporatist economic philosophy that superficially resembled the arguments of Italian fascism but lacked specificity or clear policies. In terms of action, the Jan Sangh (the BJP's predecessor) and the BJP itself in its early years supported policies such as protectionism and some forms of economic liberalism, and opposed social justice policies such as reservations—leading both to be widely known as the 'Brahmin Baniya party' (Hebbar 2023).

However, this position began to change in the 1980s, and especially in the 1990s. As Gopalakrishnan (2008) argues, the 1980s saw the rise of large mass movements by social sections, such as middle castes and middle peasants, and ethno-nationalist movements such as those in Kashmir, Punjab, and Assam, as the hegemony of Congress governance began to break down. At the same time, as repeated crises in the economic model of the Indian state led first to piecemeal regulatory liberalization in the 1980s and to more sweeping liberalization in the 1990s, Indian big capital also grew in power and came to see its interests as directly opposed to the 'particularist', 'populist', and 'vote bank' politics of the growing social movements. As neoliberalism became more deeply rooted in both India's big capitalists and in the state machinery over the 1990s, the resonances between its ideological tenets (such as the forcible breakup of collective social action, the privileging of the 'market' over state regulation and support, and the crushing of any threats to social dominance) and the right-wing ideology of the Sangh Parivar meant that the two sides began to draw closer to one another (Gopalakrishnan 2006). This also led the BJP and the RSS to alter their policy positions to more closely match those of big business. The growing alliance ultimately yielded the first BJP-led National Democratic Alliance (NDA) government of 1998–2004, which also witnessed the brutal Gujarat pogrom of 2002. The shock election defeat of 2004, however, shook up this alliance for some time and led to a level of confusion among both Indian capitalists and the more neoliberal elements of the state machinery that permitted a range of social and political experimentation in the first term of the United Progressive Alliance (UPA) government.

However, in the era of neoliberalism, India's largest businesses—like those of many other countries—have relied increasingly on rent-seeking and predatory resource expropriation to drive their profits. By 2010 or so, and in particular, as a result of the 2008 global financial crisis, the space for such activities was running into limitations, and the Congress-led government proved incapable of taking what were regarded as the necessary 'tough' measures to push the interests of big capital further. As a result, more and more elements of Indian business and their political and intellectual allies returned to supporting the BJP and the Sangh Parivar as their way forward (Gopalakrishnan 2013). This shift was particularly striking in the case of the mainstream media, which threw its weight behind anti-corruption protests targeting the Congress, presaging a role that it would later play much more strongly under the Modi government—a point I return to in the following sections and in the case of ostensibly 'liberal' intellectual figures such as Pratap Bhanu Mehta, Ashutosh Varshney, and Gurcharan Das, who helped legitimize the BJP's campaign among the English-speaking elite (Donthi 2019; Srivastava 2011). This then became the basis for a concerted, systematic campaign that channelled anger and discontent against the Congress-led government into support for the BJP—support that most likely would never have been possible without powerful backing from outside the confines of the Sangh Parivar itself.

When the BJP came to power in 2014 with the support of big capitalists and the elite, it was the culmination of a long, uneven trajectory that had begun in the late 1980s. The shift was driven by a desire for a regime that would impose 'stability' on a fractious Indian society and deliver what the most powerful sections of that society had long desired. Almost a decade later, the bet these forces placed on the BJP appears to have worked—at least at first glance.

The socio-economic project of the BJP regime

The post-2014 Indian socio-economic situation has been characterized by a number of broad tendencies. In this section, I outline the project that the BJP–RSS and their allies have attempted to push through in the decade they have been in power.

Consolidating the power of large corporates after 2014

The first apparent tendency is a rapidly growing level of concentration within the Indian economy. This has been discussed in detail in other chapters in this book, so here I offer only a summary, showing that this level of concentration has been accompanied by three corollary shifts.

The first is a change in regulations to favour the interests of large corporates, and specifically the interests of the companies that former Reserve Bank of India (RBI) deputy governor Viral Acharya (2023) refers to as the 'Big 5': the Reliance Industries (Mukesh Ambani), the Tata Group, the Aditya Birla Group, the Adani Group, and Bharti Telecom. Indeed, such changes are not only favourable to these companies but have a specific political impact as well—one that I return to in the section on attacks on economic rights.

The second is the shift in the character of the mass media, particularly the electronic media in the Hindi-speaking regions. This shift actually predates the BJP's rise to power but has been significantly accelerated after 2014. The industry has effectively collapsed, with employment in the media and publishing industry, according to the Centre for Monitoring the Indian Economy, falling from over a million people in September 2016 to 230,000 people by August 2021—a fall of over 78 per cent (Chakravarty 2021). The result has been a media without field reporting, dependent on government funds, and actively engaged in promoting hate, fake news, and the BJP's propaganda.

The third is the enormous quantity of corporate funds funnelled to political parties and, in particular, to the BJP. The primary route for this has been electoral bonds, which at the time of writing have just been struck down as unconstitutional by the Supreme Court (Das 2024). Between 2017 and 2022, electoral bonds became the foremost form of party donations in India, and the BJP received three times more donations through this route than all other national parties combined (Association for Democratic Reforms 2023). Direct corporate donations, usually routed through 'electoral trusts', have continued through this route as well, with the BJP receiving 84 per cent of all donations in the same period (ibid.). In financial terms, the BJP is now unimaginably wealthier than all other political parties in India—a 2021 analysis of expenditure by the seven national parties and eleven large regional parties showed that between 2015 and 2020, the BJP spent more than all the other parties combined on elections (Jacob and Doshi 2021). A similar deployment of financial resources by the BJP has attempted to ensure dominance on social media, particularly Facebook and WhatsApp (Menn and Shih 2023).

These shifts have ensured an unprecedented (though not total) dominance for the BJP and its corporate allies over public discourse, particularly in the Hindi-speaking parts of the country. The stark nature of the nexus emerged as the Adani Group came under international scrutiny, following the Hindenburg Research report in January 2023, with BJP leaders, troll armies, and friendly media houses launching a propaganda campaign claiming that criticism of Adani was rooted in 'anti-India' forces (K. Mehrotra 2023). The backlash was not limited to propaganda, with credible allegations that a key reporter investigating Adani had his phone hacked by the notorious Pegasus spyware (which is only provided to government agencies) less than 24 hours after he emailed a questionnaire to the company (Shih and Menn 2023).

The shift against the informal sector

While it can be argued that this consolidation only differed in degree from tendencies already present in governments that ruled India after 1991, the Modi government has undertaken another shift which appears to be *qualitatively* different from those of previous regimes. This is a series of government policies that have directly attacked India's informal sector, which still constitutes the largest part of India's economy, employs most Indians, and is constituted of middle and small enterprises as well as a large pool of 'self-employed' people, often engaged in disguised wage work.

This attack is not merely an incidental or contingent phenomenon. It appears to be central to the functioning of this government. Indeed, all three of this government's most sweeping economic policies—demonetization, the implementation of a nationwide goods and services tax (GST), and the response to the pandemic—featured what at best can be described as a breathtaking indifference to the interests of informal sector enterprises and, at worst, as a deliberate attempt to destroy their economic security and growth prospects. I will consider each of these policies in more detail.

On 8 November 2016, the government demonetized INR 500 and 1,000 notes without prior warning. The impact of this move has never truly been measured, precisely because it impacted the informal sector, which transacted (and continues to transact) primarily in cash. Agricultural trade essentially collapsed in the immediate aftermath of the move (Aggrawal and Narayanan 2016). Three months later, 73 per cent of India's manufacturers said they had not been able to undertake any new hires (Chakraborty 2017). RBI data indicated that all companies with less than INR 10 billion in sales revenue suffered in the quarter following demonetization, and the hardest hit were those with revenues of INR 250 million to INR 500 million, whose sales collapsed by more than half compared to the previous year (M. Jain 2017). By its very nature, demonetization also had distributional consequences, as both informal sector businesses and affected oppressed groups such as workers, women, and small farmers had to rush to moneylenders and formal sector enterprises for funds, resulting in a net transfer of resources from these groups to the formal sector (Gopalakrishnan 2016). The long-term impacts of demonetization are still being felt and are more than likely to be a major contributor to the growth of the current economic distress (see the discussion on economic distress).

The second policy shift was the introduction of a national GST in 2017. The new GST deprived state governments of their taxation powers and also involved a much more complex compliance regime, requiring additional documentation and formalization of transactions that had earlier occurred in cash. This once again had a disproportionate impact on the informal sector which suddenly had to invest in technology, accountants, and paperwork in a manner that only a few could afford (Chandran 2017). A year later, a Reuters report speculated that implementing the GST may have cost 'hundreds of thousands of jobs' (Reuters 2018). Once again, what remains striking about this policy—which at least had been debated in the public domain, unlike demonetization—was the sheer indifference to its impact on the informal sector.

Moreover, the GST has been part of an overall shift in taxation that has decreased the burden on large capitalists and increased the burden on other sections of society, including the informal sector. In 2019, corporate tax rates were slashed from 30 per cent to 22 per cent (*New Indian Express* 2022). By 2023, corporate tax collections had dropped below personal income tax in terms of total revenue (*The Wire* 2024). An analysis of tax data has also shown that the lower 50 per cent of the population—almost all of whom are likely employed in the informal sector—provides a disproportionate share of GST revenue (Sebastian 2023).

This indifference to the informal sector reached its most stark form during the sudden, severe lockdown imposed in 2020 in response to the COVID-19 pandemic. The policy response to the massive distress created by the lockdown bears examining in detail, because it reveals the contradictions *within* the Modi government's approach to business perhaps more starkly than any previous crisis had. With the imposition of the lockdown in 2020, the single biggest demand from the Indian capital was for increased spending in the form of a meaningful stimulus. This time, moreover, the demand came from *across* big, medium, and small businesses, from both formal and informal sectors. In May, even traditionally cautious bodies like the Federation of Indian Chambers of Commerce and Industry (FICCI) were critical of the government's refusal to spend (Chowdhury 2020). Over the following months, such criticisms were echoed by both the international financial press and international rating agencies (Kazmin 2020; Press Trust of India 2020). As the months passed, even investment banks like JP Morgan began declaring that 'what India needs right now is income support' (Choudhury 2020). By December, these voices had become uncharacteristically radical in their diagnoses: T. N. Ninan (2020), a senior financial columnist, called for 'reining in corporate power'; JP Morgan's chief India economist wrote that 'the distribution of incomes across capital and labour risks becoming very skewed in favour of capital ... this portends ominously for future demand' (Chinoy 2020); and Bloomberg columnist Andy Mukherjee (2020), in a now famous (or infamous) essay on how he was 'losing hope in India', talked of the 'concentration of economic power' and referred to the government's minimal stimulus as 'callous', citing India's 'structural demand deficit' as a fundamental problem.

Despite all this sound and fury, the government did not spend. In fact, loud announcements notwithstanding, total expenditure in 2020 was likely *less* than in previous years (Alavi 2020). Even subsidies on cooking gas were halted, and one particularly callous cut hit the health budget the next year (C. Sharma 2021; Waghmare 2021). The 'giant' COVID-19 stimulus package turned out to have not involved much actual spending (Najmi 2021). The government defended its position by claiming that it did not want an 'unsustainable' rise in the fiscal deficit (*Indian Express* 2021). This claim was deeply puzzling for two reasons. First, the agencies that would have seen the fiscal deficit as a negative signal—international rating agencies and finance capitalists—were themselves calling for increased spending. Second, the government itself *deliberately modified* its accounting methods to show a *higher* deficit for the first pandemic year (even though, as said, actual spending was lower) and the finance minister declared that this was evidence of the government's desire to spend (Press Trust of India 2021).

Thus, the government provided little stimulus but invested a certain amount of rhetoric in *acting* like it had done so. Instead of spending, the central government and BJP-ruled state governments brought in a new set of 'big bang reforms' that they claimed would address the economic devastation caused by the pandemic. These pandemic-era 'reforms' had a direct political message, but they also, as economic policy, addressed areas that once again were of specific focus for the Big 5. I return to these policies in the next section.

By its very nature, the informal sector is hard to measure at any time, and in India's case, this problem is exacerbated by the fact that data for the formal sector are often taken as a proxy for the state of the informal sector (A. Kumar 2022). However, when policies are increasing the divergence in the trajectories of these two sectors, the natural result is that data become less and less accurate. The actual impact of all of these policy steps is therefore more likely reflected in inequality and distress, which I discuss below.

From a political perspective, all these events tell us something significant about this government's character. Since it came to power, it has appeared to simply not *care* about pressure from the informal sector, despite its political importance.

This is even more striking when we consider the slew of policy changes that have been implemented in favour of big capital, as discussed elsewhere in this chapter. While the Modi government has made some measures that appear to support informal sector enterprises—such as the Prime Minister Mudra Loan Scheme for small enterprises or the PM SVANidhi (Prime Minister Street Vendor's AtmaNirbhar Nidhi) loan scheme for street vendors—these measures are presented in the government and the BJP's narrative not as support for enterprises or employment generation, but as individualistic welfare schemes, part of the 'new welfarism' that I discuss in the next section.

The approach to the informal sector seems unlikely to be an ideological imperative since the RSS has famously romanticized and idealized small business (Jaffrelot 1998). Moreover, if loyalty to big capital was an ideological imperative, one would then have to explain why, during the pandemic, the government did not appear to care about the pressure even from *large* capitalists that are not part of the handful of top corporations whose interests it seeks to serve. Instead, this approach seems to be the outcome of the hyper-centralization of decision-making and the overwhelming influence of the Big 5 corporates, a point that I return to in the conclusion.

Economic distress, the 'new welfarism', and the attack on economic rights

Data on poverty and economic distress have been becoming increasingly scarce in India, as the government has undermined the statistical system of the country and, most importantly, failed to carry out the decennial census in 2021—the first such failure since it was instituted in the late nineteenth century (Bhattacharya 2023). Moreover, data have been distorted to make claims about poverty reduction based on flimsy or obviously incorrect assumptions (S. Mehrotra 2024).

Since 2016, there have been various indicators that large sections of the Indian population are facing not merely stagnation but a decline in living standards. In 2019, a leaked statistical report based on the 2017–2018 sample survey showed that, for the first time in four decades, monthly per capita consumption expenditure had fallen. The government promptly suppressed the report (Jha 2019). Other data show a sharp rise in unemployment between 2011–2012 and 2018–2019 (Centre for Policy Research 2023), and 2021 data show employment in manufacturing has halved (Bhardwaj 2021). A 2021 private survey of consumer expenditure said that between 2016 and 2021, the incomes of the three lower quintiles of the Indian population had all fallen, and those of the poorest quintile had fallen by over 50 per cent (Mohan 2024). In January 2023, this pattern was confirmed when Oxfam India released a report stating that the top 1 per cent of the population now owned 40.5 per cent of the total wealth in the country, while the bottom 50 per cent of the population owned 3 per cent, and that the number of Indians facing hunger had increased from 190 million to 350 million (Sebastian 2023). It also noted that between the beginning of the pandemic and November 2022, the wealth of Indian billionaires increased by 122 per cent.

Given all this, the BJP government's response and approach to India's working and producing classes is instructive. This response has largely unfolded around two axes: what has been called the 'new welfarism' and an attack on what I have loosely called 'economic rights', by which I mean legal rights that are directly related to livelihoods and production. On both axes, the regime has begun to face its most entrenched challenges.

The term 'new welfarism' has become popular in policy circles to refer to an approach where the state's welfare functions are conceived of in a manner that de-emphasizes 'intangible' gains such as better health and education, in favour of 'tangible' gains such as cooking gas connections, loans for housing, and straightforward cash to farmers, Adivasis, and other social groups (Anand and Dimble 2020). Contrary to some common perceptions, this is not as 'new' as it looks—such approaches were pioneered by the Janata Dal (United) (JD[U]) government in Bihar, the Bharat Rashtra Samithi (BRS) in

Telangana, and the BJP government in Chhattisgarh, and drew upon older experiments by the Dravidian parties in Tamil Nadu.

New welfarist approaches have certain key shared features made possible by this shift in favour of commodity provision. The first is an emphasis on technocratic delivery mechanisms. Prior welfare approaches often routed welfare benefits through local governments, and even when this was not done, line department officials at the lower level had considerable discretionary and implementation powers. This is often associated with corruption and partisanship, but by their very nature, such structures also provided a key space for local political leaders and for local popular mobilization (see the subsection 'Administrative centralizsation as an exigency'). In 'new welfarist' approaches, however, welfare delivery has been centralized into the hands of the bureaucracy and, in particular, digitized through linkages with Aadhaar and other databases.

This in turn makes the second key shared feature possible, namely the personalization of benefit delivery—the items provided are associated with the name of the leader who provided them, to the extent that the prime minister's photo is now plastered on practically every welfare scheme, even those in which state governments are providing a larger share of the funds. Indeed, taking advantage of the digitization of welfare schemes and the lack of data privacy regulations, both the BJP and state-level ruling parties have begun to direct their paid workers and cadre to use lists of beneficiaries of such schemes to persuade them that they received their benefits because of the prime minister or chief minister (*The Hindu* 2019).

Such welfare approaches seem to 'work' well in electoral terms, in large part because they constitute the formalization of a much older phenomenon in Indian politics—the patron–client relationship between politicians and their supporters, in which politicians offer access to state resources to individuals or families in exchange for support (Chandra 2017). While it is important not to imagine that voters *only* vote on the basis of such transactional claims, they do play an important part in political mobilization. The BJP itself is fond of attributing its success to welfare beneficiaries (*labharthis*), to the extent that the prime minister infamously stated in a speech that those who 'have eaten Modi's *namak* [salt] will not betray him' (Shah 2022).

This form of welfarism also harmonizes with a fundamental tenet of the Sangh Parivar's mode of organizing, which relies on offering oppressed groups such as Dalits, women, and workers a de facto bargain: we will offer you material benefits, but only if you give up your collective identity and collective mobilization against social exploitation (Gopalakrishnan 2018). Welfare benefits here are not offered as a matter of right, of course, or even as a matter of welfare, but as a dole from above.

It is the second half of this bargain that has truly distinguished Modi's government. It becomes evident if we closely examine one of its most discussed features, namely the consistent attack it has mounted on regulations for big business. The first and most consistent of these attacks, mirroring the interests of the Big 5, has been against environmental, forest, and land regulations. The 2013 Land Acquisition Act, laws for forest conservation and environmental clearances, the 2006 Forest Rights Act, and other such laws have all been undermined, amended, or abolished. During the pandemic, the 'reforms' that were passed—offered as proof of the Modi government's commitment to business—followed a similar pattern. These 'reforms' attempted to dismantle India's system of agricultural regulation through the farm laws (Narayanan 2021), replace more than forty existing labour laws with four new 'labour codes' that weakened worker protections (Rajalakshmi 2020), and accelerate the privatization of the country's mining sector while reducing penalties for violations (Aggarwal 2021).

Policy changes of this type are too numerous to name, and a full discussion of their implications is beyond the scope of this chapter. It would, however, be an error to see these changes only as a favour to big business. They had an additional political characteristic—they specifically targeted institutions and legal regimes that provided space for people to collectively organize.

We see this dynamic in action clearly in the forest law. The Forest Rights Act (FRA) of 2006 was passed after a prolonged national struggle for the rights of forest-dwelling communities, particularly Adivasis (often referred to as tribals). This law not only provided for rights to forest-dwelling communities, but it also enabled democratic control of forest management, by empowering *gram sabhas* (village assemblies) to protect all forests and to manage and use 'community forest resources' (Gopalakrishnan 2017). A consequence is that the consent of the *gram sabhas* of affected communities is required before forest land can be 'diverted' (transferred) for use for infrastructure projects, extractive industries, and other such activities. The country's forest bureaucracy has consistently sought to undermine this law and in particular this provision, and prior to 2014, the requirement for the *gram sabha* consent was honoured essentially in the breach (Choudhury and Aga 2020). The BJP government, however, has taken this practice a step further. First, it has turned the environment ministry, which is the home of the Indian Forest Service, into a co-implementor of the law, when the law had consciously sought to reserve this function for the tribal welfare ministry in order to prevent sabotage by forest officials (Kukreti 2020). This has effectively stalled the implementation of the law. Second, after first amending the rules under the Forest Conservation Act, 1980, which govern the use of forest land, in 2023 the government amended the Act itself in such a fashion as to exempt broad swathes of forest land from the need for any kind of permission prior to diversion to other uses (Pardikar 2023). While the letter of the FRA continues to require *gram sabha* consent for such diversion, this new Forest Conservation Act eliminates the administrative machinery that was supposed to ensure that the law had been followed—an attempt to render the requirement for consent irrelevant in practice (Saldanha 2023; Saxena 2024).

In short, without directly attacking the rights of Adivasis and other forest dwellers, the government has marginalized or eliminated the institutional spaces that made it possible for people to seek or enforce their rights. We see the same pattern in the manner in which the new labour codes effectively render strikes illegal by making indefinite conciliation efforts mandatory before any strike (Venkataraman 2020); the attempt, through the farm laws, to eliminate the *mandi*s (market yards) that provide a space where farmers can seek and demand public procurement of their produce (Kakvi 2020); and the attempt to abolish the requirement for consent prior to land acquisition that has been provided for in the Land Acquisition, Resettlement and Rehabilitation Act of 2013 (Balachandran and Sharma 2015). In each case, the rights of the affected people are left intact on paper, but the law is sought to be modified in such a manner as to make it difficult or impossible for them to exercise those rights through collective action.

This anti-democratic approach was also made clearer by the *manner* in which most of these policies were passed. Almost all of them were pushed through using ordinances ('emergency' legislation), government orders, or hasty legislation without discussion. The intention appears to be to avoid debate on these laws and to implement them either stealthily or with a 'shock and awe' approach. Accompanied by the general repression of dissent, along with extrajudicial attacks such as 'bulldozer justice' and mob violence, the message appears to be clear: abandon notions of rights, organizing, protest and accept the welfare largess of the state—the RSS's central tenet of social policy, in short.

From all of this discussion thus far, it might appear to be working out very well. But, in fact, it is not working that well, and it is here that the cracks begin to show. In the remainder of this chapter, I explore these cracks and what they might mean.

Resistance, opposition and political trajectories

The political project of the BJP regime faces multiple challenges, most of which are not immediately apparent given the dominance of the corporate–government nexus over much public discourse in India.

The first challenge: incoherence and the scattershot approach

From a bird's eye view, which is what most of us get, the regime appears to be methodically and systematically proceeding with its objectives. Two of the three key political objectives of the Sangh Parivar as stated in the late 1990s—the Ram Temple in Ayodhya, the abrogation of Kashmir's constitutional autonomy, and the Uniform Civil Code (UCC)—appear to be through. The massive shifts in India's economy described are also underway. As the slogan goes, 'Modi hain to mumkin hai' (With Modi, anything is possible).

This is undoubtedly what the supporters of the BJP and the RSS want us to believe. But in most cases, upon closer examination of any particular domain, what emerges does not appear systematic and thorough at all. What we see instead, as I discussed in 2021, is remarkable incoherence (A. Shrivastava 2021):

- As noted previously, an initial move is made in haste and bypassing as many institutions or procedures as possible, such as through an ordinance, a decree by the central government using existing broad powers, or rushed legislation.
- This move generates chaos, opposition, or both.
- Organized opposition, if it exists, is demonized (by the media and social media allies of the regime), attacked with violence (as in the Delhi pogrom of 2020), and repressed by state force. More generalized chaos is sought to be portrayed as 'growing pains' or mistakes from honest efforts.

- Often either the repression or the policy moves themselves *fail*, and the government or the party steps back, and then it either re-attempts the whole cycle sometime later or attempts to sneak through a partial version with a less direct route.

This pattern is apparent in major policy moves such as demonetization, COVID-19 vaccines, the National Register of Citizens (NRC), or the farm laws; in smaller moves such as the new Common University Entrance Test (CUET) for university admissions; in new criminal provisions for hit and run cases; and even in non-policy areas such as attempts to set up a 'new normal' for mob violence in states (A. Shrivastava 2023).

In short, for many of its political steps, the BJP government's approach seems to be more a scattershot effort to 'throw things at the wall and see what sticks' than make a systematic plan. The results are particularly striking when it comes to many of the policies noted at the end of the previous section. The 2015 land acquisition amendment, for instance, had to be eventually withdrawn in the first major political defeat the Modi government experienced (though it was then implemented in several states through a backdoor legislative strategy) (S. Shrivastava 2015). Four years after they were rammed through during the pandemic, the four labour codes have still not been brought into force. The farm laws were greeted with what has been described as the 'world's largest protests' and eventually had to be withdrawn. For a regime that has at its disposal the entire machinery of the state as well as of the country's largest corporates, such a serial display of policy incompetence requires explanation.

On one level the explanation is simple: the ideological priorities of both the Sangh Parivar and its corporate allies are, in fact, neither as clear nor as comprehensive as they claim to be. As discussed in the first section, for the corporate sector, since the late UPA period, policy goals have been largely limited to trying to eliminate obstacles to rent-seeking and profiteering (Gopalakrishnan 2013). The Sangh Parivar faces an even more serious problem. Drawing on concepts that have a striking resemblance to European fascism, the RSS's ideological project envisions not only total social domination but a society that would be free of *all* conflict, with existing conflicts being attributed to either 'backwardness' (which requires education) or 'outsiders' (who need to be crushed). But this is a fantasy. As a result, the ideology does not equip its followers with the tools for anticipating, managing, or understanding conflict (Gopalakrishnan 2017). This proves to be a particularly severe weakness when implementing policies that face resistance.

It might be argued that, in any case, the government seems to eventually get at least part of what it sought, and it is rare for it to completely capitulate (as it did in the case of the farm laws). Many policies, such as the labour laws and the NRC, could be brought into action just by an order at any time. So is this truly a weakness in the political project or just a speed bump on the way to success?

As I argue in this chapter, on the contrary, every round of such a cycle brings significant political costs—and these costs are likely to rise over time. It is in this space that the BJP government has faced its most significant setbacks, which may eventually be the source of more serious defeats.

Administrative centralization as an exigency

A striking feature of this government has been the manner in which it has centralized power. At first glance, it appears hardly surprising, since the ideology of the RSS is inherently autocratic, and in this sense it will obviously seek to limit democratic contestation and accrue more power. However, it is important to note that the RSS's model of autocracy had its own distinct features.

Scholars of the saffron right have noted that there is a significant distinction between the RSS's understanding of the role of the Indian state and the approach of classical European fascist movements (Vanaik 2001). The stated ideology of classical European fascism privileged the role of the state as the force to remake society. As Mussolini (1932) put it in *The Doctrine of Fascism*, 'The State, as conceived and realized by Fascism, is a spiritual and ethical entity for securing the political, juridical, and economic organization of the nation, an organization which in its origin and growth is a manifestation of the spirit.' Nazism then elevated the 'Fuehrerprinzip' (or 'leader principle') as the embodiment and voice of this spirit, making it the centre of both the state and the overall mission of the fascist political project (King and King 2014).

The RSS, in contrast, envisions *its organization* as the future of Hindu (and by extension Indian) society as a whole (Gopalakrishnan 2017). One of the most abiding features of this organization is its strong focus on collective action and hierarchical discipline, in which individuals and individual leaders are supposed to subsume themselves into a collective identity (Jaffrelot

1998). Autocratic power is to be exerted by, on behalf of and through the organization, not by individual leaders.

But what we see under the BJP government is not quite this form of autocracy. Instead, it is a more 'normal' form of strongman centralization, where all decisions are centralized not in the RSS as an organization, or even in its leadership, but in the prime minister and his coterie. Every step from appointments to policies requires the approval of either the prime minister's office or the home minister, Amit Shah, at a level that has occasioned comment from both scholars and policy commentators (for instance, Echeverri-Gent, Sinha, and Wyatt 2021).

At times, this centralization reaches levels that are almost comical. For instance, in 2019 the government decided to abrogate the constitutional autonomy of Jammu and Kashmir, a stated goal of the Sangh Parivar ever since the state joined the Indian union in 1948. For such a crucial objective, held for so long by the entire organization, one would expect that every person in any significant post would be a trained RSS cadre. Instead, the leadership felt so unable to trust their own RSS comrades that they appointed Satyapal Malik, a socialist leader with a long history of party-jumping and no relationship to the RSS, as the governor of Kashmir at this crucial time. Fast forward some years and Malik is now one of the regime's most vocal critics.

Such hyper-centralization has political costs. At the most basic level, it weakens the Sangh Parivar and the BJP's own organization. Centralization of decision-making and particularly the penchant for sudden, closed-door policy decisions render other levels of leadership largely irrelevant and make it very difficult for them to mobilize either popular support or financial resources. Further, organizational structures are marginalized within the party just as the institutions of the state have been marginalized. Today, most of the saffron brigade's visible faces—such as the television anchor Arnab Goswami; Kapil Mishra, a key leader who openly engaged in hate speech and incitement during the 2020 Delhi pogrom; Uttar Pradesh's chief minister Ajay Bisht (Yogi Adityanath); and Assam's chief minister Himanta Biswa Sarma—have no connection with the RSS and are best described as self-aggrandizing bigots seeking to build personal empires. The BJP has made it a point to sideline its old prominent faces and install new faces in almost all states where it rules, including after the recent state election victories in 2023. Indeed, in a widely shared 2022 article, political scientist James Manor (2022, p. 1) described this process as 'serious degeneration that casts doubt on [the

BJP's] long term prospects', going so far as to term it the 'destruction of the BJP's organisation'.

Further, this centralization appears to narrow the circle of those the government is willing to listen to as well. In the section on the informal sector, I discussed the puzzling policy actions undertaken during the pandemic. As noted, the most plausible explanation for the government's obstinacy in responding to the demands of other businesses appears to be that those in power simply did not care what other voices, even of large capitalists, had to say—which, in turn, is unlikely in any ruling party with even a modicum of broad-based decision-making. The result is that there appear to be glimmers of hesitation among some of these capitalists as well. The business columnist quoted previously, Ninan (2023), notes in a recent article that his interlocutors in the business sector, while they 'like' this government for its 'pro-business' policies, also secretly desire that its parliamentary majority should be reduced in order to curb 'high handed' actions, given that 'stories are told of how companies being eyed by favoured businessmen find their owners getting the attention of the taxman'.

Why is such centralization underway? The government appears largely to fear the consequences of broader decision-making. Sircar (2022) argues that this centralization is driven largely by a desire to keep party leaders in line in a polity with weak affiliations. This is an ironic conclusion, considering the RSS makes much of its discipline and internal cohesion. Given the problems around conflict noted earlier, it is also probably rooted in a desire to keep party leaders, the public, and the state machinery all under control in a regime where policies seem to go wrong all the time.

Weaknesses in the new welfarism

The BJP's use of welfare schemes—part of a cocktail that the election consultant Prashant Kishor has summed up as 'nationalism, Hindutva, and "labharthi"' or beneficiaries of various welfare schemes (S. Jain 2022)—also has significant shortcomings.

First, in a point that most commentators fail to note, many schemes simply are not working very well. While they are reaching many people, they are also failing to reach many others, due to implementation failures, funding shortfalls, or just bad design. For instance, the flagship health insurance scheme, Ayushman Bharat, failed to reach many people or help with COVID-19. Five years after its initiation, it has reached only 56 per cent of eligible people, lacks facilities sufficient to cater to registered beneficiaries, and overall has not addressed or reduced out-of-pocket expenditure on health care (Iqbal 2023). A quarter of those who received cooking gas connections under the Pradhan Mantri Ujjwala Yojana were unable to purchase more than one cylinder (Porecha 2023). The crop insurance scheme has mainly served to increase insurance companies' profits (Vikram 2021). At the time of writing, news has just emerged that the agriculture ministry—supposedly a major focus of welfare schemes—has surrendered over INR 1 lakh crore (that is, a trillion rupees) over the last five years as it has been unable to spend the money (H. Sharma 2024). While the scheme to render the Public Distribution System's food rations free for most beneficiaries—ironically, a form of 'old' welfarism that has sought to be repurposed—has been extended, an estimated 110 million people are outside the distribution net entirely since the quotas have not been revised since 2011 because of the failure to carry out the census (Narayan 2021).

As a result, new welfarism also does not appear to be achieving its ostensible goal of improving people's standard of living. As discussed in the section on economic distress, standards of living for many Indians appear to be either stagnating or declining. As a result, unemployment and economic distress, whether reflected in government data or not, are now common themes of discussion across much of the country. This does not immediately negate the potency of new welfarism as an electoral tool, of course, since it remains a tangible benefit that must be weighed against largely (though not always) intangible losses. But the result is that the potential for political mobilization on these issues remains.

Such potential will likely become a more serious problem for the BJP over time, for two additional reasons. The first is that such approaches to welfarism contribute to the degeneration of the BJP's own organization by placing many BJP politicians in an invidious position. As noted earlier, patron–client relations are an inherent part of the vocabulary and praxis of electoral politics in India. But reliance on the bureaucracy, digitization, and the labelling of every scheme as a gift from the prime minister undermine the popularity of regional and local leaders, and this in turn is one of the factors leading to BJP defeats in the state elections (Centre for Policy Research 2023; Sircar 2021). Even where the BJP wins elections—as in Chhattisgarh, Rajasthan, and Madhya Pradesh in December 2023—voter surveys show a significant role of the 'Modi factor' in the sense of personally attributing credit to the prime minister (S. Kumar 2023). Weakening the role of local leaders and the BJP's organization reduces their credibility in the eyes of the public and makes it harder to resist or oppose local political forces—a point that I return to in the next section.

The second problem is that such targeted, individualistic welfare schemes are neither unique to this government nor difficult to copy. The Congress's win in Karnataka and the Trinamool Congress's win in West Bengal showed the potential for this, and the Aam Aadmi Party has practically made such schemes their trademark. The BJP attempted to undermine such opposition in 2022 and early 2023 by attacking their welfare benefits as *revdi*s (lollipops, as they would be termed in English)—with the prime minister claiming in October 2022 that 'a large section of the people' have decided to abandon '*revdi* culture' (*Indian Express* 2022, p. 1). However, this proved to be yet another poorly thought-out effort, since it cut at one of the BJP's own pillars. As a result, despite the implicit support of the Election Commission, the Supreme Court, the corporate class, and large sections of the media, by late 2023, the BJP had done a complete U-turn, going silent on *revdi*s and instead advertising 'Modi's guarantees' (*Indian Express* 2023). While voters in the most recent state elections in the north appeared to repose more faith in 'Modi's guarantees' than in those of the opposition, this is not something the BJP can take for granted, as evident from its election defeats.

Growing sections and axes of opposition

Of course, none of this ultimately matters if opposition forces are not in a position to exploit these fissures in a way that poses a serious threat to the ruling model (by 'opposition forces', I mean not only opposition political parties but also social movements and other organizations that opposed the RSS–BJP brand of politics). There is presently no easy way forward for such forces. The opposition has been faced with surveillance, violence, brutality, killings (especially of minorities), and arrests under anti-terror and money laundering laws, both of which effectively allow for indefinite detention without trial. The atmosphere of fear and intimidation that exists in large parts of the country today makes any form of opposition organizing far more difficult, and the dominance of the BJP over media and social media spaces further impedes the ability of any such organizing to have widespread impact. There is also severe fragmentation among opposition forces, which have managed to build alliances but not to have those alliances work over sustained periods of time, and have so far been unable to articulate either a single vision or a patchwork of visions to channel latent discontent into effective action at the national level.

However, to assume that the situation will remain this way is to overlook one key potential factor for change—the impact of the BJP–RSS regime's forms of political action on those it targets. Analysis of these changes is hampered by a tendency among many commentators to conflate different forms of political opposition, equating, for instance, the opportunistic dissent of some political leaders with more committed, ideological forms of political opposition. The former can often be overcome with little difficulty. But the latter is far harder to divert away, and it is this form of opposition that I am concerned with here.

As discussed, the BJP–RSS regime has a distinct approach to policymaking, rooted in the ideological praxis of both the Sangh Parivar and its corporate allies. The effect of this form of policymaking on its targets is not often discussed, but experiences in the last several years show that it can be profound. The combination of the use of the police and the media, along with either marginalizing the role of the judiciary or convincing it to be pliant, means those on the receiving end during the 'demonise and repress' phase of policymaking now must fear not just the consequences of a policy but also the loss of their freedom or lives. This galvanizes and hardens opposition. For instance, the use of such tactics against the farmers' movement in 2022 saw political shifts in the state of Punjab as well as a sharp decline in BJP support among Jat communities. The most brutally targeted community—Muslims—also discovered a new vocabulary of mass resistance in the NRC–Citizenship Amendment Act (CAA) movement, and while that has not re-emerged so far, there is no reason to believe it will not do so in the future. Such incidents happen on a smaller scale in BJP-ruled states as well and may be reflected by the fact that, even in election defeats, opposition parties have been steadily regaining a base among Dalit and tribal communities in some states (S. Kumar 2023).

This dynamic has a corollary expression in the form of federalism, a key fault line of the Indian polity. Many states that can draw on a distinct form of regional identity have precisely done this in the face of BJP onslaughts, and once again the 'demonize and repress' phase of policymaking hardens these lines as well. As a result, despite claims from 2014 that the BJP will 'penetrate the south', the political discourse in the southernmost states of Tamil Nadu and Kerala remains largely opposed to Sangh ideology (Karthik and Ashraf 2021; Sadanandan 2019). The same is now largely true of Punjab, particularly in the wake of the farmers' movement. In Bihar and West Bengal, regional forces have drawn heavily on subnational vocabularies to oppose the BJP. As a result, of course, the BJP government in Delhi has been mounting what is perhaps the most systematic attack on Indian federalism since independence (Tillin 2020). But while such tactics can be brutally effective in the short term, in the context of our present discussion, they are only likely to contribute to further polarization, as evident in the desire of the opposition parties to form the Indian National Developmental Inclusive Alliance (INDIA) in 2023.

Once again, of course, the question can be asked: does all this matter in the face of an overweening central government and the economic and discursive dominance of the BJP–RSS regime? Once again, contrary to intuitive perceptions, recent experiences show that the answer can be a qualified yes.

That is to say, the saffron project has shown a key political weakness—it is unable to respond to mass, sustained protest that is not cowed down by demonization and repression. The two best-known examples of this are the movement against the proposed NRC and the farmers' movement, but there are numerous smaller examples as well (at the time of writing, for instance, a national transport strike has just resulted in backpedalling on hit-and-run provisions). This is also true of electoral politics, in that parties that deploy organized strength and maintain it over time are far harder for the BJP to defeat.

It is precisely this kind of opposition that the cycle of policymaking under this regime is likely to continue to generate. Every attempt at rushed policymaking, whether it be on any sector or area, has the potential to result in organized opposition, which—if the regime continues with the approach its ideology requires of it—will potentially produce another social section with deepening ideological opposition, and therefore the potential for sustained mass protest that the regime finds difficult to handle (A. Shrivastava 2021). It is also important to note that, given the dominance of the BJP over public discussion (particularly in the north), the development of such constituencies is unlikely to be apparent until their opposition asserts itself (for instance, to my knowledge, no commentator or analyst predicted the scale of the NRC–CAA movement or the farmers' movement before they burst on to the scene). Meanwhile, increasing economic distress and inequality, weakening organizational coherence, hyper-centralization, and the diminished effectiveness of welfarism all mean that such protests may find larger political traction than one might otherwise assume.

At the time of writing, in January 2024, the opposition to the BJP–RSS regime has largely consolidated around three forms: ideological opposition in parts of the country such as Tamil Nadu, Kerala and Punjab; sustained mass protest, in the case of non-party organizations in many parts of the country; and competitive welfare politics in the case of the opposition political parties in much of the rest of the country. How this will play out is very difficult to predict, but what the analysis here implies is that, while the situation for the opposition is not easy, the situation for the ruling forces is not necessarily easy either. Contrary to appearances, therefore, the situation is likely to remain fluid in the years to come. The extent to which opposition forces are able to spread and consolidate their political action may, in fact, be the most crucial factor in determining what happens in the medium term.

References

Acharya, V. V. (2023). 'India at 75: Replete with Contradictions, Brimming with Opportunities, Saddled with Challenges'. BPEA Conference Drafts, 30–31 March 2023. https://www.brookings.edu/wp-content/uploads/2023/02/BPEA_Spring2023_EM-Panel_Acharya_unembargoed_updated.pdf. Accessed 1 April 2025.

Aggarwal, M. (2021). 'India's Mining Reforms Ignore Mining-Affected Communities'. Mongabay. https://india.mongabay.com/2021/01/indias-mining-reforms-ignore-mining-affected-communities. Accessed 15 March 2024.

Aggrawal, N., and S. Narayanan (2016). 'Demonetisation Alone Can't Turn Agricultural Markets Cashless'. *The Wire*, 25 November. https://thewire.in/agriculture/demonetisation-agriculture-cashless-economy. Accessed 1 March 2024.

Alavi, M. (2020). 'Despite Stimulus, Data Shows the Government May Be Spending Less, Not More'. NDTV, 23 November. https://www.ndtvprofit.com/business/despite-stimulus-data-shows-the-government-may-be-spending-less-not-more-2328975. Accessed 1 March 2024.

Anand, A., and V. Dimble (2020). 'New Welfarism of Modi Govt Represents Distinctive Approach to Redistribution and Inclusion'. *Indian Express*, 22 December. https://indianexpress.com/article/opinion/columns/national-family-health-survey-new-welfarism-of-indias-right-7114104. Accessed 27 February 2024.

Association for Democratic Reforms (2023). 'Analysis of Donations to Registered Recognised Political Parties'. https://adrindia.org/sites/default/files/Analysis_of_Donations_to_Registered_Recognised_Political_Parties_FY_2016-17_to_2021-22.pdf. Accessed 1 March 2024.

Balachandran, M., and P. I. Sharma (2015). 'Timeline: 200 Years of India's Struggle with Land Acquisition Laws'. Quartz, 5 August. https://qz.com/india/471117/timeline-200-years-of-indias-struggle-with-land-acquisition-laws. Accessed 1 March 2024.

Bhardwaj, A. (2021). 'Manufacturing Employment Halves in 5 Years'. *CEDA-CMIE Bulletin*, 6 May. https://ceda.ashoka.edu.in/ceda-cmie-bulletin-manufacturing-employment-halves-in-5-years. Accessed 5 March 2024.

Bhattacharya, P. (2023). 'India's Statistical System: Past, Present, Future'. Carnegie Endowment for International Peace. https://carnegieendowment.org/2023/06/28/india-s-statistical-system-past-present-future-pub-90065. Accessed 5 March 2024.

Centre for Policy Research (2023). 'The Evolution of India's Welfare System, 2008 to 2023'. *The Wire*, 1 February. https://thewire.in/economy/the-evolution-of-indias-welfare-system-2008-to-2023. Accessed 1 March 2024.

Chakraborty, S. (2017). 'After Demonetisation Took Away 1.5 Million Jobs, 73% Manufacturers Say No Hires for 3 Months'. *The Wire*, 18 July. https://thewire.in/economy/demonetisation-jobs-manufacturing-no-hires. Accessed 5 March 2024.

Chakravarty, A. (2021). 'How India's News Media Became an Elaborate PR Machine: It's the Economy, Stupid'. Newslaundry, 22 September. https://www.newslaundry.com/2021/09/22/how-indias-news-media-became-an-elaborate-pr-machine-its-the-economy-stupid. Accessed 10 March 2024.

Chandra, K. (2017). *Why Ethnic Parties Succeed: Patronage and Ethnic Head Counts in India*. Cambridge: Cambridge University Press. DOI: https://doi.org/10.1017/9781108573481.

Chandran, R. (2017). 'GST Makes "Untouchables" of Small Firms, Hurts Informal Workers'. Reuters, 7 July. https://www.reuters.com/article/india-tax-employment-gst-idINKBN19R231. Accessed 10 March 2024.

Chinoy, Z. S. (2020). 'A Recovery Led by Profits, at the Expense of Wages, Has Implications for Demand, Inequality and Policy'. *Indian Express*, 5 December. https://indianexpress.com/article/opinion/columns/india-gdp-economy-covid-19-worker-wages-sajjid-chinoy-7092154. Accessed 27 February 2024.

Choudhury, C., and A. Aga (2020). 'Manufacturing Consent: Mining, Bureaucratic Sabotage and the Forest Rights Act in India'. *Capitalism Nature Socialism* 31(2): 70–90. DOI: https://doi.org/10.1080/10455752.2019.1594326.

Choudhury, R. S. (2020). 'India Economy: Economists Not Impressed by Latest Fiscal Stimulus'. CNBC, 13 October. https://www.cnbc.com/2020/10/13/india-economy-economists-not-impressed-by-latest-fiscal-stimulus.html. Accessed 27 February 2024.

Chowdhury, R. J. (2020). 'Where Is the Money? Experts Fear It May Be a Case of Too Little, Too Late for Indian Economy'. *New Indian Express*, 4 May. https://www.newindianexpress.com/business/2020/may/04/where-is-the-money-experts-fear-it-may-be-a-case-of-too-little-too-late-for-indian-economy-2139166.html. Accessed 27 February 2024.

Das, A. (2024). 'Supreme Court Declares Electoral Bonds Scheme Unconstitutional, Directs SBI to Stop EB Issuance'. Live Law. https://www.livelaw.in/top-stories/supreme-court-electoral-bonds-1scheme-249553. Accessed 17 February 2024.

Donthi, P. (2019). 'The Liberals Who Loved and Lost Narendra Modi'. *The Caravan*, 17 May. https://caravanmagazine.in/politics/the-liberals-who-loved-modi. Accessed 1 January 2024.

Echeverri-Gent, J., A. Sinha, and A. Wyatt (2021). 'Economic Distress amidst Political Success: India's Economic Policy under Modi, 2014-2019'. *India Review* 20(4): 402–435. DOI: https://doi.org/10.1080/14736489.2021.1958582.

Gopalakrishnan, S. (2006). 'Defining, Constructing and Policing a "New India": Relationship between Neoliberalism and Hindutva'. *Economic and Political Weekly* 41(26): 2803–2813.

———. (2008). *Neoliberalism and Hindutva: Fascism, Free Markets and the Restructuring of Indian Capitalism* (*Radical Notes Series*). Delhi: Aakar Books.

———. (2013). 'Why Do They Love Narendra Modi?' Kafila. https://kafila.online/2013/08/24/why-do-they-love-narendra-modi-shankar-gopalakrishnan. Accessed 20 December 2023.

———. (2016). 'Demonetisation Is a Permanent Transfer of Wealth from the Poor to the Rich'. *Scroll.in*, 25 November. https://scroll.in/article/822402/demonetisation-is-a-permanent-transfer-of-wealth-from-the-poor-to-the-rich.

———. (2017). 'The Forest Rights Act'. *Economic and Political Weekly* 52(31): 71–76.

———. (2018). *Understanding the RSS and the Sangh Parivar.* New Delhi: Aakar Books.

Hebbar, N. (2023). 'Review of Abhishek Choudhary's Vajpayee: The Ascent of the Hindu Right 1924-1977'. *The Hindu*, 3 June. https://www.thehindu.com/books/books-reviews/politician-prime-minister-vajpayee-india-politics/article66896588.ece. Accessed 17 February 2024.

Indian Express (2021). 'TV Somanathan: "We Are Pulling Out of the Worst … Problem with Stimulus Is It's Easier to Start a Spending Programme Than to Stop It"'. 20 September. https://indianexpress.com/article/india/finance-secretary-t-v-somanathan-telecom-reforms-package-agr-due-india-economy-7520122. Accessed 1 March 2024.

——— (2022). 'PM Modi Slams "Revdi Culture," Says a Large Section Wants Its End'. *Indian Express*, 23 October. https://indianexpress.com/article/cities/bhopal/pm-modi-slams-revdi-culture-says-a-large-section-wants-its-end-8225638. Accessed 5 March 2024.

———. (2023). 'Decode Politics: Why "Modi Guarantees" Will Be BJP's Key Poll Pitch in 2024'. *Indian Express*, 24 December. https://indianexpress.com/article/political-pulse/decode-politics-modi-guarantees-labharthi-politics-bjp-lok-sabha-polls-9080836. Accessed 5 March 2024.

Iqbal, N. (2023). 'Three Charts on Ayushman Bharat's Achievements and Shortfalls—Indiaspend.com'. IndiaSpend. https://www.indiaspend.com/data-viz/three-charts-on-ayushman-bharats-achievements-and-shortfalls-878004. Accessed 1 March 2024.

Jacob, N, and G. Doshi (2021). 'In Charts: India's Political Parties Spent Thousands of Crores on Publicity in the Last Five Years'. *Scroll.in*, 4 October. https://scroll.in/article/1006842/in-charts-indias-political-parties-spent-thousands-of-crores-on-publicity-in-the-last-five-years. Accessed 27 February 2024.

Jaffrelot, C. (1998). *The Hindu Nationalist Movement*. New York: Columbia University Press.

Jain, M. (2017). 'Demonetisation Hit Smaller Companies Hardest, Services Sector Profits Slumped 114.5%: RBI Report'. *Scroll.in*. https://scroll.in/article/848509/demonetisation-hit-smaller-companies-hardest-services-sector-profits-slumped-114-5-rbi-report. Accessed 27 February 2024.

Jain, S. (2022). 'Prashant Kishor to NDTV–BJP's 3 Big Strengths and Prashant Kishor's Formula to Outdo Them'. NDTV, 25 January. https://www.ndtv.com/india-news/prashant-kishor-to-ndtv-bjps-3-big-strengths-and-prashant-kishors-formula-to-outdo-them-2727567. Accessed 5 March 2024.

Jha, S. (2019). 'Consumer Spend Sees First Fall in 4 Decades on Weak Rural Demand: NSO Data'. *Business Standard*, 15 November. https://www.business-standard.com/article/economy-policy/consumer-spend-sees-first-fall-in-4

-decades-on-weak-rural-demand-nso-data-119111401975_1.html. Accessed 5 March 2024.

Kakvi, K. (2020). 'New Laws Paralyse 70% of MP's Mandis in Six Months'. NewsClick, 22 December. https://www.newsclick.in/Madhya-Pradesh-New-Mandi-Law-Proves-Costly-Farmers. Accessed 1 March 2024.

Karthik, V., and A. Ashraf (2021). 'Why BJP's Hindutva Runs into the Tamil Wall'. NewsClick, 18 March. https://www.newsclick.in/Why-BJP-Hindutva-Runs-Into-Tamil-Wall. Accessed 10 March 2024.

Kazmin, A. (2020). 'Modi's Coronavirus "Stimulus" for India Leaves Business and Investors Deflated'. *Financial Times*. https://www.ft.com/content/0fbc41f8-fe43-43b9-98b8-80d1494945a8. Accessed 5 March 2024.

King, A. M., and S. J. King (2014). 'Führerprinzip'. In *The Encyclopedia of Political Thought*, pp. 1406–1407. New York: Wiley.

Kukreti, I. (2020). 'Inter-Ministerial Panel for FRA: A Giant Step Backwards, Say Experts'. Down to Earth. https://www.downtoearth.org.in/news/forests/inter-ministerial-panel-for-fra-a-giant-step-backwards-say-experts-73927. Accessed 15 January 2024.

Kumar, A. (2022). 'India Is Not the Fastest Growing Big Economy'. *The Hindu*. https://www.thehindu.com/opinion/lead/india-is-not-the-fastest-growing-big-economy/article65515195.ece. Accessed 1 March 2024.

Kumar, S. (2023). 'Pro-BJP Wave, Not Anti-Congress, Powered 2023 Assembly Election Results'. *Frontline*, 13 December. https://frontline.thehindu.com/politics/bjp-wave-welfare-schemes-modi-popularity-women-voters-2023-assembly-election-results-analysis/article67618017.ece. Accessed 15 January 2024.

Manor, J. (2022). 'The Ruination of the BJP's Organisation in 10 Steps'. *The Wire*, 3 September. https://thewire.in/politics/bjp-organisation-structure-modi-shah-ruination. Accessed 1 December 2023.

Mehrotra, K. (2023). 'Fraud Claims Targeting Indian Billionaire Gautam Adani Provoke Nationalist Backlash'. *Washington Post*, 12 February. https://www.washingtonpost.com/world/2023/02/12/gautam-adani-hindenburg-india-nationalism. Accessed 15 January 2024.

Mehrotra, S. (2024). 'Everything Wrong with NITI Aayog's Claim of 24.8 Crore Emerging Out of Poverty in 9 Years'. *The Wire*, 16 January. https://thewire.in/political-economy/niti-aayong-national-poverty-indicator. Accessed 1 March 2024.

Menn, J, and G. Shih (2023). 'Facebook Let Indian Pressure, Profits Stop Removal of Violent Content'. *Washington Post*, 26 September. https://www.

washingtonpost.com/world/2023/09/26/india-facebook-propaganda-hate-speech. Accessed 15 December 2023.

Mohan, D. (2024). 'Three Charts: What the Modi Government Wants Us to Forget before the 2024 Lok Sabha Polls'. *The Wire*, 14 January. https://thewire.in/economy/three-charts-what-really-matters-to-india-versus-what-parties-jockey-for-in-emotional-tug-to-voters-hearts. Accessed 27 February 2024.

Mukherjee, A. (2020). 'Why I'm Losing Hope in India'." NDTV, 29 November. https://www.ndtv.com/opinion/why-im-losing-hope-in-india-2331541#News_Trending. Accessed 15 February 2024.

Mussolini, B. (1932). *The Doctrine of Fascism*. https://worldfuturefund.org/wffmaster/reading/germany/mussolini.htm. Accessed 31 May 2025.

Najmi, Q. (2021). 'That Rs20 Lakh Crore Pandemic Package Expires, Bequeathing Just 15% as "Loans", Reveals RTI'. *Moneylife*, 11 August. https://www.moneylife.in/article/that-rs20-lakh-crore-pandemic-package-expires-bequeathing-just-15-percentage-as-loans-reveals-rti/64829.html. Accessed 27 February 2024.

Narayan, S. (2021). 'Time for Universal Public Distribution System: Food Mountains and Pandemic Hunger in India'. *Indian Journal of Human Development* 15(3): 503–514. DOI: https://doi.org/10.1177/09737030211049007.

Narayanan, S. (2021). 'The Three Farm Laws Were Never a Solution'. *The Hindu*, 30 November. https://www.thehindu.com/opinion/lead/the-three-farm-laws-were-never-a-solution/article37760299.ece. Accessed 5 March 2024.

New Indian Express (2022). 'In First Two Years of Corporate Tax Cut, Govt Suffers Rs 1.84 Lakh Crore Loss'. 14 August. https://www.newindianexpress.com/business/2022/Aug/14/in-first-two-years-of-corporate-tax-cut-govt-suffers-rs-184-lakh-crore-loss-2487445.html. Accessed 5 March 2024.

Ninan, T. N. (2020). 'What India Must Do to Be a Functioning Social Democracy—Stop Practising State Capitalism'. *The Print*, 12 December. https://theprint.in/opinion/what-india-must-do-to-be-a-functioning-social-democracy-stop-practising-state-capitalism/565264. Accessed 1 March 2024.

———. (2023). 'Indian Businessmen Are in Fear and Cheer Mode, but Feel Modi Govt's Still Their Best Bet'. *The Print*, 9 December. https://theprint.in/opinion/indian-businessmen-are-in-fear-cheer-mode-but-feel-modi-govts-still-their-best-bet/1878421. Accessed 5 March 2024.

Pardikar, R. (2023). 'What Will the Amended Forest (Conservation) Act Change?'. *The Hindu*, 4 August. https://www.thehindu.com/sci-tech/energy-and-environment/explained-what-will-the-amended-forest-conservation-act-change/article67146543.ece. Accessed 1 March 2024.

Porecha, M. (2023). ‘One in Four Ujjwala Yojana Beneficiaries Took Zero or One LPG Cylinder Refills Last Year despite ⊠200 Subsidy, RTI Data Reveals’. *The Hindu*, 31 August. https://www.thehindu.com/news/national/one-in-four-ujjwala-yojana-beneficiaries-took-zero-or-one-lpg-cylinder-refills-last-year-despite-200-subsidy-rti-data-reveals/article67255260.ece. Accessed 27 February 2024.

Press Trust of India (2020). ‘S&P Joins Chorus, Says Indian Economy Will Shrink 5% in Fy21, Stimulus Package Too Low’. NewsClick, 28 May. https://www.newsclick.in/S%26P-Joins-Chorus-Indian-Economy-Shrink-5%25-FY21-Stimulus-Package-Low. Accessed 27 February 2024.

———. (2021). ‘Budget Transparent and Open; Nothing Hidden Under Carpet: FM Sitharaman’. *Economic Times*, 1 February. https://economictimes.indiatimes.com/news/economy/policy/budget-transparent-and-open-nothing-hidden-under-carpet-fm-sitharaman/articleshow/80635656.cms?from=mdr. Accessed 27 February 2024.

Rajalakshmi, T. K. (2020). ‘The New Labour Codes: Labour’s Loss’. *Frontline*, 12 October. https://frontline.thehindu.com/the-nation/labours-loss/article32749705.ece. Accessed 5 March 2024.

Reuters (2018). ‘Impact of GST on Jobs: Hundreds of Thousands Laid Off Despite Growth’. Zee Business, 6 September. https://www.zeebiz.com/india/news-impact-of-gst-on-jobs-hundreds-of-thousands-laid-off-despite-growth-62341. Accessed 5 March 2024.

Sadanandan, A. (2019). ‘Why the BJP’s Hindutva Experiment Failed in Kerala’. *The Wire*, 27 May. https://thewire.in/politics/elections-2019-results-kerala-bjp-hindutva. Accessed 5 March 2024.

Saldanha, L. (2023). ‘Modi Government’s New Environmental Laws a Threat to India’s Biodiversity and Forests’. *Frontline*, 5 August. https://frontline.thehindu.com/environment/primed-for-plunder-modi-government-new-environmental-laws-biological-diversity-act-forest-conservation-act-a-threat-to-india-biodiversity-and-forests/article67158366.ece. Accessed 1 March 2024.

Saxena, K. B. (2024). ‘The Forest (Conservation) Amendment Act 2023: A Threat to Forest Lands and Forest Dwellers’. *Social Change* 54(1): 108–117. DOI: https://doi.org/10.1177/00490857231222101.

Sebastian, M. (2023). ‘Richest 1% Own 40.5% of India’s Wealth, Says New Oxfam Report’. BBC, 16 January. https://www.bbc.com/news/world-asia-india-64286673. Accessed 15 December 2023.

Shah, P. (2022). ‘People Say Can’t Betray Modi after Eating His “Namak”: PM’. *Times of India*, 21 February. https://timesofindia.indiatimes.com/

city/lucknow/people-say-cant-betray-modi-after-eating-his-namak-pm/articleshow/89712023.cms. Accessed 1 March 2024.

Sharma, H. (2024). 'Agriculture Ministry Surrendered One Lakh Crore of Its Budget in Last 5 Years'. *Indian Express*, 15 January. https://indianexpress.com/article/india/budget-hiked-agri-ministry-returned-over-rs-1-lakh-crore-in-5-years-9109498. Accessed 1 March 2024.

Sharma, C. N. (2021). 'Budget 2021: Key Public Health Schemes Receive Insufficient Funds'. *Mint*, 1 February. https://www.livemint.com/budget/news/budget-2021-key-public-health-schemes-receive-insufficient-funds-11612193102502.html. Accessed 1 March 2024.

Shih, G., and J. Menn (2023). 'Apple Warnings of Possible Government Hacking Drew Ire of Indian Officials'. *Washington Post*, 27 December. https://www.washingtonpost.com/world/2023/12/27/india-apple-iphone-hacking. Accessed 5 January 2024.

Shrivastava, A. (2021). 'The BJP's Toolkit Is Not Working That Well'. *The Wire*, 16 March. https://thewire.in/politics/the-bjps-toolkit-is-not-working-that-well. Accessed 15 December 2023.

———. (2023). 'Some Lessons in the Fight against Hate from Uttarakhand towards Deeper Democracy in India'. India Deeper, 25 November. https://indiadeeper.wordpress.com/2023/11/25/some-lessons-in-the-fight-against-hate-from-uttarakhand-english-version. Accessed 15 December 2023.

Shrivastava, S. (2015). 'Land Acquisition Legislation: Amid Central Logjam, States Move Forward'. *Indian Express*, 10 November. https://indianexpress.com/article/india/india-news-india/land-acquisition-legislation-amid-central-logjam-states-move-forward. Accessed 15 December 2023.

Sircar, N. (2021). 'Modi's Centralisation of Welfare Delivery Has a Cost That BJP's State Leaders Are Paying'. *The Print*, 11 March. https://theprint.in/opinion/modis-centralisation-of-welfare-delivery-has-a-cost-that-bjps-state-leaders-are-paying/619026. Accessed 5 March 2024.

———. (2022). 'The Roots of Political Centralization in India'. CASI Papers. https://casi.sas.upenn.edu/iit/neelanjansircar2022. Accessed 5 January 2024.

Srivastava, N. (2011). 'Is Indian Media Driving the Anti-Corruption Protests'? BBC, 25 August. https://www.bbc.com/news/world-south-asia-14660513. Accessed 5 January 2024.

The Hindu (2019). 'Delhi BJP Plans to Reach Out to Beneficiaries of Central Schemes'. *The Hindu*, 17 January. https://www.thehindu.com/news/cities/Delhi/delhi-bjp-plans-to-reach-out-to-beneficiaries-of-central-schemes/article26008642.ece. Accessed 5 January 2024.

The Wire (2024). 'K-Shape Widens: In 5 Years, Govt Tax Collection from Individuals up by 76%, from Corporates Only by 24%'. 24 January. https://thewire.in/government/k-shape-widens-govt-personal-income-tax-collection-corporate-tax. Accessed 5 January 2024.

Tillin, L. (2020). 'Why so Many Centre-State Tensions Are Breaking Out in the Open Now'. *Times of India*, 3 November. https://m.timesofindia.com/india/why-so-many-centre-state-tensions-are-breaking-out-in-the-open-now/amp_articleshow/79014564.cms. Accessed 1 March 2024.

Upadhyaya, D. (1979). 'Integral Humanism'. In *The Integral Approach*, edited by D. Upadhyaya, M. S. Golwalkar, and D. B. Thengadi, pp. 13–30. Deendayal Research Institute.

Vanaik, A. (2001). 'The New Indian Right'. *New Left Review*. https://newleftreview.org/issues/ii9/articles/achin-vanaik-the-new-indian-right. Accessed 1 December 2023.

Venkataraman, K. (2020). 'What Does the New Industrial Relations Code Say, and How Does It Affect the Right to Strike?'. *The Hindu*, 1 October. https://www.thehindu.com/news/national/the-hindu-explains-what-does-the-new-industrial-relations-code-say-and-how-does-it-affect-the-right-to-strike/article61723538.ece. Accessed 1 March 2024.

Vikram, K. (2021). 'Insurers Rolling in Money Raised for Crop Cover'. *New Indian Express*. https://www.newindianexpress.com/nation/2021/aug/23/insurers-rolling-in-money-raised-for-crop-cover-2348407.html. Accessed 1 December 2023.

Waghmare, A. (2021). 'Govt Saves 20k Crore with LPG Subsidy Pause'. *Business Standard*, 3 September. https://www.pressreader.com/india/business-standard/20210903/281689732917767. Accessed 5 March 2024.

10

Bollywood, Hindu Nationalism, and the Fascist State

Indian Identities and the Nation in *Pathaan* and *Jawan*

Rohit Chopra

Introduction

In an essay written some twenty-five years ago, Indian thinker Ashis Nandy describes popular Indian cinema as 'the slum's point of view of Indian politics and society and, for that matter, the world' (Nandy 1998, p. 2). The slum, a term for the urban lower-class settlements that constitute a significant portion of the landscape of every major Indian city, embodies the complexities of Indian society. It both aspires to and contrasts with the genteel urbanity of the upper-middle classes who are physically proximate to but separate from their slum-dwelling compatriots. The slum carries in it something of the rural and village worlds of migrants who make their home in it. It represents the profound social dislocation and alienation wrought by Indian modernity upon large sections of its population as well as new kinds of social relations that emerge as a result of these shifts and disruption. A physical space inhabited by Indian lower-middle classes and emerging middle classes but also a symbol of their aspirations, the slum is the beating heart of Indian political life. Nandy argues that the 'passions of, and the self-expressions identified with, the lower-middle class—for that matter, the middle class as a whole—now constitute the ideological locus of Indian politics' (ibid., p. 6). Inasmuch as it is a kaleidoscopic portrayal of the universe of the slum, Indian popular cinema, then, far from being an escapist fantasy or irrelevant lowbrow art, is an essential cultural form encapsulating the central concerns of Indian political and social life.

Using Nandy's formulation as a theoretical point of departure, in this chapter I seek to examine what the recent embrace of Hindutva or the ideology of Hindu nationalism in Bollywood films or popular Hindi-language Indian cinema might represent in terms of broader and deeper shifts in Indian culture, politics, and society.[1] In stark contrast to the constitutional secularism of the Indian state, Hindutva, in a nutshell, is the doctrine that claims India is culturally a Hindu society with Hindus as the rightfully privileged citizens of the nation. While Hindu nationalism has had a long, complicated, intimate, and ambivalent relationship with other notions of Indian identity, such as the constitutionally enshrined notion of a secular, syncretic, pluralistic Indianness, it has become both the reason of state and the dominant ideological force in Indian society since the sweeping victory of the Bharatiya Janata Party (BJP)-led coalition under Narendra Modi in India's 2014 general election.[2] Modi-era Hindutva, further, has increasingly taken on the character of a fascist project, with an aggressive assertion of Hindu identity, pervasive authoritarianism, muzzling of the press, and a clampdown on dissent (Stanley 2023). My analysis of the presence of fascist Hindutva in Bollywood cinema situates a close reading of two highly popular films, *Pathaan* and *Jawan*, against a genealogy of the idea of the nation in Bollywood cinema in different historical eras, with particular reference to the hardline Hindu nationalism of the present moment. Both films were released in 2023 and both starred the popular and charismatic actor, Shah Rukh Khan. Importantly, neither *Pathaan* nor *Jawan* overtly propagates Hindu nationalist ideology. On the contrary, the films were viewed as reflecting a counterpoint to the strident Hindu nationalism that had become the coin of the realm of the Indian culture and media industries, including Bollywood.

The star of the films, or SRK, as he is popularly known, is seen as a somewhat politically independent voice, in contrast to the voluble endorsement of Hindutva by prominent Bollywood figures. SRK's identity as a Muslim Indian has made him both a target of the Hindu right and magnified the symbolic value of his choices and actions, each of which is parsed and debated in terms of its endorsement of secular Indianness, critique of Hindu nationalism, or compromise with the ruling regime. Shortly after the Modi-led government came to power in 2014, Khan spoke out against a climate of intolerance in the country, for which he was attacked by BJP politicians like Yogi Adityanath and targeted through social media trolling that was carried out by the BJP's well-oiled online machine (Vohra 2023). Shortly before the release of *Pathaan*, Hindu right groups attacked the film for insulting Hinduism since the lead actress of the film was featured wearing a saffron swimsuit. The song was criticized by the Hindu right as vulgar, offensive, and demeaning to Hinduism, given that the colour saffron holds powerful symbolic significance in Hinduism. In 2021, Khan's son, Aryan, was arrested for the illegal possession of narcotics, a case that was widely seen as motivated by the goal of harassing the actor and one that was later dropped for lack of evidence (BBC 2022).

For these reasons, the two films starring Khan present a richer field for analysis than more obvious cinematic vehicles of Hindu nationalism. They enable a more nuanced reading of the political contestations over Hindutva, the extent of its credibility, and the strategies of legitimation that it deploys. These films show both the power and limitations of Hindutva while also indicating fault lines in Hindutva as a cultural project and the possible limits of its reach. Following a brief description of the ascendancy of Hindutva in political and public life in India over the course of the last decade, I present a schematic of the dominant national imaginary reflected in different eras of Bollywood. In this section, I describe how Bollywood is in the process of being transformed by the fascist character of Modi-era Hindutva. I then undertake a close reading of the two films in terms of their treatment of Indian identity, with a somewhat stronger focus on *Pathaan*, relating my reading to the spread and entrenchment of Hindutva in Indian society. I conclude with a thought on Bollywood and the current Indian political situation.

Hindutva in the era of Modi

Hindutva is a majoritarian doctrine that draws inspiration from European ethnonationalist movements and Hindu reformist trends of the nineteenth century (Jaffrelot 1998, pp. 11–12, 26–27). At the heart of the creed of Hindutva rests the idea that India is essentially a Hindu society in its cultural ethos and that religious minorities, especially Muslims and Christians, are outsiders to the Hindu nation (Savarkar 1969, p. 3; Vanaik 1997, p. 151). In the last ten years, since its victory in the 2014 Indian general election under Modi, the BJP, in concert with a host of other Hindu right-wing organizations, has managed to successfully implement a Hindu nationalist agenda across the political, cultural, economic, military, judicial, and educational fields in India.[3] As Hindutva has gone from strength to strength, its vision of chauvinistic nationalism has resulted in violent attacks on Muslims, Christians, and Dalits as well as on individuals and groups seen as critics of Modi, the BJP, and the Hindu right. This has been accompanied by the takeover and reshaping of private organizations and state institutions as instruments of the BJP and the larger Hindu nationalist apparatus (Hansen and Roy 2022, p. 1). The fusing of institutions of the state with the BJP and the weaponization of both legacy and new media have resulted in the erosion of constitutional rights, attenuated the autonomy of state bodies, and delivered a body blow to Indian democracy itself (Ganguly 2020; *The Quint* 2021; Serhan 2022). State entities, like the Central Bureau of Investigation (the main investigative agency of the country) and the Directorate of Enforcement (which falls under the Department of Revenue of the Ministry of Finance) have been deployed by the government to harass opposition leaders and critics. This situation has been complemented by a pathology of cultish devotion to Modi, the Indian prime minister, on the part of a vocal and aggressive constituency of Indians. As more than one commentator has noted, India under Modi more than meets many of the criteria of a fascist state and Hindutva can clearly be recognized as a fascist project (Pullanoor 2016; Stanley 2023; Van Zwanenberg 2022).

As is the case with other areas of Indian life, whether foreign relations or education, the military or tiger conservation, cricket or the mainstream media, Bollywood has not been immune to the influence and spread of Hindutva. Almost immediately after its 2014 election victory, the BJP government began exerting its influence on the Central Board of Film Certification, popularly known as the Censor Board, resulting in its head, Leela Samson, and nine other members resigning in protest against the interference (*Al Jazeera* 2015). Samson's replacement, Pahlaj Nihalani, an unabashed Modi loyalist, proved too controversial and was eventually sacked in 2017, only to be replaced by another loyalist, Prasoon Joshi, an advertising industry veteran who was part of the two-man team that had headed Modi's successful 2014 poll campaign (Jamkhandikar 2017). The 2019 election, which saw a spate of pro-BJP films, reflected a distinct shift from the post-independence paradigm of nation-building through development to one informed by a narrow Hindu nationalist vision of projecting national strength and unity, a change all too readily embraced by a compliant film industry (K. Sharma 2019, p. 15). As Sharma (2019, pp. 16, 18) notes, following the liberalization of the Indian economy in 1991, the process of film production was linked to the apparatus of state funding and regulatory control. The Modi government, far more astute and proactive than the Congress in recognizing and exploiting the cultural power of Bollywood, was able to successfully leverage this relationship into pressuring the industry to produce films that mirrored its agenda (p. 18).

In terms of Nandy's thesis, the metaphorical slum has both changed and adopted a new view of Indian political life. Bollywood, as its mirror and, in some cases, its megaphone, has correspondingly changed too. This latest turn to Hindutva can itself be located in terms of a genealogy of Bollywood as a space in which ideas of the Indian nation and national identity were formulated, reflected, and contested.

Bollywood, the Indian nation, and the time of fascist Hindutva

The idea of the national imaginary provides a useful heuristic with which to map significant changes in Bollywood over time, though, of course, it is not the only interpretive framework nor an exhaustive one for assessing such a rich cultural form (Doraiswamy 2002; Dwyer and Pinney 2003; Deshpande 2007; Mehta 2020; Rajadhyaksha 2009).[4] As Jaikumar (2006, p. 3) writes, 'The framework of national cinemas has become a dominant analytic trope in Film Studies because of the nation's function as a central axis along which films are regulated, produced, consumed, and canonized.'[5] Given the focus of this chapter on the current BJP government's project of remaking the nation through, among other avenues, the realm of culture, the trope is especially apposite as a theoretical frame for reading shifts in contemporary film.

The national imaginary in Bollywood can be understood in terms of four different paradigms, each related to the broader social, political, and historical context and reflecting both continuity and discontinuities with the frame that precedes it. These phases are, respectively: the era of anti-colonial nationalism from roughly 1900 to 1947; the phase of post-colonial modernity from 1947 to around 1990; the period of globalizing consumer capitalism in India from 1991 to the early 2010s; and, from around 2015 onwards, the present moment of a strident fascistic Hindutva that is simultaneously parochial yet shaped by aspirations and anxieties about global prominence or dominance. While it is the present historical phase that is most germane to the analysis undertaken in this chapter, a nuanced understanding of Bollywood's recent turn to a nakedly aggressive Hindu nationalism requires situating it in relation to earlier time periods. Each paradigm can be read as a statement of a particular idea of nationhood, while at the same time articulating a particular relationship of the Indian nation to the world. From the early days of Bollywood, a concern about India's place in the world was central to the examination of ideas of the nation. This is apposite given that cinema was a form developed elsewhere in the world but adopted, reshaped, and reimagined by Indians.

Bollywood films in the era of anti-colonial nationalism—that is, from around 1900 to 1947—are primarily mythological and religious, with moral and didactic messages and allegorical tales of good versus evil. Landmark works in the history of Bollywood and Indian cinema during this period include *Flowers of Persia* (1898), the first motion film shot in India; *The Wrestlers* (1899), the first film shot by an Indian; *Raja Harishchandra* (1913), the first full-length Indian film; and *Alam Ara* (1931), the first sound film, or 'talkie', which was a massive success. From its inception, Bollywood has taken shape as a distinctly hybrid cultural form drawing from diverse sources, including indigenous traditions of dance and dramatic art as well as Parsi theatre and Hollywood musicals. For instance, Parsi theatre itself, in turn, was influenced by Shakespearean plays in India.

Partha Chatterjee's seminal work, *The Nation and Its Fragments* (1993), provides us with a useful framework for grasping the significance of such films as culturally nationalist texts even when they are not explicitly nationalist in their content. In a critique of Benedict Anderson's thesis of the nation as an 'imagined community', Chatterjee argues that anti-colonial nationalism does not follow the universal template proposed by Anderson (1983). For Chatterjee, in a colonized society, the world is not conceptualized as being split between a private sphere and a public sphere as in the West, but between an 'inner' domain of culture, values, and religion and an 'outer' domain of statecraft, economy, and technology (Chatterjee 1993, p. 6). In the arena of the 'inner' domain of culture, the colonized in no way cede to or even acknowledge the supremacy of the colonizer, though they readily acknowledge that superiority in the outer domain. Chatterjee argues that well before the society of the colonized launches a political project of anti-colonial nationalism, it fashions an anti-colonial nationalist response in the realm of culture. In this sense, the emphasis on Indian mythology, religion, and history can be seen as an assertion of Indian cultural autonomy and a statement about Indian cultural identity.

Post-independence Bollywood broadly mirrored the ideology of Nehruvian secularism (Benegal 2007). The Nehruvian nationalist project sought to fashion India as a rational, secular, socialist society, and one that was assured of its place in the world. The Indian civilizational ethos was something that the world could learn from. A frame of secular cosmopolitanism sought to balance traditional Indian values with a modern outlook, while at the same critiquing a superficial performative modernity. Films like *Purab aur Paschim* (East and West) (1970), starring the actor Manoj Kumar, who was known as Mr Bharat (or Mr India) for his roles in patriotic films, exemplified this perspective. Popular hits like *Amar, Akbar, Anthony* (1977) promoted the idea of a unique Indian secularism, one that embodied a principle of universal belonging yet was emphatically Indian in its message of unity in diversity. As Benegal (2007, pp. 230–232) points out, the avowed secularism of the post-independence era in cinema insisted on a romanticized construction of the figure of the Muslim Indian as loyal, pious, and devout, a trope that has, till recently, had unusual staying power in the Indian cinematic imagination. In its aspirations and frustrations, Bollywood in this period also echoed the experience of other post-colonial nations, perhaps partly explaining its popularity in West Asia (the so-called Middle East), Nigeria, Turkey, and the former Soviet Union. Hindi-language popular films during this period represented not just the hopes of newly independent and developing nations and the utopian goal of social justice, but also problems of corruption, inequality, the failures of the state, and ensuing widespread social disillusionment.

Since 1991, when the Indian state turned to a programme of economic liberalization and began integrating into the global economy, Bollywood films have demonstrated a distinct shift in sensibility, one that held sway until the early 2010s, and that in some important respects persists in the current period of pro-Hindutva Bollywood (Mehta and Pandharipande 2011). In post-1947 India, the expatriate Indian was someone who had forsaken Indian values. After 1991, the non-resident Indian, or NRI, becomes singularly important for the Indian state and society. Bollywood films both soften their critique of Indian tradition and romanticize it (Uberoi 1998). There is, paradoxically, a simultaneous valorizing of an imagined 'Western way' of life in material terms, with a glorification of high-status, material objects like exotic cars, American sports like basketball, and the worked-out, ultra-fit body in films such as *Dhoom 2* (2006).

Bollywood has turned reflexive, acutely conscious of its own heritage and conventions and of itself as a global form. Some of its earlier preoccupations, such as social justice, for instance, now find articulation in global idioms such as hip-hop, as in the film *Gully Boy* (2019). With India as an increasingly important market for Hollywood, we also see an interesting cross-fertilization between Hollywood and Bollywood. Bollywood films have become more sophisticated in their production values, sporting an international look. More directors, actors, and cinematographers are trained in film schools in the United States and bring a global sensibility to their work, reflecting the influence of a wide range of filmmakers and actors from diverse global contexts, including the American, European, Iranian, Japanese, and Korean cinematic traditions. Indian actors, like Shah Rukh Khan, are now genuine global superstars, with their films premiering at prestigious international venues like the Cannes Film Festival.

During this period, the trope of the Muslim as terrorist has also entered the cinematic vocabulary of Bollywood, inaugurated by the film *Roja* (1992), adding to the repertoire of stereotypes such as the devout Muslim, the courtesan, and gangster (Islam and Rashid 2022). If Bollywood films now focus on a global Indian modernity that paradoxically is meant to be rooted in traditional Hindu values, Muslim characters largely continue to be depicted as the others of modernity. They are defined by an essential Muslimness, limited in their portrayal by the frame of religious identity and by specific perceptions about Muslim identity and Islam.

Since the early 2010s and after 2014, in particular, reflecting both Indian and global trends, Bollywood has displayed a conspicuous chauvinistic nationalism, both in its content and in its professed politics. The dominant ideological thrust of the industry, reflecting shifts in Indian society itself, in the Modi era of Hindutva, is a globalized Hindu nationalism that bears many of the hallmarks of fascism. The secularism of the post-independence era has been quite unequivocally abandoned though the imperative of globalization of the post-1991 phase has been retained. In this respect, the fascist project of Modi-era Hindutva is not necessarily inward-looking, notwithstanding its inevitable parochialism. India's newfound geopolitical importance for the US and the West as a counterweight to China and the allure of its markets have empowered it to affect a posture of an emerging global superpower that is also unrepentantly Hindu in the narrow, limited manner proposed by Hindu nationalism. Bollywood itself has become one of the main vehicles for this brand of Hindu nationalism, an instrument to reshape mass politics while the Hindu right is also engaged in ideologically reshaping the market and audience for Bollywood through other means.

In tandem, the Hindu right and the Modi-led BJP government have sought to control and tame Bollywood to ensure its complicity in their political goals, whether through organized mass campaigns of harassment directed at prominent actors and filmmakers, through incentives for films that are little more than naked propaganda, or through choreographed demonstrations of public support for BJP policies and initiatives (Das 2023; Kazmin 2020; Lateef 2022). The Modi government has also gone after streaming platforms, forcing them to cancel films that address sensitive political issues or could be seen as critical of the Hindu right or interpreted as demeaning to Hinduism. The government has followed the same pattern in exercising pressure on Big Tech companies and social media platforms in India. As Shih and Gupta (2023) note,

> Just as the BJP and its ideological allies have spread propaganda on WhatsApp to advance their Hindu-first agenda and deployed the state's coercive muscle to squash dissent on Twitter, they have used the threat of criminal cases and coordinated mass public pressure to shape what Indian content gets produced by Netflix and Prime Video.

While neither outrage at Bollywood for offending religious sensibilities nor the exploitation of such manufactured controversy for gains by political parties are new phenomena, the degree of control the BJP has imposed on the film industry is unprecedented. Its grip on Bollywood recalls the control of the German film industry by the Nazis as well as the influence they exercised indirectly on Hollywood, which consequently sought to tone down the criticism of Nazism (Denby 2012; Kürten 2020).

At the level of content, there has been an explosion of films on military themes, often centred around some aspect of the India–Pakistan conflict, terrorism, or a combination thereof, including *War* (2019), *Shershaah* (2021), *Mission Majnu* (2023), and *Uri: The Surgical Strike* (2019), with some of these conforming more categorically to a clear endorsement of the Hindu nationalist perspective. Other categories of film focus on revisionist accounts of historical events and mythology from a Hindu nationalist perspective that is, at once, absurdly anachronistic, reductive, and politically incendiary (Jain 2022). Like with the first category, these films span the gamut from crude to relatively sophisticated in their messaging and politics. Examples include films like *Bajirao Mastani* (2015), *Padmavat* (2018), *Manikarnika: The Queen of Jhansi* (2019), and *Adipurush* (2023) (ibid.; Rajendran 2022).[6] The most blatant examples of the weaponization of Bollywood are low-level works of propaganda, such as *The Kashmir Files* (2022) and *The Kerala Story* (2023), which demonize Muslims, parrot a hard Hindu nationalist line, and essentially peddle untruths (Chowdhury 2022; Mascillamani 2023). As was the case with the 2019 elections, the BJP government, by promoting films that endorse its view of history, minorities, and Hindu identity and its vision of a militaristic Hindu Indian nation-state, sought to influence voters in the 2024 general election as well but perhaps more aggressively (Lal 2023). Endorsing a Hindu right-wing ideology, such films are marked by a virulent anti-Muslim sentiment and hostility towards all the real and imagined enemies of the Hindu nationalist project, from left-liberal and secular institutions to Congress leaders, including Mahatma Gandhi (Purohit 2024). As Purohit (2024) notes, such films receive support from the BJP government in the form of tax incentives, organized screenings, and endorsements from the prime minister, Modi, himself. While such crudely propagandist films clearly impact public discourse, it is the creeping presence of themes of militarized Hindu nationalism and jingoism in seemingly mainstream 'routine' Bollywood films that is more significant. In contrast, in the past Bollywood cinema was generally associated with resolutely secular sentiments even when it dealt with overtly nationalistic themes or terrorism (D. Sharma 2020). In light of these developments, how should we view films like *Pathaan* and *Jawan* that conform to the framework of the nationalist film, yet appear to push back, in some respects, against the fascist Hindutva of the Modi era? It is to this question that I now turn in a close reading of aspects of both films.

Pathaan and *Jawan*: the presence and limits of fascist Hindutva in mainstream Bollywood

Pathaan and *Jawan* were not just the second-highest and highest-grossing Bollywood films of 2023, but of all time, earning staggering sums in the domestic and overseas markets (Malhotra 2023). Both films were seen as bucking the trend of Bollywood's wholesale adoption and promotion of Hindutva, though more than one critic noted the superficiality of the political critique in the films (Kumar 2023). The fact that the star of the films was a Muslim was also interpreted as public pushback against the Hindutva of the Modi era (Vats 2023). I want to examine three themes in untangling how the ideology of hardline Hindu nationalism that has India in its grip today plays out in the films: the valorization and uncritical endorsement of militarism; the sanctity of the Indian nation and the tension between the ideas of the nation and the state; and the role of amnesia and its relationship to Indian identity in the films.

The valorization of militarism in Pathaan *and* Jawan

It is perhaps no accident that both films squarely inhabit the discursive universe of the post-2014 mainstream Bollywood military film. No doubt, nationalism and war are tried and trusted themes that promise to reel in audiences everywhere, not just in India but in the US, the United Kingdom, and China as well. Yet the India of the Modi era has seen an uncritical endorsement and eulogization of militarism and the Indian military and, alarmingly, a weaponization and co-optation of the military for the political benefit of the BJP and the Hindu right. Retired and right-wing generals have frequently appeared on television channels like Republic, known to be mouthpieces of the government, to spew incendiary rhetoric aimed at Pakistan, Islamic terrorism, and shadowy global cabals. Publicly paying homage to the Indian military is seen as an act of patriotism while criticizing the military is considered a form of secular blasphemy, both anti-national and treasonous. A media-driven narrative, echoed on social media, relentlessly calls for India to assert itself on the global stage as a strong state and to take military action as and when needed against aggressive neighbours like Pakistan and China. Both *Pathaan* and *Jawan* affirm this perspective, though they leave out the ugly language routinely employed by the bloodthirsty, cartoonish hawks on Indian television.

Pathaan is a mishmash of Hollywood tropes, drawing inspiration from a series of action films and franchises, including the *John Wick* and *Mission Impossible* franchises, *The Bourne Supremacy*, and James Bond films, with elements of superhero films thrown in for good measure. Slick in its production values and over the top in dramatic flair, with the usual melodrama and histrionics that are grist to Bollywood's mill, its entertainment package nevertheless delivers a fundamentally hardline message about the necessity of military violence and war to protect the Indian nation. The protagonist in *Pathaan*, known simply as Pathaan (a term used to designate a member of the Pashtun community of Afghanistan), is an Indian military officer who works off the grid, while the chief villain, Jim, is a former Indian military officer who has turned against the country to which he no longer bears any allegiance. Abandoned as an infant, Pathaan's identity, ethnicity, religion, and past are unknown. Pathaan is on a quest to secure a mysterious and unknown object in Moscow that Jim is also after, the latter tasked with doing so by a rogue Pakistani general who is seeking revenge for the decision of the Indian state in 2019 to abrogate the constitutional autonomy of Kashmir.

Pathaan believes he is collaborating with Rubina Mohsin, a doctor who works for the Inter-Services Intelligence (ISI), Pakistan's intelligence services. With Mohsin betraying Pathaan, Jim gets hold of the object, which turns out to be the smallpox virus. He proceeds to mutate it into a deadly chemical weapon with the help of Indian scientists he has kidnapped. The rest of the film unfolds from there.

Jawan draws on a more conventional series of Bollywood themes, notably that of the 'angry young man' of 1970s Bollywood cinema, inaugurated by Amitabh Bachchan in the film *Zanjeer* (1973), in which a disillusioned protagonist fights a corrupt, uncaring system symbolized by rapacious politicians, evil industrialists, and morally compromised officers of the state. As stylish and melodramatic as *Pathaan*, with the usual mainstream Bollywood interludes of song and dance, *Jawan* has a prominent subplot involving the military. In short, Azad (played by Shah Rukh Khan), the jailer in a women's prison run according to progressive reformist principles, is the son of Vikram Rathore, an ex-military man who has lost his memory, also played by Shah Rukh Khan in the classic Bollywood 'double role'. Rathore had clashed with Kalee, a corrupt arms dealer, who in vengeance threw Rathore off a plane and succeeded in framing his wife, Aishwarya, for treason, a crime for which she was hanged to death. The film refers to scandals from India's past and present, offering criticism of the shortcomings and actions of both Congress and BJP governments, including the Bofors arms scandal of the 1980s and electronic voting manipulation, an issue of concern in recent elections. It also details the harassment and arrest of whistleblower paediatrician and lecturer, Kafeel Khan, punished by a Hindu nationalist state government in Uttar Pradesh for trying to remedy a shortfall of oxygen at the hospital where he worked in 2017. Father and son unite in the film, Rathore recovers his memory, justice is served, and Azad exhorts the citizens of India to do their duty by voting wisely.

The emphasis on the need for a military to protect a country and the extra-legal authority granted to or arrogated by it is arguably what grants the films a degree of ideological kinship to fascism. Justice is served through figures who are or were in the miliary but act beyond the bounds of the law. The Indian military figure in both films also serves as a protector of the innocent against a villainous foreign force.

In *Pathaan*, while on a mission in Afghanistan, Khan stops an American missile from killing a schoolteacher who has wrongly been identified as a terrorist, thus saving the lives of schoolchildren and villagers and preventing the village from being destroyed. The village of Pashtuns then adopts him as one of their own and bequeaths him with the identity of a Pathaan. In *Jawan*, the action opens with an unconscious and injured Rathore discovered by villagers in an undefined part of the north-east of India, possibly close to the border with China. The villagers tend to the comatose Rathore, who awakens from his stupor and saves the day just as members of a foreign Asian military force are about to slaughter the villagers. In both films, the villagers are painted as simple folk, naïve, innocent, and pre-political. Their religious and ethnic identities are not denigrated, but, in both villages, it is an Indian military officer, an adopted Pathaan and a privileged caste Hindu, who saves them.

The sanctity of the Indian nation in Pathaan *and* Jawan

A related theme in both films is the absolute sanctity of the idea of the nation as the axiomatic ground of identity. The nation-state is also similarly deemed essential as the larger framework of political being itself, although the state is subject to a mild or modest critique when its demands are shown to be in tension with the affective power of national belonging. Pathaan is willing to collaborate with Rubina Mohsin, not once but twice, despite being betrayed by her, because he understands that she, like him, is acting out of love for her country. Mohsin apologizes to Pathaan for betraying him and helping Jim secure the smallpox since she had not known of General Qadir's plan to unleash a deadly mutated version of the virus on an Indian city. Love of nation coexists and is perfectly compatible with love for humanity. In an interesting scene in the film, Jim states that he is a man without a country. In the context of the discourse of love of nation in *Pathaan*, it is precisely this that makes him dangerous. As someone who with no love of country, he is rendered indifferent to the suffering of humanity itself.

The abstraction of the nation, Anderson's 'imagined community', is contrasted with the concreteness of the nation-state and the actions of its representatives. It is here that there is something of a critique of the violence of the state, which manifests itself in the form of the excessive exercise of authority and power. In *Jawaan*, it is the compromised state that allows Kalee, the arms dealer, to escape unpunished and retaliate against Rathore, exacting Aishwarya's death as revenge. It is the failure of the state to protect its most vulnerable, including farmers and the poor, while protecting rich defaulters, crooked politicians, and vile industrialists that drives Azad to his vigilante actions. In *Pathaan*, Jim has turned against India because the Indian state refused to pay a ransom to free him and his pregnant wife from Somali pirates, resulting in her death and that of their unborn child. Colonel Luthra, sceptical of the secret outfit formed with Pathaan and other injured soldiers, terms them shells of broken eggs, essentially ineffectual. In a rejection of the authority of the Indian state, Pathaan frees Mohsin from her Indian interrogators as they race to stop Jim from carrying out his dastardly plot. Yet this critique of the nation-state is ultimately limited in *Pathaan* by the film's silence on the question of Kashmir. It is assumed that India's claim to Kashmir is legitimate while that of Pakistan or the Kashmiris is not. This limit is underscored by the absence of any reference to the Indian state's record of human rights violations in Kashmir and its refusal to address the legality of the abrogation of Article 370 that had granted autonomy to Kashmir (Essa 2023).

Amnesia and Indian identity in Pathaan

It is in the depiction of Muslim and Hindu identity as expressions of Indian national identity that the politics of *Pathaan* become pointedly troubling, especially when juxtaposed with *Jawaan*. Both films deal with the question of an unknown past. In Pathaan's case, his past and identity are an unknowable absence. In Rathore's case, we, as the members of the audience, know who he is, but he does not remember his past life. Nor is his son, Azad, aware that his father is alive. Essa (2023) has argued that *Pathaan* 'erases both Pathaan and SRK's direct connection to his Muslim heritage' and that it renders Islam superfluous to Indian Muslim identity. In doing so, the film reinforces a Hindu nationalist politics and legitimates the fascist turn of the Indian state.

This erasure, I suggest, is in keeping with the inability of a cultural form like Bollywood to address the Muslim question that has haunted Indian society since at least the colonial period. The two main charges levelled against Indian Muslims, when their loyalty is questioned in Hindu nationalist narratives and (often) in mainstream Indian political and public conversation, are that they are either descendants of Muslim invaders or converts who abandoned their original Hindu faith for an alien religion. Though Bollywood in the post-independence era, and, to an extent, even later, has emphasized the loyalty of the Indian Muslim, the Muslimness of the Indian Muslim has often been explained in contrast to the lurking possibility of disloyalty, secret sympathy for Pakistan, or attraction to the idea of a global *ummah*. The stereotypes of the pious Muslim or the traditional god-fearing Muslim have, in a way, functioned as shorthand forms of such explanations. In *Pathaan*, the explanation is simply eschewed. By giving Pathaan an indeterminate past, by designating his Muslimness as adopted and bestowed on him by people from a foreign land, the problem of the Muslim question is evaded. In contrast, Rathore's identity and social location are clearly spelt out. As a dominant caste Hindu, he is what historian Gyanendra Pandey (1999, p. 608) has described as the unmarked 'axiomatically natural' citizen who stands in contrast to the conspicuously 'hyphenated' minority citizen of the nation-state.[7]

Conclusion

India, it is not an exaggeration to say (even if it sounds like a cliché from a Bollywood film), is at a moment of crisis; its democracy is floundering; the autonomy of its institutions has been compromised; and its traditions of secularism, pluralism, and inclusiveness—no matter how flawed they may have been—are under attack. In critical aspects, India very much seems to resemble the past and present realities of fascist states, whether Argentina or Hungary of the present or Italy of the past. By itself, Bollywood cannot change the direction of political winds in India any more than Indian television or a social media platform might. Yet, as a mirror of Indian society, its view of the slum and much of middle-class and aspiring India reveals both the challenges and the possibilities that lie ahead for Indian society. *Pathaan* and *Jawan* can be read in at least two ways in this regard: as a sugar-coated statement of the hegemony of a fascist Hindutva that seems destined to go from strength to strength or as an articulation of limited autonomy and freedom confronting an especially virulent Hindu nationalism. If we are to adopt the more optimistic reading, nationalism, the films suggest, will be an inevitable part of the project of reviving and reclaiming Indian secular and pluralistic traditions of being and belonging. *Pathaan* and *Jawaan* both leave us with the question of how such a nationalism might look.

Notes

1. Nandy, it is worth noting, does not use the term 'Bollywood', which is an inexact and contested, though convenient, term. Scholars and commentators often prefer phrases like Hindi- or Hindustani-language cinema. It is perhaps

more accurate to refer to Bollywood as Hindi-language commercial popular cinema or the cinema of the Bombay-based or Mumbai-based film industry. People in the industry dislike the term 'Bollywood', because it implies that Bollywood copies Hollywood and because it reduces the complex history of the Hindi- or Hindustani-language film to a variant of Hollywood history. With due recognition of these concerns, the term has become popular and widespread enough to arguably exceed these semantic limitations. Bollywood is now recognized as a distinct entity with its own history, idioms, tropes, practices, and market, even as it has increasingly been shaped by and, in turn, influences processes of cultural globalization.

2. This dominance is not entirely uncontested. The results of recent state assembly elections in India in 2023 have shown a distinct north–south divide in which the BJP is dominant in most major northern Indian states but not part of any state government in the southern part of the country. Nonetheless, the BJP and Modi won a third general election in 2024.
3. The network of loosely affiliated organizations includes the Rashtriya Swayamsevak Sangh (RSS), the parent organization of the Hindu right; the Vishwa Hindu Parishad (VHP); the Akhil Bharatiya Vidyarthi Parishad (ABVP); and the Bajrang Dal. The BJP is the political wing and face of the Hindu right network, or the Sangh Parivar.
4. The literature on Bollywood is voluminous. In this section, I have cited works that will provide the reader with a sense of the critical issues related to the themes identified in the chapter.
5. Jaikumar's own analysis does not, for instance, prioritize the nation as an 'organizing principle' (2006, p. 3).
6. Films from the south of India like *RRR* (2022) are also open to the same charge of promoting Hindutva.
7. Pandey argues that this hierarchy is constitutive of the very idea of the modern nation-state (1999, p. 608).

References

Anderson, B. (1983). *Imagined Communities: Reflections on the Origin and Spread of Nationalism*. London: Verso.

Al Jazeera (2015). 'India Film Censor Quits Over "Interference"'. 17 January. https://www.aljazeera.com/news/2015/1/17/india-film-censor-quits-over-interference. Accessed 5 April 2024.

BBC (2022). 'Aryan Khan: Drug Charges Dropped Against Shah Rukh Khan's Son'. https://www.bbc.com/news/world-asia-india-61548614. Accessed 10 December 2023.

Benegal, S. (2007). 'Secularism and Popular Indian Cinema'. In *The Crisis of Secularism in India*, edited by A. D. Needham and R. S. Rajan, pp. 225–238. Durham: Duke University Press.

Chatterjee, P. (1993). *The Nation and Its Fragments: Colonial and Postcolonial Histories*. Princeton: Princeton University Press.

Chowdhury, D. R. (2022). '*The Kashmir Files:* How a New Bollywood Film Marks India's Further Descent into Bigotry'. *Time*, 30 March. https://time.com/6162035/kashmir-files-india-hindu-muslim. Accessed 2 December 2023.

Das, A. (2023). 'Bollywood: The Politics Behind the Scenes'. ABC News, 10 August. https://www.abc.net.au/news/2023-08-10/bollywood:-the-politics-behind-the-scenes/102714842. Accessed 10 December 2023.

Denby, D. (2013). 'Hitler in Hollywood'. *New Yorker*, 16 September. https://www.newyorker.com/magazine/2013/09/16/hitler-in-hollywood. Accessed 4 December 2023.

Deshpande, A. (2007). 'Indian Cinema and the Bourgeois Nation State'. *Economic and Political Weekly* 42(50): 95–103.

Doraiswamy, R. (2002). 'Image and Imagination: Reconstructing the Nation in Cinema'. *India International Centre Quarterly* 29(3–4): 211–223.

Dwyer, R., and C. Pinney (2003) (eds.). *Pleasure and the Nation: The History, Politics and Consumption of Public Culture in India*. Delhi: Oxford University Press.

Essa, A. (2023). 'How Shah Rukh Khan's Pathaan Will Strengthen Hindu Nationalism'. Middle East Eye, 3 February 2023. https://www.middleeasteye.net/opinion/india-shah-rukh-khan-pathaan-hindutva-strengthen-how. Accessed 6 December 2023.

Ganguly, S. (2020). 'India's Democracy Is under Threat'. *Foreign Policy*, 18 September. https://foreignpolicy.com/2020/09/18/indias-democracy-is-under-threat. Accessed 18 November 2023.

Hansen, T. B., and S. Roy (2022). 'What Is New about "New Hindutva"?' In *Saffron Republic: Hindu Nationalism and State Power in India*, edited by T. B. Hansen and S. Roy, pp. 1–24. New York: Cambridge University Press.

Islam, F. U., and M. Rashid (2022). 'How Bollywood Perpetuates Stereotypes and Myths about Kashmir, and Muslims'. *Outlook*, 2 April. https://www.outlookindia.com/culture-society/how-bollywood-perpetuates-stereotypes

-and-myths-about-kashmir-and-muslims-news-189760. Accessed 5 December 2023.

Jaffrelot, C. (1998). *The Hindu Nationalist Movement in India.* New York: Columbia University Press.

Jaikumar, P. (2006). *Cinema at the End of Empire: A Politics of Transition in Britain and India.* Durham: Duke University Press.

Jain, A. (2022). 'How Hindi Film Adaptations Align with the Hindutva Project'. *The Caravan*, 31 August 31. https://caravanmagazine.in/film/adaptations-foreign-films-hindi-cinema-hindutva. Accessed 7 December 2023.

Jamkhandikar, S. (2017). 'Pahlaj Nihalani Sacked as India's Censor Board Chief'. Reuters, 11 August. https://www.reuters.com/article/idUSKBN1AR1VQ. Accessed 5 April 2024.

Kazmin, A. (2020). 'Hindu Nationalists Take Aim at Bollywood'. *Financial Times*, 16 October. https://www.ft.com/content/9604b441-28d6-4563-9c4a-d69ba15e555a. Accessed 9 December 2023.

Kumar, A. (2023). 'Decoding the Political Messaging of Shah Rukh Khan's "Jawan"'. *The Hindu*, 14 September. https://www.thehindu.com/entertainment/movies/decoding-the-political-messaging-of-shah-rukh-khans-jawan/article67307072.ece. Accessed 14 December 2023.

Kürten, J. (2020). 'The Film Industry under the Nazis'. DW, 7 May. https://www.dw.com/en/how-the-film-industry-under-the-nazis-survived-until-the-very-end/a-53353463. Accessed 4 December 2020.

Lal, N. (2023). 'Bollywood Becomes Political Battleground as India's Election Looms'. *Nikkei Asia*, 8 August. https://asia.nikkei.com/Spotlight/Asia-Insight/Bollywood-becomes-political-battleground-as-India-s-election-looms. Accessed 14 December 2023.

Lateef, S. (2022). 'In India, Modi's Hindu Nationalists Declare War on Bollywood's Muslim Superstars'. *Haaretz*, 29 September. https://www.haaretz.com/world-news/2022-09-29/ty-article/.premium/in-india-modis-hindu-nationalists-declare-war-on-bollywoods-muslim-superstars/00000183-8870-d06a-a3e7-b8f376f30000. Accessed 4 December 2023.

Malhotra, R. (2023). 'Jawan Is Poised to Become Second-Biggest Bollywood Movie in Global Box Office History'. Collider, 24 September. https://collider.com/jawan-global-box-office-118-million. Accessed 4 December 2023.

Mascillamani, K. (2023). '"The Kerala Story" Ushers in a New Era of Malicious Hindutva Propaganda'. *The Wire*, 3 May. https://thewire.in/film/kerala-story-new-era-malicious-hindutva-propaganda. Accessed 6 December 2023.

Mehta, R. B. (2020). *Unruly Cinema: History, Politics, and Bollywood.* Urbana: University of Illinois Press.

Mehta, R. B., and R. V. Pandharipande (eds.) (2011). *Bollywood and Globalization: Indian Popular Cinema, Nation, and Diaspora.* London: Anthem Press.

Nandy, A. (1998). 'Introduction: Indian Popular Cinema as a Slum's Eye View of Politics'. In *The Secret Politics of Our Desires: Innocence, Culpability and Indian Popular Cinema*, edited by A. Nandy, pp. 1–18. New Delhi: Oxford University Press.

Pandey, G. (1999). 'Can a Muslim be an Indian?' *Comparative Studies in Society and History* 41(4): 608–629.

Pullanoor, H. (2016). 'India Is Displaying Classic Signs that Foreshadow Fascism'. *Quartz*, 23 November. https://qz.com/india/844672/along-with-narendra-modis-rise-india-has-displayed-classic-signs-that-foreshadow-fascism. Accessed 26 November 2023.

Purohit, K. (2024). 'Bollywood "Takeover": Pro-Modi Films Swamp Indian Voters Ahead of Election'. *Al Jazeera*, 9 March. https://www.aljazeera.com/features/2024/3/9/bollywood-take-over-pro-modi-films-swamp-indian-voters-ahead-of-election. Accessed 5 April 2024.

Rajadhyaksha, A. (2009). *Indian Cinema in the Time of Celluloid: From Bollywood to the Emergency.* Bloomington: Indiana University Press.

Rajendran, S. (2022). 'How Blockbuster Films Are Aiding the Hindutva Nationalism Project'. News Minute, 6 April. https://www.thenewsminute.com/news/how-blockbuster-films-are-aiding-hindutva-nationalism-project-162635. Accessed 11 December 2023.

Savarkar, V. D. (1969). *Hindutva: Who Is a Hindu?* (5th ed.). Bombay: Veer Savarkar Prakashan.

Sharma, D. (2020). '*Filmfare* Recommends: Top Bollywood War Films from the '60s to '80s'. *Filmfare*, 3 July. https://www.filmfare.com/features/filmfare-recommends-top-bollywood-war-films-from-the-60s-to-80s_-41930.html. Accessed 5 April 2024.

Sharma, K. (2019). 'Supporting Role: How Bollywood Acted under the Modi Government'. *The Caravan*, April 2019, pp. 15–18.

Serhan, Y. (2022). 'The Hinduization of India is Nearly Complete'. *The Atlantic*, 7 May. https://www.theatlantic.com/international/archive/2022/05/narendra-modi-india-religion-hindu-nationalism/630169. Accessed 4 November 2023.

Shih, G., and A. Gupta (2023). 'Facing Pressure in India, Netflix and Amazon Back down on Daring Films'. *Washington Post*, 20 November. https://www.

washingtonpost.com/world/2023/11/20/india-netflix-amazon-movies-self-censorship. Accessed 27 November 2023.

Stanley, J. (2023). 'The US Should Not Normalize Modi's Autocratic and Illiberal India at the G20'. *The Guardian*, 8 September 2023. https://www.theguardian.com/commentisfree/2023/sep/08/biden-india-modi-g20-autocrat. Accessed 19 November 2023.

The Quint (2021). '"RSS Used Digital Tech to Adapt": Jaffrelot at Dismantling Global Hindutva Event'. 11 September. https://www.thequint.com/news/dismantling-global-hindutva-multidisciplinary-perspectives-dgh-a-three-day-global-scholarly-conference-begins#read-more. Accessed 5 November 2023.

Uberoi, P. (1998). 'The Diaspora Comes Home: Disciplining Desire in DDLJ'. *Contributions to Indian Sociology* 32(2): 305–336. DOI: https://doi.org/10.1177/006996679803200208.

Van Zwanenberg, R. (2022). 'Hindu Nationalism: BJP in Historical and Comparative Perspective of Fascism.' *Policy Perspectives* 19(1): 95–109.

Vanaik, A. (1997). *The Furies of Communalism: Religion, Modernity and Secularisation*. London: Verso.

Vats, V. (2023). 'How a Muslim Movie Star Triumphed in Hindu Nationalist India'. *The Atlantic*, 9 October 2023. https://www.theatlantic.com/international/archive/2023/10/bollywood-modi-hindu-nationalism-shah-rukh-khan/675800. Accessed 4 December 2023.

Vohra, A. (2023). 'Modi Is Losing His War on Bollywood'. *Hasht e Shubh Daily*. https://8am.media/eng/modi-is-losing-his-war-on-bollywood. Accessed 28 November 2023.

11

The Distributed Sovereignty of Fascist Violence

Rohit Varman

> *Is baar danga bahut bada tha,*
> *khoob hui thi khoon ki baarish*
> *Agale saal achhi hogi fasal*
> *matadaan ki.*
>
> Riots were big this time,
> plenty of blood was shed.
> Harvest will be good next year,
> of votes.
>
> —Gorakh Pandey, 'Danga'

Several scholars have researched religious violence in India (for example, Brass 1997; Engineer 1994; Varshney 2002) and have offered insights into the role of the state in furthering pogroms (I. Ahmad 2022; Brass 2006; Khalidi 2003; Vanaik 2009; Varshney and Gubler 2012). Many writers have also emphasized the role of electoral politics in triggering pogroms (for example, Wilkinson 2006). Yet the role of violence remains under-examined from the perspective of a capitalist political economy. Put differently, past studies have paid less attention to how pogroms are used as political tools to advance the economic interests of big capital by mobilizing lower classes under the guise of distributed sovereignty. This is a significant oversight, particularly when mass violence against Muslims is systematically deployed to shape fascist politics that advances the interests of big capital (Desai 2014, 2016).

This chapter addresses the aforementioned lacuna by examining the 2020 pogrom in north-east Delhi, which began on February 23 and lasted six days. Without being economistic in my reading of fascism, as Kershaw (1989) warns against, and acknowledging some autonomy of the Sangh Parivar, I draw attention to the political economy of fascist violence. The pogrom in which Muslim lives and property were disproportionately harmed witnessed fifty-three deaths, and thousands of businesses and homes were destroyed (Gowda et al. 2020). Victims allege that north-east Delhi did not witness a spontaneous riot between Hindus and Muslims, but claim there was a pogrom. A pogrom is deliberately organized with 'state-supported killings and the destruction of property of a targeted group' (Brass 2006, p. 19). The Muslim victims interpret pogroms as part of the larger agenda of the current Indian government to establish absolute control in the name of Hindutva, or Hindu nationalism (Varshney 2022). Many argue that India is turning to fascism led by the Sangh Parivar (the Bhartiya Janata Party [BJP] and various arms of the Rashtriya Swayamsevak Sangh [RSS]) that draws inspiration from Mussolini's and Hitler's ideas for its propounding of Hindutva (Basu et al. 1993; Casolari 2000; Desai 2014, 2016; Sud 2022).

Pogroms and fascism are closely intertwined. Unlike Weber's (1918) reading of the state as a monopoly on the legitimate use of physical force, fascism unfolds somewhat differently. A fascist state can share this monopoly, under the guise of distributed sovereignty, with its stormtroopers, who are mobilized as instruments of violence against clearly identified enemies (J. Banaji 2016; Parenti 1997; Rosenberg 2016). Through distributed sovereignty, a government can delegate to its followers the power to kill and punish with impunity as part of a technique of governance.

Fascism is a political behaviour that is characterized by 'obsessive preoccupation with community decline, humiliation, or victimhood and by compensatory cults of unity, energy, and purity' (Paxton 2005, p. 218). It usually builds on a mythical past and lost glory, and singles out a population group to blame for the past humiliations that fascists seek to rectify (Stanley 2020). In so doing, fascism rests on three pillars: (*a*) abandoning some lives that are othered in the name of nationalism, humiliating them, and holding them responsible for the plight of a majority; (*b*) deploying petty bourgeoisie and working-class stormtroopers to wage the struggle against democratic rights of people and controlling private sphere; and (*c*) using authority, centralism, and violence to further corporate interests (Rosenberg 2016).

There are two dominant approaches to understanding fascism within the critical tradition. First, emphasizing the political economy, Rosenberg (2016) identifies the role of capitalism and suggests that under fascism, big capital does away with its liberal façade to replace it with chauvinistic nationalism to mobilize people to further the interests of the upper classes. Accordingly, fascism is a capitalist counter-revolution wearing a popular mask that relies on the support of the masses because capitalists can only rule indirectly and have to depend on the lower classes, who produce or become instruments of violence for the ruling elite. These unorganized lower classes, made vulnerable by social and economic inequalities, are recruited as stormtroopers by a fascist state to carry out violence (J. Banaji 2016). Mass violence is used to intimidate the racial/religious 'other', socialists, trade unionists, and other political opponents (Rosenberg 2016). As a result, as Walter Benjamin (2008, pp. 35–36) notes, 'Fascism seeks to organize the newly emergent proletarianized masses without touching the property relations.... Fascism sees its salvation in allowing the masses to find their voice (not, of course, to receive their due).' Here, Benjamin refers to capitalist spectacles with the aestheticization of politics through which the masses are engaged. Hence, fascism adopts what Rosenberg (2016, p. 82) describes as a 'dual character' in which the rhetoric of anti-elitism is deployed to advance anti-working-class measures. As Poulantzas (2018) notes, fascism is a capitalist exception to safeguard corporate interests that emerges in response to political crises. Although Hobsbawm (1994) refuses to attribute the rise of fascism to the interests of monopoly capital, he acknowledges that corporations benefit from the repressive apparatus of fascist rule. Neoliberalism and finance capital, it is argued, require fascist authority to further capitalist accumulation (Patnaik 2019).

The second complementary perspective adds psychological and social dimensions to the material context and explains fascism as a psycho-social phenomenon in addition to an economic one (Fromm 1994; Reich 1970). Capitalism, Fromm (1994) posits, destroys traditional social arrangements, and the unfettering of the newly emergent individual exposed to freedom is vulnerable to fears of powerlessness and meaninglessness. Such an individual seeks refuge in a totalizing fascist order. When there is an economic or social crisis, such individuals preserve or accept the identities of hate spewed by fascists (Stanley 2020) and support their anti-enlightenment ideology (Mason 2021). Fascism is not capitalism gone sour but is inherent in the social relations, subjectivity, and rationality it produces (Langman 1998).

In examining the testimonies of the Muslim victims of the 2020 pogrom in north-east Delhi, this chapter helps to comprehend how violence is a political project to mobilize lower classes to further fascist domination and the interests of big capital. Lower classes here refer to a combination of working classes and lower middle classes. Fascist violence creates the degraded other with the help of the lower classes. Degradation of the other entails humiliation and de facto curtailment of the political rights of citizenship. It also involves looting and destruction of Muslim property. Fascist violence engages lower-class Hindus to obfuscate their immiseration by big capital as they seek material and symbolic compensation from the other. It furthers a delusion of exalted status through the guise of distributed sovereignty; the delusional exaltation is particularly significant for lower classes because fascism is not meant to ameliorate material conditions or deepen democratic rights. The requirement of delusional exaltation becomes particularly necessary under neoliberalism when there is an accelerated transfer of wealth from the poor to the rich. Fascism facilitates accumulation for big capital by sharpening the repressive state apparatus. Unlike the traditional bourgeois political formations that are required to work within a liberal framework of political rights and economic guarantees, fascists suture the political sphere by mobilizing lower classes (under the guise of distributed sovereignty) as stormtroopers who are deployed to degrade the other. This violent control of the political sphere facilitates the accumulation for big capital without the necessity of economic redistribution or the deepening of democratic rights for the majority. As instruments of fascist violence, lower-class Hindus intensify the structural violence of corporate accumulation, of which they are, as a majority, the prime victims. The following sections elaborate on these insights.

Hindutva and communal violence

Communal violence in the form of riots is rarely spontaneous in India (Brass 1997; Engineer 1994; Varshney and Gubler 2012; Wilkinson 2006). Political parties and governments play essential roles in shaping the responses of the police and other law-enforcement arms to communal violence (Brass 2006; Khalidi 2003; Vanaik 2009). Moreover, the presence of a politician–criminal nexus in the absence of inter-religious and inter-ethnic civic organizations (such as trade unions, business associations, and so on) or local bridging capital contributes to communal violence (Varshney 2002). Although the country witnessed violence against different religious groups (for example, the anti-Sikh pogrom of 1984) in which the Indian National Congress was involved, such pogroms were not part of the conscious agenda to remould the Indian state (J. Banaji 2016). The conscious remoulding of the Indian state through anti-Muslim violence is central to the fascist project of Hindutva advanced by the Sangh Parivar (J. Banaji 2016; Desai 2014; Simeon 2016).

In the last few decades, anti-Muslim violence has increased because of the rise of the BJP (and the RSS) to power, with a pattern in its intensification (Jaffrelot 2021; Sud 2022; Vanaik 2009). This pattern can be explained as follows:

> [The RSS] represents Hindu revivalism of the worst sort; in its heart, it is still taking revenge against Aurangzeb, the Mughal Emperor…. [D]uring communal tension, its impact is wide, and RSS members become the most dangerous clandestine force, determined to provoke violence. (Akbar 1988, p. 22)

The most appropriate example of fascist violence is the Gujarat 2002 pogrom that left more than a thousand dead (Desai 2014). It has been suggested to have been organized to help the BJP make electoral gains and control the state (Dhattiwala and Biggs 2012; see also Wilkinson 2006). The Gujarat pogrom was particularly significant because it offered, as S. Banaji (2018, p. 342) adds, 'a template for the consolidation of a vigilante public, with a high tolerance for mass-murder, and without conscience or regret'. Such a pogrom was made possible by widespread state support for Hindutva and mass participation in the violence against Muslims (Ayyub 2016; Mukhopadhyay 2019; Noorani 2019). In fact, in such pogroms, there exist what Brass (2006, p. 20) has called 'institutionalized riot systems', in which 'the organizations of militant Hindu nationalism are deeply implicated'.

Fascism involves mobilizing populations and converting them into instruments of violence against clearly marked enemies (Paxton 2005; Rosenberg 2016). The Sangh Parivar has long been instigating the public (S. Banaji 2018; Basu et al. 1993; Patnaik 2019; Simmeon 2016), making the RSS arguably the longest-surviving fascist organization globally (Zachariah 2020). The founding of the RSS in 1925 is based on the furtherance of Hindutva, and its founder, Keshav Baliram Hedgewar, was committed to building a Hindu cadre-based organization for achieving Hindu unity against its enemies (Basu et al. 1993; Mukhopadhay 2019). M. S. Golwalkar (1966), the second head of the RSS, identified Muslims (along with communists and Christians) as threats to India. Consider Golwalkar's (2020 [1939], p. 12) observation: 'Ever since that evil day when Moslems first landed in Hindusthan, right up to the present moment, the Hindu Nation has been gallantly fighting on to shake off the despoilers.' Such a reading echoes Stanley's (2020) insight that fascism is about fetishization of an imagined past that is based on selective erasures and memories. Golwalkar (2020 [1939], p. 35) even praised the methods deployed by Hitler in purging Jews to create a pure nation and viewed it as 'a good lesson for us in Hindusthan to learn and profit by'. Hindutva was romanticized by another important influence on the RSS, Vinayak Savarkar, who instilled a sense of victimhood among Hindus (Mukhopadhay 2019). In these narratives, Muslims were held responsible for the plight of Hindus. Indeed, a detailed historical analysis shows Hindutva borrowed from European fascism (Casolari 2000).

In the last few decades, the rise of the BJP and the politics of communal hatred have coincided with the economics of a pro-corporate governance agenda that allows the upper classes to corner the national resources further (Desai 2014; Patel 2020; Varman and Vijay 2022). Hence, economy of hatred should be understood; the BJP gets the backing of the majority of upper-class and upper-caste votes, and in recent years has displaced the Congress as the prime beneficiary of their support (Vanaik 2009). The state and corporations in neoliberal India are deeply penetrated by Hindutva that combines economic extraction with the terror of stormtroopers (A. Ahmad 1993). Corporations provide overwhelming support to the BJP, and between 2016 and 2018, the party received 93 per cent of its funding from 1,731 corporate sources and 86 per cent of these funds from trusts set up by corporations for electoral funding (Association for Democratic Reforms 2018; Rodriques et al. 2019). As Stanley (2018) points out, the forces of capital are the prime financers and beneficiaries of the politics of us and them. The resulting communal politics happen as a violent engagement alongside unprecedented oppression and exploitation of lower classes as part of neoliberalism (Patnaik 2019). Further, the current regime seeks to create an entrepreneurial consumer whose behaviour is regulated by Hindu majoritarianism's cultural framework and aims to advance the Hindu nation (Chacko 2019). Accordingly, 'in the Hindu nationalist conception of market citizenship, the individual is an entrepreneurial consumer who is regulated in his/her behaviour by the cultural framework of Hindu majoritarianism and is driven by a desire to strengthen the Hindu nation. This is, therefore, the distinctive variant that I term, "virtuous market citizenship"' (Chacko 2019, p. 3).

Such agendas are actively supported by the upper classes, who are eager to be conscripted into the global flows of capital, and by corporations that fund the activities of the BJP (Poruthiyil 2021; Varman and Vijay 2022). The political crisis of liberalism evident in the anti-corruption protests across the country paved the way for the BJP to come to power in 2014. There was a widespread disenchantment with the Congress government, disaffection with the traditional elite, and paralysis of governance that contributed to the popularity of the BJP. Hence, it is not surprising that some echo Rosenberg's (2016) reading of fascism and view the current BJP regime as a 'counter-revolution' through which the upper-class hold on the Indian polity is cemented (Jaffrelot 2021, p. 139). The intertwining of fascism and elite interests makes it necessary to understand how, despite their material losses, the majority comprising lower-class Hindus is drafted into the project of Hindutva.

The participation of the lower classes is furthered by carefully capturing media to propagate fascist messages (S. Banaji 2018; S. Sarkar 2016; T. Sarkar 2022). Indeed, Indian television news channels have become prime peddlers of Hindutva messages and hatred against Muslims (Naqvi 2019). In addition, as Vasudeva and Barkdull (2020) observe, technological tools such as WhatsApp have become novel media for fascist propaganda among lower classes through the circulation of derogatory and hateful representations of Muslims (see also Mason 2021).

In short, contemporary India fulfils many of the conditions of fascism in terms of violent othering, chauvinistic nationalism, dominance of a leader, upper-class alignment, control of private sphere, and paralysis of progressive politics. These conditions of fascism make it necessary to interrogate further the politics of pogroms through which a part of the population is segregated, stripped of its rights, and degraded to mobilize lower classes and further elite interests. I turn to this interrogation in the remainder of the chapter.

Research context and methodology

Research context

To understand the north-east Delhi pogrom, I conducted a three-year study from 2020 to 2023. North-east Delhi is one of the 11 administrative districts in Delhi with a population of 2.2 million, a high population density of

36,155 inhabitants per square kilometres, and the literacy rate of 83 per cent (Government of Delhi 2011). Although the Aam Admi Party ruled Delhi until February 2025, its police were under the jurisdiction of the central government ruled by the BJP.

While there has been an increase in violence against Muslims after the BJP came to power in 2014, an important prelude to the pogrom was the passing of the Citizenship Amendment Act (CAA) by the Indian parliament on 11 December 2019 (Mason 2021). This amended the Citizenship Act of 1955 to relax the citizenship requirements for Hindus, Sikhs, Buddhists, Jains, Parsis, and Christians who entered India from the neighbouring Muslim-majority countries of Pakistan, Bangladesh, and Afghanistan before 31 December 2014. However, the CAA excluded Muslims. The discriminatory amendment was greeted with protests across the country, including Delhi. Muslim women most notably led the anti-CAA protests in Shaheen Bagh, Delhi. The Shaheen Bagh sit-in non-violent protest began on 15 December 2019 and lasted until the announcement of the nationwide COVID-19 lockdown on 24 March 2020. It became a site of heroic struggle led by Muslim women, attracting activist groups and Hindus (Mustafa 2020). Victims allege that BJP members threatened by the protest targeted Muslims for asserting their rights as citizens. As Gowda et al. (2020, pp. 118–119), in their report, observe, 'Shaheen Bagh and its courageous women were painted as the enemy; the symbol of secular India became, for the BJP, the target for its politics of hate.'

Beyond the political challenge posed by anti-CAA protests, there is a broader context of economic inequity and immiseration in contemporary India that requires greater attention, as summarized by a recent Oxfam (2023, p. 7) report:

> Following the pandemic in 2019, the bottom 50 percent of the population have continued to see their wealth chipped away. By 2020, their income share was estimated to have fallen to only 13 percent of the national income and they have less than 3 percent of the total wealth. Its impact has been exceptionally poor diets, increase in debt and deaths.... The wealthiest 10 percent own more than 72 percent of the total wealth, with the top 5 percent owning nearly 62 percent of total wealth, and the top 1 percent nearly 40.6 percent. The country still has the world's highest number of poor at 228.9 million. On the other hand, the total number of billionaires in India increased from 102 in 2020 to 166 in 2022.

The north-east Delhi pogrom should be seen in this context in which there is an ongoing transfer of wealth from the poor to the rich. Neoliberalism has been aggressively pursued by the BJP regime, which has caused incalculable miseries to the lower classes and is reflected in a reduced labour force participation rate from 51.4 per cent in 2014 to 46.2 per cent in 2020 and 60 per cent of the population dependent on government food doles (Patel 2022). In the last ten years, unemployment in the age group of 15–29 years has tripled, and poverty has increased (Mehrotra and Parida 2021). Despite a state of crisis for the lower classes, the state has not provided any substantial package for economic revival (Ghosh 2020). The BJP government allows corporations to extract various concessions, and valuable public assets are offered to them at distress prices to bridge fiscal deficits (RUPE 2020). In addition, various institutions of democratic accountability have been further weakened (Chowdhury and Keane 2021). In fact, the weakening of the post-independence democratic institutions, privatization of public assets, and increasing exploitation of the poor have created conditions for the fascification of society (Patnaik 2019). In such a situation, to keep the working classes engaged and mobilized, Muslims have to be demonized and made objects of fascist violence. To further explain this facet of fascist violence in the face of political challenge, inequality, and impoverishment, I elaborate on the methods used in this study.

Methods

In 2020, with the help of a colleague from a local university, I collected oral testimonies from the Muslim victims of the pogrom. I conducted two more rounds of the collection of oral testimonies in 2022 and 2023 to understand how victims interpreted the roles of both the state and the perpetrators of violence. For some testimonies in the first round, a research assistant (RA) was hired to conduct the interviews. We briefed the RA about the research objectives and gave a broad set of questions to guide the collection of testimonies. We deployed snowballing to include participants and used personal acquaintances to recruit the initial set of participants, subsequently asking the initial participants for more references. Despite the trauma of violence, we found that the victims were willing to testify and share their experiences.

We collected the 2020 testimonies individually from fifteen Muslim victims. We asked the victims to describe the events of February 2020 and who they saw as the perpetrators of violence. We also asked about the activities of political parties, police, and other state agencies. We inquired into how they were reconstructing their lives after the pogrom. We also interviewed three lawyers and two activists who supported the victims. In 2022, we contacted one of the key participants from the 2020 round for further testimonies, and he invited us to his locality. This participant's business and home were burnt in 2020. In this round, we collected testimonies in groups of five to six because the participants invited other victims to share their pain and corroborate their experiences and interpretations of the perpetrators. We recorded these group testimonies in three separate sittings that included another fifteen individuals. In the third round of data collection in 2023, we went to another riot-affected area in north-east Delhi and collected seven more individual testimonies from Muslim victims. I have assigned the participants pseudonyms to ensure their anonymity. The victims gave their testimonies over periods of 45 to 120 minutes. These testimonies were originally in Hindi and later translated and transcribed into English.

As part of the data, I also collected media articles and reports published by independent groups (for example, Delhi Ruins by Gowda et al. 2020; *Delhi Minorities Commission Report* 2020; *Uncertain Justice* by Lokur et al. 2022). These secondary sources included WhatsApp messages, and interviews with the perpetrators of violence were particularly helpful to understand how the lower classes were mobilized to participate in the pogrom. Some victims shared videos of the violence and their media appearances, and I included these in the dataset. The data analysis was ongoing and iterative, with simultaneous analyses of testimonies in a process consistent with the emergent design and constant comparative method (Strauss and Corbin 1990). The coding started with an emphasis on inductively identifying broad data categories in the form of open codes. The next step was to combine the open codes into axial codes and convert them into selective codes to help understand the political economy of NE Delhi pogrom.

Findings

Fascist violence is premised on the othering of Muslims as traitors and mobilizes lower classes as perpetrators of violence. I use the tropes of 'exaltation by degrading the other', 'material compensation through marketplace violence and destruction', and 'in the anomic space of law' to structure my findings.

Exaltation by degrading the other

Hindutva casts Muslims as harmful to the interests of the nation. Such branding is used to humiliate Muslims as dishonest or insincere Indians and to cast them outside the domain of right-bearing citizenship. Branding some people as traitors and blaming them for the ills in a society is a defining aspect of totalitarianism (Arendt 2017). Since its inception, there has been a concerted attempt by the RSS and its affiliates to create a narrative of nationalism branding Muslims as traitors. Their hate campaigns help the BJP to divide the population for electoral dividends (Jaffrelot 2021). In a way, learning to do violence involves acquiring a normative language of justification to present oneself as a victim (Ray 2011). Presenting Muslims as traitors and Hindus as an injured community harmed by anti-nationals helps to create a religious divide and frames perpetrators of violence as exalted entities delivering justice under the guise of distributed sovereignty. A stigmatized identity becomes the target of justified violence.

Indeed, in the Delhi assembly election in February 2020 that preceded the pogrom, there were repeated direct and indirect attempts to frame Muslims as traitors. The slogan 'Desh ke gaddaron ko, goli maron salo ko' (Shoot the traitors) was explicitly deployed in the election by several BJP leaders. For instance, in his election speech on 27 January 2020, Anurag Thakur, a central minister in the previous Modi government, along with the crowd, resorted to the slogan (Bhatia 2020). Another BJP leader, Kapil Mishra, now a cabinet minister in the Delhi government, targeted universities associated with Muslims and gave slogans such as 'AMU [Aligarh Muslim University] ke gaddaron ko, goli maron salon ko' (Shoot the traitors from AMU) and 'Jamia [Milia Islamia Univerity] ke gaddaron ko, goli maron salon ko' (Shoot the traitors from Jamia) (Ara and Mahaprashasta 2021). Such slogans mobilize riot squads (Brass 1997). However, despite attempts to create hatred, the BJP lost the 2020 Delhi assembly election.

Some victims allege that in order to overcome the loss of political control, the BJP engineered the Delhi pogrom. Several victims and also news reports (for example, Sagar 2021) pointed to the role of the ruling party leaders in starting the pogrom. For instance, as victim Rahim observed, 'There is no doubt that the BJP had done it.' This corroborates what Brass (2006, p. 20) saw as part of an institutionalized riot system in which political leaders 'keep inter-group tensions alive through various inflammatory and inciting acts …

lead and address mobs of potential rioters and give a signal to indicate if and when violence should commence'.

Saira, an activist, shared, 'Kapil Mishra ... tweeted in January [2020] that Pakistan has entered Shaheen Bagh and mini Pakistans are being created.' There are frequent references to Muslims as Pakistanis in the Hindutva narrative harking back to the division of the region into India and Pakistan at the time of independence in 1947 (Basu et al. 1993). Khalid, a victim, confirmed the role of Mishra and added, 'It [the violence] is because of Kapil Mishra. He gave an instigating hate speech and asked everyone to gather; it is because of him and his hate speech.' Saira also referred to the speech by Mishra on 23 February in Maujpur, in which he warned the police that if they did not remove anti-CAA protesters within three days, he and his supporters would throw them out. Saira believes that Mishra could not have given the hate speeches without the patronage of the BJP government. The victims allege that the speech by Mishra became an immediate trigger, and his frequent calls to shoot the traitors incited violence (*Delhi Minority Commission Report* 2020). Such calls frame and justify pogroms *as natural reactions to the evil designs of the other* (Ghassem-Fachandi 2022).

A quick look at the RSS doctrines reveals that Mishra, Thakur, and the other BJP leaders repeated what has been propagated by the RSS for decades. In RSS doctrines, Muslims are viewed as anti-nationals and are identified as enemies of the nation (Basu et al. 1993). For instance, the second head of the RSS, Golwalkar (1966, p. 184), wrote that 'all over the country wherever there is a masjid [mosque] or a Muslim mohalla [neighbourhood], the Muslims feel that it is their own independent territory'. Therefore, Muslims have to be contained to curb their anti-national activities. A little later in the same text, Golwalkar (1966, p. 185) interpellated Muslims as 'pro-Pakistani elements' and hence traitors:

> Within the country, there are so many pockets, i.e., so many 'miniature Pakistans', where the general law of the land is to be enforced only with certain modifications, and the whims of the miscreants have to be given the final say. This acceptance, indirect though it may be, implies a very dangerous theory fraught with possibilities of destruction of our national life altogether.

By branding Muslims as enemies, Golwalkar made violence against them natural and defensive rather than predatory. After a group is branded as a traitor, it can be violated with impunity (Arendt 2017). In fact, in such interpellations, it becomes a patriotic duty of the other citizens to eradicate traitors.

In eerie similarities with fascism in Europe (J. Banaji 2016), the mobilization of stormtroopers by BJP leaders is done in the guise of national duty. The pogrom in Delhi followed the same script. Consider the following instance of killings shared by Rahim:

> Two brothers had gone to their grandmother's house, and they were returning and had reached the Gokulpuri *nala* [drain]. They called up their home [on the 24th and told them that they had almost reached home. Within five minutes of their calls, their phones were found switched off, and they went missing. After three days, their bodies were found in the nala.

On the morning of 27 February, the lifeless and lacerated bodies of the two brothers—Mohammad Aamir and Hashim Ali, aged thirty and sixteen, respectively—were found in a drain. Ara (2020), examining the WhatsApp messages of Kattar Hindut Ekta (a Hindutva group), reports that they boasted with pride the murders of the two brothers. A message read, 'Tumhare Bhai ne abhi 9 bje k krib b.vihar m 2 mulla mare hai' (Your buddy has just killed two *mullah*s [a derogatory word used for Muslims] in Bhagrirathi Vihar at around 9 p.m.). Such violence inflicted on the other exalts the status of the perpetrators and helps these violators to have a share in distributed sovereignty.

The testimonies of the victims repeatedly point to how Hindutva riot squads stripped Muslims of dignity. Majid explained this feature: 'The rioters were abusive. They were constantly shouting and yelling at us, "Come, *mullah*s, we will show you, we will give you freedom" [*mullah*, as mentioned earlier, is a pejorative reference to Muslims in the region].' Moreover, there is a constant refrain of 'giving freedom' in these humiliating narratives because 'azadi', or 'freedom', was frequently deployed in Shaheen Bagh to protest against the state's communal and discriminatory agenda (Chakrabarti 2019). Reports that have published chats from a Hindutva WhatsApp group identify messages such as 'Inke Masjid me aag laga di hai' (We burnt their mosques) and 'Haan bhai shi h rnki ma chodni h ab' (Yes, brother, very good; now we have to rape their mothers) (Ara 2020). In such messages, there were derogatory references to Muslims with clear calls to inflict violence on them and their religious sites. For instance, Ara (2020) reports messages such as

'Masjidon ki maa chodo' (F**k mosques) and 'Jo bahar baithi thi … mullani unhe chodo' (The *mullanis* [slur used for Muslim women] sitting outside the mosque … rape them). It is unsurprising that, in light of such messages, fourteen mosques were destroyed in a brief period of six days (Jayaprakash 2020).

The mobilization of lower-caste/class Hindus for the pogrom was done in the name of a unified Hindu identity. For example, a WhatsApp message by Kattar Hindut Ekta exhorted its members thus: 'Listen brothers. Hindus need to become one. No caste and no jati. We are only hindus—that's it' (Lalwani and Daniyal 2020). In a similar vein, a young Hindu stormtrooper asserted, 'It was necessary to suppress Muslims.... Earlier, they were like lions, and now they are scared mice.... They know now that Hindus are united, and they will not think about attacking us' (Pandey and Tantray 2020). Such calls for Hindu unity to become part of riot squads are meant to overcome class- and caste-based divisions. It becomes a moment of distributed sovereignty through which lower classes are given the sovereign right to injure the other. These moments of united participation as stormtroopers are essentially about degrading Muslims and destroying their lives and property. The WhatsApp messages (shared on 25 February at 9:08 p.m.) also include 'Are sabki maa chodo' (Rape their mothers), 'Dekha jaega' (We will see), and 'Dekho bhaiyo jo hoga ab bo to hoga hi par kisi mulle ko chordna mat sale ko jane se marna' (Now whatever has to happen, will happen. But don't leave any mullahs—kill them) (Ara 2020). The exaltation of the lower-class stormtroopers is purely based on their ability to destroy the property of Muslims. Those who could not inflict the violence 'were often called "impotent" and "cowardly"' (ibid.). Although the moment of distributed sovereignty is limited to the sphere of violence against the other, its ability to engage lower classes through the creation of 'H-' and 'M-class' hierarchy of citizenship (that is, Hindu and Muslim classes of citizenship as articulated by Ghassem-Fachandi 2022) is a key outcome for fascist politics. It should be added that in some areas where Muslims were in larger numbers, there were retaliations. As Saira explained in her interview, 'Muslims have also attacked in retaliation when they have been attacked. They also burnt houses.' As a result, thirteen Hindus died and their houses were destroyed. However, the losses were disproportionate, and Muslims bore the brunt of the violence.

Muslims, as a result of discourse of traitor, are reduced to what Agamben (1998) describes as bare lives. Agamben interprets a bare life as a *homo sacer*, or, according to Roman law, a person without political rights and who may be killed by anybody without incurring any legal punishment. A bare life is neither a being nor a non-being but a physical body that occupies a threshold (Colebrook and Maxwell 2016). In other words, a Muslim as a *homo sacer* is an *aporia*, that is, a human impasse without a border between the pure and defiled or the proper and improper. As a result, distributed sovereignty becomes a combination of two antithetical principles of violence and justice. That is, a sovereign can erase zones of separation between bare life and good life, and lawful and lawless or inclusion and exclusion, as rightful citizens (Gupta 2012).

Material compensation through marketplace violence and destruction

Discourse of traitor unfolded in Delhi with a clear market dimension and was allegedly deployed by Hindutva stormtroopers to destroy Muslim businesses/homes and to loot their property. Thousands of businesses and homes owned by Muslims were burnt or looted (Gowda et al. 2020; Singh and John 2020). Confirming this part, Lala (another victim) provides a tragic account of how the six-day pogrom began and how his business was targeted:

> I used to run a chicken food outlet. At around 8–8:15 p.m. on 23rd February [2020], there was a crowd of around 250–300 at Sherpur Chowk, which is 200 metres from my outlet, and they were shouting slogans: 'Jai Shree Ram' [Victory to Lord Ram], 'Delhi Police *zindabad*' [Long live Delhi Police], 'Mohan Singh Bisht *zindabad*' [Long live Mohan Singh Bisht], and 'Desh ke gaddaron ko, goli maron salo ko' [Shoot the traitors].

Lala also alleged that the same crowd, under the stewardship of the BJP leaders (such as the local member of legislative assembly [MLA] Mohan Singh Bisht), went on to burn his outlet. It is instructive that lower classes were mobilized in the name of shooting the traitors. Lala's allegations were confirmed by Gowda et al. (2020, p. 126), who added, 'Mohan Singh Bisht was not only present but reportedly gave a hate-filled speech and incited the crowds.' Lala further testified how there was collusion among the riot squad, his acquaintances, and the state in the violence that he faced. On 23 February, he discovered, after the cries of shoot the traitors, a crowd of pro-CAA protesters at Sherpur Chowk, about 200 meters from his food outlet:

> I was relieved to see the BJP MLA Mohan Singh Bisht and his associate Karampal leading the crowd. I had good relationships with them because I had been working in their party before. I had their party office in my house. Before the riots, we supported the BJP and canvassed for the party in elections. I, my brother, and our whole family used to be involved in the canvassing for them. So I thought when Bisht and Karampal were around, there was nothing to fear, and I returned to my outlet. My father had purchased the land [for building their home] from Karampal twenty-five to thirty years back. I was certain that nothing would happen to us because they were all known to us.

Lala's family shifted to the area in 1976 and had never experienced such violence. Lala had been running the business (Panjar Chicken Corner) since 2015. It was indeed ironic that despite being a supporter of Bisht and working for the BJP, Lala's business was not spared. In a video interview given to a news outlet, which Lala shared, he also mentioned that he heard Bisht telling the crowd, 'We have burnt the shops of these Muslims, and now we should not leave them so that they don't raise a voice against us or dare to protest.' As part of degrading Muslims so that they did not have the courage to protest, their homes were also destroyed. Lala explains the impunity with which the BJP leaders led the riot squads that burnt Muslim houses:

> On the 25th, at around 10 a.m., we saw that SHO [station house officer, or a police officer in-charge of an area] Talkeshwar with a mob, along with the nearby Mother Dairy's person Surender and his son and other RSS activists in our locality.... They were a mix of locals and outsiders as the locals were guiding them and informing them because none of the houses had any nameplates. One by one, the Muslim houses were set on fire.... There was a 10,000 to 20,000 strong crowd, and we were watching from a terrace, hiding so that nothing happened to us.

In the violence that followed, for six days Muslim businesses and homes were targeted with impunity. As Farhan said,

> On the 24th all Muslim shops on the road were burnt. Khan Medical was burnt. There was another showroom, poor man it was a new showroom,

> and that showroom was burnt…. Then on the 25th our houses were set on fire.

Victims allege that the violence was not spontaneous but carefully planned by the Sangh Parivar (see also Sagar 2021). They highlighted how Muslim businesses and homes were meticulously identified. Majid explained,

> These people had planned everything, and they had planned much before about this…. How do they know in our streets who lives in which house and how these people came with their full preparation; they had petrol bombs and they had brought everything. One thing is that like you have come for some protest, and then there is a scuffle, so you fight with your hands, and you abuse each other something like that but not like this as they came prepared. So if it had been only this, then the situation could be brought under control. But here it wasn't like this; here it was like they had come fully prepared.

Most houses and businesses are in close proximity to each other; and in the absence of proper signage, for an outsider it is difficult to determine the ownership of homes. The very fact that Muslim property was targeted with precision gives credence to Majid's belief that the pogrom was meticulously planned. A description of how the Sangh Parivar facilitated the mobilization through the use of social media is provided by Sagar (2021). Indeed, this resonates with Brass's (1997) observations that communal violence in India is rarely spontaneous and often involves organizational networks. Moreover, several victims elaborated on what Majid meant by 'fully prepared'. They explained how firearms, bombs, and gas cylinders were systematically used to target them and their establishments. They allege that such organized violence could not have taken place without the knowledge of the state and the involvement of neighbours with whom they had lived for decades. As Appadurai (1999) suggests with the idea of 'vivisectionist violence', instead of interpreting such pogroms as impersonal violence by a faceless riot squad, there is a need to see the intimate brutality of the perpetrators.

Social media played a key role in shaping the intimate brutality of fascist violence. Hindutva groups used social media to impart a specific cultural twist to market transactions to justify the pogrom. Consider the following WhatsApp message from a Hindutva group that Lokur et al. report:

> *Wo apney chetra me ladies tailor ki dukaan kholengey ya chudi bechengey, aisey kaam karnengey jissey mahilaaon sey unka sampark badh sake aur love jihad ko badhaya jaa sake.*
>
> Muslims will open tailor shops in our areas or sell bangles, they will do such jobs that will ensure they can come in contact with Hindu women and love *jihad* will increase. (Lokur et al. 2022, p. 100)

In this patriarchal and communal narrative of love *jihad*, which has been popularized and weaponized by the Sangh Parivar, Muslim men supposedly use love to convert Hindu women to Islam (Strohl 2019). As a result, laws have been enacted in some states to restrict such relationships and there is an active Hindutva discourse to stop Muslim men from using markets to form relationships with Hindu women. *Hindutva culturalizes markets and the economy in a specific manner and turns them into fertile grounds for hatred.* In the WhatsApp chat, the Hindutva group exhorts the riot squad to protect Hindu women and their faith by removing Muslim presence from markets.

Such market access is crucial in north-east Delhi, which is one of the poorest and most densely populated areas of Delhi. A large section of the population is in the unorganized sector and works as welders, carpenters, painters, scrap dealers, street vendors, manual workers, construction workers, and so on (Gowda et al. 2020). Forty-one per cent of the district's population is self-employed in petty businesses, which is the highest in the state (Government of Delhi 2020) and further indicates high levels of poverty in the area. It is also a site of a large number of home-based garment factories that are owned by Muslims (Chakravarty 2020). Prasad further corroborates the widespread poverty in the district and notes,

> According to the latest Economic Census of Delhi, only about one-third of the working-age population is classed as a 'worker' who is engaging in some sort of economic activity. The rest of the working people may be categorised as undocumented workers, many of whom are self-employed. Many of the enterprises in the area are home-based and employ less than two people. Another 45 per cent of the enterprises work from sheds outside the house. Only 5 per cent of the businesses could be classed as 'shops and establishments', of which about one-fifth were owned by Muslims (Government of Delhi 2013). A recent study of

> informal labour in the region showed that the average monthly income of a household where there was home-based work was INR 5000–10000. (Prasad 2020, p. 169)

The district's demographic composition sheds more light on the economy of hatred. While its large Muslim population magnifies the bogey of the other, north-east Delhi (29.3 per cent) has a smaller proportion than central Delhi, where Muslims are 33.4 per cent (Census of India 2011) The pogrom, however, did not take place in central Delhi. The Government of Delhi (2020) employment survey may help to explain this phenomenon. The unemployment rate in north-east Delhi in January/February 2020 was 15.9 per cent, which was much higher than central Delhi's 10.3 per cent and the state's average of 11.1 per cent. Moreover, unlike the state's average of 39.5 per cent and central Delhi's 47.3 per cent residents with regular wages/salaries, only 31.7 per cent in north-east Delhi had that privilege (ibid.). It is also notable that 23.8 per cent of those employed in north-east Delhi were casual/contract workers as compared to 17.3 per cent in central Delhi (ibid.). It is safe to conclude that north-east Delhi is a site of greater economic precarity than central Delhi. It is this economic precarity that plausibly becomes an enabling condition for fascist mobilization and violence. Chakravarty (2020) elaborates on the economy of hatred in north-east Delhi and identifies unemployment as a key problem:

> Most of the rioters who have unleashed violence in the streets of Delhi are men between the age of 20 and 30 years. The national capital has around 10 lakh unemployed men and women in this age group. These youths become the pawns of those inciting communal riots. While they are on the streets taking lives and losing their own, the leaders who incite them sleep peacefully in their lavish houses.

He adds that unemployed youth are angry, frustrated, and can be easily mobilized as instruments of mass violence, as happened in the pogrom. Delving into the economic logic of hatred, Chakravarty (2020) also notes that Muslims are *framed* as more affluent and blamed by the Sangh Parivar for the poverty of Hindus. A common myth propagated by the Sangh Parivar is about the increasing population of Muslims limiting the economic opportunities for Hindus (*The Wire* 2023). Echoing this myth, the young Hindu stormtrooper interviewed by Pandey and Tantray (2020) claimed that Muslims have 'ten children … that their population has risen a lot'. As a result, Muslims become prime targets of the anger of the lower classes, who seek to eliminate them to reduce the competition for the limited economic resources.

Victims identified the lower classes as perpetrators from nearby localities that housed some of the poorest and lowest caste Hindus in the district. As Jha (2017, p. 73) describing Bajrang Dal, a key Sangh outfit in the region, notes, '[A]ctivists are poorly educated young people who are either unemployed or who regard their jobs as unsatisfactory. Though the leadership belongs to the upper or intermediary castes, a substantial segment of foot soldiers is drawn from the backward castes and even Dalits.' Aleem's testimony also confirmed this: 'The mob consisted of people who are basically unemployed.… When they are rioting, and under somebody's protection then even the administration does not act against them. In such a case [of patronage by the ruling party and the state], they are bound to do evil acts.' Such accounts resonate with Brass's (2006, pp. 20–21) observation that as part of the institutionalized riot system, 'criminals and the poorest elements in society, [are] recruited and rewarded for enacting the violence'.

Other features of the pogrom include the displacement of Muslims from their property and the looting of their houses and businesses. Lala explained to us how, after vandalising and looting, his shop had been replaced by a store owned by a Hindu. Several victims shared the details of how Muslim houses/businesses were systematically looted. Consider Amir's testimony in which he said, 'They looted and took away air conditioners, refrigerators, televisions, etc., all expensive things in rickshaws.… They were looting homes before burning them.' In the right-wing narratives, corporations or the upper classes are not blamed for the plight of the lower classes. Instead, Muslims are held responsible and are the sources from whom property has to be retrieved to ensure a fair redistribution. Sagar (2020) provides evidence of how such narratives influence lower classes and shape their quest for economic gains:

> [A Hindu involved in the pogrom] proudly showed me the burnt houses and shops of Muslims, noting that they deserved it. '*Hinduon ki jagah kabza karke rakha tha inn logon ne*'—These people had occupied the property of Hindus, he claimed. '*Bhenchod saath lakh, aath lakh mangte the* property *bechne ko. Abh ho gaya Hinduon kabza. Ladte raho* case *abh*' (The fuckers would ask for seven or eight lakhs [INR 700,000–800,000] for a property. Now the Hindus have occupied it. Keep fighting the case now.)

Such loot and destruction help the lower classes make economic gains at the expense of the other. In this context, calls for Hindu unity are meant to target Muslims and to engage the lower-class youth in such a way as to obfuscate their immiseration and the activities of big capital that cause dispossession. Such engagement of the lower classes as instruments of violence against the other resonates with Benjamin's (2008) observation that fascism does not give rights to such classes, but instead allows them to express themselves through spectacles of violence. Without ameliorating their material losses, lower classes are offered the freedom to inflict violence on the other as symbolic and economic compensation for their marginalization.

In the anomic space of law

A state of exception entails inclusion in law through exclusion (Agamben 2005). Such a state is not outside the law, but the law is absent by design so that some people can be stripped of their citizenship rights. The state of exception is a disoriented space in which there is no distinction between the law and what is outside the law. In north-east Delhi, the victims witnessed a state of exception for the six days of the pogrom. Although there were some instances of the protection of Muslims, the victims primarily described two roles of the police. First, they found that the police refused to protect them and their property. Second, in some cases, the police joined the riot squads in inflicting violence.

Describing the first feature of their exclusion, Insaan testified, 'The police gave them [the riot squad] total support. Not only us, but so many also called them; they did not answer. A minimum of 200 calls were made [to the police], and they went unanswered.' Insaan refers to the calls several victims made to the police seeking their intervention. However, the police refused to provide protection to the victims. Indeed, Khan (interviewee) adds,

> We are suffering after getting injured and our homes and businesses are destroyed, but the ones who beat us, threatened us, and even shot at us are all going around freely, and no action has been taken against them. We have given their names to the police, and still, no action has been taken.

Despite the traceability of subjective violence (Zizek 2009) in such accounts, in the official police records, the perpetrators remain untraceable.

Lala, whose shop was burnt, described in detail how his repeated pleas to the police for protection were not answered:

> When I saw my shop on fire, I immediately called the emergency helpline number, but they did not answer. After trying for some time, when the police answered the call, they told me that they had dispatched the force to the riot site, but for the next three hours nobody came, and my outlet was completely burnt. After waiting for the police to show up, I went to the Dayalpur Police Station…. The duty officer heard me and told me to come later because there were riots in the city…. Later at 2 a.m. that night, the police came and asked me to accompany them to the police station to lodge a complaint about the store…. When I went there with my uncle, the officer refused to lodge a report and told me to come later. He told me, 'There is a meeting going on, and you come later.' That night (despite my second visit to the police station), no complaint was lodged.

Lala's initial police report with the names of the culprits was not lodged, and he was asked by the police to file a 'simple FIR [first information report] without their names', which he eventually did. The police also asked him to remove any reference to the Hindu slogan of 'Jai Shree Ram' (Victory to Lord Ram). Accordingly, the police, in order to protect the key leaders involved in the pogrom, deleted their references. Irfan (interviewee) added, 'The police either just kept on watching and did not do anything, or they supported them [riot squads].' Explaining the complicity of the state, Fakir (interviewee) lamented, 'If on the 23rd police force had been posted and they had been active, then the story would have been different. No house would have been burnt. Had there been a curfew on the 23rd, it wouldn't have happened.' Omar added, 'Delhi Police played a major role…. They controlled the mob and told them not to fear, and nothing has happened, and nothing is going to happen, they assured the mob.' Saira further pointed to the complicity of the BJP government and stated, 'The police acts mainly on order from the top. There are very few officers who have the guts to defy'. There were intelligence reports, claimed Jayaprakash (2020), that warned the police of possible violence, but they chose to ignore them. Lala corroborated this charge of the state–riot squad nexus:

> On the 24th morning, I got a call from the police station that your burnt stuff is lying outside on the road and I should collect it; otherwise, they

> would send it to the municipal corporation. When I got there, I found that it was SHO Talkeshwar from our police station, and he told me to remove my stuff. I requested him to give me ten minutes as I had to arrange for a vehicle because the goods were heavy. He replied that I could pick up the stuff within half an hour, and I requested him to stay because the situation was tense. As I was collecting my stuff, I could see Mohan Singh Bisht's car going towards Chand Bag, and following it was a convoy of motorcycles. After five minutes, the SHO got a call from Satpal, a BJP MP, and I could hear the police officer tell him, 'Today no Katulla [a pejorative reference to Muslims] would be left alive.' This is what the SHO said standing in front of me.... After that, he told me that the riots had spread to Chand Bag, and he had to leave. As soon as he left, I could see a mob rushing towards me, and I had to leave my stuff and run for my life.

Lala lamented that the people who burnt his outlet and home were left scot-free, and, instead, a Muslim by the name of Sulaiman was accused of the crime. Some victims alleged that they faced false police charges and some were implicated in crimes they had never committed. Several reports (for example, Ellis-Peterson 2020; Ellis-Peterson and Rahman 2021) allege that more than 900 Muslims, of which the majority is of victims, have been jailed while the real perpetrators of the pogrom have gone scot-free. The testimonies show, as Varshney (2020) notes, that '[w]e have reached a point in India's history now that the state in BJP-ruled states is openly abandoning the principle of neutrality vis-à-vis religious groups. And in some cases, [the state is] a "mute spectator" as you put it, and in some cases a very open participant in anti-Muslim violence.'

Although some victims have subsequently received partial compensation for every floor of their homes destroyed, they consider it insufficient and paltry in the face of the destruction. Hence, there is an overwhelming feeling of abandonment by the state among the victims and of existence as bare lives (Agamben 1998). Majid, another Muslim victim, explained,

> Police were involved. Instead of targeting the rioters, the police were throwing tear gas at us and targeting our homes.... They were firing, and the police were standing behind them and protecting them so that no one attacked them.

There were several accounts of how the police mocked the victims when they sought protection. For instance, Lala lamented, 'Cops were saying, "Aur manglo azadi, le lo azadi" [You asked for freedom, now this is your moment of freedom], and refused to protect the victims.' Irfan shared another account:

> I have seen a video that has become viral in which three or four Muslim boys are lying on the ground, and the police are badly beating them up. The cops were asking them to recite 'Vande Matram' and the national anthem. One of the boys died because of the violence.

Irfan refers to an incident in Kardam Puri on 24 February, in which several policemen allegedly beat five injured Muslims (Manral 2021). The video of the incident circulating on social media shows the young Muslims lying on the ground with the police beating them and forcing them to recite the national anthem and 'Vande Matram'. One of the young men, Faizan, later succumbed to his injuries (ibid.). Such acts of violence reinforce the belief among victims that the police support the Hindutva agenda and commit atrocities by treating Muslims as traitors. Saira adds, 'One thing is very clear: any riot can be stopped within a few hours if the administration wants it. It was planned by them [the state], it was encouraged by them, and it was allowed by them to continue.' Gowda et al. (2020, p. 168) concur, 'Clearly the top officials in charge of law and order in the Capital allowed this to happen. Yet none of them have been held responsible. Is it because the Home Ministry instructed them to remain silent and indifferent?' Thus, the creation of bare lives in a state of exception is about violence and persistent degradation that is not outside the law but actively facilitated through the law enforcement apparatus (Agamben 2005). As witnessed in Delhi, these bare lives can be violated within the boundaries of law and without traces in official records. Hence, bare lives in a state of exception exist as lives that do not count and can be erased without a consequence.

In summary, the victims allege persistent degradation as a crucial feature of the pogrom. The violence that the ruling establishment allegedly supported exalts the identities of lower-class perpetrators under the guise of distributed sovereignty with the mandate to humiliate the other, strip them of political rights, and rob them and destroy their property. The testimonies show that violence against those who were reduced to bare lives proceeded with impunity in a state of exception as Muslim businesses and homes became the prime targets of looting and destruction.

Conclusion

Fascism is a form of capitalist rule that appears as a response to a political crisis (Poulantzas 2018). Fascism attempts to control the political sphere through a combination of mass mobilization and repression. Fascist repression is not merely about physical violence that the state monopolizes through its juridical apparatus. It begins with the extra-juridical casting aside of some people as bare lives. The creation of bare lives allows sovereign violence to be inflicted by other citizens in a state of exception, as in the case of the north-east Delhi pogrom. Unlike the liberal bourgeois parties that have to rely on some measures of economic redistribution and deepening of democratic rights for popular appeal, mass violence helps fascists mobilize lower classes under the guise of distributed sovereignty. The rise of fascism has its roots in the failure of the liberal bourgeois parties to control the political sphere and in the undoing of the post-independence consensus that allowed capitalist accumulation to coexist with limited welfare and the democratic agenda of the state.

The undoing of the post-independence political consensus accelerated with the neoliberal turn of the Indian economy in the 1980s. Neoliberalism has resulted in high levels of inequality and transfer of wealth to the upper classes (Das 2020; Oxfam 2023; Patel 2022; RUPE 2020). The increasing inequality creates new fault lines and contributes to popular resentment. The last few decades have also witnessed a destabilization of the traditional caste hierarchy and the rise of Dalit and lower-caste participation in the political sphere (Jaffrelot 2003). With these shifts in the structures of domination and new fault lines, the traditional elite struggled to suture the political sphere hegemonically. The resulting political crisis was palpable before the 2014 election, with the Congress government embroiled in several corruption scandals and losing the legitimacy to govern the country. This paved the way for a further rise in the fascist politics, built on decades of the Sangh Parivar's groundwork, and the BJP's electoral victory in 2014. The BJP's victory was also a result of the overwhelming support of upper-class/caste voters (Chibber and Verma 2014). As Poruthiyil (2019, p. 128) writes, 'neoliberal Hindutva' is meant to reinstate the domination of the upper-class/caste elites.

The BJP reinstates the domination of elites through a mix of mass mobilization and repression. Along with the use of state agencies to intimidate opponents, it controls the political sphere by recruiting lower classes to quell any political dissent (such as anti-CAA protests). To mobilize lower-class Hindus, as the pogrom in north-east Delhi demonstrates, Hindutva demonizes Muslims. It creates a delusional exaltation for lower-class Hindus that shifts the registers from class-based struggles to that of religious identities. In so doing, fascism engages the lower-class majority in such a way that obfuscates its material losses and occludes the neoliberal transfer of wealth to the upper classes and corporations. As Stanley (2018, p. 183) adds, 'Fascist politics preys on the human frailty that makes our own suffering seem bearable if we know that those we look down upon are being made to suffer more.'

Fascist violence creates 'the "H"' and the "M-Class" of citizens' (where the H stands for Hindus and M for Muslims) (Ghassem-Fachandi 2022, p. 299). By participating in pogroms such as the one in north-east Delhi, lower-class Hindus reinforce the religious hierarchy of citizenship. In so doing, lower-class Hindus also further the conditions of structural violence in the form of immiseration because of corporate accumulation, of which they are, as a majority, the prime victims. The structural violence is evident in hundreds of millions of lower-class Indians dying untimely deaths due to lack of food, medicine, and care or living lives of hunger, poverty, and extreme exploitation (Chowdhury and Keane 2021; Das 2020). Put differently, under the fascist guise of distributed sovereignty, lower-class Hindus become instruments of violence against themselves by allowing the forces of Hindutva to control the political sphere, which, in turn, advances the interests of big capital in the economic sphere. Thus, fascism serves big capital through a violent suturing of the political sphere. It means that while Paxton (2005) is right in noting that fascism involves mobilizing populations and *converting them into instruments of violence* against clearly marked enemies, he overlooks the intensification of structural violence under fascist rule against the mobilized populations. Paxton ignores how fascism entails the use of stormtroopers to inflict violence, not just on the other but on the self. In a state of exception that contributes to capitalist accumulation, lower classes are used in the name of religion to degrade the other and, as Benjamin (2008) notes, to obfuscate property relations and their own violent dispossession.

Mass violence and degradation of the other helped Hindutva to create an impression of distributed sovereignty for the lower classes. Distributed sovereignty does not rely on law, and neither does it claim to be outside it. Such sovereign violence stems from a state of exception in which the law is present in its absence (Agamben 2005). The law that is based on

India's constitution has limited application and is suspended during such pogroms to apply the natural or 'civilizational' law that Hindutva claims (see also Arendt 2017). Moreover, the violence through distributed sovereignty unfolds without moral compunctions, and there is indifference to moral commandments against killing or harming others because fascist violence draws upon the morals embedded in its hateful ideology (ibid.). The violence in north-east Delhi unfolded in the name of nationalism and religious duty. The very categories of nation and religion are already sacred in popular discourses and require no other justification. In such a context, it is not surprising, as a Hindutva chat group shows (Ara 2020), that it became a sacred and patriotic duty of stormtroopers to inflict violence on Muslims. It makes fascist violence an act of justice and high morality that exalts the identities of its perpetrators and provides them with some economic relief.

Such a distributed sovereignty advances fascist politics in several ways. It helps to unite a large population of lower classes from whom fascists draw their stormtroopers. Mass violence strengthens fascism by 'mobilizing masses from below' (Hobsbawm 1994, p. 117); it also makes lower classes complicit in the use of violence against clearly identified enemies (see also Hamm 1994; Ray 2011). Moreover, fascist violence unfolds through intimate networks of distributed sovereignty from below and, as Lala alleges, is inflicted by those who lived together as neighbours for decades (see also Appadurai 1999). Intimacy is needed to identify and mark the other. It is this intimacy that makes fascist distributed sovereignty so diabolical because it destroys the existing bonds of trust and class solidarities and replaces them with a toxic religious hierarchy that leads to further violence.

Acknowledging the violence and discrimination against Muslims, Chacko (2019, p. 16) writes,

> [A]n examination of the BJP's social and economic policies suggests an emphasis on the creation of entrepreneurial individuals who, unlike the self-regulating autonomous individual of discussions of neoliberal capitalist transformation in the West, are circumscribed within 'culturally' defined (Hindu nationalist) social frameworks and whose purpose is to strengthen the Hindu nation. In this state-society-market relation, the state's role is to act as a facilitator of 'market citizenship' in a way that promotes a Hindu majoritarian ethos and advances the Hindu nation.

Chacko's reading of 'virtuous market citizenship' and neoliberalism requires further clarification. While neoliberalism may disguise its motives as a system that advances marketization of the economic sphere, in practice it is a system that displaces markets and strengthens monopoly capital (Hathaway 2020; Sawyer 2022). In a similar vein, the current political project of Hindutva is not about market citizenship but about the *culturalization of markets and economy* to turn the lower classes into corporate foot soldiers and stormtroopers in the guise of distributed sovereignty. These stormtroopers are not expected to be entrepreneurial but are trained to follow the commands of fascist masters and fulfil the requirements of big capital to control the economic sphere. In such a role, the 'virtuous market citizenship' translates into the recruitment of the lower classes to become instruments of fascist violence and hate that further market destruction and looting.

In conclusion, this chapter has examined the politics of fascist violence based on the testimonies of Muslim victims in north-east Delhi. It shows how lower classes are deployed in the guise of distributed sovereignty to humiliate, loot, and destroy property and to curtail the political rights of Muslims. Such a combination of mobilization and repression helps the BJP to control the political sphere and also to serve the interests of big capital. Indeed, fascist violence is based on a delusion that becomes necessary under neoliberalism to obfuscate the transfer of wealth from the poor to the rich. It is evident that fascism threatens the gains India made through a liberal constitution with an emphasis on plurality as lawful existence. In so doing, fascism parasitically makes use of the very people it harms the most—the lower classes. In these circumstances, the only way to stop fascism from casting its dark shadows on the future of the republic is through working-class mobilizations and political consciousness that disrupt the economy of hatred and challenge the hegemony of big capital. Perhaps it is appropriate to close this chapter with the haunting verses of Sahir Ludhianvi:

Aaj agar khamosh rahe to
Kal sannata chayega.
Har basti mein aag lagegi
Har ghar jal jayega.
Aur us sannate se phir
Ek sada yeh ayegi.
Koi nahi hain, koi nahin hain
Koi nahi hain, koi nahin.

If we keep silent today
Our tomorrow will fall still
Every neighbourhood will burst into flames
Every house will burn
And from the stillness will arise
This echo,
Nobody here, there is nobody here
There is nobody here, nobody.

References

Agamben, G. (1998). *Homo Sacer.* Chicago: University of Chicago Press.

———. (2005). *The State of Exception*, Chicago: University of Chicago Press.

Ahmad, A. (1993). 'Fascism and National Culture: Reading Gramsci in the Days of Hindutva'. *Social Scientist* 21(3–4): 32–68.

Ahmad, I. (2022), 'Violence after Violence: The Politics of Narratives over the Delhi Pogrom'. In *Saffron Republic: Hindu Nationalism and State Power in India*, edited by T. M. Hansen and S. Roy, pp. 251–274. New Delhi: Cambridge University Press.

Akbar, M. J. (1988). *Riots after Riots: Reports on Caste and Communal Violence in India.* Delhi: Penguin Books.

Appadurai, A. (1999) "Dead Certainty: Ethnic Violence in the Era of Globalization." In *Globalization and Identity: Dialectics of Flow and Closure*, edited by Birgit Meyer and Peter Geschiere, 305–325. Oxford: Blackwell.

Ara, I. (2020). '"Tear Them Apart": How Hindutva WhatsApp Group Demanded Murder, Rape of Muslims in Delhi Riots'. *The Wire*, 6 July. https://thewire.in/communalism/delhi-riots-hindutva-whatsapp-muslims-murder-rape. Accessed 28 March 2025.

Ara, I., and A. A. Mahaprashasta (2021). 'Watch: BJP Leader Kapil Mishra Says "Nothing Wrong With "Goli Maro Saalon Ko" Slogan'. *The Wire*, 24 February 2021. https://thewire.in/communalism/watch-bjp-kapil-mishra-interview-delhi-riots. Accessed 28 March 2025.

Arendt, H. (1966). *The Origins of Totalitarianism*. London: Penguin Books.

———. (2017). *The Origins of Totalitarianism*. London: Penguin.

Association for Democratic Reforms (2018). 'Analysis of Donations from Corporates and Business Houses to National Parties for FY 2016–17 & 2017–18'. https://adrindia.org/content/analysis-donations-corporates

-business-houses-national-parties-fy-2016-17-2017-18-0. Accessed 28 March 2025.

Ayyub, R. (2016). *Gujarat Files: Anatomy of a Cover Up*. Delhi: Createspace.

Banaji, J. (2016). *Fascism: Essays on Europe and India*. New Delhi: Three Essays Collective.

Banaji, S. (2018). 'Vigilante Publics: Orientalism, Modernity and Hindutva Fascism in India'. *Javnost: The Public* 25(4): 333–350.

Basu, T., P. Datta, S. Sarkar, T. Sarkar, and S. Sen (1993). *Khakhi Shorts, Saffron Flags*. New Delhi: Orient Blackswan.

Benjamin, W. (2008). *The Work of Art in the Age of Its Technological Reproducibility, and Other Writings on Media*. New York: Penguin Books.

Bhatia, S. (2020). 'Anurag Thakur's Incendiary Speech Is Part of the Sangh Parivar's Smoke and Mirrors Show'. *The Wire*, 28 January 2020. https://thewire.in/politics/anurag-thakur-incendiary-speech-sangh-parivar-show. Accessed 28 March 2025.

Brass, P. R. (1997). *Theft of an Idol: Text and Context in the Representation of Collective Violence*. Princeton: Princeton University Press.

———. (2006). *Forms of Collective Violence: Riots, Pogroms, and Genocide in Modern India*. New Delhi: Three Essays Collective.

Casolari, M. (2000). 'Hindutva's Foreign Tie-Up in the 1930s: Archival Evidence'. *Economic and Political Weekly* 35(4): 218–228.

Census of India (2011). 'North East Delhi District Population Census 2011-2021-2024, Delhi Literacy Sex Ratio and Density'. https://www.census2011.co.in/census/district/170-north-east-delhi.html. Accessed 30 May 2024.

Chacko, P. (2019). 'Marketizing Hindutva: The State, Society, and Markets in Hindu Nationalism'. *Modern Asian Studies* 53(2): 377–410.

Chakrabarti, S. (2019), 'Shaheen Bagh Heralds a New Year with Songs of Azaadi'. *The Wire*, 31 December. https://thewire.in/rights/delhi-shaheen-bagh-anti-caa-protest. Accessed 28 March 2025.

Chibber, P., and R. Verma (2014). 'The BJP's 2014 "Modi Wave": An Ideological Consolidation of the Right'. *Economic and Political Weekly* 49(39): 50–56.

Chowdhury, D. R., and J. Keane (2021). *To Kill a Democracy: India's Passage to Democracy*. New Delhi: Macmillan.

Das, R. (2020). *The Political Economy of New India*. New Delhi: Aakar.

Delhi Minorities Commission Report (2020). 'Report of the DMC Fact-Finding Committee on North-East Delhi Riots of February 2020'. https://ia801906.us.archive.org/11/items/dmc-delhi-riot-fact-report-2020/-Delhi-riots-Fact-Finding-2020.pdf. Accessed 22 November 2023.

Desai, R. (2014). 'A Latter-Day Fascism?' *Economic and Political Weekly* 49(35): 48–58.

———. (2016). 'The Question of Fascism'. In *Making Sense of Modi's India*, edited by H. Suroor, pp. 56–79. New Delhi: HarperCollins.

Dhattiwala, R., and M. Biggs (2012). 'The Political Logic of Ethnic Violence: The Anti-Muslim Pogrom in Gujarat, 2002'. *Politics and Society* 40(4): 483–516.

Ellis-Peterson, H. (2020). 'Delhi Police Accused of Filing False Charges over February Riots'. *The Guardian*, 23 June. https://www.theguardian.com/world/2020/jun/23/delhi-police-accused-after-charging-activists-over-february-riots. Accessed 28 March 2025.

Ellis-Peterson, H., and S. A. Rahman (2021). 'Delhi Muslims Fear They Will Never See Justice for Religious Riot Atrocities'. *The Guardian*, 28 February 2021. https://www.theguardian.com/world/2021/feb/28/delhi-muslims-fear-they-will-never-see-justice-for-religious-riot-atrocities. Accessed 28 March 2025.

Engineer, I. (1994). 'Backward Communities and Migrant Workers in Surat Riots'. *Economic and Political Weekly* 29(22): 1348–1360.

Fromm, E. (1994). *Escape from Freedom*. New York: Macmillan.

Ghassem-Fachandi, P. (2022). '*Pratikriya*, Guilt, and Reactionary Violence'. In *Saffron Republic: Hindu Nationalism and State Power in India*, edited by T. M. Hansen and S. Roy, pp. 284–305. New Delhi: Cambridge University Press.

Ghosh, J. (2020). 'A Critique of the Indian Government's Response to the COVID-19 Pandemic'. *Journal of Industrial and Business Economics* 47(3): 519–530.

Golwalkar, M. S. (2020 [1939]). *We or Our Nationhood Defined* (*with A Critique by Shamsul Islam).* New Delhi: Pharos.

———. (1966). *Bunch of Thoughts*. Bangalore: Sahitya Sindhu Prakashan.

Government of Delhi (2011). 'Demography | District North East, Government of Delhi | India'. https://dmnortheast.delhi.gov.in/demography. Accessed 28 March 2025.

——— (2013). *Sixth Economic Census, 2013.* https://des.delhi.gov.in/sites/default/files/DES/generic_multiple_files/final_book12.pdf. Accessed 21 November 2023.

——— (2020). *Employment Survey in Delhi.* https://ddc.delhi.gov.in/sites/default/files/reports/delhi_employment_survey_report.pdf. Accessed 25 November 2023.

Gowda, V. G., T. M. Krishna, V. Prashad, N. Ram, T. Setalvad, N. Shah, K. M. Tiwari, and M. Velayudhan (2020). *Delhi's Agony*. Delhi: LeftWord Books.

Hamm, M. S. (ed.). (1994). *Hate Crime: International Perspectives on Causes and Control*. Academy of Criminal Justice Sciences, Northern Kentucky University. Cincinnati, OH: Anderson Pub. Co.

Hathaway, T. (2020). 'Neoliberalism as Corporate Power'. *Competition and Change* 24(3–4): 315–337.

Hobsbawm, E. (1994). *Age of Extremes: The Short Twentieth Century (1914–1991)*. New Delhi: Viking.

Jaffrelot, C. (2003) *India's Silent Revolution: The Rise of the Low Castes in North Indian Politics*. Delhi: Permanent Black.

———. (2021). *Modi's India: Hindu Nationalism and the Rise of Ethnic Democracy*. Princeton: Princeton University Press.

Jayaprakash, N.D. (2020). 'Delhi Riots 2020: There Was a Conspiracy, But Not the One the Police Alleges'. *The Wire*, 15 July. https://thewire.in/communalism/delhi-riots-2020-there-was-a-conspiracy-but-not-the-one-the-police-alleges. Accessed 28 March 2025.

Jha, D. K. (2017). *Shadow Armies: From Yogi Adityanath to Those Charged in the Murder of Gauri Lankesh*. New Delhi: Juggernaut.

Kershaw, I. (1989). 'The Nazi State: An Exceptional State?' *New Left Review* 1 (176) (July–August): 47–67.

Lalwani V. and S. Daniyal (2020). 'From Planning Murder to Praising Modi: WhatsApp Chats Offer a Window into the Mind of Delhi Rioters'. *Scroll.in*, 9 July. https://scroll.in/article/966775/from-planning-murder-to-praising-modi-whatsapp-chats-offer-a-window-into-the-minds-of-delhi-rioters. Accessed 21 November 2023.

Langman, L. (1998). 'I Hate, Therefore I Am'. *Social Thought and Research 21*(1–2): 151–183.

Lokur, M. B., A. P. Shah, R. S. Sodhi, A. Parekh, and G. K. Pillai (2022). 'Uncertain Justice: A Citizens Committee Report on North East Delhi Violence'. https://constitutionalconduct.files.wordpress.com/2022/10/uncertain-justice-executive-summary-of-citizens-committee-report-on-north-east-delhi-violence-2020.pdf. Accessed 28 March 2025.

Manral, M. S. (2021), 'Delhi Riot-Injured Forced to Recite National Anthem: 3 Policemen Identified'. *Indian Express*, 19 August. https://indianexpress.com/article/cities/delhi/northeast-delhi-riot-injured-forced-to-recite-anthem-3-policemen-identified-7460425. Accessed 28 March 2025.

Mehrotra, S., and J. K. Parida (2021). 'Poverty in India Is on the Rise Again'. *The Hindu*, 20 October 2019. https://www.thehindu.com/opinion/lead/poverty-in-india-is-on-the-rise-again/article35709263.ece. Accessed 28 March 2025.

Mukhopadhyay, N. (2019). *The RSS: Icons of Indian Right*. Delhi: Tranquebar.

Mustafa, S. (ed.) (2020). *Shaheen Bag and the idea of India*. New Delhi: Speaking Tiger.

Naqvi, B. (2019). 'How Indian News Channels Are Peddling Hatred against Muslims on Primetime TV'. *Gulf News*. https://gulfnews.com/world/asia/india/how-indian-news-channels-are-peddling-hatred-against-muslims-on-primetime-tv-1.67265166. Accessed 28 March 2025.

Noorani, A. G. (2019). *The RSS: A Menace to India*. Delhi: LeftWord Books.

Oxfam (2023). 'Survival of the Richest: The India Story'. https://d1ns4ht6ytuzzo.cloudfront.net/oxfamdata/oxfamdatapublic/2023-01/India%20Supplement%202023_digital.pdf?kz3wav0jbhJdvkJ.fK1rj1k1_5ap9FhQ. Accessed 28 March 2025.

Pandey, A., and S. Tantray (2020). 'Hate Speech: A Hindu Rioter Speaks'. *The Caravan*, 31 July. https://caravanmagazine.in/crime/delhi-rioter-testimony-hindu-revenge-muslims-police-free-reign. Accessed 28 March 2025.

Parenti, M. (1997). *Blackshirts and Reds: Rational Fascism and the Overthrow of Communism*. San Francisco: City Lights Books.

Patel, A. (2020). *Our Hindu Rashtra: What It Is, How We Got Here*. Delhi: Penguin Books.

———. (2022). *Price of the Modi Years*. Delhi: Penguin Books.

Patnaik, P. (2019). 'Shadow of Fascism'. *Monthly Review*. https://mronline.org/2019/04/08/the-modi-years. Accessed 9 September 2021

Paxton, R. O. (2005). *The Anatomy of Fascism*. London: Vintage.

Poruthiyil, P. V. (2021). 'Big Business and Fascism: A Dangerous Collusion'. *Journal of Business Ethics* 168(1): 121–135.

Poulantzas, N. (2018). *Fascism and Dictatorship: The Third International and the Problem of Fascism*. London: Verso.

Prakash, B. (2022). 'Why the Toxic Beats of "Disc Jockey Hindutva" Are So Dangerous for India'. *Scroll.in*, 25 April. https://scroll.in/article/1022502/how-the-toxic-beats-of-disc-jockey-hindutva-are-inspiring-violence. Accessed 28 March 2025.

Prasad, A. (2020). 'Communal Violence and Informal Labour: The Case of North East Delhi Carnage'. *Global Labour Journal* 11(2): 23–28.

Ray, L. (2011). *Violence and Society*. London: Sage Publications.

Reich, W. (1970). *The Mass Psychology of Fascism*. New York: Macmillan.

Rodriques, J., A. Choudhary, and H. Dormido (2019). 'A Murky Flood of Money Pours into the World's Largest Election'. *Bloomberg*, 17 March.

https://www.bloombergquint.com/elections/a-murky-flood-of-money-pours-into-the-worlds-largest-election#gs.21os45. Accessed 28 March 2025.

Rosenberg, A. (2016). 'Fascism as a Mass Movement'. In *Fascism: Essays on Europe and India*, edited by J. Banaji, pp. 19–96. New Delhi: Three Essays Collective.

RUPE (2020). *Crisis and Predation: India, COVID-19, and Global Finance*. New York: Monthly Review Press.

Sagar (2020). 'Driven by Islamophobia, Gokalpuri's Hindus Justify Targeted Arson of Mosque, Muslim Homes'. *The Caravan*, 28 February. https://caravanmagazine.in/conflict/driven-islamophobia-gokalpuri-hindus-justify-targeted-arson-local-mosque-muslim-homes Accessed 21 November 2023.

——— (2021). 'Delhi Violence Unmasked: Part One'. *The Caravan*, 1 March. https://caravanmagazine.in/amp/politics/part-one-how-rss-bjp-members-invoked-hindu-identity-to-mobilise-hindutva-mobs-at-maujpur. Accessed 21 November 2023.

Sarkar, S. (2016). 'The Fascism of the Sangh Parivar'. In *Fascism: Essays on Europe and India*, edited by J. Banaji, pp. 135–152. New Delhi: Three Essays Collective.

Sarkar, T. (2022). *Hindu Nationalism in India*. New Delhi: Permanent Black.

Sawyer, M. (2022). 'Monopoly Capitalism in the Past Four Decades'. *Cambridge Journal of Economics* 46(6): 1225–1241.

Simmeon, D. (2016). 'The Law of Killing: A Brief History of Indian Fascism'. In *Fascism: Essays on Europe and India*, edited by J. Banaji, pp. 153–214. New Delhi: Three Essays Collective.

Singh, P., and A. John (2020). 'Crime and Prejudice: The BJP and Delhi Police's Hand in the Delhi Violence'. *The Caravan*, 1 September. https://caravanmagazine.in/politics/the-bjp-and-delhi-police-hand-in-the-delhi-violence. Accessed 28 March 2025.

Stanley, J. (2020). *How Fascism Works: The Politics of Us and Them*. New York: Random House.

Strauss, A. L., and J. M. Corbin (1990). *Basics of Qualitative Research: Grounded Theory Procedures and Techniques*. Thousand Oaks, CA: Sage Publications.

Sud, N. (2022). 'The Actual Gujarat Model: Authoritarianism, Capitalism, Hindu Nationalism and Populism in the Time of Modi'. *Journal of Contemporary Asia* 52(1): 102–126.

The Wire (2023). 'Why Nirmala Sitharaman Is Wrong to Say 'Growing' Muslim Population Means All Is Well'. *The Wire*, 11 April. https://thewire.in/

communalism/nirmala-sitharaman-muslim-population-growth-analysis. Accessed 23 November 2023.

Vanaik, A. (2009). 'India's Paradigmatic Communal Violence'. *Socialist Register* 45: 141–162.

Varman, R., and D. Vijay (eds.) (2022). *Organizing Resistance and Imagining Alternatives in India*. New Delhi: Cambridge University Press.

Varshney, A., and J. Gubler (2013). 'The State and Civil Society in Communal Violence: Sparks and Fires'. In *Routledge Handbook of Indian Politics*, edited by A. Kohli and P. Singh, pp. 155–166. London: Routledge.

Varshney, A. (2002). *Ethnic Conflict and Civic Life: Hindus and Muslims in India*. New Delhi: Oxford University Press.

———. (2020). 'The Rise in Communal Violence'. *The Wire Talks*, episode 60. https://www.youtube.com/watch?v=NP3gLdE9CyE&t=346s. Accessed 23 May 2025.

———. (2022). 'Full Text: Ashutosh Varshney on BJP's Communal Plan, Rights and the Future of India'. *The Wire*, 16 May. https://thewire.in/rights/full-text-ashutosh-varshney-on-bjps-communal-plan-rights-and-the-future-of-india. Accessed 23 November 2023.

Vasudeva, F., and N. Barkdull (2020). 'WhatsApp in India? A Case Study of Social Media related Lynchings'. *Social Identities* 26(5): 574–589.

Verma, A. (2012). 'Role of Police in Containing Mob Violence'. *Economic and Political Weekly* 47(36): 65–73.

Weber, M. (1918). *Politics as a Vocation*. http://fs2.american.edu/dfagel/www/Class%20Readings/Weber/PoliticsAsAVocation.pdf.

Wilkinson, S. (2006). *Votes and Violence: Electoral Competition and Ethnic Riots in India*. Cambridge, UK: Cambridge University Press.

Zachariah, B. (2020). 'India Has the Longest Running Fascist Movement in the world— the RSS'. *The Wire*, 27 January. https://thewire.in/politics/benjamin-zachariah-fascism-sangh-parivar. Accessed 10 September 2021.

Zizek, S. (2008). *Violence*. London: Picador.

12

The Role of Business during the Erosion of Liberal Democracy in Modi's India

Daniel Kinderman

While Donald Trump's ruthless, reckless, aggressive, multi-pronged assaults are threatening American democracy in unprecedented ways, India nevertheless stands out when viewed against broader trends of democratic backsliding (Haggard and Kaufman 2021). Since 2014, liberal democracy in India has come under increasing pressure from Hindu nationalism. Commentators and scholars who are sympathetic to liberal democracy express grave concern, if not alarm, about the state of Indian democracy: 'The blaze is at our door' (A. Roy 2022) and 'The Hindu Rashtra [Hindu Nation] is … indeed underway' (Jaffrelot 2019a, p. 64). One writes that 'India's Democracy Is Dying' and notes that democracy watch organizations now classify India as a 'hybrid regime', an 'electoral autocracy' or a 'flawed democracy' (Tudor 2023).

Electoral democracy remains intact in India, but civil freedoms, minority rights, and institutional constraints on executive power have been substantially weakened (Varshney 2022), and 'India's standing as an inclusive, diverse nation with an independent judiciary, rule of law and free media was degraded' (Patel 2021, p. 460).

During the past decade, prime minister Narendra Modi's Bharatiya Janata Party (BJP) government has 'tethered religious nationalism to right-wing populism' (Basu 2021, p. 278) and prioritized Hindu nationalism over the Indian constitution, as 'an ideology that promotes the idea that Hinduism is the authentic religious and cultural identity of the Indian people' (Yilmaz and Morieson 2023, p. 185). 'The BJP has thus moved Hindutva beyond right-wing nationalism and toward a civilisational struggle between Hindus and "others"' (ibid., p. 198). New Hindutva has fashioned Indian politics into an emotional drama running on anger, fear, and resentment (Hansen and Roy 2022, p. 20). This means India 'is not a case of democratic collapse but one of democratic erosion or democratic backsliding' (Varshney 2022, p. 34). According to the V-Dem Institute (2023, p. 10), India is 'one of the worst autocratisers in the last 10 years'.

To a large extent, these developments are a result or a manifestation of Hindu nationalism, the Indian variety of ethnonationalism (Sahoo 2020) and religious majoritarianism (Patel 2001). India's constitution states that India is a secular nation, and India's first prime minister, Jawaharlal Nehru, declared, 'We accept as Indian anyone who calls himself a citizen of India' (Mander 2021, p. 632). But 'Modi has taken India to a place where political parties dare not speak of secularism and pluralism though it is the basic structure of our [India's] Constitution' (Patel 2001, p. 3). For Hindu nationalists, India is an ethnic democracy (Jaffrelot 2019a). If all members of the polity were of the same ethnicity, this would not necessarily threaten democracy, but in a diverse society such as India, anti-pluralism has resulted in a 'systematic erosion of equal citizenship ... [for] Muslims, Christians and many Dalit people, first in Modi's Gujarat and now in Modi's India' (Mander 2018, p. xxxii). For 'Hindutva adherents, the removal of inauthentic and foreign religions can be perceived as a "cleansing" of India, and a way of returning the nation to its civilizational roots' (Yilmaz and Morieson 2023, p. 186).

Since Hindu nationalists have taken control of the state, 'freedom of expression, independence of civil society, and minority rights, [are] ... under severe erosion' (Varshney 2022, p. 63). This suggests that

> Hindutva nationalism mandates that every Indian must accept and willingly submit to the cultural, social and indeed political dominance of the Hindu faith as interpreted by the Sangh.... The 'nationalist' duty to demonstrate your love for your nation, in the Hindutva doctrine, requires the ultimate litmus test of hating.... I can be a proud Hindu only if I hate Muslims. ... I can love India only if I noisily hate Pakistan. (Mander 2018, p. 156)

> [S]ince 2014, when Narendra Modi was elected Prime Minister ... India has hurtled rapidly and treacherously downward to become a country increasingly dangerous and unwelcoming to its vast Muslim populace, as well as to liberal voices of dissent who speak out to fight for their rights. Elected leaders flaunt hate speech, thereby legitimizing

> and valorizing bigotry and hatred, which have become the dominant markers of social life. Crowds gather to beat Muslims and Dalits to death in the name of protecting the cow or preventing a Muslim man from having a romantic relationship with a Hindu woman (which they call 'love jihad') and then proudly post videos of the murders on social media. (Mander 2021, p. 633)

Modi's re-election in 2019 'was interpreted by the leadership as a mandate to implement its alternate vision for India as a country owned, dominated, and controlled by Hindus' (ibid.). The rise of Hindu nationalism or the

> saffronisation of India comes at a huge cost. Modi's Hindutva political narrative has eroded democracy and the secular state, and given the power to Hindu vigilantes who are attempting to reestablish a civilization rooted in largely fictitious tales of glory.... The result is an India less tolerant, riven by civilisational divisions, and in which the secular democracy of the Indian National Congress—however flawed—is being replaced by a new system in which Hindutva is merged with the state. (Yilmaz and Morieson 2023, p. 208)

Within India, as within any large country, there is substantial sub-national variation, and opposition parties have recently won a few state legislative assembly elections. Thus, while we must not underestimate the dangers of collusion between fascism and big business (Poruthiyil 2021), it is doubtful that India can be considered truly fascist in 2023: elections are meaningless in fascism, which destroys democracy, establishes an ultraviolent dictatorship, and views violence as an end in itself (Finchelstein 2017). However, Hindutva is clearly anti-pluralist. Perhaps, India can be characterized as a 'fascist democracy', in which 'fascist elements are entwined with democracy' (I. Roy 2023, p. 47): 'Modalities of Hindutva violence are significantly influenced by the populist and religious nationalist character of the current regime. The BJP's success rests on continual populist-style mobilization, accompanied by violence, to secure and expand its base' (Basu 2021, p. 290). This makes this movement a danger to democracy, and the violence could spread through contagion—a slippery slope from an electoral autocracy towards a fascist regime cannot be ruled out.

These political developments have important implications for business, which is a powerful interest group in all capitalist democracies. How has Indian business responded to these developments? This chapter builds on historical and contemporary literature and interviews to advance our understanding of the role(s) that Indian business has played in this conjuncture. Conceptually, Feldmann and Morgan's (2021) heuristic is helpful. Feldmann and Morgan extend Albert O. Hirschman's 'exit, voice, and loyalty' framework to identify the strategies businesses deploy in response to right-wing populists: exit, implicit loyalty, explicit loyalty, soft voice, and loud voice.[1]

As one scholar using this heuristic points out, 'So far, business has been unable or unwilling to resist Modi's political aggrandisement. The rise of aggressive nationalism and personalist politics has mostly been met with "implicit loyalty" and a more cautious approach to politics by business' (Wyatt 2023, p. 197). In large corporations, at the top of India Inc., there are examples of 'explicit loyalty' to Modi's BJP government: the Adani Group and Reliance Industries are prominent examples (ibid., p. 193).[2]

Of course, that is not the whole story. In early 2017, an Indian scholar asked, 'Can India Inc speak up against hate like Silicon Valley has done against social issues?' (Mirza 2017). There are some examples of business voice in India: in 2020, Rajiv Bajaj, the chief executive officer (CEO) of Bajaj Group and one of India's biggest industrialists, withdrew advertising from three television channels that were a source of hate-mongering and toxicity. He stated, 'I don't want my child to inherit an India built on hate.' To be sure, this was a criticism or denunciation of one of religious nationalism's most pernicious consequences, rather than of religious nationalism itself, but it was an example of loud voice in support of pluralism, nevertheless. Bajaj had previously stated that he firmly believes in the 'idea of India' and in India's diversity (Nair 2012). Other Indian companies have shown advertisements that sought to promote harmonious relations between Hindus and Muslims, and they received significant backlash for doing so. Overall, there is widespread agreement that India Inc., which includes corporate interests and India's largest companies, such as the Tata Group, Reliance Industries, and the Adani Group, cultivate close and perhaps even cosy relations with Modi's BJP government.

Poruthiyil (2018) submits that there are two major reasons why many business people in India have been relatively quiet in the face of the erosion of democracy in India: greed and fear, or carrots and sticks. My analysis in this chapter builds on and supports Poruthiyil's argument: the BJP's overall business-friendliness allows them to 'buy' support from an undisclosed number of businesses. In addition, the fact that a large majority of India's population is Hindu increases the incentives for business people to jump on the BJP and Hindutva bandwagon. It is safe to assume that the pro-business stance and policies of Modi's BJP have increased the number of businesses that are willingly on board the Hindutva bandwagon. Of course, businesspeople may be motivated by values, by what Max Weber called 'ideal interests', in addition to material ones. If those values are strong and opposed to Hindu nationalism, material incentives may be insufficient, and fear and state repression assume great importance. On the other hand, if corporate leadership and business people share the Hindu supremacist values that the BJP seeks to promote, those people may support Modi's BJP, quite apart from their material interests as businesses.

There is widespread agreement that Modi's government uses the power of the state to suppress dissent and target those—including businesses—who refuse to toe the party line. This makes loud and soft voices more risky and costly. While implicit loyalty is almost certainly the default mode for most businesspeople in India, it may be useful to differentiate more sharply between corporate interests and business interests when it comes to supporting Modi's regime. In this latter category, which is much wider, there are courageous business people who are willing to take risks to defend liberal democracy. In line with this, I draw attention to some examples of soft and loud voices, which involve strong public positions, by small businesses, petty traders, and others in the micro, small, and medium enterprises (MSMEs) category, in the context of the Bharat Jodo Yatra marches in 2022–2023. I conclude by comparing business responses to anti-pluralism in other countries and offer some programmatic advice for business people who are concerned about the state of liberal democracy in India.

The chapter is organized as follows. The following section discusses the important role of material interests and greed. The third section discusses the role of state repression and fear. The fourth section addresses the role of religious nationalism and cultural supremacism. The fifth section draws on interviews to discuss business participation in the Bharat Jodo Yatra marches in 2022–2023. The sixth section points out that while Indian business faces challenges in opposing Hindutva due to a combination of pro-business incentives and state repression, some do resist humanistic values. Business leaders must define and defend these. The conclusion compares India to other cases and offers some recommendations for business leaders.

Material interests and greed

CEOs, managers, and businesspeople in general are strongly motivated by material interests, and they will generally pursue business opportunities and support or make deals with anyone who may be able to further their interests. Business opportunities present themselves not only in liberal democracies, but also in authoritarian capitalist states, which have become increasingly business-friendly in recent decades, and where, at least until recently, these states' illiberalism and authoritarianism lacked significant drawbacks for large segments of business (Kinderman 2021). Corporate collusions with neoliberal and fascist forces have become a major topic in recent years given the rise of authoritarian politics in many countries across the globe (Poruthiyil 2021). Taking a more historical perspective, it is by now very well known that Germany's wealthiest and most prominent industrialists embraced the Nazi regime as it offered many attractive business opportunities (de Jong 2022).

In addition, historians have found that even businesses in what are today liberal democracies—such as the United States (US)—sought out business opportunities in fascist regimes. Thus, in different ways, Ford, General Motors, and International Business Machines Corporation (IBM) decided to do business with Nazi Germany, even though many of their investments in Nazi Germany were unprofitable. Even those who were not antisemitic and pro-Nazi, like Henry Ford was (Weixelbaum 2018), were enticed by the possibility of future profits. In general, illiberal governments or political parties will engender business support if they are otherwise business-friendly (Kinderman 2023). By contrast, those on the political left who support political liberalism but have an explicitly anti-business or anti-capitalist orientation will encounter fierce business resistance and business collective action.

Thus, one of the major reasons why business opposition to Modi's BJP government has been muted is the BJP's pro-business and pro-market orientation. The BJP has a long history as a pro-business party: already in the early 1990s, the BJP had prominent business support (Malik and Singh 1992). When the BJP first came to power in Delhi in 1998, urban traders were the oldest layer in the BJP's support base. Given the BJP's commitment to private enterprise, '[b]usiness's support is readily understandable' (Kohli 1998, pp. 11–12). When Modi was the chief minister of Gujarat, the state was business-friendly (Jaffrelot 2019b). Indeed, shortly after Modi had become prime minister of India, the World Bank ranked Gujarat as the best state in India to do business. Although the World Bank's Ease of Doing Business Index has been discontinued, an examination of historical data shows that India's global ranking improved substantially under Modi's BJP since 2014.

Figure 12.1 shows that for a decade, from the mid-2000s until 2016, India's ranking in the World Bank's Ease of Doing Business Index remained stable at around number 130. Between 2016 and 2019, India's ranking improved considerably. This is relevant to my argument—it can be safely assumed that many business people will appreciate the removal of red tape. Along these lines, at the time of writing, media outlets discussed India's transition from red tape to red carpet. The business friendliness of Modi's BJP and the policies it has enacted, which include changes in labour laws, reductions in corporate taxes, and the sale of public assets (Chowdhury 2023), reduces the likelihood that businesspeople will stand up and speak out against the government. In 2019, the BJP government lowered the base corporate tax rate from 30 per cent to 22 per cent, which significantly lowered the corporate tax to GDP ratio in India (ibid., p. 155).

Needless to say, profits are more important for business than the corporate tax rate. Nor does a general growing ease of doing business imply that all segments of Indian business have benefitted equally. While Modi's government has strongly supported large businesses, it has been suggested

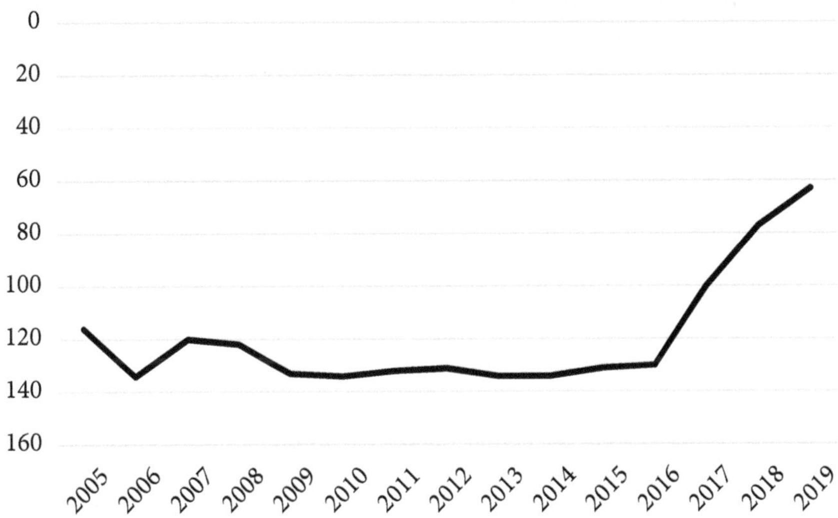

Figure 12.1 India's ease of doing business ranking, 2005–2019

Source: World Bank, https://archive.doingbusiness.org/en/data (accessed 18 April 2025).

that demonetization and the goods and services tax (GST) have hurt India's vast array of MSMEs (Sinha and Nayak 2021). If that is indeed the case, it may have increased the inclination of businesspeople in the MSME sector to support the opposition and/or voice their discontentment with the government.

Since communalism can be problematic and costly for business, it is important to consider the possible business costs of the BJP's illiberalism and religious nationalism. Business people who are enthusiastic, full-throated supporters of the Hindu Rashtra project may be willing to engage in extreme actions, even if those actions end up being costly for them. But businesspeople without strong illiberal values and/or extreme prejudices may hesitate to engage in such actions if they end up being costly for their business, which could be the case if there is a loss of consumer demand. The fact that Indian Muslim households are generally poorer, and on average have lower incomes and less wealth than Hindu households (Khan 2020; Rakshit 2023), makes Hindu discrimination against and/or persecution of Muslims less costly than it otherwise would be. In addition, the fact that Muslims account for 14 per cent of the Indian population, as opposed to 80 per cent of Hindus, makes it less costly in aggregate terms for the latter to discriminate against the former than would be the case if Muslims made up a larger chunk of the Indian population.

Many other factors are relevant, including the demographic composition of the business in question. If a small company is owned and run by Hindus and has Hindu suppliers and customers, Hindutva may not pose a big problem from a strict and narrow business point of view. By contrast, for larger firms with diverse employees, customers, and suppliers, communalism may be more costly if it increases tensions among employees or disrupts the company's relations with its important stakeholders. By extension, businesspeople may be more hostile towards communalism in large, diverse companies than in smaller, more homogeneous ones. It would be interesting to see if this hypothesis is borne out, for example, in an examination of the companies in the pro-Modi and pro-Hindutva 'Resurgent Group of Gujarat'.

Ultimately, businesses need to make money, and ceteris paribus, more profitable businesses are likely to be happier with the political powers that be than less profitable businesses. In the absence of comprehensive data for the Indian business class, Figure 12.2 shows the wealth share of the Indian business and propertied elite. More specifically, it shows the wealth share of India's top decile and centile, which Thomas Piketty calls the 'dominant class', over time.

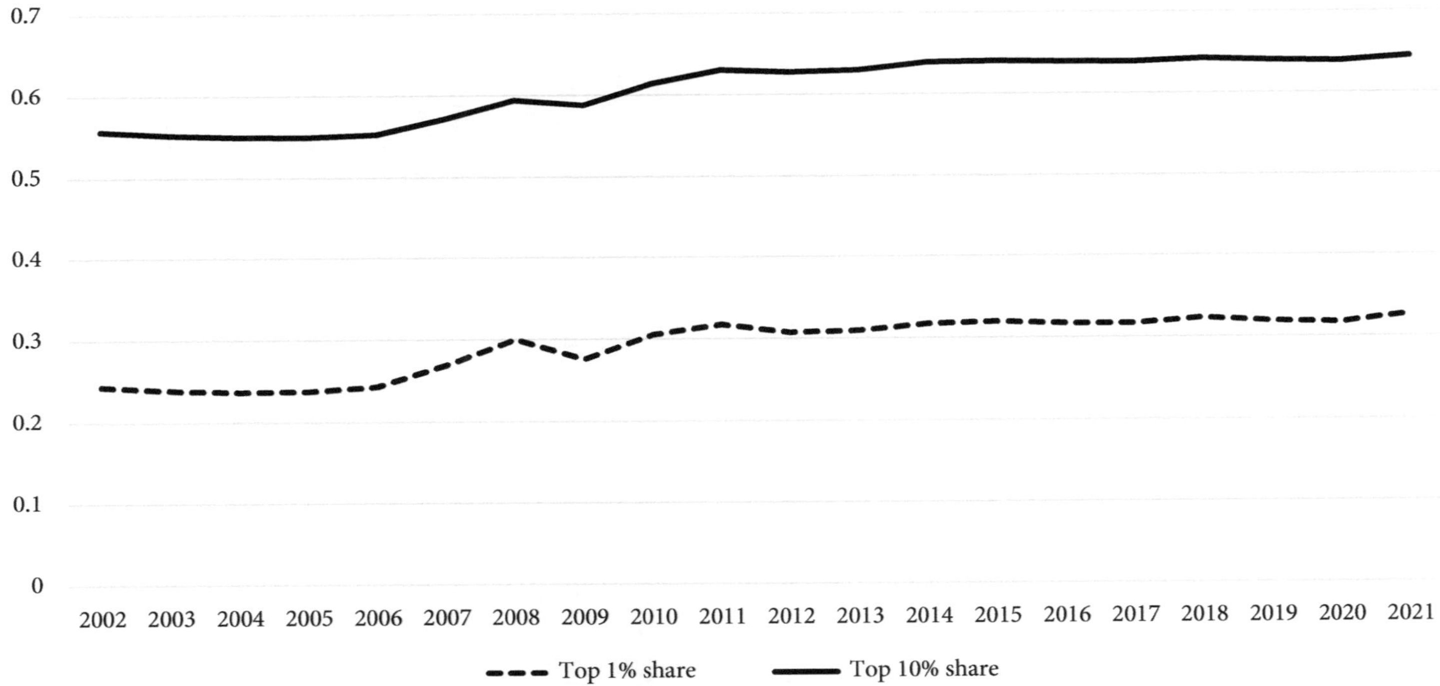

Figure 12.2 Top 10 per cent and top 1 per cent wealth share in India, 2002–2021

Source: World Inequality Database, https://wid.world (accessed 18 April 2025).

The overall trend is clearly upward. Interestingly, the wealth share of the top 10 per cent and top 1 per cent increased more rapidly under Congress-led governments between 2004 and 2014 than it has under Modi's BJP since 2014. However, it has continued to increase during the past decade. More granular data would be helpful. If India's 20 most profitable firms have recently generated 70 per cent of the country's profits, up from 14 per cent three decades ago (Marcellus 2020), it seems likely that this segment of India Inc. has been strongly supportive of Modi's BJP government. This too would need to be substantiated through empirical research, perhaps by comparing the political donations of large firms to the BJP.

To sum up this section, the BJP benefits from being a pro-business, pro-market party, and it appears that some businesspeople have done quite well for themselves in Modi's India. These incentives increase the business support for Hindutva, but they do not render anti-pluralism costless for Indian businesses. Nor is it true that businesspeople are motivated exclusively by material interests. The next section explains how state repression and fear help to silence and discourage those who would otherwise be inclined to speak out against anti-pluralists in the government and/or in society.

Fear and state repression

Fear powerfully motivates human action. In 2019, as the late Rahul Bajaj, chairman emeritus of the Bajaj Group industry conglomerate and 'the last bastion of Gandhian industrialists' (*Fortune India* 2022), stated, 'There is an environment of fear in India, where everyone is afraid of criticising the government.' This statement by one of India's leading industrialists struck a chord with many. This section sketches how fear and state repression have shrunk the space for voice against Hindutva and Modi's BJP government by making it both more risky and more costly. This chapter is not the place for a comprehensive review of state repression by Modi's BJP government, but the following example illustrates this broader dynamic:

> Among the first legislative acts of the second Modi government was the amendment of the laws related to terrorism and 'public safety'. The government now has the power to designate any individual as a terrorist (based on writings, speeches, even possession of certain kinds of literature), and the room for judicial appeals against such detentions has

> been substantially reduced. A similar legal dictum applies to preventive detention on grounds of public safety. Essentially, with these laws, imprisonment for political dissent is perfectly possible, something not practiced on a significant scale since the Emergency but increasingly being practiced now. (Varshney 2022, pp. 65–66)

The following two figures provide evidence of growing authoritarianism. Figure 12.3 shows the V-Dem Institute's Liberal Democracy Index, which measures civil liberties, checks and balances, the rule of law, and aspects of electoral democracy.

Between 2002 and 2014, India's Liberal Democracy Index score tended gradually downward, but since Modi and the BJP came to power in 2014, this decline has accelerated, leading to a precipitous drop. Figure 12.4 shows that press freedoms have also deteriorated in India between 2002 and 2023.

In 2002, under prime minister Atal Bihari Vajpayee's BJP-led National Democratic Alliance, India's press freedoms were ranked number 80 in the world. When the BJP conceded defeat and the Congress returned to power in 2004, India's press freedoms were ranked number 120 in the world. By the time the BJP returned to power and Modi became the prime minister in 2014, India's ranking had deteriorated to number 140. By 2023, India's global score had declined even more, and its ranking had deteriorated to number 161, which placed it in the bottom 11 per cent of the countries ranked by Reporters Without Borders.

My anonymous interviewee refers to a high level of 'viciousness' and coercion in the media sector in recent years. This person states that the Indian government threatens companies that it will 'destroy their reputation' if they do not tow the party line. As this person continues, if the company does not comply with the government's wishes, the government will launch an income tax raid and close the office down.[3] The 'large media houses are totally coopted' by Modi's BJP government. Comparing India's media ecosystem with the US, this person says, 'The Indian media is Fox News and rightward'.[4] This suggests that India's improvement in the Ease of Doing Business Index is somewhat misleading: it has only become easier to do business in India if one does not criticize or come into the crosshairs of government. If one does, doing business can quickly become difficult or impossible.

It should be noted that the use of state power, more specifically the deployment of the enforcement directorate and income tax officials, to shape business behaviour and extract resources from them was already practised

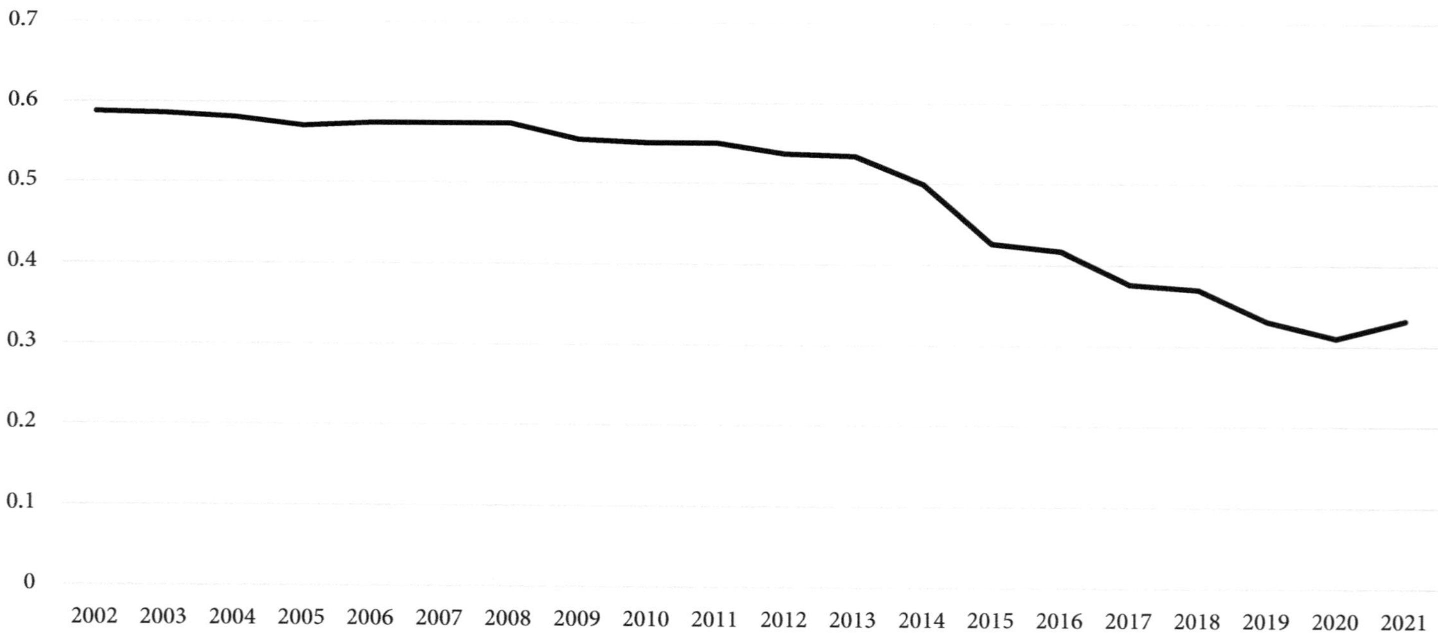

Figure 12.3 Liberal Democracy Index in India, 2002–2021

Source: V-Dem Institute, https://www.v-dem.net (accessed 18 April 2025).

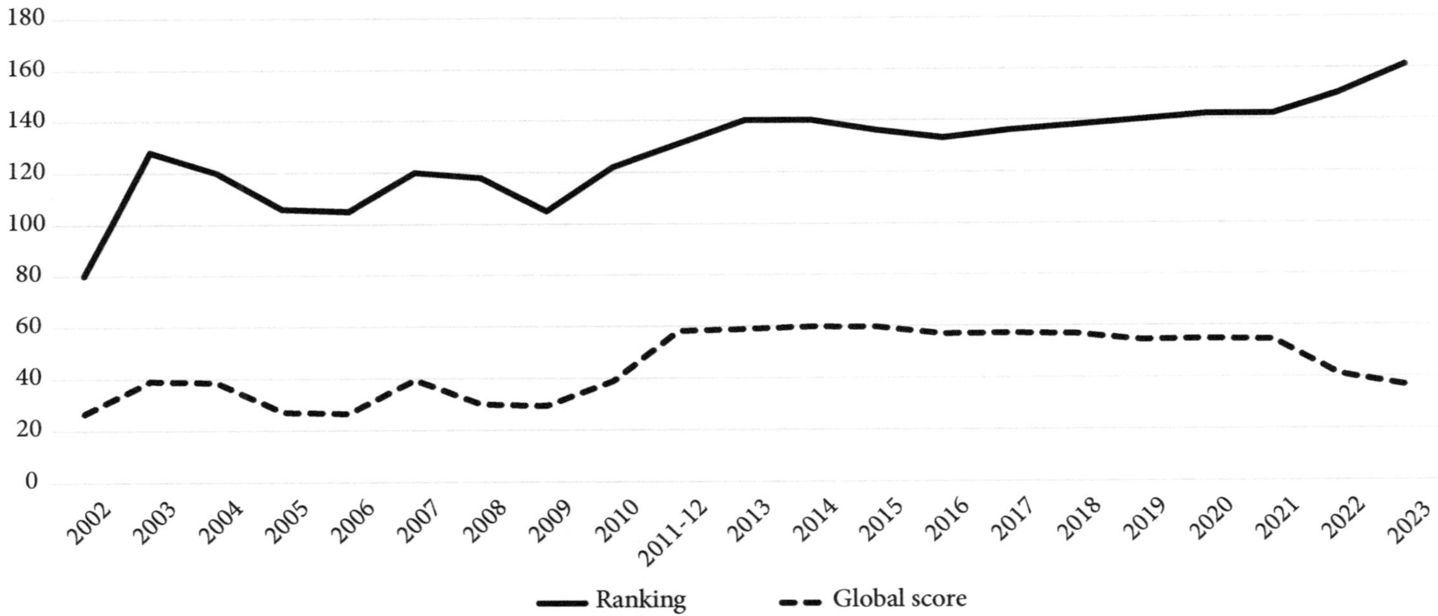

Figure 12.4 World press freedom ranking and score for India, 2022–2023

Source: Reporters Without Borders, https://rsf.org/en/index (accessed 18 April 2025).

under the Congress in the 1970s (Kochanek 1987)—it did not begin with the BJP. Further research will determine whether Modi's BJP government is making more widespread and aggressive use of these tools than previous governments. Given the state's ability to use state machinery, such as law and coercion, to achieve its goals, it is feared by dissidents: most people prefer to stay out of jail. But fear can also emanate from fellow citizens who propagate hate, engage in hate speech (also digitally), practise economic boycotts, or engage in various kinds of violence, such as mob lynchings.

India's economy, some scholars maintain, should be understood as a system of 'oligarchic state capitalism' (Chaterjee 2023) or as a system of 'crony capitalism' (Khatri and Ojha 2016). This implies a lower degree of business autonomy and a higher degree of direct business dependence on politics, and vice-versa. The 'symbiotic relationship between the state leadership and a small coterie of favored businessmen' (Chaterjee 2023, p. 129) shrinks and narrows the space for business voices from the affected firms. I do not mean to suggest that Adani, Ambani, and the like fear state repression by Modi's government, but if they were to criticize the government in public in certain ways, that could easily change.

A fusion of greed and fear: the electoral bonds scheme

Greed and fear can be particularly powerful when they are fused or used jointly. There is scarcely a better example of the fusion of greed and fear than the Electoral Bonds Scheme (EBS), which came into effect in 2018 and which the Supreme Court of India (led by Chief Justice D. Y. Chandrachud) struck down in 2024, before this volume went to press. A very large share of all bonds sold went to the ruling BJP. What motivated companies to buy these bonds and support the BJP government?

As the Supreme Court put it, 'Contributions made by companies are purely business transactions made with the intent of securing benefits in return.' In other words, purchases of electoral bonds and corporate donations to the government were motivated by a quid-pro-quo system which benefitted both parties, albeit not necessarily to the same extent. The BJP government used the EBS to extract resources from companies: when government agencies such as the Central Bureau of Investigation (CBI), Enforcement Directorate, and the Income Tax Department raided them, companies in turn would purchase electoral bonds to curry favour with the government and perhaps also end the agency action. It is unclear to what extent the EBS allowed the government to extract financial resources from companies and businesspeople who had done nothing wrong, and companies and businesspeople who had been justly prosecuted for breaking the law were able to use electoral bonds to get themselves out of legal trouble (see Goyal 2024; Goyal et al. 2024).

States coerce their citizens in various ways, and the government of India has used this power, coupled with the EBS, to extract resources from fearful businesses for the BJP. But the corporate agency and greed have been important too. Businesspeople have used electoral bonds to get contracts, licenses, leases, clearances, and approvals worth thousands and sometimes lakhs of crores (*The Wire* 2024). Electoral bonds were also used to obtain more favourable rulings and policy changes, which could have major benefits for the affected businesses, and stall or stop agency action (ibid.). While the former examples provide businesses with clear material benefits, the latter shows that they can also use their financial resources to buy freedom from unjust state coercion or to free themselves from being accountable under the law.

Fear and greed powerfully motivate human action. Although the EBS has been declared illegal, the money that the BJP made through them has already tilted the scale, perhaps irreversibly.

Religious nationalism and cultural supremacism

Although fear and greed powerfully motivate business, this greed–fear categorization may not be comprehensive enough to explain corporate attitudes. While businesses are constrained and influenced by market demand and competition as well as state regulation and coercion, human beings, including businesspeople, are not economic automatons. Values and cultural interests, 'political or religious interests … can be much stronger than economic interests' (Swedberg 2005, p. 69), as Max Weber recognized long ago.

Along this line of thinking, some members of the Indian corporate elite may support Modi's BJP government because they subscribe to its Hindu nationalist ideology—the belief that India is a Hindu nation rather than a pluralistic one. To avoid any misunderstanding, greed and fear are powerful, but these forces do not apply equally to all firms and all business people in all market segments. There are some business people for whom these influences do not matter very much. Cultural or religious beliefs may be more important than more narrowly conceived business interests. For some businesspeople, the defence of cultural traditions or religious values may take priority or precedence over material interests.

This claim becomes more plausible when one considers the role religion plays in the lives of many Indian citizens. For example, Soper and Fetzer point out that according to the World Values survey, two-thirds of respondents in India indicated that religion is a very important part of their lives (2018, p. 201). Over the past few decades, the proportion of respondents in India for whom religion is very important has increased substantially, according to the survey (ibid., p. 208). From this perspective, it makes sense to rally Indian voters along religious lines (ibid., p. 201), and that is exactly what the BJP has done. As a result of these trends, 'secular nationalism is hardly dead in India, but it clearly is on the decline' (ibid., p. 223).

The division or distinction between material interests and cultural values is not always clear-cut. Religious nationalists will strive to provide their followers in business with material rewards and benefits, and if businesspeople who align themselves with the cultural or religious values of the majority receive economic benefits or business rents for doing so, material benefits and cultural values can reinforce each other. Conversely, taking a strong secularist or anti-government stance may be costly for business. Some groups support Modi's BJP government because they view the government as defending their cultural privileges vis-à-vis other groups in Indian society. In this vein, Modi, Heller (2020, p. 605) argues, represents a reactionary movement that seeks to protect and defend the accumulated privileges, values, and social structures of elites from social movement pressure from below. Cultural supremacist values and economic interests shape each other in complex ways.

Despite these serious pressures—incentives from the business-friendly BJP, harsh sticks in the form of fear and (threats of) state repression, and the ascendance of religious nationalism—there are soft and loud voices, quiet and loud resistance to communalization in the Indian business community. The next section shows that some businesspeople are willing to join a movement to voice their dissent if there is a political vehicle that enables them to do so.

Business participation in the Bharat Jodo Yatra

The Bharat Jodo Yatra (BJY) was a 'unite India march' that took place from September 2022 until January 2023 from Kanyakumari to Kashmir, across twelve states of India, a distance of approximately 3500km. Former president of the Congress, Rahul Gandhi, around whom the BJY was organized, stated, 'The spirit of this yatra is to bring Indians together regardless of religion, community and remind them that this is one country and it will be successful if we stand together and are respectful to each other.' The underlying ideology and programmatic message of the BJY are pluralist, a clear contrast to the BJP's Hindutva.

We will never know the exact number of businesspeople who participated in the BJY, but we know that some did participate. The evidence in this section suggests that pluralistic values/convictions and courage played a very important role in motivating businesspeople to participate in the BJY marches. It is possible also that the perceived or actual mistreatment of MSMEs by Modi's BJP government in favour of very large companies in Modi's inner circle also helped motivate business participation. Rahul Gandhi highlighted the plight of MSMEs in a YouTube video, 'Wake up MSMEs, you are under attack!', which aired in early January 2023. Also, it cannot be ruled out that some of these people may be Congress loyalists. In the writings of those who joined the BJY, we find moving descriptions of businesspeople from the MSME sector who joined the march:

> Hoimee Dey had travelled from Kolkata to join the Yatra. She was a manager in a small firm, and had asked for leave to join the Bharat Jodo Yatra. When leave was refused, she resigned and came to Rajasthan to join the Yatra. 'I will get a job when I return but such an opportunity will not come again,' she said. 'I do not like what is happening in the country, and the hate being spread; so I had to join and protest.' (Atkuri 2022)

In this example, liberal democratic values took precedence over shorter-term material interests. In a related vein, Darshan Mondkar, a businessman from Pune who runs a manufacturing MSME, said he was grappling with an 'internal tussle' between his socialist side and his capitalist side. 'I am a businessman, so honestly Modi has been good to me.... but the targeting of minorities and women and communalization of issues is what bothers me' (Sodhi 2022).

My interviewees—MSME businesspeople who participated in the BJY—were motivated first and foremost by values: by the disapproval of the dominant anti-pluralism. This is confirmed by the following extracts (a full list of the interviews can be found in Appendix 12A), first from Darshan Mondkar, who states,

> My participation in the Bharat Jodo Yatra was more from a social standpoint than from a business one. However, I am of the view that both do go hand in hand to some extent. A business-based economy cannot thrive in an atmosphere filled with hate. The Bharat Jodo Yatra, according to me, was making a concentrated effort in bringing people together instead of pushing them apart, as is the current narrative being hyped in India.
>
> The actions of the BJP government do seem to be favouring the businesses, but this is not the case. A targeted effort is being made by their actions to ensure that the MSME sector is not supported. Instead, their sops are aimed to benefit the larger corporate houses at the cost or demise of the MSME sector.
>
> I think the Bharat Jodo Yatra is already making a difference.... The very fact that the BJY received such a huge response shows that the people are generally fed up with the hate narrative and want to have a peaceful coexistence. With the right guidance from the top echelons of the government, this would very much be achievable and wholeheartedly supported by the people. Right now, in India, the peace-loving majority is being outshouted by the hate-mongering minority (number-wise, not community). The trolls do not outnumber the rational voices; it is just that the trolls get their voices heard better thanks to the BJP support for this narrative.
>
> The businesspeople will be the last to speak out about this since their businesses can be shut down at a snap of the fingers. The 'raid culture' has scared everyone, and even the biggest grouse is being whispered about mainly in closed circles.[5]

Rahul Rajamuthiah, a retail professional based in Mumbai, states,

> My rationale was humanitarian, which is far simpler and [more] basic than bigger abstract ideas like politics and economics. Let me explain.

> The rise of the BJP has been on the back of placing Muslim lives as dispensable. Lynching, vigilante executions, local-level rioting, and pogroms are the basis on which the BJP has garnered its core vote bank. I feel even if India is the most populous country, it doesn't mean that any human life is dispensable. By othering the Muslims and letting people get lynched, and ensuring there is no form of justice available to the families of the ones killed or maimed, the BJP has accentuated a cleavage which remained buried in the polity.
>
> India, which should be seen as a continent (an analogous one would be Europe), already has many cleavages, ethnic, linguistic, caste, and food habits. While politics is about appealing to segments with an affirmative or enabling support from the state, the BJP's model is one of creating enemies which can then be annihilated for electoral purposes.
>
> The Bharat Jodo Yatra was approaching from exactly the opposite end, saying that we need to unite this country rather than create enemies within. My participation was to demonstrate solidarity with that idea.
>
> It is risky, not just as a businessman, but as a human, more so, if you are an Indian citizen. If the BJP government sees you as a source which is challenging their idea, they haven't hesitated to use all means (which could even be illicit) to trap the individual under the Indian legal system.
>
> While I am not sure, I feel there were people of all shades who participated in the yatra. These were the silent ones who do not have any direct affiliation, but grieve for this sad state the Idea of India is going through.[6]

Shyama Iyer, a sociopolitical activist who recently retired from the Indian Institute of Technology Bombay as a project manager, spoke to two businesspeople who had participated in the BJY: one who runs a cybercafe/ computer training institute and another who has a construction company. According to these interviewees, the financial effect of the BJP's economic policies, which include demonetization and the perception or reality of support given to big business, to the detriment of MSMEs, played an important role in motivating business participation in the BJY (Iyer, 2023). But values were also important:

> There is a strong wish for a change in government, hence the support to the BJY. People came because they wanted to have played some part

in protesting against the present policies. They would not want to face their children, who would question them in the future on their silence. Another motivation was to support the message of love over hate, which would create an environment conducive to purchase, spend, and consumer happiness.

Fear of being persecuted for having participated in the Yatra was very much seen but the businessmen accepted the risk. They felt that there is no other way to highlight their problems to the government at large.[7]

Finally, Dipali Sikand is a businesswoman based in Bengaluru, who runs several businesses, mainly in the hospitality field. Sikand's value orientation is very strong:

I live by the courage of my convictions. I believe in the ideology of the Congress party and in a secular democratic scientific tempered country where civil society dialogue happens without polarization and institutions are respected. Being a businesswoman comes second to being a proud Indian where for me the constitution of my country is the Bible. If you have nothing to hide, if you have run your business and personal life without a single compromise to the laws, what is there to fear?

Is it risky to speak as a businesswoman? The choice is simple for me: what is the legacy I want to leave behind? A woman who lived by her convictions and beliefs or a woman to lived in fear of speaking out because there could be imminent repercussions? I believe political and religious beliefs are personal and each has their right to their own opinions.

Risk comes from all sources. Customers, clients and the government at various levels.... It is true many do not speak out as they don't want to be trolled or harassed or perceived as anti-government. But I personally have to sleep with my conscience, and I can't hide behind excuses. I haven't personally lost a client because of my beliefs. And I guess because my business records are transparent and at all stages lawful the govt cannot find fault with at least my business.... Some fear business, some fear putting their families at risk. Some are just not bothered and feel this too shall pass. Most feel: will their views even matter, and most don't have the guts![8]

Sikand states that she participated in the MSME meetup in Tamil Nadu with approximately two dozen other MSME owners. She concludes by saying, 'Local MSMEs will speak up. It's the bigger business houses and owners who fear more and therefore appear to toe the line the government wants them to.'[9]

Although the interview evidence in this section is from a small sample, it suggests that liberal and pluralistic values, courage, and a sense of concern about the state of their country motivated MSME business owners to participate in the BJY. If participation in the BJY entailed risks for these businesspeople, this did not deter them from participating. A business voice is possible in Modi's India. However, current evidence suggests that large corporations have played a very minute role in the BJY movement. Further research could adjudicate between competing explanations and expose whether large corporations are more vulnerable to pressure by state officials who support Modi's BJP, or whether the upper echelons of these companies are more uniformly Hindu supremacist in their orientation than the MSME sector.

Conclusion, comparative outlook, and recommendations for business leaders

I began this chapter with a survey of the trends of illiberalism, autocratization, and anti-pluralism in Modi's India. Given its power in capitalist democracies, business has the ability to shape, influence, and resist these developments. In the central empirical sections of my chapter, I discussed some major reasons why there has been relatively little public business opposition to Hindutva. First, the carrots (or material incentives) of Modi's BJP are strongly pro-business in orientation. India's business elite has done well for itself during the past decade. Even if some of them do not approve of the communalization of India and rising tensions between Hindus and Muslims, their pocketbooks are likely to influence their political views and allegiances. Of course, business people are not motivated exclusively by material interests: people are also motivated by material/economic interests and by cultural and religious as well as political values. Business people who strongly subscribe to the idea of a Hindu Rashtra will jump aboard the Hindutva bandwagon whether it serves their material interests or not. For supporters of pluralism and secularism, state repression and fear play an important role: by raising the risks and costs of speaking out against the powers that be, these influences discourage and, in many cases, silence those who would otherwise be inclined to speak out against anti-pluralism.

In spite of this inhospitable environment, my chapter does draw attention to some examples of soft and loud voices, or quiet and loud resistance to communalization, by parts of the Indian business community. In addition to the well-known cases in which some companies have 'said no to hate' by withdrawing their advertising from channels with toxic and hateful content, the evidence I collected suggests that a substantial number of businesspeople in the MSME sector participated in the BJY marches in 2022–2023. It is certainly possible that business challenges helped motivate MSMEs to participate in the BJY marches, but the interview evidence I collected suggests that pluralistic and humanistic values and courage also played an important role in motivating these people. Over a century ago, the founder of modern-day sociology, Max Weber, stressed the importance of ideal interests, and we see that values, norms, and convictions do lead some businesspeople to stand up and speak out in defence of democracy and minority rights in India, in spite of the risks that this entails. A cursory comparison with two well-established liberal democracies helps show why it can be difficult for Indian business to speak up against Hindutva.

During Donald Trump's first presidency (2017–2021), the US was roughly equally divided between Democrats and Republicans. This made it comparatively easy for at least some segments of American business to resist Trump: they had more than half of the country behind them, and companies that were more clearly based in one of the two American political tribes—Democratic or Republican—could do well by appealing to their side and mobilizing against the other side. With Trump's return to the presidency in 2025 with a Republican trifecta, many businesspeople and business organizations that had been vocal and outspoken critics of Trump's first administration became quieter and more cautious. This reflects the second Trump presidency's authoritarian attacks on its political opponents and enemies, which have dramatically raised the risks and costs of dissent. Although I expect business voice and opposition to continue, the US under Trump 2.0 has moved closer to Modi's India.

The environment in Germany (Kinderman 2020) is even more favourable for businesses that speak out against the right-wing populist Alternative für Deutschland (AfD). Although support for the AfD has grown, over two-thirds of the German population opposed the AfD at the time of writing, and perhaps even more importantly, the AfD so far has very little power over the German state—one mayor and one district administrator belonged to the AfD. This is a stark contrast to the BJP, which not only has an extremely popular prime minister, but also has a majority of seats in India's parliament, the Lok Sabha. This gives it very far-reaching political power. The environment and topology of power is much more challenging for business opponents of Modi's BJP government in India than it was under Trump 1.0 or in contemporary Germany. The environment and topology of power may be somewhat more favourable when opposition parties are in power at the level of state governments.

This chapter concludes with some programmatic advice (which builds on Doty and Kinderman 2022): in the face of the current threats to liberal democracy in India, businesspeople need to know where they stand. At a minimum, they should avoid actively or financially supporting people or political parties that threaten democracy. More generally, they need to ask: What are their red lines? What democratic values are they willing to stand up for? Will they stand up against aggressive Hindutva? Can they find a way to forcefully stand up against communalism and resurrect and popularize a traditional multicultural identity, which has receded in the face of Hindu nationalism? Some extremists have called for genocide in order to fulfil their vision of a Hindu Rashtra. These calls are not only morally reprehensible and despicable, but they are also extremely dangerous. They must be denounced by businesspeople and by all citizens in the strongest possible terms.

Furthermore, '[i]f Modi's appointees to the Election Commission were to overturn the results of an election, or deprive voters opposed to Modi of their franchise' (Varshney 2022, p. 63), it would be imperative for business leaders of all stripes and colours to stand up, speak out, and take action. If business owners are also respected members of the community, they are positioned to have a significant impact. Can business muster the courage to speak out against aggressive Hindutva, and to help to breathe fresh new life into a pluralistic liberal democratic counter-narrative to ethno-nationalism? As one scholar recently observed, 'At no other point in independent India has there been more need for a counter-narrative than at this juncture' (Poddar 2019).

Given the support of Hindutva and Modi's BJP in important segments of Indian business, developing a successful counter-narrative will not be easy: 'Modi belongs to this new "Aspirational India" that also desires more, and, he believes, it belongs to him. It is a social class that does not think or dream in English.... This class does not constitute India's power elite but it has begun to matter more—socially, politically, and economically' (Baru 2021, p. 37). On the other hand, those who support pluralism and political liberalism need not think or dream in English—any of the many languages spoken in India will do the trick. The strong values that motivated some of the MSME participants in the BJY marches provide grounds for hope—business voice is possible in Modi's India.

The brief survey in this chapter is not a comprehensive overview of the businesspeople in India who act against hate. Beef lynchings are a category of communal violence and religiously motivated hate crimes that have increased since Modi took office: 'once lynchings began, there was little or no effort from the State to end the violence against India's minorities, predominantly Muslims' (Patel 2021, p. 212). In this context, the Karwan e Mohabbat—Caravan of Love—supports the survivors of hate crimes and targeted violence, powered by human rights activist Harsh Mander and his team and 'the universal values of the constitution, of solidarity, equality, freedom, justice and compassion'.

Karwan e Mohabbat requires material resources to do its work, and some businesspeople have risen to the occasion: 'Karwan e Mohabbat has been supported by individual as well as institutional donations by business houses'.[10] Can these activities be scaled up? Can businesspeople come up with creative ideas to defend and reinvigorate pluralism and pluralist values in India as an alternative to the ascendant Hindu nationalist identity? Can additional pressure be put on multinationals and on Western technology companies such as Meta/Facebook, which generate large profits in India and have been at the very least complicit in the upsurge of communalist violence in India?

As Sharma (2023) points out, Internet Hindus, disinformation, and online propaganda in the current era were preceded by audio cassettes, which delivered emotionally charged messages helping to provoke vigilante violence and communal unrest in India. In recent years, '[t]he attack on free speech in the Modi years is accompanied by hate speech flowing freely from the ruling party on Facebook, which lets the government get away with inciting murder in India' (Patel 2021, p. 63). Acting against the BJP would damage Facebook's business interests in India (ibid., p. 64), but it should be easier to get companies such as Facebook/Meta to take a much more proactive stance against online hate and communal violence, which many Indians, including Hindus, oppose.

Given the treacherous terrain that lies ahead, businesspeople need to ask themselves: What are my red lines? What democratic values am I willing to stand up for? And, in the end, they need to stand up and speak out and act.

There is much at stake, but the situation is far from hopeless. There is always a fighting chance, and Indian democracy is still alive and kicking.

Appendix 12A

List of Interviewees

Anonymous, 22 February 2023.
Shyama Iyer, 27 January 2023.
Karwan e Mohabbat, 6 August 2023.
Darshan Mondkar, 22 February 2023.
Rahul Rajamuthiah, 23 February 2023.
Dipali Sikand, 15 February 2023.

Notes

1. Feldmann and Morgan modify Hirschman's typology in some key ways (see Feldmann and Morgan 2023).
2. In the 2019 general election, Mukesh Ambani publicly announced support for Milind Deora, a candidate from the Congress party, which created a storm in Mumbai.
3. Anonymous, interview with the author, 22 February 2023.
4. Anonymous, interview with the author, 22 February 2023.
5. Darshan Mondkar, interview with the author, 22 February 2023.
6. Rahul Rajamuthiah, interview with the author, 23 February 2023.
7. Shyama Iyer, interview with the author, 27 January 2023.
8. Dipali Sikand, interview with the author, 15 February 2023.
9. Dipali Sikand, interview with the author, 15 February 2023.
10. Karwan e Mohabbat, interview with the author, 6 August 2023.

References

Atkuri, R. 2022. 'Faith, Courage and Discipline: Conversations with Participants in the Bharat Jodo Yatra'. *Scroll.in*, 31 December. https://scroll.in/article/1040808/faith-courage-and-discipline-on-the-road-with-the-bharat-jodo-yatra. Accessed 17 April 2025.

Baru, S. (2021). *India's Power Elite: Class, Caste and Cultural Revolution*. New Delhi: Penguin Random House.

Basu, A. (2021). 'Changing Modalities of Violence: Lessons from Hindu Nationalist India'. In *Negotiating Democracy and Religious Pluralism: India, Pakistan, and Turkey*, edited by Karen Barkey, pp. 277–300. New York: Oxford University Press.

Chaterjee, E. (2023). 'India's Oligarchic State Capitalism'. *Current History* 122(843): 123–130.

Chaudhury, S. B. R. (2023). 'How India's Economy and Hindutva Rise Together' *The* Wire, 26 August.

Chowdhury, S. (2023). 'Economics and Politics under Modi Government: A Synoptic View'. In *Human Geography* 16(2): 146–161.

de Jong, D. (2022). *Nazi Billionaires: The Dark History of Germany's Wealthiest Dynasties*. New York: HarperCollins Publishers.

Doty, E., and D. Kinderman (2022). 'Recognizing and Countering Authoritarian Threats to Democracy: What Role for Business?' Erb Institute, University of Michigan, Ann Arbor.

Feldmann, M., and G. Morgan (2021). 'Business Elites and Populism: Understanding Business Responses'. *New Political Economy* 27(2): 347–359.

——— (2023). 'Business and Populism: The Political Economy of the "Odd Couple"'. In *Business and Populism: The Odd Couple?* Edited by Magnus Feldmann and Glenn Morgan, pp. 3–35. Oxford: Oxford University Press.

Finchelstein, F. (2017). *From Fascism to Populism in History*. Berkeley: University of California Press.

Fortune India (2022). 'Rahul Bajaj: The Last Bastion of Gandhian Industrialists'. 13 February. https://www.fortuneindia.com/people/rahul-bajaj-the-last-bastion-of-gandhian-industrialists/107104. Accessed 17 April 2025.

Goyal, P. (2024). 'Part 1: Behind the BJP's Rise and Rise, Bonds, Trusts and Raids on Corporates'. Newslaundry, 20 February.

Goyal, P., K. Abraham, N. Chandrashekar, and B. Kumar (2024). 'Part 2: 30 Firms Who Donated Rs 335 Cr to BJP Were Also Stung by I-T, ED'. Newslaundry, 21 February.

Haggard, S., and R. Kaufman (2021). *Backsliding: Democratic Regress in the Contemporary World*. New York: Cambridge University Press.

Hansen, T. B., and S. Roy (2022). 'What Is New about "New Hindutva"?' In *Saffron Republic: Hindu Nationalism and State Power in India*, edited by Thomas Blom Hansen and Srirupa Roy, pp. 1–23. New York: Cambridge University Press.

Heller, P. (2020). 'The Age of Reaction: Retrenchment Populism in India and Brazil'. *International Sociology* 35(6): 590–609.

Iyer, S. (2023). 'Business Support and Business Opposition for Hindu Nationalism: Summary of Key Findings'. Unpublished report.

Jaffrelot, C. (2019a). 'A De Facto Ethnic Democracy? Obliterating and Targeting the Other, Hindu Vigilantes, and the Ethno-State'. In *Majoritarian State: How Hindu Nationalism Is Changing India*, edited by Angana P. Chatterji, Thomas Blom Hansen, and Christophe Jaffrelot, pp. 41–67. Oxford: Oxford University Press.

——— (2019b). "Business-Friendly Gujarat Under Narendra Modi" in: Christophe Jaffrelot, Atul Kohli, and Kanta Murali (eds.) Business and politics in India. Oxford: Oxford University Press, pp. 211–233.

Khan, S. (2020). 'Social Exclusion of Muslims in India and Britain'. *Journal of Social Inclusion Studies* 6(1): 56–77.

Khatri, N., and A. Ojha (eds). (2016). *Crony Capitalism in India: Establishing Robust Counteractive Institutional Frameworks.* Basingstoke: Palgrave Macmillan.

Kinderman, D. (2020). 'German Business Mobilization against Right-Wing Populism'. *Politics and Society* 49(4): 489–516.

——— (2021). 'Authoritarian Capitalism and Its Impact on Business'. In *Symposium on Authoritarianism and Good Governance*, pp. 1–22. Herdon, VA: International Institute of Islamic Thought.

——— (2023). 'Business Associations and Right-Wing Populism'. In *Business and Populism: The Odd Couple?* Edited by Magnus Feldmann and Glenn Morgan, pp. 263–284. Oxford: Oxford University Press.

Kochanek, S. A. (1987). 'Briefcase Politics in India: The Congress Party and the Business Elite'. *Asian Survey* 27(12): 1278–1301.

Kohli, A. (1998). 'Enduring Another Election'. *Journal of Democracy* 9(3): 7–20.

Malik, Y. K., and V. B. Singh (1992). 'Bharatiya Janata Party: An Alternative to the Congress (I)?' *Asian Survey* 32(4): 318–336.

Mander, H. (2018). *Partitions of the Heart: Unmaking the Idea of India.* New Delhi: Penguin Random House.

——— (2021). 'Contested Citizenship: Struggles over Belonging'. *PS: Political Science and Politics* (October 2021): 632–633.

Mirza, A. (2017). 'Can India Inc Speak Up against Hate Like Silicon Valley Has Done against Social Issues?' *Dailyo.in*. https://www.dailyo.in/voices/donald-trump-silicon-valley-india-inc-modi-government-19288. Accessed 13 April 2025.

Nair, A. (2012). 'I Believe in the "Idea of India", Diversity, Says Rahul Bajaj'. *Times of India*, 9 December.

Patel, A. (2021). *Price of the Modi Years*. Chennai: Westland.

Poddar, G. (2019). 'Ascendance of New India: Whither Our civilisation?' *Deccan Herald*, 20 October. https://www.deccanherald.com/opinion/ascendance-of-new-india-whither-our-civilisation-769897.html. Accessed 18 April 2025.

Poruthiyil, P. V. (2018). 'Beef Lynchings and the Silence of Corporate India'. In *Reconciliation: Karwan e Mohabbat's Journey of Solidarity through a Wounded India*, edited by Harsh Mander, John Dayal, and Natasha Badhwar, pp. 93–107. New Dehli: Westland Books.

——— (2021). 'Big Business and Fascism: A Dangerous Collusion'. *Journal of Business Ethics* 168: 121–135.

Rakshit, D. (2023). 'Marginalization of Indian Muslims Is Systemic'. *The Swaddle*, 4 2023. https://www.theswaddle.com/why-the-economic-marginalization-of-indian-muslims-is-systemic. Accessed 13 April 2025.

Roy, A. (2022). 'Roy on Religious Nationalism, Dissent, and the Battle between Myth and History: Our Hopes Have Been Cauterized, Our Imaginations Infected'. Literary Hub, 21 April. https://lithub.com/arundhati-roy-on-religious-nationalism-dissent-and-the-battle-between-myth-and-history. Accessed 13 April 2025.

Roy, I. (2023). 'India's Fascist Democracy'. In *The Rise of the Radical Right in the Global South*, edited by Rosana Pinheiro-Machado and Tatiana Vargas-Maia, pp. 36–57. Abingdon: Routledge.

Sahoo, N. (2020). 'Mounting Majoritarianism and Political Polarization in India'. In *Political Polarization in South and Southeast Asia: Old Divisions, New Dangers*, edited by Thomas Carothers and Andrew O'Donohue, pp. 9–23. Washington, DC: Carnegie Endowment for International Peace.

Sharma, A. D. (2023). 'Political Moblization in an Era of "Post-Truth Politics"' In *The Rise of the Radical Right in the Global South*, edited by Rosana Pinheiro-Machado and Tatiana Vargas-Maia, pp. 141–155. Abingdon: Routledge.

Sinha, G., and B. S. Nayak (2021). 'Rise of Hindutva Politics, Demonetisation, and Its Impact on Micro, Small and Medium Enterprises in India'. In *Emerging Markets*, edited by Vito Bobek and Chee-Heong Quah, pp. 133–143. London: IntechOpen.

Sodhi, T. (2022). 'Emergency Prisoners, Farmer Leaders, Journalist: Who Are the Non-Congress People with Bharat Jodo Yatra?' Newslaundry, 14 November. https://www.newslaundry.com/2022/11/14/emergency-prisoners-farmer

-leaders-journalist-who-are-the-non-congress-people-with-bharat-jodo-yatra. Accessed 13 April 2025.

Soper, J. C., and J. S. Fetzer (2018). *Religion and Nationalism in Global Perspective.* New York: Cambridge University Press.

Swedberg, R. (2005). *Interest.* Berkshire: McGraw Hill/Open University Press.

The Wire (2024). 'Bulk of Electoral Bonds Given as Quid Pro Quo Arrangements: Plea in SC Seeks SIT Probe'. 24 April. https://thewire.in/law/bulk-of-electoral-bonds-given-as-quid-pro-quo-arrangements-plea-in-sc-seeks-sit-probe. Accessed 13 April 2025.

Tudor, M. (2023). 'Why India's Democracy Is Dying.' *Journal of Democracy* 34(3): 121–132.

V-Dem Institute (2023). 'Democracy Report 2023: Defiance in the Face of Autocratization'. https://v-dem.net/documents/29/V-dem_democracyreport2023_lowres.pdf. Accessed 13 April 2025.

Varshney, A. (2022). 'India's Democratic Longevity and Its Troubled Trajectory' In *Democracy in Hard Places*, edited by Scott Mainwaring and Tarek E. Masoud, pp. 34–72. Oxford: Oxford University Press.

Weixelbaum, J. (2018). 'At the Crossroads of Fascism: The Decision of Ford, General Motors, and IBM to Do Business with Nazi Germany'. PhD dissertation, Department of History, American University, Washington, DC.

Wyatt, A. (2023). 'India: Populism, Personalism and Economic Governance'. In *Business Elites and Populism: The Odd Couple?* Edited by Magnus Feldmann and Glen Morgan, pp. 181–201. New York: Oxford University Press.

Yilmaz, I., and N. Morieson (2023). *Religions and the Global Rise of Civilizational Populism*. Singapore: Palgrave Macmillan.

13

The Making of *Ram Ke Naam**

Anand Patwardhan

In 1984, after her Sikh bodyguards assassinated Indira Gandhi, a revenge pogrom took the lives of over 3,000 Sikhs on the streets of Delhi. Congress Party members led many killer mobs, but some were led by the Rashtriya Swayamsevak Sangh (RSS) and the Bharatiya Janata Party (BJP) as well. This is a fact forgotten by history but recorded in newspaper headlines of the day. It was this massacre that set me on the road to fight communalism with my camera. For the next decade, I recorded different examples of the rise of the religious right, as seen in diverse movements from the Khalistani upsurge in Punjab to the glorification of sati in Rajasthan and the movement to replace the Babri Mosque in Ayodhya with a temple to the Hindu god Ram. The material I filmed was very complex and if I had tried to encompass it all into a single film, it would have been too long and confusing. Eventually, three distinct films emerged from the footage shot between 1984 and 1994, all broadly describing the rise of religious fundamentalism and the resistance offered by secular forces in the country. *Una Mitran Di Yaad Pyaari* (*In Memory of Friends*), the first film to get completed, spoke of the situation in the Punjab of the 1980s where Khalistanis as well as the Indian government were claiming Bhagat Singh as their hero, but only people from the left remembered the Bhagat Singh who, from his death cell, wrote the booklet *Why I Am an Atheist*.

---

* An earlier version of this chapter was published as Anand Patwardhan, 'The Making of *Ram Ke Naam*', Sabrang, 22 January 2024, https://sabrangindia.in/the-making-of-ram-ke-naam-a-hinduism-that-is-the-mirror-opposite-of-hindutva.

The second film was *Ram Ke Naam* (*In the Name of God*), which was about the rise of Hindu fundamentalism as witnessed in the temple–mosque controversy in Ayodhya. The third was *Pitra, Putra aur Dharmayuddha* (*Father, Son and Holy War*) on the connection between religious violence and the male psyche. All three films tackled communalism, but each used a different prism to analyse what was happening. *In Memory of Friends* highlighted the writings of Bhagat Singh, suggesting that class solidarity was the antidote to religious division. *Father, Son and Holy War* looked at the issue from the prism of gender.

The long march

For this chapter, I will focus on *Ram Ke Naam*, the middle film of what became a trilogy on communalism. While the film covers a two-year span from 1990 onwards, the backstory begins in the mid-1980s when the Vishva Hindu Parishad (VHP) and sister organizations of the Hindutva family (the Sangh Parivar) were searching for a way to capture the imagination of the Hindus of India, who at 83 per cent constitute the real vote bank of this country. A 'Dharam Sansad' (Parliament of Priests) in 1984 (the year Indira Gandhi was assassinated and the Congress rode to power on a sympathy wave) identified 3,000 sites of potential conflict between Hindus and Muslims that could mobilize the sentiments of Hindus and polarize the nation. The top three sites chosen were Ayodhya, Kashi, and Mathura. The 'Dharam Sansad' decided to start with the Ram Temple/Babri Mosque in Ayodhya.

Soon, a nationwide village-to-village campaign began to collect bricks and money to build a grand Ram temple in place of the Babri mosque. The campaign went international as non-resident Indians (NRIs) chipped in from distant lands. By design or by a remarkable coincidence, India's state-controlled television (TV) channel, Doordarshan, started to run a never-ending series on the Hindu epic Ramayana. There were few other TV channels in those days, and the whole nation was hooked on mythology. These were the ingredients already at play when the BJP stalwart L. K. Advani set out on his chariot of fire. *Ram Ke Naam* follows the *rath yatra* of Advani, who, in 1990, traversed the Indian countryside in an air-conditioned Toyota dressed up by a Bollywood set designer to look like a mythological war chariot. The stated objective was to gather volunteers, or *kar sevaks*, to demolish a sixteenth-century mosque built by the Mughal emperor Babar in Ayodhya and build a temple to Ram in its exact location. The rationale for this act of destruction and construction was that Babar had supposedly built this mosque after demolishing a temple to Ram that had marked the exact location of Ram's birth. This was justified as an act of historic redress for the many wrongs inflicted by Muslim invaders and rulers on their native Hindu subjects—a theme that runs through all Hindutva discourse like a flaming torch.

I started the film instinctively, shooting the *rath yatra* when it arrived in Bombay in 1990 and then following it through various segments of its journey. At many places the *rath* passed through, it left a trail of blood as *kar sevak*s attacked local Muslims either for not showing due respect or just to display their might. By the end of its journey, over sixty people had been killed and many more injured in the wake of the *rath yatra*.

Basic equipment

Most of our shoot was done with a two-person crew consisting of myself with an old 16 millimetre camera and colleagues who accompanied me on different legs of the shoot. Pervez Merwanji recorded sound on our portable Nagra for the leg that eventually reached Ayodhya. Pervez was a dear friend and a filmmaker in his own right, having just made his brilliant debut feature *Percy*, which went on to win a major award at the Mannheim International Film Festival. Despite this, he was not too proud to don the mantle of sound recordist on an unheralded independent documentary project like ours. It turned out to be the last film he would ever work on. Pervez contracted jaundice, probably during our shoot, and seemed to recover, but then his liver failed him, and he passed away, never having seen the final edit of our film.

Our actual filming was staggered over a year and a half, and we were able to research and shoot during this period. We learned that contrary to the theory that votaries of Hindutva were propagating, which claimed that there was a temple underneath the mosque, the artefacts that archaeologists had originally found in digs in the vicinity had nothing to do with any temple. According to historians, in the seventh century at the location of present-day Ayodhya, there probably stood the Buddhist city of Saket. We learned that the proliferation of *akhada*s (military wings attached to temples) in Ayodhya had nothing to do with the long war to liberate the birthplace of Ram as was being claimed by Hindutva ideologues but owed their origin to the ongoing rivalry between armed Shaivite and Vaishnavite sects in the middle ages.

Most importantly, we learned that in the sixteenth century, the poet Tulsidas visited Ayodhya many times as he composed his famous *Ram Charit Manas*, a text that converted the relatively obscure Sanskrit Ramayana into *khadi boli*, a form of Hindi that popularized the story of Ram for the ordinary folk of north India. Not only does Tulsidas never mention that a temple marking the birthplace of Ram was just demolished by Babar, but there is another telling fact. Until the sixteenth century, the Ram legend was largely restricted to the few Brahmins who knew Sanskrit. It was only after Tulsidas's Hindi version had spread that Ram became a popular god for the masses, and Ram temples sprouted across the country. In other words, in the middle of the sixteenth century, when the Babri Mosque was built, it is highly unlikely that there were any Ram temples at all. Today, Ayodhya is full of Ram temples, and at least twenty of them claim to be built at the birthplace of Ram. The reason is obvious. Any temple that establishes itself as the birthplace of Ram gets huge donations from its devotees.

Making it cinematic

Some of this research is hinted at in the finished film but rarely made explicit as I felt that it would be more powerful for our film to rely on the logic of events unfolding before the camera in 1990–1991 rather than become a theoretical and didactic treatise. Ideally, I, or someone else, should have made an accompanying booklet to point out the many footnotes and annotations that such a film really needs.

30 October 1990 had been declared by Advani as the target date for *kar seva* at the disputed Ram Janmabhoomi/Babri Mosque site in Ayodhya. Pervez and I headed to Uttar Pradesh. We were trying to catch up with the *rath* at some of its scheduled stops. The trains were already jam-full. We squeezed into a third-class compartment where we could barely sit on top of our luggage. We had got on the wrong train, but it was impossible to get out! It turned out to be a stroke of luck as the train took us to Patna, Bihar, where the Left Front, along with Bihar's then chief minister, Lalu Prasad Yadav, was holding a huge anti-*rath* rally at the Gandhi Maidan.

A. B. Bardhan of the Communist Party of India (CPI) made a brilliant appeal to preserve India's syncretic culture, and Lalu Prasad Yadav gave a stern warning telling Advani to turn back from the brink. A few days later, he kept his promise. Advani was arrested, and the *rath yatra* finally came to a halt in Bihar. Not so the *kar sevaks* who used all modes of transport to continue to head towards Ayodhya.

We caught a train back to Lucknow. There, we spent almost ten days trying to get permission to enter Ayodhya. Chief Minister Mulayam Singh Yadav had vowed to protect the Babri Mosque and claimed that he had turned Ayodhya into an impenetrable fortress where not just 'kar sevaks' but also 'not a bird could fly across' (parinda par na kar payega) (Jaiswal 2019). As it turned out, in the end the only people who had difficulty getting into Ayodhya were journalists and documentarians like us.

We finally reached Ayodhya on 28 October, two days before the planned assault on the mosque. Here we met Shastriji, an old *mahant* (temple priest) who in 1949 had been part of the group that had broken into the Babri Mosque at night and installed a Ram idol in the sanctum sanctorum. From that day on, the site had become disputed territory as district magistrate K. K. Nair refused to have the idols removed. As *Ram Ke Naam* points out, Nair, after retiring from government service, went on to join the Bharatiya Jana Sangh (precursor of the BJP) and became a member of parliament.

Shastriji, the *mahant*, was proud of installing the idols and a little miffed that everyone had forgotten his role. Hindutva videos, audio, and literature proclaimed that what happened in 1949 was a 'miracle' where Lord Ram appeared at his birthplace. Shastriji was arrested and released on bail by the district magistrate, Nair. Till the day we met him forty-one years later, he had remained free.

On the other side

We went across the Saryu bridge to Ayodhya's twin city, Faizabad. Here we met the old Imam of the Babri Mosque and his carpenter son, who recounted the 1949 story from their perspective. The district magistrate had told them after the break-in that order would soon be restored and by next Friday they could re-enter their mosque for prayers. As the Imam's son said, 'We are still waiting for that Friday.'

As 30 October dawned and we made our way on foot to the Saryu bridge at Ayodhya, we could see that chief minister Mulayam Singh Yadav's promise that no one would get through to Ayodhya was proving to be false. Already several thousand had gathered by the bridge despite the curfew. There had been a small *lathi* charge while shoes and footwear were scattered all over the bridge. Busloads of arrested *kar sevaks* were being driven away after arrest. What we did not notice at the time was that many of these buses would stop at a short distance, and the *kar sevaks* would disembark to rejoin the fray. By the side of the bridge, thousands were chanting at the police 'Hindu Hindu bhai bhai; beech mein vardi kahan se aayee?' (All Hindus are brothers; why let a uniform get between us?)

As the day progressed, it was heartbreaking to those of us who knew that any attack on the mosque would rent apart the delicate communal fabric of the nation. We believed in Mulayam Singh's strong rhetoric that he would stop *kar sevaks* long before they reached the mosque. What we saw on the ground was bewildering. Not only were thousands pouring in despite the curfew but in many places there was active connivance from the police and paramilitary forces. There was utter confusion. In the end, some *kar sevaks* did break through to attack the mosque, but at the very last instance, the police opened fire. Some *kar sevaks* reached the top of the mosque's dome and tied their saffron Hindutva flag. Others broke into the sanctum sanctorum where the idols were kept, but police firing prevented the larger crowd from demolishing the mosque. In all, twenty-nine people, young and old, lost their lives. Later, BJP and VHP propaganda would claim that over a thousand had been killed and thrown into the Saryu River. The think tank of Hindutva then initiated another *rath yatra* across the country carrying the ashes of their Ayodhya 'martyrs'.

On the night of the 30th, in the sombre mood that the attack had spawned, we met Pujari Laldas, the court-appointed head priest of the disputed Ram Janmabhoomi/Babri Mosque site. Laldas was an outspoken critic of Hindutva despite being a Hindu priest and had received death threats. The Uttar Pradesh government had provided him with two bodyguards. It is this wonderful interview of one of independent India's unsung heroes that gives *Ram Ke Naam* its real poignancy. Laldas spoke out against the VHP, pointing out that they had never even prayed at the site but were using it for political and financial gain. He spoke of the syncretic past of Ayodhya and expressed anguish that Hindu–Muslim unity in the country was being sacrificed by people who were cynically using religion. He predicted a storm of mayhem that would follow but expressed confidence that this storm, too, would pass and sanity would return.

Finding a lens

For *In Memory of Friends*, I used a prism of class as seen through the writings of Bhagat Singh to speak of the Punjab of today. In reality, by the late 1980s, classical Marxist analysis and class solidarity were no longer exclusively effective tools in an India and a world where the ideas of the left were losing out to consumer capitalism. The Soviet Union was collapsing, and China was embracing state capitalism. The United States (US) was the only superpower left in the world, which itself was fragmenting into its religious and ethnic sub-parts. Yugoslavia disintegrated into internecine warfare. The US, with its ally, Saudi Arabia, stoked Islamic fundamentalism in Afghanistan and Pakistan to fight communism, which in turn helped Kashmiri militants take up the gun. In Punjab, Sikh militants were rising, and in northern India, Hindu militants came into their own.

For *Ram Ke Naam*, the sane voice of the Hindu priest Laldas played the role that Bhagat Singh's writings had done in my previous film. The left antidote to communalism was still present through the Patna speech of the CPI's Bardhan. But it was now joined by a liberation theologist in the form of Laldas. The violent reaction of upper-caste Hindus to the attempt by the then prime minister, V. P. Singh, to implement a Mandal Commission report granting reservations to 'backward' castes had led to upper-caste Hindus embracing Hindutva and the Mandir movement. This had not yet trickled down the caste order. Wherever we went in Uttar Pradesh, Dalits and 'backward castes' spoke out against the Ram Temple movement. This caste factor became the third spoke in the anti-communal wheel.

The film was complete by late 1991. We had some hiccoughs and delays from the censors but finally cleared this hurdle without cuts. The film went on to win a national award for Best Investigative Documentary as well as a Filmfare award for Best Documentary. Jaya Bachchan was the head of the jury at the 1992 Bombay International Documentary Film Festival. *Ram Ke Naam* did not get a mention. Several critics commented that the film was raking up a dead issue as the Babri Mosque was intact, and the film would unnecessarily give the country a bad name abroad. Later that month, I attended the Berlin Film Festival with *Ram Ke Naam*. I learned, to my horror, that Amitabh and Jaya Bachchan, who were also guests at this festival, had told the festival authorities that they should not have selected such an 'anti-India' film.

On the strength of our national award, I submitted it for telecast on Doordarshan. Any government that actually believed in a secular India would have shown such a film many times over so that our public could realize how religious hatred is manufactured for narrow political and financial gains. Widespread exposure may have undermined the movement to demolish the mosque. The BJP was not in power. Yet Doordarshan refused to telecast the film, so I took them to court. Five years later, we won our case, and the film was telecast, but the damage had long been done.

The aftermath

After the 30 October attack in 1990 and the death of twenty-nine *kar sevaks*, the BJP, which had been in coalition with V. P. Singh's Janata Dal government at the centre, pulled out its support. Chandra Shekhar briefly came to power at the centre but quickly lost to Narsimha Rao's Congress in the wake of Rajiv Gandhi's assassination. In Uttar Pradesh, Mulayam Singh Yadav's government gave way to a BJP government. One of its first steps was to have Laldas removed as the head priest of the Ram Janmabhoomi/Babri Mosque site and then to remove his bodyguards. Conditions were now ripe for the major assault.

On 6 December 1992, with the BJP in power in Uttar Pradesh, and a strangely acquiescent Narasimha Rao-led Congress government at the centre, the Hindutva brigade finally succeeded in demolishing the Babri Mosque. Laldas's predictions of large-scale violence in the region came true. The old Imam and his son from Faizabad I had interviewed were put to death on 7 December 1992. While Muslims were slaughtered across India, in neighbouring countries, Pakistan and Bangladesh, the Hindu minority was targeted and temples destroyed. In March 1993, bomb blasts in Mumbai organized by Muslim members of the mafia killed over 300 people. The chain reaction set into motion since those days has still to abate.

Back in 1991, our première had been held in Lucknow, the capital of Uttar Pradesh. Laldas came for the screening and asked for several cassettes of the film. When I asked about his own safety, he laughed and said he was happy that now his views would circulate more widely. As he put it, if he had been afraid, he would not have spoken out in the first place.

A year later, a tiny item on the inside pages of The *Times of India* noted, 'Controversial priest found murdered'. Laldas had been killed with a country-made revolver. The article never told us that the real 'controversy' was the fact that this brave priest believed in an inclusive Hinduism that is the mirror opposite of Hindutva.

An epilogue

That a state-run national TV broadcaster, Doordarshan, commissioned and broadcast the quasi-religious mythological TV serial *Ramayana* in the years preceding and during the attacks on the Babri Mosque was ironic because a supposedly progressive Congress, which carried the legacy of India's predominantly secular independence struggle, was in power at the time.

It must be said that by the 1990s, secularism was already under threat globally. Economic liberalization quickly followed the decline of the Soviet Union, even as communist China openly embraced state capitalism. As a direct consequence, religious sectarianism erupted in many parts of the world that had experimented with socialism and secularism. Yugoslavia is a case in point. In India, advocates of secularism were feeling the heat, and perhaps Doordarshan airing mythological series was a result of this global change. The *Ramayana* serial proved to be immensely popular and was followed by another Indian epic, the Mahabharata.

Doordarshan, which was expected to promote scientific thought and reason, in fact, shut its doors to audiovisual material that adhered to the directive principles of the Constitution of India. My own films could only be shown after we won court cases against Doordarshan for trying to suppress my freedom of expression and the public's right to information. After an order by the Bombay High Court, *Ram Ke Naam* was finally aired on Doordarshan in prime time in 1997, six years after it was first made and five years after the Babri Mosque had been demolished. The warning about what would happen to India if religious fundamentalists were allowed to run riot reached the public only after damage had been irrevocably done. Two decades later, India installed those who had ridden a fake religious chariot on the road to Ayodhya into power. Another decade later, the Supreme Court of India, instead of punishing religious vandals who demolished a protected national monument, rewarded them with the object of their desire—the construction of a new Ram temple at the very spot where the mosque once stood.

References

Jaiswal, P. (2019). 'Mulayam Singh Yadav, an Astute Politician Who Once Nursed PM Ambitions'. 10 April. https://www.hindustantimes.com/people/mulayam-singh-yadav-an-astute-politician-who-once-nursed-pm-ambitions/story-IVgYoXFksl4D7AzKE8sTYM.html. Accessed 24 May 2025.

Merwanji, P. (dir.) (1989). *Percy*. Produced by National Film Development Corporation. https://www.youtube.com/watch?v=y8Hnfw-NYWQ. Accessed 1 April 2025.

Patwardhan, A. (dir.) (1990). *Una Mitran Di Yaad Pyaari*. https://patwardhan.com/in-memory-of-friends. Accessed 1 April 2025.

——— (dir.) (1992). *Ram Ke Naam*. https://patwardhan.com/ram-ke-naam. Accessed 1 April 2025.

——— (dir.) (1995). *Pitra, Putra aur Dharmayuddha*. https://patwardhan.com/fshw. Accessed 1 April 2025.

About the Contributors

Marzia Casolari is Associate Professor of Asian History at the University of Turin and Deputy Director of the Institute of the Studies on Asia (Centro di Studi sull'Asia; ISA), Turin. She has been teaching at the University of Bologna and the University of Perugia. Among her publications, there are three authored books, *L'Asia agli asiatici: La politica 'indiana' del regime fascista e i rapporti con il nazionalismo radicale* (2024), *In the Shadow of the Swastika: The Relationships Between Indian Nationalism, Italian Fascism and Nazism* (2020), and *The British Strategic Imperative in South Asia and Its Role in India's Partition: 1942–1947* (2017), and two edited books, *Sguardi sull'Asia: Scritti in onore di Michelguglielmo Torri* (2018) and *Gandhi After Gandhi: The Relevance of the Mahatma's Legacy in Today's World* (2022). In addition, she has published about forty articles and book chapters on Indian and South Asian history and politics.

Rohit Chopra is Associate Professor in the Department of Communication at Santa Clara University. He has been a visiting scholar at the Center for South Asia, Stanford University; Assistant Professor at Babson College, Wellesley, Massachusetts; and a visiting assistant professor at Emory University, Atlanta. Before his academic career, he worked in the Indian legacy media and academic publishing industries and in the corporate web solutions division of rediff.com, a pioneering start-up and India's first online portal. He has authored *The Gita for a Global World: Ethical Action in an Age of Flux* (2021), *The Virtual Hindu Nation: Saffron Nationalism and New Media* (2019), and *Technology and Nationalism in India: Cultural Negotiations from Colonialism* *to Cyberspace* (2008), and is the co-editor of *Global Media, Culture, and Identity: Theory, Cases, and Approaches* (2011).

Radhika Desai is Professor in the Department of Political Studies, University of Manitoba, Winnipeg, Canada, and Director of the Geopolitical Economic Research Group at the university. She has authored *Geopolitical Economy: After US Hegemony, Globalization and Empire* (2013), and co-edited *Revolutions* (2021) and *Karl Polanyi for the Twenty First Century* (2020). She also writes in the *Economic and Political Weekly, International Critical Thought, New Left Review, Third World Quarterly, World Review of Political Economy*, and other journals and in edited collections on parties, political economy, culture, and nationalism. She co-edits the book series *Geopolitical Economy* and *Future of Capitalism* and serves on the editorial boards of many journals, including the *Canadian Political Science Review, Critique of Political Economy, E-Social Sciences, Pacific Affairs, Global Faultlines, Research in Political Economy, Revista de Economía Crítica, World Review of Political Economy*, and *International Critical Thought*.

Ajay Gudavarthy is Associate Professor, Centre for Political Studies, Jawaharlal Nehru University, New Delhi. He is also an associate member at the Institute for Humanities, Simon Fraser University, Burnaby, Canada. He was previously a visiting professor at the Centre for Modern Indian Studies, University of Göttingen (2014); visiting fellow at the Centre for Citizenship, Civil Society, and Rule of Law, University of Aberdeen (2012); visiting faculty, Goldsmith College, University College London (UCL) (2010); and Charles Wallace visiting fellow, SOAS (School of Oriental and African Studies), University of London (2008). His published works include *Politics of Post-Civil Society* (2013), *Maoism, Democracy and Globalization* (2014), and *India After Modi: Populism and the Right* (2018). He has also edited the books *Re-Framing Democracy and Agency* (2012), *Revolutionary Violence versus Democracy* (2017), and *Secular Sectarianism: Limits of Subaltern Politics* (2019). His forthcoming book is titled *Politics, Ethics and Emotions in 'New India'* (2022). He is a regular contributor to leading news dailies in India that include *The Hindu, Indian Express, The Telegraph, The Wire*, and NewsClick. He has appeared on and shared his views with various international print media and news channels, including Channel News Asia (Singapore), Al Jazeera, The Conversation, *South China Morning Post*, BBC, *The Independent, Time, Friday Times, Khaleej Times*, and *Dawn*, among others.

Vijay Gudavarthy is Assistant Professor at the School of Economics, University of Hyderabad. He was awarded his doctorate in Development Studies from the Institute of Social Studies, the Hague, in 2004. He was the recipient of the Sanjay Thakur Young Labour Economist Award from the Indian Society of Labour Economics in 2008. He was the conference secretary for the international conference on 'Pharmaceuticals in Developing and Emerging Economies: Production, Innovation, and Access to Medicines in the Wake of TRIPS', organized by the School of Economics, University of Hyderabad, together with Deakin University, Victoria, in 2010. He has published research papers in various national and international journals as well as chapters in books. His latest publication is 'Development through Informalization and Circulation of Labour: The Emerging Anatomy of an Uncivil Society', in *B. R. Ambedkar: The Quest for Justice*, vol. 3: *Legal and Economic Justice* (2021), edited by Aakash Singh Rathore.

Daniel Kinderman is Associate Professor in the Department of Political Science and International Relations, University of Delaware. He is also the director of the European Studies Program, University of Delaware. He specializes in comparative and international political economy and corporate social responsibility (CSR), with a geographical focus on Europe. He teaches courses on European politics, the European Union (EU), CSR, comparative political economy, and international political economy. His current research focuses on business responses to right-wing populism, the impact of responsible business associations on the CSR performance of their member companies, and the relationship between CSR and political-economic institutions. He has been a visiting scholar at the WZB Berlin Social Science Center and the Max Planck Institute for the Study of Societies in Cologne, Germany.

Ashok Kumbamu is a medical sociologist and health services researcher at Mayo Clinic. He focuses on exploring the significance of caring, character, and practical wisdom in promoting human flourishing in health care. He is dedicated to addressing diversity, equity, and inclusion issues to create fair and equitable clinical and learning environments. He uses social theory and qualitative research methods to examine the complex interplay among social structures, institutional settings, cultural practices, and individual experiences in health care delivery. His commitment to social justice drives him to contribute to a more compassionate, sustainable, and equitable health care system that is responsive to the needs of marginalized communities.

Arvind Narrain is the author of *India's Undeclared Emergency: Constitutionalism and the Politics of Resistance* (2021), the co-author of *Of Law and Life: Conversations with Upendra Baxi* (2024), and the co-editor of *Law Like Love: Queer Perspectives on Law* (2011), as well as the co-author of *Breathing Life into the Constitution* (2016). He was the founding member of the Alternative Law Forum (www.altlawforum.org). He was also a part of the team of lawyers challenging Section 377 of the Indian Penal Code (IPC) right from the High Court of Karnataka in 2009 to the Supreme Court in 2018.

Prabhat Patnaik has taught Economics at the University of Cambridge and at Jawaharlal Nehru University, New Delhi, where he held the Sukhamoy Chakravarty Chair at the time of his retirement and is currently Professor Emeritus. His special interests are macroeconomics, political economy, and development economics. His books include *Accumulation and Stability under Capitalism* (1997), *The Retreat to Unfreedom* (2003), *The Value of Money* (2009), *Re-Envisioning Socialism, Capital and Imperialism* (co-authored with Utsa Patnaik) (2012), and *Beyond Liberalism* (2024). He was the executive head of the State Planning Board of Kerala and is an editor of the journal *Social Scientist*.

Anand Patwardhan has been making sociopolitical documentaries for over five decades, pursuing diverse and controversial issues that are at the crux of social and political life in India. Many of his films were at one time or another banned by state television channels in India and became the subject of litigation by him, who successfully challenged the censorship rulings in court. Anand received a BA in English literature from the University of Bombay in 1970; won scholarships to get another BA in Sociology from Brandeis University, Waltham, Massachusetts, in 1972; and a master's degree in Communications from McGill University, Montreal, in 1982. He has been an activist ever since he was a student: he participated in the anti-Vietnam War movement, was a volunteer in Caesar Chavez's United Farm Workers Union, worked in a rural development and education project in central India, and participated in the Bihar anti-corruption movement in 1974–1975 and in the civil liberties and democratic rights movement during and after the 1975–1977 emergency. Since then he has been active in movements for housing rights of the urban poor and for communal harmony and has participated in movements against unjust, unsustainable development, militarism, and nuclear nationalism.

Amit Shrivastava is an independent researcher and activist.

Anand Teltumbde is a writer, columnist, civil and education right activist, and a commentator on policy issues. A regular contributor to the *Economic and Political Weekly,* wherein he wrote a monthly column named 'Margin Speak' for nearly a decade. He has written over thirty books on contemporary issues, which are widely translated in most Indian languages. Formally trained in technology and management, he ended his corporate career after working as the chief executive officer of a holding company. He was invited by Indian Institute of Technology (IIT) Kharagpur as a professor of Business Management, and later by the Goa Institute of Management as a senior professor and chair, Big Data Analytics.

Rohit Varman is Professor at Birmingham Business School, University of Birmingham. His research interests are broadly in the field of critical management studies. He has published his research in notable journals, including *Human Relations*, the *Journal of Consumer Research, Organization Studies*, and *Organization Science*. He has co-edited books published by the Press on alternative organizations and organizing resistance in India. He is the editor-in-chief of *Marketing Theory* and serves on the editorial boards of the *Journal of Marketing Management, Journal of Macromarketing*, and *Journal of Historical Research in Marketing.* He is also an associate editor of *Consumption Markets, and Culture.*

Index

www.ingramcontent.com/pod-product-compliance
Ingram Content Group UK Ltd.
Pitfield, Milton Keynes, MK11 3LW, UK
UKHW040359250426
470365UK00013B/433
* 9 7 8 1 0 0 9 6 0 5 5 0 2 *